THE POLITICAL VOICES OF GENERATION Z

This book explores the political expression of members of Generation Z old enough to vote in 2018 and 2020 on issues and movements including MeToo, Supreme Court nominations, March for Our Lives, immigration and family separation, and Black Lives Matter. Since generational dividing lines blur, we study 18–25-year-olds, analyzing the oldest members of Generation Z along with the youngest Millennials. They share similarities both in their place in the life cycle and experiences of potentially defining events. Through examining some movements led by young adults and others led by older generations, as well as issues with varying salience, core theories are tested in multiple contexts, showing that when young adults protest or post about movements they align with, they become mobilized to participate in other ways, too, including contacting elected officials, which heightens the likelihood of their voices being heard in the halls of power. Perfect for students and courses in a variety of departments at all levels, the book is also aimed at readers curious about contemporary events and emerging political actors.

Laurie L. Rice is Professor of Political Science at Southern Illinois University Edwardsville. Her research interests include political communication, the presidency, elections, social media, and civic engagement. She is the coauthor of *Web 2.0 and the Political Mobilization of College Students* and coeditor of *American Political Parties under Pressure*. Her work has appeared in journals such as *Presidential Studies Quarterly*, *Social Science Computer Review*, and *Journal of Information Technology and Politics*. She provides expertise to regional, national, and international media on elections, social media, and the presidency and has written pieces for *The Hill*, *The Huffington Post*, and the *St. Louis Post Dispatch*.

Kenneth W. Moffett is Professor of Political Science at Southern Illinois University Edwardsville. His research interests lie in American politics and policy. He is coauthor of *Web 2.0 and the Political Mobilization of College Students*, and specializes in American politics and policy. His work has appeared in the *Journal of Information Technology and Politics*, *Social Science Computer Review*, *Party Politics*, *Legislative Studies Quarterly*, *Congress & the Presidency*, and other journals. He has also written essays that have appeared in *The Hill*, *The Huffington Post*, the *St. Louis Post-Dispatch* and *The Washington Post*'s Monkey Cage blog.

MEDIA AND POWER

David L. Paletz, Series Editor
www.routledge.com/Media-and-Power/book-series/MP

Media and Power is a series that publishes work uniting media studies with studies of power. This innovative and original series features books that challenge, even transcend, conventional disciplinary boundaries, construing both media and power in the broadest possible terms. At the same time, books in the series are designed to fit into several different types of college courses in political science, public policy, communication, journalism, media, history, film, sociology, anthropology, and cultural studies. Intended for the scholarly, text, and trade markets, the series should attract authors and inspire and provoke readers.

Published Books

Star Power
American Democracy in the Age of the Celebrity Candidate
Lauren Wright

Politics, Journalism, and the Way Things Were
Martin Tolchin

The Political Voices of Generation Z
Laurie L. Rice and Kenneth W. Moffett

Fixing American Politics
Solutions for the Media Age
Edited by: Roderick P. Hart

THE POLITICAL VOICES OF GENERATION Z

Laurie L. Rice and Kenneth W. Moffett

NEW YORK AND LONDON

First published 2022
by Routledge
605 Third Avenue, New York, NY 10158

and by Routledge
2 Park Square, Milton Park, Abingdon, Oxon OX14 4RN

Routledge is an imprint of the Taylor & Francis Group, an informa business

© 2022 Laurie L. Rice and Kenneth W. Moffett

The right of Laurie L. Rice and Kenneth W. Moffett to be identified as authors of this work has been asserted by them in accordance with sections 77 and 78 of the Copyright, Designs and Patents Act 1988.

All rights reserved. No part of this book may be reprinted or reproduced or utilised in any form or by any electronic, mechanical, or other means, now known or hereafter invented, including photocopying and recording, or in any information storage or retrieval system, without permission in writing from the publishers.

Trademark notice: Product or corporate names may be trademarks or registered trademarks, and are used only for identification and explanation without intent to infringe.

Library of Congress Cataloging-in-Publication Data
Names: Rice, Laurie L., 1976– author. | Moffett, Kenneth W., author.
Title: The political voices of Generation Z/Laurie L. Rice and Kenneth W. Moffett.
Identifiers: LCCN 2021014364 (print) | LCCN 2021014365 (ebook) |
ISBN 9780367769055 (paperback) | ISBN 9780367769062 (hardback) |
ISBN 9781003168898 (ebook)
Subjects: LCSH: Generation Z–Political activity–United States. |
Generation Z–United States–Attitudes. |
United States–Politics and government–2017-2021.
Classification: LCC HQ799.9.P6 R53 2022 (print) |
LCC HQ799.9.P6 (ebook) | DDC 305.23509 73–dc23
LC record available at https://lccn.loc.gov/2021014364
LC ebook record available at https://lccn.loc.gov/2021014365

ISBN: 978-0-367-76906-2 (hbk)
ISBN: 978-0-367-76905-5 (pbk)
ISBN: 978-1-003-16889-8 (ebk)

DOI: 10.4324/9781003168898

Typeset in Bembo
by Newgen Publishing UK

Access the Support Material: routledge.com/9780367769055

To Larry and Bobbie
and
To Beverly

CONTENTS

List of Illustrations ix
Acknowledgments xi

1 Introduction: Why Young Adult Political Expression Deserves a Fresh Look 1

**PART I
Posting, Protesting, and Civic Engagement:
Causes and Movements That Mobilized** 29

2 The MeToo Movement: How an Online Social Movement Sparked Civic Engagement 31

3 Brett Kavanaugh and Amy Coney Barrett: How Controversial Supreme Court Nominations Provided Opportunities to Get Involved 61

4 School Shootings: How Gun Violence Encouraged Civic Involvement 96

5 Immigration and Family Separation: When Political Expression Fails to Expand Participation 127

6 Black Lives Matter: How a Surging Movement Engaged Young People in 2020 160

PART II
Moving from the Outside in: The Link between Posting and Protesting and Contacting Elected Officials **191**

7 Messages Received? Examining the Link between Young Adults Posting Political Views Online and Sharing Views with Elected Officials 193

8 Discontent Heard? Examining the Link between Young Adults Engaging in Protests and Sharing Views with Elected Officials 227

9 Conclusion: Assessing Young Adult Political Power 265

Index *297*

ILLUSTRATIONS

Figures

1.1	Voter Turnout by Age in 2014 and 2018	9
1.2	Generational Experiences by Age among Those 18–29	15
2.1	Google Trends Searches for MeToo in the United States, 2017–2020	35
4.1	Threats to School Aged Children	99
4.2	Media Coverage of School Shootings	100
4.3	Mean Civic Engagement Levels by Concern about School Shootings	106
5.1	Opinions about a Border Wall	129
5.2	Media Coverage of DACA	131
6.1	Media and Public Attention to Black Lives Matter, 2013–Election Day 2020	161
7.1	Posting and Contacting Elected Officials by Age in 2012	195
9.1	Job Approval of Then-President Trump by Age and Partisan Affiliation	266
9.2	Views of Global Warming by Party and Generation	286

Tables

1.1	Comparison between Pew Surveys (September 2018 and June 2020) and mTurk Samples (November 2018 and 2020) (%)	18
2.1	Civic Engagement and the MeToo Movement	47
3.1	Opinions about Supreme Court Nominations and Civic Engagement	79

3.2	Civic Engagement, Posting, and Participating in Protests Related to Supreme Court Nominations	80
4.1	Civic Engagement and Posting and Protesting about Gun Control	115
5.1	Civic Engagement and Posting and Protesting about Immigration and Family Separation	147
5.2	Civic Engagement and Opinions about Family Separation and DACA	148
6.1	Civic Engagement and Black Lives Matter	178
7.1	Contacting Elected Officials and Posting about Politics	207
7.2	Contacting Elected Officials about the MeToo Movement and Supreme Court Nominations and Posting about Those Issues	209
7.3	Contacting Elected Officials about Gun Control or Immigration and Family Separation and Posting about Those Issues	212
7.4	Contacting Elected Officials about Black Lives Matter and Posting about that Social Movement in 2020	214
8.1	Contacting Elected Officials and Participating in Protests	245
8.2	Contacting Elected Officials about the MeToo Movement or Supreme Court Nominations and Participating in Protests Related to Those Issues	247
8.3	Contacting Elected Officials about Gun Control or Immigration and Family Separation and Participating in Protests about That Issue	249
8.4	Contacting Elected Officials about Black Lives Matter and Participating in Protests Related to That Movement in 2020	251
9.1	Civic Engagement, Contacting Elected Government Officials, and Presidential Approval	272

ACKNOWLEDGMENTS

When performing the research and writing for this manuscript, we have benefited significantly from the support of many in our profession and their generous advice. We thank numerous colleagues within our discipline for their comments on varying portions of the analyses that we present in this manuscript. These analyses were presented at the annual meetings of the Midwest Political Science Association (2019), American Political Science Association (2019 and 2020), the Southern Political Science Association (2020), and the Western Political Science Association (2021). Specifically, we thank Andrew Menger, Steve Utych, David Amaral, John Cluverius, Mebs Kanji, Melissa Michelson, Robert Pallitto, Elizabeth Bennion, Anthony Orlando, and manuscript reviewers for their thorough read of the varying analyses that are interspersed throughout this manuscript. Their feedback has improved this work immeasurably. Of course, any errors or omissions are ours. We also thank the Department of Political Science at Southern Illinois University Edwardsville for its financial support of the surveys on which this research is based.

We thank the superb team at Routledge for their belief in our research, and the collegial, careful, intelligent, and efficient way that they operate. We thank Jennifer Knerr for her initial interest in our project, and for her support throughout the review and publication processes. We thank her for the guidance that she has provided, and for continually encouraging us to connect our analyses more clearly to political realities that affect young people. She has done everything that we could ever ask for or want in an editor. We thank David Paletz for his interest in our project, too, and his work in editing the Media and Power series in which this book appears.

Laurie thanks her mentors who never made her choose between studying political behavior and political institutions. Specifically, she thanks Sam Kernell for his continued mentorship and encouragement of her work and her colleagues in the political science department at Southern Illinois University Edwardsville for the supportive environment they maintain. She is thankful for the love of all the members of the Rogers family and joins them in celebrating the entry of Myka into this world – may you never struggle to find your voice. She is grateful for the support and encouragement of the women who gather with her on Monday evenings as well as her friends scattered around the globe. Although she is saddened that her uncle, Rich, who loved debating politics, and her dear friend, Jean Shen, passed away during the writing of this book, she is thankful for their prayers and knows they would celebrate this book's completion.

Finally, she dedicates her portion of the book to her parents, Larry and Bobbie Rice. There are few greater blessings in life than to grow up in a home full of love and encouragement. Their support and prayers enabled her to soar. They set an inspiring example of faith, perseverance through life's challenges, kindness, love, and generosity and have always gladly dropped whatever they were doing whenever she needed them. As small business owners, their dedication meant they went many years without taking a day off but when she was severely ill, they didn't think twice about rushing to get to her so they could hold her hand and help nurse her back to health. They have always cheered her on in everything she has done from nerve-wracking childhood spelling bees to becoming the first in her family to obtain a college degree, completing her PhD, getting promoted to Professor, and to finishing this book. She is grateful to have their continued support through life's adventures.

Kenneth thanks those who have supported him professionally and personally. Many of his colleagues and friends in the profession have encouraged his interest in and have honed his thinking about American politics, and more specifically, about political participation. Professionally, he thanks Charles Shipan, Tracy Slagter, Scott Ainsworth, Brian Harward, Ashley Moraguez, Jason Macdonald, McKenzie Ferguson, Morris Taylor, and his excellent departmental colleagues at Southern Illinois University Edwardsville for their numerous insights on American politics. He also thanks his friends and family, including his nephew, Boede; his sister, Becky and her husband, David. He is grateful for their unconditional love, support, and encouragement. He also thanks his grandmother, Jean, for being there no matter what and for encouraging him to enjoy life while being mindful of the larger picture. He thanks his dad, Vern, for his sound advice regardless of the situation and for many political conversations over the years that encouraged him to become a political scientist. He thanks his wife, Grete, for her love, intelligence, wit, companionship, and for happily reading more copies of his work than anyone should. He thanks his mother-in-law, Lori, for being one of the kindest, most gracious people that he could ever have met.

He thanks his mother, Beverly Bowling, for her love, support, prayers, and encouragement that she has provided since day one. She was the first person who never doubted that he would accomplish anything meaningful, as he was born on the autism spectrum. She supported and fought for him as he endured numerous hardships while being in special education until the fourth grade, and through continual difficulties with the K-12 educational system. She has also supported him professionally and personally throughout his life and never ever doubted that he would be successful, become the first person in his immediate family to complete a PhD, and get promoted to Professor. During his childhood, she also rose through the ranks of her workplace when she began as a cashier and culminated in her becoming a service manager at a large car dealership in California. As one of the few female service managers anywhere, she endured countless instances of sexism from many colleagues and customers. She met this challenge, handled the haters deftly, and held this position with distinction for over 25 years until her retirement that occurred while this book was written. For these reasons and more, he is proud of her and happily dedicates his portion of this book to her.

1
INTRODUCTION

Why Young Adult Political Expression Deserves a Fresh Look

Introduction

The voices of young activists suggest that the generation coming of political age today responds differently to the challenges they inherit. Instead of responding with resignation or apathy, or waiting on their elders to fix it, they act and believe that they can advance change. Amel Viaud, a 21-year-old organizer of the Black Boston 2020 march after the killing of George Floyd in Minneapolis, said: "I think young people today are trying to break generational problems, and systemic issues that are going on in their environment" (Moore 2020). One of her partners in organizing the march, then 22-year-old Toiell Washington, stated:

> The other generations already had their turn. They already went through it. They already did it, so not only should we not expect it of them, but we should be starting to expect it ourselves. We should be holding each other accountable. People think that in moments like these, we're reaching out and waiting for someone to save us, but we are the next generation, so we have to save each other.
>
> *(Moore 2020)*

These sentiments were not confined to young activists in Boston. Alesia Robinson, 23 years old at the time and who identified herself as one of the oldest members of a group organizing similar marches in Orange County, California, stated:

> It seems to be youth at the forefront of this movement. They always say that young people are the ones who are going to make the change. The fact that they are leading this protest almost guarantees that change in my eyes.
>
> *(Walker 2020)*

DOI: 10.4324/9781003168898-1

Meanwhile, then 20-year-old Sara Wunete who helped organize a protest in Howard County, Maryland, that drew thousands said: "There is a room of adults who are in positions to do something and they underestimate youth to make that happen" (Faguy 2020).

This belief in acting themselves and distrust in older generations to bring about change was not unique to the Black Lives Matter protests of 2020. Two years earlier Parkland shooting survivor Cameron Kasky, then aged 17, posted on Facebook shortly after the tragedy at his high school, "I just want people to understand what happened and understand that doing nothing will lead to nothing. Who'd have thought that concept was so difficult to grasp?" (Witt 2018). As he and other survivors turned movement organizers met a few weeks later at one of their March for Our Lives planning sessions, he stated: "The adults know that we're cleaning up their mess" to which Emma Gonzales added "It's like they're saying, 'I'm sorry I made this mess,' while continuing to spill soda on the floor" (Alter 2018). Thus, Kasky concluded: "We want the grownups we need in this, and nothing more. We only have people doing the things that as 17-year-olds we cannot" (Alter 2018).

Social media helped young adults organize for change. Jaclyn Corin, then aged 17, another young leader of the #NeverAgain movement against gun violence, just days before the first March for Our Lives Protest, told a reporter, "People always say, 'Get off your phones,' but social media is our weapon. Without it, the movement wouldn't have spread this fast" (Alter 2018). Two years later, organizers of Black Lives Matter protests in Howard County, Maryland, credited their quick organization of large protests to social media with then 18-year-old Dumebi Adigwe adding "social media…is one of the best ways to get things in the faces of people who didn't want to see it before" (Faguy 2020).

Young people have been at the forefront of social movements before, including in the 1930s and 1960s (Braungart and Braungart 1990b). Young Baby Boomers played meaningful roles in the civil rights movement and the anti-Vietnam War protests in the 1960s. Yet, youth activism seemingly waned in the years afterward. Both young adults in Generation X as well as young adult Millennials were criticized for low levels of political participation. The stereotype of the politically unengaged young adult dominated.

Yet, since Donald Trump's election as president in 2016, there has been a new wave of activism in American society. The seeds for this activism began after he took office in 2017 and have accelerated across issues since, particularly from the approach of the 2018 midterm elections onward. This bent toward activism appears particularly strong among young adults and coincides with a world networked on social media at levels like never before and a new generation coming of political age. Young adults have become deeply involved in sharp debates about multiple political and social issues that gripped the headlines. Among these were immigration policy, gun violence, sexual harassment and assaults, and racism in American society and politics. Those seeking change took both to the streets and to social media to register their views. Media accounts showed young adults at the center of many of these activities. For an age group often portrayed in the past as politically uninvolved, young adults were seemingly everywhere.

Immigration

As a presidential candidate, Donald Trump made resistance to unauthorized immigration a central campaign plank, promising to build a wall to stop immigrants at the border with Mexico and to deport unauthorized immigrants (Trump 2015). In his first years as president, several actions in pursuit of this policy sparked protests from young adults. The first was an action that directly targeted young adults – ending the Deferred Action for Childhood Arrivals (DACA) policy of the Obama administration and threatening these so-called Dreamers with deportation. The night the policy was announced, more than 6,000 of the 400,000 members of the immigrant youth organization United We Dream collaborated on a conference call to commiserate and strategize (Preston 2017). Both Dreamers and their U.S. citizen peers joined together to protest the move. The day of the announcement, protests blocked traffic in Washington, DC, and New York (Preston 2017). Two months later in November 2017, Washington, DC, area high school and college students, supported by United We Dream, staged a walkout, marching to Capitol Hill and streaming into the Hart Senate Office Building chanting "Si Se Puede" and "Dream Act" and demanding that Congress pass a clean Dream Act that would offer a pathway to citizenship for the Dreamers without additional anti-immigration measures paired with it (Stein 2017).

By the late spring of 2018, a different anti-immigration policy dominated the headlines – family separation. The Trump administration had begun separating and detaining undocumented immigrant families crossing the Southern border. In the first six weeks of the policy alone, nearly 2,000 children were separated from their parents and held at detention facilities and shelters (Rhodan 2018). Both the policy itself and the conditions within these facilities sparked protests. On June 14, 2018, protests occurred in about 60 cities across more than a dozen states (Silva and Johnson 2018). The protests drew extensive media coverage. *Teen Vogue* even summarized news coverage of these protests for their readers, noting that some of the protests had been organized by those with no experience with activism and providing multiple examples of people tweeting about the issue (Beck 2018). Then, on June 30, a crowd of roughly 50,000 protesters gathered in Washington, DC, at a protest event featuring both celebrities and the stories of young people (Newkirk 2018). The same day, protesters gathered in more than 600 cities to demand the return of children to their parents (McCausland, Guadalupe, and Rosenblatt 2018). Young adults featured prominently in many of the pictures of protesters accompanying these news articles.

#MeToo and the Kavanaugh Hearings

The MeToo Movement went viral after a tweet from actress Alyssa Milano invited those who had been sexually harassed or assaulted to respond "Me Too" (Garcia 2017). The response was overwhelming and the online movement that followed was especially visible to young adults as they form the highest share of Twitter users (Smith and Anderson 2018) and are especially likely to follow celebrities (Hargittai and Litt 2011). But it was more than simply more visible to young adults, it touched on a value that is particularly important to them – gender equality (Shushok and Kidd 2015, 38) – and it targeted predatory behaviors that young adults are more likely to experience than their elders (Kearl 2018). Young adults quickly joined the movement.

This online movement produced offline consequences. The movement addressed sexual harassment and assault in numerous career fields and institutions, including college campuses. The movement did more than support survivors – lists emerged naming alleged perpetrators. For example, a student at Middlebury College posted a "List of Men to Avoid" on Facebook, listing 30 names and identifying them as rapists, harassers, or abusers (Bauer-Wolf 2018).

In the midst of the MeToo Movement, Dr. Christine Blasey Ford came forward with allegations that Supreme Court nominee Brett Kavanaugh had sexually assaulted her when they were both in high school. Young adults, far less likely than other age groups to have a very favorable opinion of Kavanaugh (YouGov 2018), joined with others in opposition to his nomination and led protests. Signs went up at his alma mater, Yale University, stating "We believe Dr. Christine Blasey Ford," undergraduates there rallied against him, and law school students held a sit-in (Wood 2018). Such actions were not limited to his alma mater, though. For example, students at both the University of Massachusetts and Harvard held protests opposing Kavanaugh's nomination (Esten 2018; Hailu 2018).

Gun Violence

On February 14, 2018, a gunman entered Marjorie Stoneman Douglas High School in Parkland, Florida, killing 17 (Alter 2018). Active shooters attacking schools was not new but the response to this particular tragedy was markedly different. Survivors spoke out immediately to national news outlets (Grinberg and Muaddi 2018) calling for change, launching the hashtag #NeverAgain within a day (Alter 2018). Within four days of the attack they announced plans for a march for their lives in Washington, DC, on March 24 (Grinberg and Muaddi 2018). They gathered Florida students to rally the state capitol and successfully pushed the governor to sign legislation increasing the state minimum age to purchase a firearm to 21 and the waiting period to three days (Yee and Blinder 2018). The movement quickly spread outside the state, with student-led walkouts on March

14 held nationwide in schools from California to New York (Yee and Blinder 2018). At one rural Wisconsin school, a single student walked out while protests in Washington drew thousands (Yee and Blinder 2018). Two weeks later, hundreds of thousands gathered in Washington, DC, for the March for Our Lives protests and they were joined by protesters at more than 800 events across the United States (Hays and McFarland 2018). The march focused on three demands – banning assault weapons, outlawing the sale of high-capacity magazines, and more stringent background checks for gun purchases (Grinberg and Muaddi 2018). More protests followed and survivors eventually developed an 11-point strategy to address the problem of school shootings (Hogg and Hogg 2018). Young adults were leading calls for change.

Black Lives Matter

The Black Lives Matter movement predated the movements discussed thus far, but it resurged to prominence in 2020. While being assisted or watched by other officers, Officer Derek Chauvin of the Minneapolis Police Department killed African American George Floyd by placing and holding his knee on his neck on May 25, 2020 (Walker 2020). A growing crowd filmed and pled with Chauvin to stop, but he did not. The footage was viewed on millions of cell phone and television screens. Most Americans had spent several months social distancing due to Covid-19, but they quickly took to the streets in protest.

Many of these protests were organized by young adults. Although these young leaders had an array of interests, they united under a common goal: to eradicate systemic racism in America (Moore 2020).

On May 28, 2020, then 21-year-old Amel Viaud tweeted, "Boston, I say we unify and go downtown this Sunday evening and stand with Minneapolis" (Moore 2020). Using the name Black Boston 2020, she and two other black women led tens of thousands of protestors to march to the Massachusetts state capitol building (Moore 2020). By doing so, Viaud joined many other young adults and teens in Nashville, New York City, and other cities in leading the charge for social change and against pervasive racism in American society (Moore 2020).

While under lockdown due to Covid-19, these young people watched rapidly circulating images of mass resistance to police violence directed against members of racial minority groups and took to the streets to protest and demand social change (Moore 2020). And, social media allows many leaders to emerge, because it is so decentralized (Moore 2020). In fact, many of the protests involving Black Lives Matter and race relations in America have been organized through social media, and these helped spread protests beyond major cities.

A group of 17 people, 18–21-year-olds, some of whom knew each other previously from involvement in March for Our Lives, organized a Black Lives Matter protest that became the biggest protest in the history of Howard County, Maryland (Faguy 2020). The group created HoCo for Justice accounts on Instagram, Facebook, and Twitter, with Instagram swelling to 2,000 followers in just two days (Faguy 2020). Ryan Staples, a young black man who had just graduated from high school in the predominantly white suburban community of O'Fallon, Missouri, and two of his classmates organized a protest in their hometown via social media (Grimsley 2020). "I had no idea that 1,500 plus people were going to come and throw their support behind us," said Staples (Grimsley 2020). Even small towns saw youth-led protests spread via social media. Keon Singleton, a college athlete started his own one-man protest in his college town of Ashland, Ohio, by going jogging every day with a Black Lives Matter sign (Smith and Huey-Burns 2020). Someone posted it on Facebook and it soon became a march of 80 people (Smith and Huey-Burns 2020).

A Generational Shift?

Each of these vignettes of political activism stand counter to the reputation of young adults, cultivated over the last few generations, as politically unengaged. While some have argued that this caricature of young adults as politically unengaged is misleading or incomplete because norms of an engaged citizenry are changing (Dalton 2008), the events seen between 2017 and 2020 seemed to challenge even that characterization. The fact that these activities continued beyond the 2018 midterm elections (Alemony and Viser 2019) suggest this rising political activism is more than a temporary aberration, particularly with young people leading many of the protests surrounding racism in American politics and society. This rising activism also coincides with a new generation coming of political age – Generation Z. Members of that generation were at the forefront of protests against gun violence and racism in American society and politics, not Millennials.

Some of this activism, especially related to the Parkland shootings and Black Lives Matter, even attracted those not yet old enough to vote. But the activism among this group did not end there. In March 2019, even elementary and middle school students worldwide staged walkouts and other protests to pressure lawmakers to do something about climate change in a global movement inspired by Swedish teenager Greta Thunberg (Paris 2019). And in 2020, young adults across the country and even around the world, some of whom just graduated from high school, have been at the forefront of the resurgence of the Black Lives Matter movement, organizing protests after the killing of George Floyd (Grimsley 2020; Faguy 2020; Walker 2020). A generation is finding and using its voice to push for political change in levels not seen in decades. These changing patterns of political activity combined with a new generation coming of political age suggest it is time for another look at young adults' political participation.

Mischaracterization of Millennials

New generations can easily be mischaracterized. As Millennials came of political age, scholars began comparing their political activity to those of prior generations. The popular media stereotype of uninvolved Millennials was shown to be a mischaracterization (Novak 2016). While Millennials came up far short in some respects, they lead the way in others. They have been less likely than older generations to vote and to follow politics (Wattenberg 2016). However, they prefer civic engagement over political engagement and do not necessarily lag behind participation rates of other generations when it comes to more civic-oriented activities like "buycotting," joining groups, and volunteering (Zukin et al. 2006; Dalton 2008). They value tolerance and social justice (Dalton 2008; Rouse and Ross 2018) and are more likely than older generations to believe that protesting advances political change (Rouse and Ross 2018). They were also quick to take to a variety of online forms of political engagement, which fostered additional offline engagement (Moffett and Rice 2016; Kahne and Bowyer 2018).

What Changed?

Yet this mischaracterization of Millennials alone does not explain the high levels of participation among young adults seen from the lead up to the 2018 midterm elections to the 2020 election and beyond. Perhaps there was something different about these years that produced increased activism and young adults were more active because everyone was more active. Politics became more contentious as partisan polarization increased. Increased polarization perceptually increases the stakes and heightens participation (Abramowitz and Saunders 1998; Abramowitz and Stone 2006). Further, what was seen in many circles as a surprise victory for President Trump in 2016 drove home the importance of voter turnout.

Like all age groups, young adults are not uniform in their political proclivities. During the 2016 campaign, Donald Trump had both vocal and silent supporters who were under the age of 25. Yet, these were in the minority. The Democratic advantage among Millennials runs nearly two-to-one (Pew Research Center 2018a), but does not necessarily translate into votes on Election Day, as young adults have historically had the lowest turnout rates (Miller and Shanks 1996; Wattenberg 2016). Complicating matters further, the young left had been especially enthusiastic supporters of Bernie Sanders during the 2016 Democratic primaries. As the Democratic nominee, Hillary Clinton struggled to win over this enthusiasm. Most young Sanders supporters preferred Clinton over Trump (Booker 2016), but many were still reluctant to vote for her. Some young Democratic voters, convinced Trump had no chance, thought they could safely stay home or cast their vote for the Green Party as a message to the Democratic establishment (Richmond, Zinshteyn, and Gross 2016). These young adults did not dream that a candidate whom they saw as a threat to the generation's strongly held norm of equality would become president of the United States. In the days after the election there were reports that some young people were so distraught over Trump's election night victory in 2016 that universities offered students counseling and other forms of emotional support and some professors canceled classes or postponed exams because students were in such shock (Korn and Belkin 2016; Mascarenhas 2016). A clear lesson emerged – electoral participation has drastic consequences – and Generation Z, nearly all of whom were too young to vote in 2016, waited in the wings watching.

Perhaps this lesson took root. The 2018 election drew unusually high turnout for a midterm election year. The issues introduced at the beginning of this chapter remained highly important to voters. While the decision to end DACA was blocked by court injunctions in early 2018 (Feuer 2018) and the controversial policy of separating children from parents when families crossed the border illegally was suspended in June 2018 (Jervis and Gomes 2019), a substantial portion of voters said immigration would help guide their vote choice for Congress in 2018. In fact, immigration was virtually tied in first place in importance to voters with the perennial election issues of the economy and healthcare; 78–80% of voters said each issue would be extremely or very important in guiding their vote for Congress (Newport 2018).

Although the MeToo movement saw some successes, Brett Kavanaugh was confirmed to the U.S. Supreme Court just a month before the 2018 midterm elections. Both issues remained important to voters, with 74% saying the way women are treated in society would be extremely or very important in guiding their vote for Congress and 64% saying the same for Kavanaugh's confirmation (Newport 2018). Finally, while the March for Our Lives movement against gun violence was seeing some success at the state level (Vasilogambros 2018), Congress had yet to take meaningful action to help curb gun violence. Voters watched this debate closely, with 72% of Americans saying gun policy would be extremely or very important in helping guide their vote for Congress (Newport 2018). These issues not only guided vote choice; they propelled voter turnout in 2018.

Since the strongest piece of evidence provided of young adults' lack of political engagement has been their lower voter turnout rate compared to older generations, their comparative level of electoral participation in 2018 bears examination. Figure 1.1 shows voter turnout by age in both the 2014 and 2018 midterm elections. While in 2018, young adults remained the least likely of all age groups to use their right to vote, they also exhibited the steepest increase in turnout. All generations were more active but young adults were especially so. This suggests there was something different about 2018 and that its effects were particularly strong among young people. While similar data from the U.S. Census Bureau Current Population Survey for the 2020 election will not be available until 2022, preliminary estimates of youth voter turnout in 2020 show a bigger increase than did total ballots counted among the voting eligible population (CIRCLE

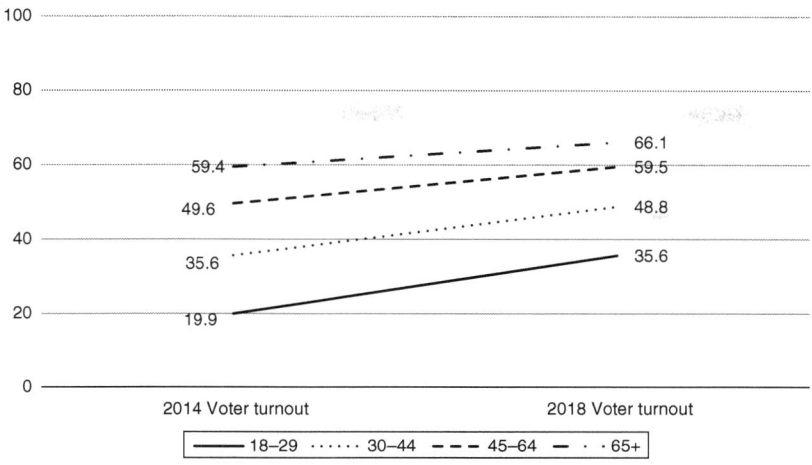

FIGURE 1.1 Voter Turnout by Age in 2014 and 2018.
Source: U.S. Census Bureau Current Population Survey Voting and Registration Supplements.

2020; United States Election Project 2020). Young adult political participation is increasing.

Reexamining Young Adult Participation

From the streets to the ballot booth, participation among young adults has increased. Could a generational shift be taking place? Is this partially the result of a rising Generation Z with sharply different norms about political participation? Will politically unengaged young adults become a thing of the past? Or is this heightened participation issue driven and likely to fade? Whatever the answers, it is time to reexamine our conclusions about young adult participation.

We explore how young adults express themselves politically, how this shapes the participation patterns of young adults, and the consequences this may have on the representation of their views and the implementation of their preferred policies. In doing so, we focus in part on the issues introduced earlier in this chapter: the MeToo movement, Brett Kavanaugh's nomination to the U.S. Supreme Court, gun violence and gun control, immigration and family separation. Gallup Polls showed these issues were four of the top ten issues to voters in 2018 (Newport 2018) and the only four in the top ten that sparked significant activism. While these are not the only issues in which young adults engage, the examination of them allows us to apply diverse theoretical perspectives to better understand young adult political expression and its consequences.

Yet, this heightened activism among young adults endured beyond the 2018 midterm election, and right through 2020. Young adults have continued to raise their voice and lead calls for change. We examine activism on many of the same issues in 2020, with activism related to Justice Kavanaugh replaced by activism related to the nomination of Amy Coney Barrett to the Supreme Court.

In addition, we add to this list of issues one in which this youth activism was particularly apparent in 2020: the resurgence of the Black Lives Matter movement. #BlackLivesMatter was born in 2013 after George Zimmerman was acquitted for the killing of Trayvon Martin, an unarmed black teenager, and became a rallying cry in the protests that emerged after police officer Darren Wilson shot and killed Michael Brown in Ferguson, MO, and police officers in Staten Island, New York, fatally restrained Eric Garner (Chase 2018). While the movement stayed active throughout this period, the killing of George Floyd in Minneapolis sparked a resurgence that spread the movement further across America than ever before, into its suburbs and small towns (Smith and Huey-Burns 2020), with young adults leading their communities in protest (Grimsley 2020; Moore 2020). For African Americans, protests were already part of a proven strategy by which to confront discrimination and racial inequality in a way that places them on the public agenda (Gillion 2020; Lee 2002). Yet, social media helped spread them further and faster than before. As 20-year-old HoCo for Justice organizer Sara Wunete pointed out to reporters,

> Protesting and marching isn't something that just started existing in this day and age; it's been happening for years. As for us being young, utilizing social media because of how quick it can get to people, that's why we were able to make something like this happen in four days.
>
> *(Faguy 2020)*

These issues share something else in common besides sparking activism that social media helps spread and being important to large numbers of voters – they disproportionately affect young adults While adults of all ages have been engaged in activism on these issues, young adults' disproportionate risks and experiences related to these issues make them particularly important to study. Young adults share a disproportionate risk of sexual assault and a high incidence of sexual harassment. A majority of those who are sexually assaulted are under the age of 30 (RAINN 2020). Female college students between the ages of 18 and 24 are three times more likely to experience sexual assault than are women in other age groups (RAINN 2020). In addition, a survey found that 74% of women between the ages of 18–24 reported having experienced sexual harassment (Kearl 2018).[1,2] These unwelcome experiences and statistics suggest that most young adults and their friends have their own stories to add to the MeToo movement.

Young adults, by virtue of their age, can expect a longer time horizon of being affected by the influence of Justices Kavanaugh and Barrett on Supreme

Court decisions than other age groups. This may have raised the stakes of their nominations for young adults compared to older Americans. Young adults also have a greater likelihood of knowing an immigrant whose future in the country is uncertain. As the 2018 election neared, two-thirds of those who would face potential deportation if the Obama administration's DACA policy ended were under the age of 25 (Lopez and Krogstad 2017). This makes young adults particularly likely to be directly affected by this policy or have friends that could be directly affected by changes in U.S. immigration policy, a factor associated with increased empathy for immigrants and support for more liberal immigration policies (Knoll 2009).

Young adults also face disproportionate risks of being killed with a firearm and of being killed by police. Young adults have grown up under the threat of school shootings and the gun homicide rate among 18–25-year-olds is more than twice the rate for Americans as a whole (Kochanek et al. 2019). Also, across all racial and ethnic groups and genders, the risk of being killed by the police peaks between the ages of 20 and 35, with the risk particularly high for young black men (Edwards, Lee, and Esposito 2019). While 0.05% of all male deaths in the United States is caused by police use of force, 1.6% of the deaths of black males between the ages of 18 and 24, 1.2% of the deaths of Latino and Native American males aged 18–24, and 0.5% of the deaths of white and Asian/Pacific Islander males aged 18–24 is due to police use of force (Edwards, Lee, and Esposito 2019). These disproportionate impacts give young adults strong incentives to raise their political voice.

Yet, while the issues we examine all disproportionately impact young people, they also involve key variations that provide additional analytical leverage for testing our hypotheses. The MeToo movement, the March for Our Lives/# Never Again movement against gun violence, and the Black Lives Matter movement all share characteristics of social movements. Some of these, like March for Our Lives, were led exclusively by young people, while the MeToo movement was led primarily by members of another generation (Generation X). Meanwhile, the Black Lives Matter movement was started by women at the older end of the Millennial generation but most of the protests related to it in 2020 were organized by members of Generation Z. By examining some movements led by young adults and some led by older generations, we can test our core theories in several contexts. This allows us to investigate whether when young adults post or protest about movements they align with, regardless of whether those movements are led by their own generation or older ones, they become mobilized to participate in other ways, too.

We investigate issues with varying degrees of salience to young people in varying years. For example, the MeToo movement and the March for Our Lives movement had both faded to the background in 2020, eclipsed by other issues in many voters' minds. Yet, by examining young adults' political expression related to these issues in 2020, we can investigate whether their activism continues to spread even when an issue is no longer on center stage.

Yet, we do not limit our examination of young adults using their political voice to social movements. We also test our hypotheses on issues with limited time horizons like Supreme Court nominations and the policy of family separation. These issues generated active involvement from organized interest groups. They were less important to young adults collectively than some of the social movements we examine, but among young adults who cared enough to post or protest, did such activity lead to other forms of engagement? By testing our hypotheses in these varying contexts, we hope to gain greater insights into the stretch and impact of young adult political expression.

Young adults may be growing more politically active, but that does not guarantee they will be any more effective in getting their voices heard. As Figure 1.1 shows, while young adult voter turnout rates increased more substantially than any other age group in 2018, they still voted at much lower rates than their elders. This persistent differential turnout rate by age continues to send elected officials the signal that young adults can be safely ignored. But, can they, and if so, for how long?

We focus on three forms of political expression: posting one's political views online, protesting, and contacting elected officials about political issues. The forms of participation young adults seem to favor – protesting and posting online – are not necessarily the ones most likely to provoke a response from elected officials, at least as long as young adult turnout remains low. However, Millennials think protesting is effective (Rouse and Ross 2018) and recent events suggest Generation Z favors it even more. Whatever the cause of this increased activism, if all this generation does is protest, how much impact will they have? Gillion (2020) finds that voter turnout increases in electoral districts in which protest activity occurred. Outsider tactics such as protests often operate based on implicit threats – if elected officials fail to act or hear their voices, it could hurt them electorally in the next election (Gillion 2020; Lee 2002). Elected officials must weigh how seriously to take this threat against the messages they are hearing directly from constituents and campaign supporters – those most likely to sway election outcomes. As long as young adults vote at lower rates, they may be unlikely to be counted among this group.

Online communications have featured prominently among young adults' recent activism. Parkland survivors started #NeverAgain on Twitter the day after a gunman stormed their school (Alter 2018) and also used #MarchForOurLives to coordinate protests. #MeToo was used more than 19 million times in the year after Milano's tweet went viral (Anderson and Toor 2018) and #FamiliesBelongTogether was used to organize protests against the family separation policy, with various celebrities promoting the hashtag, heightening its visibility (Nyren 2018). #BlackLivesMatter and #blm emerged on Twitter in 2013 after George Zimmerman's acquittal for the shooting of Trayvon Martin (Anderson et al. 2018) and have remained a helpful organizing tool for protests in 2020. And while a growing line of research shows posting about politics – either on blogs or social media – leads to other forms of offline engagement (Shah et al. 2005; Gil de Zuniga, Puig-I-Abril, and Rojas 2009; Moffett and Rice 2016), does expressing oneself online reach the ears of politicians? And if it does, how seriously are these online messages taken? These are important empirical questions with normative consequences for democratic representation. To the extent young adults avoid electoral politics more than other age groups, elected officials might safely ignore their protests and posts with little consequence. However, if this increase in activism through outsider tactics helps produce increased electoral and governmental involvement, then young adults' voices are more likely to matter.

How Young Is a Young Adult?

To answer this question, we focus on young adults between the ages of 18–25 because we believe the common age grouping of 18–29 is overbroad. First, the relationship between age and voting is a particularly strong one. Voter turnout is lowest at age 18 and the estimated turnout rate at age 29 is roughly ten points higher than the turnout rate at 19 (Franklin 2018). It is important to examine where participation has been lowest, especially since these are the ages that were unusually visible in the timespan we examine.

Examining ages 18–29 may also be overbroad from both life cycle and generational perspectives about political participation.[3] Life cycle perspectives tie age differences in political participation to factors specific to different stages of life that shape participation rates. For example, participation increases as people move into their thirties because people in this decade become more likely to buy houses and have children reach school age. This increased participation comes because they have greater incentive to pay attention to local politics, as this impacts their property values and quality of their children's education. Meanwhile, declines in voting seen among the oldest Americans may be tied to their increased likelihood of ill health. Generational perspectives instead focus on the defining events that shape a generation, its views, and its participatory rates. The generation's unique experiences, particularly as they come of political age, are expected to stick with them throughout their lifetimes.

From a life cycle perspective, those aged 18–25 are more likely to have more in common with each other than with those in their late twenties. The age span of 18–25 marks the period of transitioning into adulthood, both legally and functionally. At this age, young adults establish independence from their parents. Some go off to college while others find their first full-time job. Young adults gain rights throughout this period, becoming eligible to vote at 18, to drink alcohol at 21, and to rent a car without added stipulations at 25. Throughout this period, young adults are eligible to remain on their parents' insurance. By 26, independence is expected; most young adults are expected to have settled into adult life, establishing a career and perhaps a family of their own.

While generational focuses are commonplace, generational dividing lines are typically unclear and the subject of much debate. Pew Research Center places the end of the Millennial generation with those born in 1996 and characterizes those born in 1997 or later as Generation Z (Dimock 2019). This made the youngest possible Millennial a little under two months shy of 22 years old at the time of the 2018 midterm election and nearly 24 for the 2020 presidential election.

From a generational perspective, there are likely to be sharp divisions between the younger half of the oft-used 18–29 range than the older half. Most of those aged 18 at the time of the 2018 midterm elections were born in 2000 while most of those aged 29 were born in 1989. These age differences are likely to shape how they experienced potentially defining events of their generation. One such defining event was the September 11 terrorist attacks. Others involve the launch of popular social media platforms. Panel A of Figure 1.2 shows the age of those between 18 and 29 at the time of the 2018 midterm elections would have been at the time the September 11 terrorist attacks occurred and at the time Facebook and Twitter launched. Nearly all of Generation Z would be too young to remember the September 11 terrorist attacks while most Millennials under age 25 would only have vague direct memories. Meanwhile, older Millennials will remember when they first heard the news and watching the vivid images of the aftermath on television. This difference in experience could potentially have a distinct impact on worldviews. In addition, older Millennials lacked the ability to use social media to connect with friends as they first entered their teenage years. Their experience will have differed from their younger compatriots who grew up in a socially networked world. From a generational perspective, focusing on the ages of 18–25 allows us to examine the political participation of the oldest four years of Generation Z and the youngest four years of Millennials in 2018, those most likely to have experienced these defining events similarly.

By 2020, the ages of 18–25 encompass the six oldest years of Generation Z and the two youngest years of Millennials. As Panel B of Figure 1.2 shows, this was the first major election when some of those not yet born at the time of the September 11 terrorist attacks were eligible to vote. Almost no one in the age range of 18–25 during the 2020 election year had reached the start of their tweens before Facebook launched and nearly all would have still been elementary school aged when Twitter launched a few years later. This age range's generational experiences would have far more in common with each other than they would with those aged 29 in 2020 who were ten at the time of the September 11 terrorist attacks, 13 when Facebook was launched and 15 when Twitter first launched.

Our Data

Those aged 18–25 deserve focus due to differences in participatory rates, life cycle similarities, and experiences within generational cohorts but they are also notoriously hard to survey representatively (Pew Research Center 2018a; Cantrell

a. At the time of the 2018 midterm elections

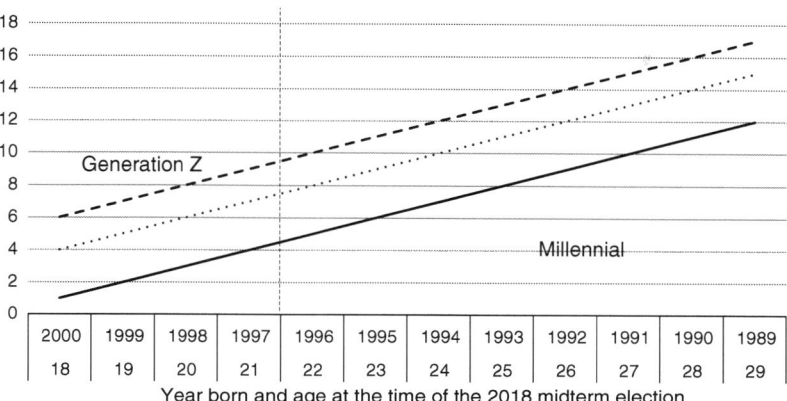

b. At the time of the 2020 presidential elections

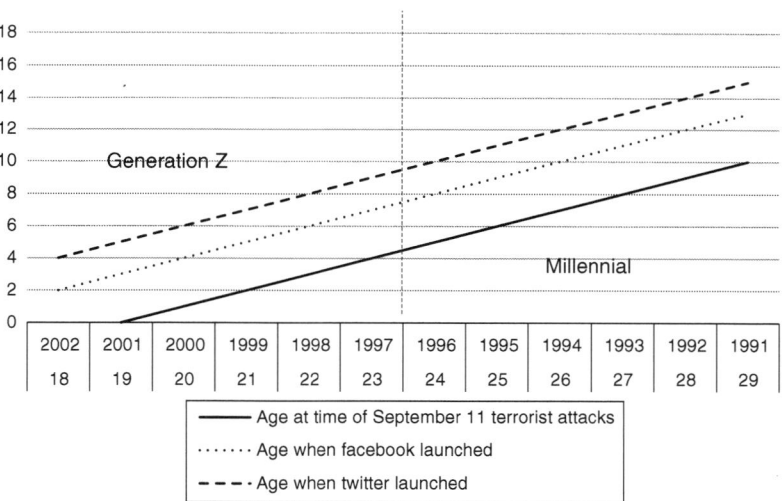

FIGURE 1.2 Generational Experiences by Age among Those 18–29.
(a) At the Time of the 2018 Midterm Elections.
(b) At the Time of the 2020 Presidential Elections.

et al. 2018). There is no list available to survey researchers of the contact information of every American between the ages of 18–25 of which to sample from, so a truly representative sample is impossible. When studying adults as a whole, survey researchers typically turn either to random digit dialing (RDD) so that all who have a phone are equally likely to be selected into the sample or to taking a random sample of a large (several million) internet panel in the hopes of closely approximating the characteristics of a truly random sample. Neither of these approaches does particularly well at accurately capturing young adults.

Although including cell phones in sampling frames has helped reduce age disparities in surveys, young adults remain significantly underrepresented in random digit dialing surveys (Keeter et al. 2017). Likewise, some studies indicate that young adults participate in internet-based surveys at significantly lower rates than do older age groups (Giglotti and Dietsch 2014), and internet-based surveys have been found to significantly underrepresent young adults (Chang and Krosnick 2009). Large internet panels like Harris Interactive or Ipsos can direct surveys to 18–25-year-olds within their panels, but panels like these have been found to have significantly lower percentages of young adults in them than in the population (Chang and Krosnick 2009) and they struggle to recruit enough young adults to participate. Meanwhile, using RDD to survey young adults might require calling tens of thousands of households or more just to find 1,000 young adults. Then, low response and completion rates might necessitate calling hundreds of thousands of numbers to get 1,000 completed surveys of young adults. This adds significantly to the costs of such effort. Together, this suggests that young adults may be both harder to reach in the first place and less likely to respond when they are reached. This complicates any effort to survey young adults.

To study this age group, we performed online surveys on the day after the 2018 midterm election (November 7, 2018) and the day after the 2020 presidential election (November 4, 2020) of Americans between 18 and 25 years old. Instead of sampling within a large internet panel, we used Amazon's Mechanical Turk (mTurk) platform to carry out this survey, a website that allows members of the public to earn money for completing many kinds of tasks, including participating in survey research. Each participant was paid $1.50 for completing the survey. A total of 1,010 participants completed the survey in 2018, and 969 participants did so in 2020; we removed any incomplete responses.[4]

Some may see the use of Amazon mTurk as potentially problematic because it is not a random sample where all in the sample frame have an equal opportunity to participate. Yet, as we discussed previously, this is a pitfall RDD and internet-based panels share when they are used to study young adults. Still, mTurk workers could differ systematically from the population in potentially unobservable ways. For example, mTurk workers are more likely to be white and self-identify as members of the LGBTQ community than the U.S. population writ large (Casey et al. 2017). Similarly, Casey et al. (2017) identify other, small effects on mTurk survey respondents such as the weekday and hour in which they are recruited.[5]

Most importantly for our research, mTurk workers tend to be younger than the U.S. population at large (Casey et al. 2017). Thus, using mTurk to recruit our sample is less concerning than it would be if we performed a survey that claimed to generalize to all American adults, not just ones between 18 and 25.[6] What might otherwise be a problem thus turns into an asset for us since the nature of our research questions requires a younger sample than that which exists in the broader population of U.S. adults.

In addition, many scholars have used mTurk to obtain representative samples of their target population in survey and experimental research (see Berinsky, Huber, and Lenz 2012; Chandler, Mueller, and Paolacci 2014; Huff and Tingley 2015; Towner 2018), particularly young adults or college students (Lupton 2019). Thus, we believe that the results that we have generated can generalize to the population of American 18–25-year-olds.

Yet, we do not rely solely on the fact that mTurk has produced representative samples for others to determine whether we can safely draw conclusions about young adults from our survey. First, we compared the characteristics of our sample to other recent research that has examined young adults (Rouse and Ross 2018) and found that the characteristics are similar. Then, to explore whether our dataset is sufficiently representative to use in our study of young adult participation, we also acquired data from surveys taken by the Pew Research Center (2018a, 2020) in September 2018 and June 2020 to compare young adults in their nationally representative samples with the ones that we acquired via mTurk. To perform this comparison, we used Pew's sample weights for the Pew sample, and constrained by those between the ages of 18 and 25 in 2018, and the ages of 18 and 29 in 2020.[7] Table 1.1 illustrates this comparison on four characteristics: partisan identification, approval of President Trump's job performance, ideology, and race.[8]

This table illustrates that the 2018 mTurk sample is slightly more Democratic and liberal, and has a higher percentage of disapproval of President Trump's job performance than Pew's. Given that the issues drawing young adult activism in the time period we examine tend to be left-leaning largely Democratic ones, this should not pose a significant problem. The 2020 mTurk data, though, is less Democratic and more conservative than the Pew data. However, the Pew and mTurk data in 2020 both show a majority of Democratic party identifiers and those who disapproved of then-President Trump's job performance. Also, the racial composition of both samples is similar to Pew's. Thus, the mTurk samples are similar enough to other national-level surveys taken around the same time on several dimensions that we can use the data acquired from the mTurk samples to analyze young adult political participation in 2018 and 2020.

Finally, some might express concerns that our mTurk samples might attract those with more interest in the 2018 and 2020 elections. We note this is an issue for large internet nonprobability panels as well (Chang and Krosnick 2009). Yet, while such surveys may disproportionately attract those interested in the subject, this quality is also associated with more accurate self-reporting by respondents

TABLE 1.1 Comparison between Pew Surveys (September 2018 and June 2020) and mTurk Samples (November 2018 and 2020) (%)

Characteristic	Pew Survey (18–25 Only) (2018)	mTurk Sample (2018)	Pew Survey (18–29 Only) (2020)	mTurk Sample (2020)
Partisan Identification				
Democratic	57.31	65.45	67.87	52.64
Republican	31.50	33.86	28.83	47.05
Approval of President Trump's Job Performance				
Approve	25.95	32.35	24.31	39.31
Disapprove	58.92	67.65	73.57	60.69
Ideology				
Very Conservative	8.21	8.55	4.27	20.65
Conservative	16.27	14.81	14.28	26.80
Moderate	35.24	26.54	38.96	18.14
Liberal	24.32	28.73	23.61	25.65
Very Liberal	12.20	20.48	15.46	8.76
Race				
Whites	66.82	68.86	66.89	65.81
African Americans	13.80	11.04	10.54	13.43
Asian Americans	4.32	6.27	8.40	6.61

(Chang and Krosnick 2009; Holbrook and Krosnick 2010). Provided our survey shows significant variations on key measures of political expression and factors known to influence political participation (something we establish in the chapters that follow), it will allow us to test our hypotheses with more accurate self-reports of political expression than we might acquire through other methods.

Analytic Methods

To analyze the extent to which posting or protesting about differing political issues or opinions about those issues affect civic engagement and contacting elected government officials, we use a series of matching analyses. This approach estimates the impact of a treatment on an outcome, while controlling for other factors that may influence the outcome. Although the method may be unfamiliar for some of our readers, the result is simple and intuitive to grasp. It provides a precise estimate of the change in an outcome, such as amount of civic activity or the likelihood of contacting an elected official that is attributable to the treatment, such as posting about an issue.

We choose this estimator for three reasons. First, nearly all regression techniques (including ordinary least squares (OLS)) presume a linear relationship between the dependent and independent variables (see Greene 2011). Our theoretical arguments posit a positive relationship between our treatment variables and both dependent variables. However, we make no prediction beyond a positive sign about the treatment effects at each specific level of our treatment variables. Consequently, the relationship between the dependent and treatment variables is unlikely to be linear and would be inappropriate to examine using a method that presumes linearity. Matching analyses do not assume linearity, which is one reason why these are better suited to examine the phenomena that we investigate throughout this book (Imbens and Rubin 2015).[9]

This discussion implies an additional justification for the matching approach: individuals likely have different treatment effects, depending on the frequency with which they have engaged in the different activities or opinions specified in our treatment variables. Any regression-based analysis assumes treatment homogeneity, which is unlikely given that linearity is uncertain. Matching analyses deal nicely with this issue because they assume neither linearity nor homogeneity (Abadie and Imbens 2011; Imbens and Rubin 2015). Instead, matching-based approaches produce several treatment estimates depending on the level of treatment that a respondent received (Imbens and Rubin 2015). Thus, we can generate several, more accurate estimates of our effect sizes.

In Chapter 2, for example, we examine the effects of posting about the MeToo Movement (the treatment) on civic engagement. Our posting variable has five levels: never, rarely, sometimes, very often, and frequently. We estimate separate matching analyses for each of the other treatment levels relative to what would have happened if one had never posted about this movement. In doing so, we get a more accurate estimate that gets closer to making causal inferences about the effects of posting about the MeToo movement on civic engagement. We perform analogous estimations throughout this book.

Plan of the Book

In Part I of the book, we examine how issues mobilize in more depth. We rely on our mTurk surveys of young adults' political expression and activity to test the pathways between the #MeToo Movement, the Kavanaugh and Barrett Supreme Court nominations, the March for Our Lives/#NeverAgain movement, immigration and family separation, and the #BlackLivesMatter movement and civic engagement, but we also place political expression of young adults in context, using surveys from Gallup, Pew Research Center, and others to help identify how young adults' views and actions may differ from older Americans.

Whenever we refer to civic engagement, we reference a combination of both political and civic activity. Specifically, these encompass elements of what Zukin et al. (2006, 57–58) identify as civic activities, political activities, cognitive engagement with politics, and public voice activities. We expect that posting and protesting about political issues helps increase engagement across this variety of activities. This can include engaging in both civic and political activities, as well as the desire to acquire additional political information. Our measure of civic engagement adds together survey respondents' reported engagement in activities including: paid attention to political campaigns; used the internet to research a candidate's positions or view speeches by a candidate; wore a campaign button or shirt, put a campaign sticker on your car, or placed a sign in your window or in front of your residence; tried to talk to people and explain why they should vote for or against one of the parties or candidates; contacted a newspaper, radio, or TV talk show to express your opinion on an issue; attended any political meetings, rallies, speeches, dinners, or things like that in support of a candidate or party; worked or volunteered on a political campaign for a candidate or party; worked with a group to solve a problem in a community; made a purchasing decision based on the conduct or values of a company; and contributed money to a candidate, political party, or affiliated organization.

Those who study political behavior will recognize many of these as measures routinely queried in the American National Election Studies. One of the principal exceptions is the question on making a purchasing decision based on the conduct or values of a company. This is a relatively new form of engagement that is sufficiently favored by young adults that we thought it important to add due to Zukin et al. (2006) seminal work.

Then, to create our index of civic engagement, we added together the frequency with which respondents reported engaging in this array of 12 political and civic activities. Respondents were asked the extent they engaged in these ranging from "never" having done so to having done each of them "very often," using a five-point scale. The means of this index of 14.56 (2018) and 26.01 (2020) are relatively low and the standard deviations, 10.75 (2018) and 14.61 (2020), indicate substantial variance around this mean. Thus, despite the tendency of internet surveys to attract those who participate at higher rates (Holbrook and Krosnick 2010), we can be confident we have captured both low and high participators in our surveys.

Since we are combining many measures that others like Zukin et al. (2006) examined separately, it is important to consider whether these items can be combined to measure a single concept. When creating an index of items, Cronbach's alpha can be used to determine the extent to which the items in the index provide a consistent measure of a concept. It takes on values ranging from 0 to 1, with values closer to 1 indicating the measures in the index are reliably measuring the same concept. Our index of civic engagement has a Chronbach's alpha of .92 in 2018 and a Chronbach's alpha of .95 in 2020, giving us very high confidence in the reliability of these items in measuring a single concept, which we label civic engagement.

In Chapter 2, we investigate how support for the MeToo Movement or posting about it or engaging in protests related to it heightened young adults' civic and political activity as measured in our civic engagement index. Drawing on the social movement literature, we develop a theory about why support for a social movement that was not explicitly political helps extend the civic and political engagement of young adults.

Then, in Chapter 3 we examine how opposition to the nominations of Brett Kavanaugh or Amy Coney Barrett to the U.S. Supreme Court, posting about their nominations, or participating in protests related to their nominations increased young adult participation. We turn to prospect theory and the impact of threats to core values to help explain who might be most responsive to calls for action. However, we also argue that opinions do not necessarily translate into action – it's the willingness to act on these opinions, either via posting or protesting, that provides the clearest pathway to higher levels of civic engagement.

Chapter 4 focuses on young adult involvement in the movement to prevent gun violence. We trace the history of movements against gun violence, identify the factors that contributed to a movement of young adults emerging in 2018, and investigate whether this movement that emerged out of shared threat and collective grievance helped broaden civic engagement.

Chapter 5 turns to the issues of immigration and family separation. Large increases in immigration produce different emotions in different people. For some, it triggers anxiety and a focus on self-interest where for others it triggers empathy for the plight of immigrants. Strong emotions on either side might stimulate individuals to act. Do those who posted or protested about these issues become more civically engaged as a result? Chapter 6 focuses on the Black Lives Matter movement in 2020. Does support for this movement and participation in it through posting and protesting about it help young adults expand their civic engagement as the Civil Rights Movement did decades earlier?

Two large-scale findings emerge from these chapters. First, posting about political issues is associated with higher levels of political participation. For example, those who posted about the MeToo Movement, Supreme Court nominations, and gun control had significantly higher civic engagement levels than those who did not do so. Second, the story of young adult participation is more nuanced in that not every issue young adults care about broadens their rate of civic engagement. In particular, young adults viewed immigration and family separation policies as important in 2018, but their views about these policies, posting about them, or participating in protests related to them was not connected to higher levels of participation.

Part II of the book examines the link between protesting and posting about politics with contacting elected officials. More specifically, do the outsider tactics of young adults that were so prominent in the media accounts of young adult activism make young adults any more likely to turn their attention inward to the halls of power? Outsider and insider tactics provide distinct strategies for political influence, but they are not mutually exclusive. In the past, young adults have been highly unlikely compared to other age groups to engage in insider strategies like contacting elected officials. Given the recent change in levels of activism, their likelihood of contacting elected officials bears revisiting.

In Chapter 7, we focus on whether posting online about the issues explored in Part I makes young adults any more likely to share these views directly with elected officials while Chapter 8 investigates whether engaging in protests on these issues makes young adults any more likely to contact elected officials directly about their views. The answers we uncover to these questions suggest that a new politically active generation may be emerging and that these young adults will be increasingly likely to have their policy concerns listened to by elected officials. Chapter 9 considers a potential alternative explanation for young adults' heightened involvement – opinions about then-President Trump, and concludes with what our findings, taken together, suggest for the future of young adult participation and the effectiveness of young adults' political voices in the years to come.

To facilitate chapter-by-chapter access, we have included References at the end of each chapter in the book. A full-book, consolidated Reference list is available on the Webpage for the book:

Notes

1 While the highest rates of ever experiencing sexual harassment and assault were reported among women and men aged 25–49, the study's author points out that more years alive might make the reports of ever experiencing these more likely (Kearl 2018).
2 Men also experience sexual harassment and assault, albeit at far lower rates than women.
3 For further discussion of these perspectives, see Beck (1984) and Zukin et al. (2006).
4 We constrained the eligibility of participants in this survey to those with human interface task (HIT) approval rates of at least 95% and whose location is in the United States. Although we were unable to constrain by age here, we did so through the first question asking respondents whether they were between the ages of 18 and 25. If they responded no, the survey ended.
5 We had little control over the weekday in which we fielded our survey (Wednesday), as the date on which these elections are held is always the first Tuesday after the first Monday in November.
6 We did not ask about membership in the LGBTQ community, as mTurk does not permit researchers to ask personally identifiable information in surveys.
7 The age categories available in the 2020 data differ from those in the 2018 data.
8 These were the only topics on which the surveys offered comparable questions.
9 Throughout this book, we follow King and Nielsen's (2019) advice in implementing this matching technique, propensity score matching, by appropriately scaling our variables, reporting imbalance statistics before and after matching in our online appendix, and have used this technique on a set of data with high levels of imbalance.

References

Abadie, Alberto and Guido W. Imbens 2011. "Bias-Corrected Matching Estimators for Average Treatment Effects." *Journal of Business and Economic Statistics* 29(1): 1–11. https://doi.org/10.1198/jbes.2009.07333. Accessed online June 19, 2021.

Abramowitz, Alan I. and Kyle L. Saunders 1998. "Ideological Realignment in the U.S. Electorate." *Journal of Politics* 60(3): 634–652. https://doi.org/10.2307/2647642. Accessed online June 19, 2021.

Abramowitz, Alan I. and Walter J. Stone 2006. "The Bush Effect: Polarization, Turnout, and Activism in the 2004 Presidential Election." *Presidential Studies Quarterly* 36(2): 141–154. https://doi.org/10.1111/j.1741-5705.2006.00295.x. Accessed online June 19, 2021.

Alemany, Jacqueline and Matt Viser 2019. "Parkland Students Unveil Sweeping Gun-Control Proposal and Hope for a Youth Voting Surge in 2020." *The Washington Post*, August 21. www.washingtonpost.com/politics/parkland-students-unveil-sweeping-gun-control-proposal-and-hope-for-a-youth-voting-surge-in-2020/2019/08/20/145f4574-c36f-11e9-9986-1fb3e4397be4_story.html. Accessed online April 17, 2020.

Alter, Charlotte 2018. "The School Shooting Generation Has Had Enough." *Time* March 22, 2018. https://time.com/longform/never-again-movement/. Accessed online January 30, 2020.

Anderson, Monica and Skye Toor 2018. "How Social Media Users Have Discussed Sexual Harassment since #MeToo Went Viral." Pew Research Center. October 11, 2018. www.pewresearch.org/fact-tank/2018/10/11/how-social-media-users-have-discussed-sexual-harassment-since-metoo-went-viral/. Accessed online June 6, 2019.

Anderson, Monica, Skye Toor, Lee Rainie, and Aaron Smith 2018. "An Analysis of #BlackLivesMatter and Other Twitter Hashtags Related to Political or Social Issues." Pew Research Center. www.pewresearch.org/internet/2018/07/11/an-analysis-of-blacklivesmatter-and-other-twitter-hashtags-related-to-political-or-social-issues/. Accessed online June 9, 2020.

Bauer-Wolf, Jeremy 2018. "A College's List of Alleged Rapists." *Inside Higher Ed*. www.insidehighered.com/news/2018/01/30/metoo-movement-inspires-similar-campaigns-among-colleges. Accessed online August 21, 2019.

Beck, Paul Allen 1984. "Young vs. Old in 1984: Generations and Life Stages in Presidential Nomination Politics." *PS: Political Science and Politics* 17(3): 515–524. https://doi.org/10.1017/S1049096500024483. Accessed online June 19, 2021.

Beck, Robyn 2018. "Over 60 Cities Protest Family Separation at the United States Border." *Teen Vogue*. www.teenvogue.com/story/families-belong-together-rallies-and-other-grassroots-events-protest-family-separation-at-the-united-states-border. Accessed online August 21, 2019.

Berinsky, Adam, Gregory Huber, and Gabriel Lenz 2012. "Evaluating Online Labor Markets for Experimental Research: Amazon.com's Mechanical Turk." *Political Analysis* 20(3): 351–368. https://doi.org/10.1093/pan/mpr057. Accessed online June 19, 2021.

Booker, Brakkton 2016. "Harvard Poll: Millennials Yearn for Bernie but Prefer Clinton over Trump." *National Public Radio*. www.npr.org/2016/04/25/475658752/harvard-poll-millennials-yearn-for-bernie-but-prefer-clinton-to-trump. Accessed online August 23, 2019.

Braungart, Richard G. and Margaret M. Braungart. 1990b. "Generational Themes in the American Student Movements of the 1930s and 1960s." *Journal of Political and Military Sociology* 18(2): 79–121.

Cantrell, Jennifer, Elizabeth C. Hair, Alexandria Smith, Morgane Bennett, Jessica Miller Rath, Randall K. Thomas, Mansour Fahimi, J. Michael Dennis, and Donna Callone 2018. "Recruiting and Retaining Youth and Young Adults: Challenges and Opportunities in Survey Research for Tobacco Control." *Tobacco Control* 27(2): 147–154. http://dx.doi.org/10.1136/tobaccocontrol-2016-053504. Accessed online June 19, 2021.

Casey, Logan S., Jesse Chandler, Adam Seth Levine, Andrew Proctor, and Dara Z. Strolovitch 2017. "Intertemporal Differences among mTurk Workers: Time-Based Sample Variations and Implications for Online Data Collection." *Sage Open* 7(2): 1–15. https://doi.org/10.1177/2158244017712774. Accessed online June 19, 2021.

Chandler, Jesse, Pam Mueller, and Gabriele Paolacci 2014. "Nonnaivite among Amazon Mechanical Turk Workers: Consequences and Solutions for Behavioral Researchers." *Behavior Research Methods* 46(1): 112–130. https://doi.org/10.3758/s13428-013-0365-7 Accessed online June 19, 2021

Chang, Linchiat and Jon A. Krosnick 2009. "National Surveys via RDD Telephone Interviewing versus the Internet: Comparing Sample Representativeness and Response Quality." *The Public Opinion Quarterly* 73(4): 641–678. https://doi.org/10.1093/poq/nfp075. Accessed online June 19, 2021.

Chase, Garrett 2018 "The Early History of the Black Lives Matter Movement, and the Implications Thereof." *Nevada Law Review Journal* 18(3): 1091–1112.

CIRCLE. 2020. "Election Week 2020: Young People Increase Turnout, Lead Biden to Victory." https://circle.tufts.edu/latest-research/election-week-2020#youth-voter-turnout-increased-in-2020. Accessed online June 19, 2021.

Dalton, Russell J. 2008. "Citizenship Norms and the Expansion of Political Participation." *Political Studies* 56(1): 76–98. https://doi.org/10.1111/j.1467-9248.2007.00718.x. Accessed online June 19, 2021.

Dimock, Michael 2019. "Defining Generations: Where Millennials End and Generation Z Begins." January 17. www.pewresearch.org/fact-tank/2019/01/17/where-millennials-end-and-generation-z-begins/. Accessed online April 17, 2020.

Edwards, Frank, Hedwig Lee, and Michael Espisito 2019. "Risk of Being Killed by Police Use of Force in the United States by Age, Race-Ethnicity, and Sex." *Proceedings of the National Academy of Sciences of the United States of America* 116(34): 16793–16798. https://doi.org/10.1073/pnas.1821204116. Accessed online June 19, 2021.

Esten, Kathrine 2018. "Kavanaugh Rally Brings Student Activists Together." *The Massachusetts Daily Collegian*. https://dailycollegian.com/2018/10/anti-kavanaugh-rally-brings-student-activists-together. Accessed online August 21, 2019.

Faguy, Ana 2020. "Youth-Led Group behind Columbia's Black Lives Matter Protests Discusses What It Takes to Organize in 2020." *Baltimore Sun*. www.baltimoresun.com/aryland/howard/cng-ho-youth-organizing-protests-20200605-gwfdwqdxmfaapkymmq2pvc27km-story.html. Accessed online June 9, 2020.

Feuer, Alan 2018. "Second Federal Judge Issues Injunction to Keep DACA in Place." *The New York Times*. www.nytimes.com/2018/02/13/nyregion/daca-dreamers-injunction-trump.html. Accessed online May 12, 2020.

Franklin, Charles 2018. "Age and Voter Turnout." https://medium.com/@PollsAndVotes/age-and-voter-turnout-52962b0884ef. Accessed online April 17, 2020.

Garcia, Sandra E. 2017. "The Woman Who Created #MeToo Long Before Hashtags." *The New York Times*. October 20. www.nytimes.com/2017/10/20/us/me-too-movement-tarana-burke.html. Accessed online June 6, 2019.

Giglotti, Larry and Alia Dietsch 2014. "Does Age Matter? The Influence of Age on Response Rates in a Mixed-Mode Survey." *Human Dimensions of Wildlife: An International Journal* 19(3): 280–287. https://doi.org/10.1080/10871209.2014.880137. Accessed online June 19, 2021.

Gil de Zúñiga, Homero, Eulalia Puig-I-Abril, and Hernando Rojas 2009. "Weblogs, Traditional Sources Online and Political Participation: An Assessment of How the

Internet Is Changing the Political Environment." *New Media and Society* 11(4): 553–574. https://doi.org/10.1177/1461444809102960 Accessed online June 19, 2021.

Gillion, Daniel Q. 2020. *The Loud Minority: Why Protests Matter in American Democracy.* Princeton, NJ: Princeton University Press.

Greene, William H. 2011. *Econometric Analysis.* 7th Ed. New York, NY: Pearson.

Grimsley, Brooke 2020. "Ft. Zumwalt West Grad Lead Peaceful Protest: 'It's Truly a Blessing to Bring People Together.'" KMOV News. www.kmov.com/news/ft-zumwalt-west-grad-leads-peaceful-protest-its-truly-a-blessing-to-bring-people-together/article_98d194b2-a913-11ea-8482-0387620ff5d0.html. Accessed online June 9, 2020.

Grinberg, Emanuella and Nadeem Muaddi 2018. "How the Parkland Students Pulled Off a Massive National Protest in Only 5 Weeks." CNN. www.cnn.com/2018/03/26/us/march-for-our-lives/index.html. Accessed online August 9, 2019.

Hailu, Ruth A. 2018. "Harvard Student Vow Continued Activism after Kavanaugh's Confirmation to Supreme Court." *The Harvard Crimson.* www.thecrimson.com/article/2018/10/11/kavanaugh-confirmation-activism. Accessed online August 21, 2019.

Hargittai, Eszter and Eden Litt 2011. "The Tweet Smell of Celebrity Success: Explaining Variation in Twitter Adoption among a Diverse Group of Young Adults." *New Media and Society* 13(5): 824–842. https://doi.org/10.1177/1461444811405805. Accessed online June 19, 2021.

Hays, Brooks and Susan McFarland 2018. "March for Our Lives: Students around the Country Rally against Gun Violence." UPI. www.upi.com/Top_News/US/2018/03/25/March-for-Our-Lives-Students-around-the-country-rally-against-gun-violence/1451521897434. Accessed online August 9, 2019.

Hogg, David and Lauren Hogg 2018. *#NeverAgain: A New Generation Draws the Line.* New York, NY: Random House.

Holbrook, Allyson L. and Jon A. Krosnick 2010. "Social Desirability Bias in Voter Turnout Reports: Tests Using the Item Count Technique." *Public Opinion Quarterly* 74(1): 37–67. https://doi.org/10.1093/poq/nfp065. Accessed online June 19, 2021.

Huff, Connor and Dustin Tingley 2015. "Who Are These People? Evaluating the Demographic Characteristics and Political Preferences of mTurk Survey Respondents." *Research and Politics* 2(3): 1–12. https://doi.org/10.1177/2053168015604648. Accessed online June 19, 2021.

Imbens, Guido W. and Donald B. Rubin 2015. *Causal Inference for Statistics, Social, and Biomedical Sciences: An Introduction.* New York, NY: Cambridge University Press.

Jervis, Rick and Alan Gomez 2019. "Trump Administration Has Separated Hundreds of Children from Their Migrant Families since 2018." *USA Today.* www.usatoday.com/story/news/nation/2019/05/02/border-family-separations-trump-administration-border-patrol/3563990002/. Accessed online October 23, 2019.

Kahne, Joseph and Benjamin Bowyer 2018. "The Political Significance of Social Media Activity and Social Networks." *Political Communication* 35(3): 470–493. https://doi.org/10.1080/10584609.2018.1426662. Accessed online June 19, 2021.

Kearl, Holly 2018. "The Facts behind the #metoo Movement: A National Study on Sexual Harassment and Assault." www.stopstreetharassment.org/wp-content/uploads/2018/01/Full-Report-2018-National-Study-on-Sexual-Harassment-and-Assault.pdf. Accessed online June 4, 2020.

Keeter, Scott, Nick Hatley, Courtney Kennedy, and Arnold Lau 2017. "What Low Response Rates Mean for Telephone Surveys." Pew Research Center. www.pewresearch.org/methods/2017/05/15/what-low-response-rates-mean-for-telephone-surveys. Accessed online June 9, 2020.

King, Gary and Richard Nielsen 2019. "Why Propensity Scores Should Not Be Used for Matching." *Political Analysis* 27(4): 435–454. https://doi.org/10.1017/pan.2019.11. Accessed online June 19, 2021.

Knoll, Benjamin R. 2009. "'And Who Is My Neighbor?' Religion and Immigration Policy Attitudes." *Journal for the Scientific Study of Religion* 48(2): 313–331. https://doi.org/10.1111/j.1468-5906.2009.01449.x. Accessed online June 19, 2021.

Kochanek, Kenneth D., Sherry L. Murphy, Jiaquan Xu, and Elizabeth Arias 2019. "Deaths: Final Data for 2017." *National Vital Statistics Report* 68(9): 1–77.

Korn, Melissa and Douglas Belkin 2016. "Colleges Try to Comfort Students Upset by Trump Victory." *Wall Street Journal*. https://blogs.wsj.com/washwire/2016/11/09/colleges-try-to-comfort-students-upset-by-trump-victory. Accessed online August 21, 2019.

Lee, Taeku 2002. *Mobilizing Public Opinion: Black Insurgency and Racial Attitudes in the Civil Rights Era.* Chicago, IL: University of Chicago Press.

Lopez, Gustavo and Jens Manuel Krogstad 2017. "Key Facts about Unauthorized Immigrants Enrolled in DACA." Pew Research Center. www.pewresearch.org/fact-tank/2017/09/25/key-facts-about-unauthorized-immigrants-enrolled-in-daca. Accessed online June 9, 2020.

Lupton, Danielle L. 2019. "The External Validity of College Student Subject Pools in Experimental Research: A Cross-Sample Comparison of Treatment Effect Heterogeneity." *Political Analysis* 27(1): 90–97. https://doi.org/10.1017/pan.2018.42. Accessed online June 19, 2021.

Mascarenhas, Nataha 2016. "Here's How Universities Are Offering Support to Students after Trump's Election." *USA Today*. www.usatoday.com/story/college/2016/11/15/heres-how-universities-are-offering-support-to-students-after-trumps-election/37424377. Accessed online August 9, 2019.

McCausland, Phil, Patricia Guadalupe, and Kalhan Rosenblatt 2018. "Thousands across U.S. Join 'Keep Families Together' March to Protest Family Separation." NBC News. www.nbcnews.com/news/us-news/thousands-across-u-s-join-keep-families-together-march-protest-n888006. Accessed online August 21, 2019.

Miller, Warren E. and J. Merrill Shanks 1996. *The New American Voter.* Cambridge, MA: Harvard University Press.

Moffett, Kenneth W. and Laurie L. Rice 2016. *Web 2.0 and the Political Mobilization of College Students.* Lanham, MD: Lexington Books.

Moore, Dasia 2020. "Young People Have the Megaphone. Here's What They Want Everyone Else to Hear." *The Boston Globe.* June 13. www.bostonglobe.com/2020/06/13/metro/young-people-have-megaphone-heres-what-they-want-everyone-else-hear/?s_campaign=breakingnews:newsletter. Accessed online June 15, 2020.

Newkirk, Vann R. 2018. "Family Separation Protests Shift the Narrative." *The Atlantic.* www.theatlantic.com/politics/archive/2018/06/a-rally-for-families-by-families/564239. Accessed online August 21, 2019.

Newport, Frank 2018. "Top Issues for Voters: Healthcare, Economy, Immigration." https://news.gallup.com/poll/244367/top-issues-voters-healthcare-economy-immigration.aspx. Accessed online May 12, 2020.

Novak, Alison N. 2016. *Media, Millennials, and Politics: The Coming of Age of the Next Political Generation.* Lanham, MD: Lexington Books.

Nyren, Erin 2018. "Celebrities Support Families Belong Together March: 'Let's Put an End to This Madness.'" *Variety.* https://variety.com/2018/biz/news/families-belong-together-march-celebrities-hollywood-supports-1202862773. Accessed online August 24, 2019.

Paris, Francesca 2019. "Photos: Youth Climate Change Demonstrations across the World." NPR. www.npr.org/2019/03/16/704050431/photos-youth-climate-change-demonstrations-across-the-world. Accessed online August 23, 2019.

Pew Research Center 2018a. "Wide Gender Gap, Growing Educational Divide in Voters' Party Identification." www.people-press.org/2018/03/20/1-trends-in-party-affiliation-among-demographic-groups. Accessed online August 9, 2019.

Pew Research Center 2020. "Election 2020: Voter Are Highly Engaged, Nearly Half Expect To Have Difficulties Voting." www.pewresearch.org/politics/2020/08/13/election-2020-voters-are-highly-engaged-but-nearly-half-expect-to-have-difficulties-voting. Accessed online February 2, 2021.

Preston, Julia 2017. "How the Dreamers Learned to Play Politics." *Politico*. www.politico.com/magazine/story/2017/09/09/dreamers-daca-learned-to-play-politics-215588. Accessed online August 21, 2019.

RAINN 2020. "Victims of Sexual Violence: Statistics." www.rainn.org/statistics/victims-sexual-Violence. Accessed online June 9, 2020

Rhodan, Maya 2018. "Here Are the Facts about President Trump's Family Separation Policy." *Time*. https://time.com/5314769/family-separation-policy-donald-trump. Accessed online August 23, 2019.

Richmond, Emily, Mikhail Zinshteyn, and Natalie Gross 2016. "Dissecting the Youth Vote." *The Atlantic*. www.theatlantic.com/education/archive/2016/11/dissecting-the-youth-vote/507416. Accessed online August 23, 2019.

Rouse, Stella M. and Ashley D. Ross 2018. *The Politics of Millennials: Political Beliefs and Policy Preferences of America's Most Diverse Generation*. Ann Arbor, MI: University of Michigan Press.

Shah, Dhavan V., Jaeho Cho, William P. Eveland, Jr. and Nojin Kwak 2005. "Information and Expression in a Digital Age: Modeling Internet Effects on Civic Participation." *Communication Research* 32(5): 531–565. https://doi.org/10.1177/0093650205279209. Accessed online June 19, 2021.

Shushok, Frank Jr. and Vera Kidd 2015. "Millennials in Higher Education: As Students Change, Much about Them Remains the Same." In *Positive Psychology on the College Campus*, John C. Wade, Lawrence I. Marks, and Roderick D. Hetzel (Eds.). New York, NY: Oxford University Press.

Silva, Daniella and Alex Johnson 2018. "Thousands Nationwide Protest Family Separations at U.S.-Mexico Border." NBC News. www.nbcnews.com/storyline/immigration-border-crisis/family-separations-border-being-protested-nationwide-thursday-n883171. Accessed online August 23, 2019.

Smith, Aaron and Monica Anderson 2018. "Social Media Use in 2018." Pew Research Center. www.pewinternet.org/2018/03/01/social-media-use-in-2018/. Accessed online January 11, 2019.

Smith, Kate and Caitlin Huey-Burns 2020. "Black Lives Matter Protests Extend into America's Suburbs and Towns." CBS News. June 10. www.cbsnews.com/video/black-lives-matter-protests-extend-into-americas-suburbs-and-towns/. Accessed online June 16, 2020.

Stein, Perry 2017. "'Undocumented, Unafraid.': DACA Recipients Storm the U.S. Capitol." *The Washington Post*. www.washingtonpost.com/local/undocumented-unafraid-daca-recipients-storm-the-us-capitol-for-their-cause/2017/11/09/4d9ae0bc-c558-11e7-aae0-cb18a8c29c65_story.html. Accessed online August 21, 2019.

Towner, Terri L. 2018. "The Infographic Election: The Role of Visual Content on Social Media in the 2016 Presidential Campaign." In *The Presidency and Social Media; Discourse,*

Disruption, and Digital Democracy in the 2016 Presidential Election, Dan Schill and John Allen Hendricks (Eds.). New York, NY: Routledge.

Trump, Donald J. 2015 "Here's Donald Trump's Presidential Announcement Speech." *Time*. https://time.com/3923128/donald-trump-announcement-speech/. Accessed online October 21, 2019.

United States Elections Project. 2020. Voter Turnout. www.electproject.org/home/voter-turnout/voter-turnout-data Accessed online June 19, 2021.

Vasilogambros, Matt 2018. "After Parkland, States Pass 50 New Gun-Control Laws." Stateline. www.pewtrusts.org/en/research-and-analysis/blogs/stateline/2018/08/02/after-parkland-states-pass-50-new-gun-control-laws. Accessed online May 12, 2020.

Walker, Theresa. 2020. "When Black Lives Matter to Everyone: A New Generation Leads Call for Change, Sparked by the Killing of George Floyd." *The Orange County Register*. www.ocregister.com/2020/06/05/when-black-lives-matter-to-everyone-a-new-generation-leads-call-for-change-sparked-by-the-killing-of-george-floyd. Accessed online June 9, 2020.

Wattenberg, Martin P. 2016. *Is Voting for Young People?* 4th Ed.. New York, NY: Routledge.

Witt, Emily 2018. "How the Kavanaugh Nomination Has Intensified the Feminist Protest Movement." *The New Yorker*. www.newyorker.com/news/news-desk/how-the-kavanaugh-nomination-has-intensified-the-feminist-protest-movement. Accessed online April 15, 2020.

Wood, Josh 2018. "Yale Students Condemn Kavanaugh Case as 'Symptom of a Larger Problem.'" *The Guardian*. www.theguardian.com/us-news/2018/sep/29/yale-students-protest-brett-kavanaugh. Accessed online August 23, 2019.

Yee, Vivian and Alan Blinder 2018. "National School Walkout: Thousands Protest Against Gun Violence across the U.S." *The New York Times*. www.nytimes.com/2018/03/14/us/school-Walkout. Accessed online August 9, 2019.

YouGov 2018. The Economist/YouGov Poll. September 23–25.

Zukin, Cliff, Scott Keeter, Molly Andolina, Krista Jenkins, and Michael X. Delli Carpini 2006. *A New Engagement? Political Participation, Civic Life, & the Changing American Citizen*. New York, NY: Oxford University Press.

PART I
Posting, Protesting, and Civic Engagement

Causes and Movements That Mobilized

2
THE METOO MOVEMENT
How an Online Social Movement Sparked Civic Engagement

Introduction

On October 15, 2017, Alyssa Milano (2017) wrote, "If you've been sexually harassed or assaulted, write 'Me Too' as a reply to this tweet" to encourage Twitter users to provide an indication of how widespread these experiences are among women (Garcia 2017). In doing so, she unknowingly co-opted the words of a movement begun by Tarana Burke approximately ten years earlier. Once Milano became aware of this movement, she reached out to Burke to collaborate and thereafter publicly credited Burke as its founder (Garcia 2017). Sparked by a series of high-profile allegations against famous names in Hollywood, this rapidly spreading movement soon generated serious allegations against politicians, reporters, academics, doctors, business leaders, and others (Johnson and Hawbaker 2019).

MeToo quickly went viral, as many tweeted to share their stories and express their support. In the year following Milano's tweet, #MeToo was used more than 19 million times, spiking at various times, including during the confirmation hearings for Supreme Court Justice Brett Kavanaugh (Anderson and Toor 2018). The hashtag was so widespread that 65% of social media users reported seeing at least some content on sexual harassment or assault (Anderson and Toor 2018).

MeToo has also had some successes. In particular, it generated heightened awareness of sexual harassment and assault, particularly by famous people. For example, MeToo had a significant role in publicizing allegations of sexual harassment by (now former) politicians like Senator Al Franken (D-MN) (Johnson and Hawbaker 2019) and Representative Pat Meehan (R-PA) (Opsahl 2018). As of October 29, 2018, MeToo was responsible for over 200 prominent men losing their jobs after public accusations of sexual harassment or assault, with almost half of their replacements being women (Carlsen et al. 2018). Further, state legislatures

DOI: 10.4324/9781003168898-3

passed approximately 10% more bills to protect the public from sexual harassment and assault in 2018 than were passed in 2017 (Kelly and Hegarty 2018).

Prior research on personal mobilization after an experience of sexual harassment may offer one reason this movement gained so much attention – decisions to come forward and report incidents are heavily influenced by the presence of support by friends (Blackstone, Uggen, and McLaughlin 2009). This creation of an online support network encouraged people to share their stories of harassment and assault. The large number of people who did so helped generate societal outrage over the pervasiveness of sexual harassment and assault and demands for change.

The MeToo movement may have been led by members of Generation X, but there is good reason to think that young Millennials and members of Generation Z would be particularly responsive to the movement's calls for action. Since young adults comprise a disproportionately high share of Twitter and other social media users (Smith and Anderson 2018), they were more likely than other age groups to be exposed to MeToo. Further, young adults are already likely to be a sympathetic audience, as they "expect progress toward equalization of genders to continue" (Shushok and Kidd 2015, 38) and are more apt to post on social media about women's rights than older generations (Cai and Clement 2016). In addition, a nontrivial percentage of young adults have experienced sexual harassment or assault, as a study of young adults at ages 25 and 26 found that about 25% reported having experienced perceived sexual harassment as adults (Blackstone, Uggen, and McLaughlin 2009). Moreover, even higher percentages reported experiences that could be classified as sexual harassment even if the respondents did not perceive it as such (Blackstone, Uggen, and McLaughlin 2009). Young adults are also more likely than older age groups to experience sexual assault (Kearl 2018). Together, these factors suggest young adults may be disproportionately likely to be mobilized by MeToo. But, did young adults become primed to do more than just post about MeToo?

In this chapter, we consider how three types of individual responses to MeToo may have fostered increased civic engagement: self-identifying as MeToo supporters, posting online about MeToo, or participating in protests related to MeToo. Self-identifying as a MeToo supporter does not automatically carry cost or public commitment. However, posting a message about or participating in protests related to MeToo can be costly because of the public commitment and potential time involved. Posting messages is a relatively new and low-cost form of expression, especially related to a movement with little formal organizational structure. In comparison, participating in a protest carries higher costs, both in terms of time and public commitment.

Yet, we argue that posting about and participating in protests related to MeToo had the potential to mobilize young adults to civically participate. If true, then young adults who posted about or participated in protests related to MeToo should exhibit higher levels of civic engagement than otherwise similar young adults who declined to post or participate in protests. We test our expectations using surveys of approximately 1,000 American voters between the ages of 18–25 fielded through mTurk on November 7, 2018, a period when interest in the MeToo movement, as measured by Google Trends, was high. We also test them in a second mTurk survey on November 4, 2020, a year when Google Trends indicates interest had faded to low but steady levels. We find that that merely supporting the MeToo movement had no impact on young adult civic engagement. Rather, the evidence suggests that posting about MeToo on social media and participating in protests in 2020 related to the MeToo movement were connected with higher levels of other forms of civic activity.

Social Movements and Mobilization

Social movements are typically based on a moral imperative and have historically provided multiple opportunities to engage with the political process even if they do not have intrinsically political goals (Andrews 1997; Braungart and Braungart 1990a; Chua 2015; Cowell-Meyers 2014; Gamson 1990). For example, the women's suffrage movement generated opportunities for people to participate, worked within states to give women the right to vote, and ultimately was successful in passing the 19th Amendment, granting women suffrage nationwide (Ryan 1992). Likewise, the civil rights movement produced significant social, legal, and political change (Lewis 2005). Likewise, the feminist movement gives people numerous opportunities to participate politically. And, the feminist movement has had successes at the local, state, and national level in policy areas like abortion, and laws that prohibit sexual harassment (Banaszak, Beckwith, and Rucht 2003). In sum, social movements can potentially galvanize civic activity (Baumgartner and Mahoney 2005), help shape local electoral politics (Andrews 1997), spark the formation of a political party (Cowell-Meyers 2014), change the policy agendas that governments pursue (Banaszak 1996; Symanski 2003; Amenta et al. 2010), or cause governments to provide new benefits or enact new coercive policies (Fording 2001).

While these and other social movements have had many policy successes, they have not been uniformly successful. For example, conservative organizations countermobilized against the feminist movement, and successfully reversed some of the feminist movement's successes on abortion policy (Banaszak, Beckwith, and Rucht 2003). Mobilization and countermobilization in response to social movements is consistent with the overarching literature, as some movements have been more successful than others in enacting significant, enduring policy change (Fording 2001; Giugni; McAdam and Tilly 1999; Meyer 2007; Meyer, Jenness, and Ingram 2005; Piven and Cloward 1977). Regardless of the ultimate policy success or lack thereof of a particular social movement, many large-scale movements consistently mobilize people toward political action (Piven and Cloward 1977; Meyer 2007).

MeToo as a Social Movement

Although the #MeToo hashtag went viral, drew millions of responses, and led to the removal of accused harassers from positions of power, is MeToo a social movement? Tarrow (1989, 2011, 6) argues that ordinary people engage in contentious politics and join forces to confront authorities and opponents. However, those engaged in social movements mount, coordinate, and sustain those confrontations against powerful opponents (Tarrow 2011, 6). Further, social movements do not always have politically oriented goals, as many movements seek changes in access to institutions of power (Andrews 1997; Cowell-Meyers 2014), acceptance for marginalized groups (Gamson 1990; Cowell-Meyers 2014; Chua 2015), or broader social changes (Braungart and Braungart 1990a).

MeToo began quietly in 2006, but did not become a household name until Milano's tweet went viral in 2017. In part, Traister (2018) argues that this tweet went viral because many women are angry about a range of issues from gender equality to sexual harassment and assault. While the impact of this tweet persisted throughout 2018 because of the underlying anger into which it tapped (Traister 2018), as evidenced by use of the hashtag #MeToo, there were six time points scattered across the year when its use spiked considerably above average (Anderson and Toor 2018). Google Trends data of searches in the United States for MeToo, displayed in Figure 2.1, also suggest sustained interest in this movement between Milano's initial tweet and the 2020 election, with several significant peaks, especially in 2017 and 2018. Although interest in 2019 and 2020 lessened, curiosity in the topic persisted. The Google Trends metric still averaged in the double digits these years. This suggests a sustained confrontation of organizational cultures that have sheltered harassers and abusers from consequences. Although MeToo has a loosely defined organizational structure, it seeks broader social changes and has coordinated action online to achieve these. It has called attention to the prevalence of sexual harassment and assault in society, and has led the charge in calling for the removal of hundreds of offenders from their positions of influence. It has also supported survivors, and has sparked conversations about acceptable behavior in academia, business, and government.

Thus, MeToo fits the criteria for a social movement. The MeToo movement has addressed discrete societal maladies (e.g., sexual harassment and assault) that frequently are not discussed, go unnoticed, or are not dealt with appropriately. This is consistent with Kitschelt's (1993, 14) characterization[1] of one branch of "new social movements" in general, as they practice:

> a politics of social identity, in which participants work toward a redefinition and re-constitution of individual and collective identities as well as social relations that would go beyond the stereotypes generated by contemporary market relations, political institutions, and cultural conceptions.

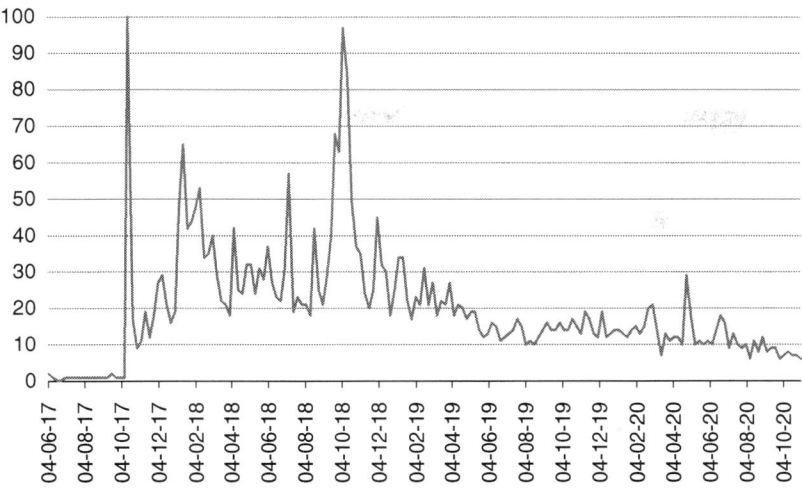

FIGURE 2.1 Google Trends Searches for MeToo in the United States, 2017–2020.

The MeToo movement does this, as its participants seek to redefine and reconstitute social relations between people and especially reduce the prevalence of sexual assault and harassment in society.

Simultaneously, the MeToo movement differs from what scholars have traditionally considered to be a social movement because it uses social networks in different ways than how social movement scholars usually examine. Scholars have long acknowledged networks as important in mobilizing people and influencing behavior (see e.g., Christakis and Fowler 2009; Tilly 1978). Online social networking platforms like Facebook and Twitter facilitate rapidly expanding networks beyond those of face-to-face connections to include friends and followers one has never met (Bond et al. 2012). Social movements have capitalized on these platforms, as new forms of communications technology were important for MoveOn (McAdam and Tarrow 2010) and have also played a significant role in youth movements in Serbia, Georgia, and Ukraine (Nikolayenko 2007). These new forms of technology were vital in the rise of the MeToo movement, as it exists more as an online social network than it does as a formalized organizational structure.[2] Through the #MeToo hashtag, this movement quickly gained followers, and through its support base, created the kind of latent networks of relationships and communications upon which it can draw during periods lacking protests (Kitschelt 1993).

MeToo and Civic Engagement

These differences matter because the MeToo movement employs outsider tactics that attract those who do not typically participate (Cowell-Meyers 2014), like online communications. These communications have received less attention from those who study social movements because posting and spreading messages online is a form of participation that was not available until the advent of a publicly available internet, the birth of blogs in the late 1990s, and the invention of social media platforms like Facebook in 2004 and Twitter in 2006.

Since this movement spread through online social networks, it is particularly likely to engage young adults, a group that historically participated at lower rates (Dalton 2015; Rouse and Ross 2018), perhaps in part due to its lower levels of political knowledge (Delli Carpini and Keeter 1996; Zukin et al. 2006).Yet, the MeToo movement offered a way to increase political knowledge as following the #MeToo hashtag brought exposure to political information. Although the MeToo movement did not have explicitly political goals, 7% of #MeToo tweets mentioned politics or specific politicians (Anderson and Toor 2018). Thus, it had the potential to provide participants with politically relevant information.

Young adults comprise a disproportionately high share of online social network users (Smith and Anderson 2018) and also have social attitudes that differ from their elders (Parker, Graf, and Igielnik 2019; Rouse and Ross 2018; Shushok and Kidd 2015) in ways that make them more likely to be receptive to the MeToo movement. More specifically, members of Generation Z and Millennials are more liberal than preceding generations, particularly on social issues like gay marriage (Parker, Graf, and Igielnik 2019; Ross and Rouse 2015; Rouse and Ross 2018). They support higher levels of diversity (Parker, Graf, and Igielnik 2019) and "expect progress toward equalization of genders to continue" (Shushok and Kidd 2015, 38). Since MeToo strikes right at the heart of these values, these generations were particularly ripe for mobilization.

Yet, people can support causes without taking any action to help advance them. For example, not everyone who identified as a supporter of the civil rights movement engaged in marches, demonstrations, or sit-ins (Stewart, Settles, and Winter 1998). Similarly, many people support the environmental movement who have never contacted their elected officials about environmental issues, donated money to environmental causes, or joined an environmental interest group. While support for a movement may encourage civic action, it does not guarantee that individuals will act. Olson (1973) identified this as the free rider problem, a behavior that impedes successful group action even when individuals all support a cause and an action that advances it. The free rider problem inhibits successful collective action because those who support a cause but do not act receive the same level of benefits as those who actively work on behalf of the group toward receiving those benefits (Olson 1973). Thus, support for the MeToo movement alone might not be enough to propel young adults to take further action, as MeToo supporters receive as many benefits from the successes of that movement as those who participated in it. Thus, we expect that supporting the MeToo movement is not connected with any changes in civic activity among young people.

Posting about MeToo and Civic Activity

Posting a message about the MeToo movement is a relatively low-cost way to express support or opposition. A post can be written quickly and involves little effort for young adults who have grown up expressing themselves in a social media world. However, posts do involve some level of public commitment to a cause. Specifically, posting a message in support of the MeToo movement allows people to become connected to something more meaningful. While some might dismiss posting as a low-cost action with limited power, those who post about this movement may be similar to the "engaged observers" of previous social movements – those who engage in "interested observation of, and moral support for, a social movement" but do not take action (Stewart, Settles, and Winter 1998, 64). Yet, even young engaged observers of the women's movement, the civil rights movement, and the anti-Vietnam War movements experienced enduring impacts, including being more likely to belong to political and community organizations later in life (Stewart, Settles, and Winter 1998). In this vein, posting about the MeToo movement may be connected with higher levels of civic activity.

Posting was the most obvious way for young adults to participate in the MeToo movement. Research shows engaging in varying civic activities online is connected with higher levels of political participation away from the internet (Best and Krueger 2005; Towner and Munoz 2018), especially political expression (Boulianne 2019). In particular, informational uses of the internet are connected with higher levels of participation (Kenski and Stroud 2006; Shah, Kwak, and Holbert 2001, 2005; Min 2007; Towner 2013), as is online discussion about politics (Shah et al. 2005). Generally, expressing oneself politically online can lead to higher levels of civic activity away from the internet (Moffett and Rice 2016, 2018). What is more, online deliberation increases political efficacy and generates a moral imperative to act politically (see e.g., Alberici and Milesi 2016). Thus, we expect that those who post messages online about the MeToo movement are more likely to have higher levels of civic engagement. We expect, though, that the size of these effects may vary between 2018 and 2020. In 2018, when the movement was most visible, young adults with varying levels of commitment to this cause would be likely to post. These varying levels of commitment might help shape the likelihood of getting involved in other ways, weakening the overall gains seen in civic engagement. In 2020, when the movement was far less visible, we expect only those with strong levels of commitment to this issue would be likely to post. As a result, while posting about MeToo may be less prevalent in 2020, those who do post would likely feel more connected to this movement and be more likely to increase their offline civic engagement as a result. In addition, offline engagement was significantly more difficult in 2020 than it was in 2018 due to the Covid-19 pandemic. This also suggests that a more significant commitment to a cause might be needed to take the risks of offline engagement in 2020.

Protests Related to MeToo and Civic Activity

Engaging in a protest related to MeToo also involves a public commitment that is a particularly costly form of expressing one's views about the movement relative to posting. Protesting involves foregoing one's regular activities, traveling to a protest location, and subjecting oneself to some degree of risk that might range from heckling to violence or arrest (Alamanzar and Herring 2004). Individuals without a strong commitment to a cause are far less likely to be willing to endure these costs. Instead, anger and threats to group interests often provide the motivational strength needed to be willing to participate in a protest (van Stekelenburg and Klandermans 2013). Thus, protesting often indicates a stronger commitment to a cause than other less costly types of action.

Young adults who protested in the Women's March were motivated by a variety of issues and causes, including MeToo. For example, 20-year-old Liza Jane told reporters in 2017:

> I felt as if there was no choice to march, it is something I simply must do. So many have felt silenced by this election, so I must use my voice and gifts for activism. I will be using this opportunity to come out as a sexual assault survivor, and it will be my first time to speak out about it.
>
> *(Gutowitz 2017)*

Madison Thomas, a 19-year-old college student and the national coordinator for college engagement of the Women's March, estimated 50,000 college students participated in the 2017 Women's March on Washington (Tate 2017). One of these college students, Sophia Myszkowski, when asked why she marched, said:

> It's important that we send a message to our new president that a lot of people care about women's issues, a lot of people care about injustice. And we're not willing to let injustice be normalized, to let sexual assault, sexual harassment and bigotry be normalized.
>
> *(Tate 2017)*

Protesting is also a social activity, or a form of not just individual but collective behavior. While most protesters are accompanied to protests by people they know, a nontrivial percentage of protesters attend alone (Whalstrom and Wennerhag 2014). Through their participation, they become connected to something larger than themselves. Once at a protest, protesters meet others passionate about the same causes. They have opportunities to make new friends and become connected to organizations helping to support the protest. These new friends and organizational contacts are likely to encourage additional forms of participation. Protesters are likely to be a particularly receptive audience to these mobilization attempts. After all, those willing to endure the costs involved in expressing their views through protests might be far more responsive to additional mobilization attempts aimed at less costly activities.

At each Women's March, some marchers were accompanied by friends, some families marched together with mothers bringing their sons or daughters, while other marchers came alone (Gutowitz 2017; Rosenblatt 2019). Some left with new friendships that were rekindled at the Women's March the following year (Burns and Attar 2018). At Women's March events, marchers expressed their support for other causes and movements, too, including the March for Our Lives movement against gun violence, climate change, and LGBTQ issues (Rosenblatt 2019). One participant, Rachel Jackson, told reporters:

> One of the things I found from the march is…it doesn't matter if I'm marching because I want to show the power of women's education and another person is marching for equality and someone else is marching for immigration – we can all coalesce and join forces.
>
> *(Tate 2017)*

Connections like these facilitate participants branching out to engage on other issues, too, potentially increasing protestors' civic engagement levels.

However, the costs of engaging in both protests and various forms of offline civic engagement varied between 2018 and 2020. Those joining protests in 2020 faced added risks to their health due to the prevalence of the Covid-19 pandemic. While these may have been underestimated in their January 2020 event, the risks of Covid-19 were clearly evident in their second march of the year in October 2020. Less people would be expected to be willing to pay these costs in 2020, which is reflected in the differences in Women's March attendance in 2020, which drew an estimated 117,000 participants nationwide, compared to 2017 and 2018 when millions participated (Hauck 2020). Those who protested in 2020, then, would be expected to possess stronger support and be even more willing to engage in other forms of action. Yet, young adults were better positioned to shoulder these costs than older Americans who, on average, faced more significant health risks from Covid-19. Young adult protesters may have felt a need to step up for those who could not safely do so, and this may translate into other forms of offline activity as well.

In the following sections, we examine whether identifying as a supporter of the MeToo movement is associated with higher levels of civic activity and suspect that support for the movement alone may not increase young adults' civic activity. We then explore whether posting about the MeToo movement and engaging in protests related to MeToo are associated with increased levels of civic activity. As these actions involve more costs than support that stops short of action, they are likely to reflect a stronger moral and emotional imperative. This might make individuals who take these actions more receptive to other mobilization attempts, something they become more likely to be subject to through these public commitments to the cause. Thus, we expect young adults who post about MeToo or participate in protests related to it will have higher levels of civic engagement.

Data

To test our hypotheses, we performed separate online surveys via Amazon's Mechanical Turk (mTurk) platform on the day after the 2018 (November 7) and 2020 (November 4) general elections. The survey population was Americans between 18 and 25 years old – an age range that includes both older members of Generation Z and younger Millennials.[3] This platform allows members of the public to earn money for completing a multitude of tasks, including participating in survey research. A total of 1,010 participants completed the survey after we eliminated any incomplete responses in 2018.[4] Also, 969 participants completed the survey after eliminating any incomplete responses in 2020. Each participant was paid $1.50 for completing each survey in 2018 and 2020.

Dependent Variable

The dependent variable is the extent to which each respondent participated in an array of civic and political activities, with each activity measured on a five-point scale that ranged from "never" to "very often." These activities included attending political functions in support of a candidate or party, talking to people and explaining why they should vote for or against a particular candidate or party, and making purchasing decisions based on a company's conduct or values. We summed the values for each of the 12 activities to produce a civic engagement index that was based on answers to this set of questions ($\alpha = .92$, 2018; $\alpha = .95$, 2020). The means of this index (M = 14.56, 2018; M = 26.01, 2020) are relatively low as this indicates an activity level equivalent to having done 4 of the 12 activities in this index very often in 2018, and 6 of the 12 activities in this index very often in 2020. Both standard deviations (SD = 10.75, 2018; SD = 14.61, 2020) indicate substantial variance around this mean. Thus, we have captured both low and high participators in our survey. The question wording, response categories, and precise variable measurement for our dependent variable, treatment variables, and all matching covariates can be found in the online appendix.

To test our theoretical expectations, we use a series of matching routines. This allows us to match respondents who are similar with respect to a variety of variables known to influence participation levels and isolate the separate effects of supporting the MeToo movement, posting about it, and participating in protests related to it on civic engagement.

Treatment Variables

We examine the effects of supporting the MeToo movement on civic activity by asking each respondent whether they self-identified as a supporter of this movement, measured as a binary coded one for support. To determine the effects of posting messages on social media about the MeToo movement, or participating in protests related to it on civic engagement, we asked each respondent separate questions about how often they posted messages about this movement on social media, and how frequently they participated in protests related to the MeToo Movement. The response options ranged from never having done so to having done so four or more times for both questions.

Matching Covariates

We used two variables to investigate the effects of political engagement away from the internet. First, we asked each respondent three questions about the extent to which their friends engaged in a set of activities. We built an additive index based on the responses to these questions to examine the effects of peer civic activities on civic engagement ($\alpha = .63$, 2018; $\alpha = .58$, 2020).[5,6] Second, each respondent was queried about the extent to which they are interested in politics, measured on a four-point scale.

We also match based on political engagement using the internet as several researchers have found a link between activities on social media and offline civic engagement (see e.g., Kahne and Bowyer 2018; Ley and Brewer 2018; Loader, Vromen, and Xenos 2014). Through separate questions, each respondent was asked about the extent to which they had relied on social media for news, posted about politics on social media, read social media feeds about politics, liked or shared posts about politics on social media, or read or watched posts about politics on social media, and we combined these into an additive index ($\alpha = .84$, 2018; $\alpha = .83$, 2020).[7]

Second, each respondent was asked how frequently they read news on the internet about politics. Third, we asked each respondent how often they read blogs online about politics as blogs can act as outlets that foster enhanced civic activity, either online or offline (Kerbel and Bloom 2005; Moffett and Rice 2018). Fourth, each respondent was asked a series of questions about the extent to which they posted messages on social media about gun control, immigration, Supreme Court nominations (Kavanaugh in 2018, Barrett in 2020), Black Lives Matter (in 2020 only), and about other issues. This allows us to isolate the effect of posting about the MeToo movement compared to posting on other issues. Fifth, each respondent was asked a set of questions about the extent to which they participated in protests related to each of these issues.

We employed five variables to account for the effects of issue importance, as issues can sometimes prompt higher levels of political participation (Converse 1964; Carmines and Stimson 1989; Reny, Collingwood, and Valenzuela 2019). Using separate questions, we asked each respondent about the importance of congressional stances on immigration, as well as gun control, in influencing their vote choice. We also asked each respondent about the extent to which they supported or opposed the family separation policy implementation under the Trump administration and the extent to which they supported or opposed the DACA program. Finally, we asked whether they self-identified as a supporter of the Black Lives Matter movement (in 2020 only).

Moreover, we employed several variables to account for the effects of personal characteristics on offline civic activity. First, we examined the effects of ideology on civic engagement, by creating a binary for those who identified as liberals as Achen and Bartels (2016) find that ideological self-identification shapes political participation. Second, we queried the extent to which each respondent strongly identifies with either the Republican or Democratic parties, as this attachment is associated with an array of other political activities (see e.g., Flavin and Griffin 2009; Verba, Brady, and Schlozman 1995). We computed a binary variable that is coded one for those who self-identified as having strong partisan attachments. Third, we asked each respondent whether they disapproved or approved of the job that Donald Trump is doing as president, as presidential approval is connected with changes in participatory patterns (Abramowitz and Stone 2006).[8]

Fourth, we asked each respondent for their sex, and we coded this variable one for females, two for males, and three for those who self-identified in another category. Fifth, we asked each respondent for their race and collapsed that information into a binary that is coded one for whites, and zero otherwise. Sixth, we acquired data on each respondent's age by asking each to report their month and year of birth. Then, we computed each respondent's age based on the month and year of the 2018 midterm election, or for the 2020 general election.[9] Finally, we asked each respondent for their level of education.[10]

Methods

To investigate whether our treatment variables are linked to civic engagement, we use a matching analysis to compute the average treatment effect on the treated (ATET). We choose a matching estimator for several reasons. First, nearly all regression-based techniques (including OLS) assume a linear relationship between the dependent and independent variables (see Greene 2011). Our theory advances a positive relationship between our treatment variables and civic engagement, but makes no prediction about the treatment effects at each level of supporting the MeToo movement, posting about or participating in protests related to this movement beyond a positive sign on each of them. Thus, the phenomenon that we examine is likely to be nonlinear, and is ill suited to investigate using a method that assumes linearity (like OLS). Fortunately, matching analyses do not assume linearity, allow for a more flexible functional form, and have many other statistical properties that make them a better choice to test our hypothesis (Imbens and Rubin 2015).

What is more, individuals have differing probabilities of supporting the MeToo movement, posting about it or participating in protests related to it with varying frequencies. OLS estimators presume treatment homogeneity, which is unlikely to hold. Individuals likely have different treatment effects, particularly depending on their support for this movement, or the frequency with which they have posted about or participated in protests related to this movement (see Abadie and Imbens 2011). Thus, the effects of supporting this movement, posting about, or participating in protests related to the MeToo movement may vary depending on level or frequency. By construction, OLS-based estimators assume that we observe a linear, homogeneous relationship between supporting, posting about, and participating in protests related to this movement and offline civic activity. Matching-based approaches deal effectively with this issue because they assume neither linearity nor homogeneity (Imbens and Rubin 2015). Rather, they produce several treatment estimates depending on the level of treatment that a respondent received (Imbens and Rubin 2015). Thus, we can generate several, more accurate estimates of the effect that supporting, posting about or participating in protests related to this movement had on offline civic engagement.

Moreover, OLS does not permit us to estimate what happens to offline civic activity in the absence of either self-identifying as a supporter of the MeToo movement, posting about it, or participating in protests related to it (Nichols 2007). Matching analyses use the existing data to generate a dataset that includes observations that are as similar as possible, given the values of the remaining predictors (Stuart 2010). Thus, we can estimate what would have happened in the absence of supporting this movement, posting about it, or participating in protests related to it (see Gelman and Hill 2007). Then, we can use this dataset to estimate the effects of supporting or posting or participating in protests at varying frequencies on civic engagement relative to not having posted or participated in protests at all, or not having supported this movement. Finally, if we used OLS estimates to obtain the results, our results would likely be biased because any estimate of the treatment effect is conditioned on the values of the remaining independent variables. Consequently, OLS-based approaches do not compute ATETs.

Matching analyses manage each of these issues because they let us examine whether supporting, posting about, or participating in protests related to the MeToo movement are associated with higher levels of civic engagement. By matching based on each of the predictor variables to make inferences, we can separate the effect of posting about or participating in protests related to this movement beyond individuals' other predispositions to participate. Thus, doing so enables us to compare people with similar inclinations to civic activity who only vary in their support, or frequency of posting about or participating in protests related to this movement. Moreover, matching allows us to calculate ATETs for each treatment level, and by doing so, to calculate more precise effect sizes with observational data.

Assumptions

Before performing our matching analyses, we must fulfill four assumptions. The validity of any matching analyses hinges on satisfying these assumptions.[11] First, we presume that each treatment variable is binary. The first treatment variable, supporting the MeToo movement, is already binary. The other treatment variables, posting about and participating in protests related to the MeToo movement, are not. To make the posting and protesting variables binary, we generated a series of dichotomous variables for each response option, relative to never having posted (or protested) about the MeToo movement. These binaries are coded one for each of these categories, zero for never having participated in the respective activity (e.g., posting or participating in protests), and missing for those who declined to answer the question, and for the remaining scalar options.

There are three binaries for posting once, posting two or three times, and for having posted four or more times. For instance, the binary for having posted once about this movement is coded one for those who did so, zero for never having done so, and missing for those who declined to answer this question, and for those who reported having posted more than once. Similarly, there are three dichotomous variables for participating in protests once, participating in protests twice or three times, and for having participated in protests four or more times, coded in a similar manner to the posting binaries. We expect positive signs for the ATET for each variable.

Second, we assume common support (or overlap), which means that it is possible that treated units may face an intervention that could have assigned them to the control group (see Imbens and Rubin 2015; King, Lucas, and Nielsen 2017). The data that we use meet this requirement because all respondents could have chosen not to post about or participate in protests related to this movement, or not to support it.

Third, we must fulfill the stable unit treatment value (SUTVA) assumption, which means that "the potential outcomes for any unit do not vary with the treatments assigned to other units, and for each unit, there are no different forms or versions of each treatment level, which lead to different potential outcomes" (Imbens and Rubin 2015, 10). We have met the first part of this assumption because the possible outcomes for civic activity do not vary with the levels of having posted about or participated in protests related to this movement, or with having been a MeToo supporter.[12]

The second aspect of this assumption is more complex because we have different variations on two of our treatment variables (posting about or participating in protests related to the MeToo movement): once, two or three times, and four or more times about this movement. Yet, we can compare the effects of having posted with varying frequencies about this movement relative to those who never did so. For example, we can compare those who posted once about this movement to those who never did so, provided that we exclude those who posted at all other frequencies from that analysis.[13] Similarly, we can compare the effects of having participated in protests with varying frequencies related to this movement relative to those who never did so. We must perform an equivalent procedure to compare those who had posted or participated in protests two or three times, and four or more times about this movement if we hope to execute a matching analysis without an alternative treatment. When we compute our ATETs in this manner, we ultimately satisfy the SUTVA assumption because we have neither interference nor any hidden variations of the treatments (Imbens and Rubin 2015, 10–11).

Finally, the treatment assignment must be conditionally independent of the outcome variable given a set of matching covariates (D'Agostino 1998, 2266). Thus, each respondent's assignment to either treatment (i.e., posting about the MeToo movement, participating in protests related to this movement, or self-identifying as a supporter) is unconnected with their level of civic engagement, given the values of the remaining explanatory variables. We observe greatly varied participatory levels with respect to civic activity, and the mean level of civic activity is fairly low (M = 14.56, 2018; M = 26.01, 2020), given the minimum (0) and maximum values (48) possible with this index. Moreover, the activities that comprise offline civic activity do not cause an individual to be assigned to one or more treatment categories.

Matching Technique

To perform our matching analyses, we use one-to-one genetic matching with replacement (Diamond and Sekhon 2013; Sekhon 2011). We incorporate a propensity score into the analysis, as knowing estimated values of this score meaningfully improves the accuracy of this method (Diamond and Sekhon 2013). Propensity score matching allows us to compare observations that are otherwise similar across other predictors, but have experienced different treatments. We perform our analysis with replacement, as matching discrepancies are reduced because we can use untreated units as a match multiple times (see Abadie and Imbens 2006).[14] To remove any bias that results due to the choice of the matching estimator without affecting the variance of that estimator, we employ a bias correction (Abadie and Imbens 2016).

Results

Before analyzing the results testing a link between each of our treatment variables and higher levels of civic engagement, we need to investigate how similar the control and treatment groups are to one another (King, Lucas, and Nielsen 2017). If these groups substantially differ, then we cannot use matching to estimate effect size. The imbalance statistics for these models are available in Tables A1 through A5 for 2018, and A6 through A10 for 2020. For 52.17% (2018) and 48.15% (2020) of the variables contained in the model in Table 2.1 for self-identifying as a MeToo movement supporter, the Kolomogorov-Smirnov (KS) tests or t-tests are not significant at the .05 level after matching has occurred. In most of these cases, it is only one of these tests that is significant at the .05 level, post-matching. However, in the remaining 5 of 23 cases (or 21.74%) in 2018, and 11 of the remaining 27 cases (or 40.74%) in 2020, the KS test and the t-test are significant.

For 92.75% of the variables contained in the models in Table 2.1 regarding posting about the MeToo movement for 2018, the KS tests are not significant at the .05 level after matching has occurred. In 2018, for the remaining 5 of 69 cases (or 7.25%), the KS test is significant. In 2020, the KS tests are not significant at the .05 level after matching has occurred for 67.90% of the variables contained in the models in Table 2.1. In 2020, for the remaining 26 out of 81 cases (or 32.10%), the KS test is significant.

When we examine the models in Table 2.1 for protesting about the MeToo movement in 2018, for 84.06% of the variables in these models, the KS and t-tests are not significant at the .05 level after matching has occurred. In the remaining 11 of 69 cases (or 15.94%) that occurred in 2018, the KS and t-tests are significant. In 2020, for 67.90% of the variables in the protesting models, the KS and t-tests are not significant at the .05 level after matching has occurred. In the remaining 26 out of 81 cases (or 32.10%) that occurred in 2018, the KS and t-tests are significant. Overall, it appears that matching has helped eliminate the majority of preexisting differences across the models in Table 2.1.

In many of the remaining cases, the KS and t-tests indicate statistically significant differences between the treatment and control groups with respect to issues we examine in other chapters: opinions about Kavanaugh's (2018) or Barrett's (2020) nominations (examined in Chapter 3), protesting about Supreme Court nominations (examined in Chapter 3), protesting about gun control (examined in Chapter 4), opinions about then-President Trump's implementation of the family separation policy (examined in Chapter 5) opinions about the DACA program (examined in Chapter 5), and posting about and participating in protests related to Black Lives Matter (2020) (both examined in Chapter 6). While these significant differences exist across the models in varying places, we have reduced imbalance sufficiently. The matched groups for these models have similar enough observable characteristics such that we can attribute any remaining differences across levels of posting about the MeToo movement to the effects of our treatment variables, not to preexisting differences (Eggers and Hainmueller 2009).[15]

In Table 2.1, we provide the results from each matching routine. The results indicate that there is no statistically significant difference in civic engagement by virtue of having supported the MeToo movement in either 2018 or 2020.[16] In addition, the results indicate that we find slight evidence in 2018 that having posted once about the MeToo movement is connected with higher levels of civic engagement, relative to those who did not post at all.[17] Since we are testing

TABLE 2.1 Civic Engagement and the MeToo Movement

	Supporting the MeToo Movement		Posting about the MeToo Movement						Protesting about the MeToo Movement					
	2018	2020	2018			2020			2018			2020		
	Model	Model	Once	Two or Three Times	Four or More Times	Once	Two or Three Times	Four or More Times	Once	Two or Three Times	Four or More Times	Once	Two or Three Times	Four or More Times
Effect on Offline Civic Engagement	-.140	1.886	2.239	1.647	-.999	-2.903	17.643	9.891	6.527	-11.270	8.804	1.554	4.410	13.116
Abadie-Imbens Standard Error	1.121	1.541	1.208	1.366	5.027	3.331	7.757	2.982	2.962	11.657	3.877	4.483	2.608	2.616
95% Confidence Interval Lower Bound	-2.345	-1.147	-.158	-1.063	-11.023	-9.562	2.269	3.939	.573	-34.759	.763	-7.461	-.775	7.874
95% Confidence Interval Upper Bound	2.063	4.919	4.636	4.357	9.025	3.756	33.017	15.843	12.481	12.219	16.845	10.569	9.595	18.358
T-Statistic	-.124	1.224	1.854	1.205	-.199	-.871	2.2756	3.317	2.204	-.967	2.271	.347	1.691	5.015
P-Value (two-tailed)	.901	.221	.064	.228	.842	.384	.023	.001	.028	.334	.023	.729	.081	$5.308*10^{-7}$
P-Value (one-tailed)	.451	.111	.032	.114	.421	.192	.012	.0005	.014	.167	.012	.365	.041	$2.654*10^{-7}$
N	367	284	99	99	71	63	110	68	50	45	23	49	87	56

Notes: For the two columns for supporting the MeToo movement, supporting the MeToo movement is compared to those who do not support the MeToo movement (or have no opinion). Then, for each three-column set, the number of times that one has posted or protested about the MeToo Movement in a particular year is compared with one who has never done so about that subject. Second, the covariates on which the matching is based are described in the text. Third, the effects on off-line civic engagement are the ATET. Finally, the matching results are from 1:1 genetic matching with post-matching bias adjustment. Thus, the N represents the matched number of observations.

a directional hypothesis, a one-sided t-test is more appropriate, rather than a two-sided test. When we use such a test (p = .032), the results now indicate that there are statistically significant differences in civic engagement between those who posted once, relative to those who did not do so at all. More specifically, those who posted once about this movement had civic engagement levels that were approximately two points higher. A two-point increase is the equivalent of participating in two activities at one level higher, or one activity at two levels higher.[18]

In 2020, though, we uncover a different set of results. More specifically, the model appears to indicate that posting two or three times about this movement in 2020 is connected to an approximately 18-point increase in civic engagement. However, this result is not robust, as we will discuss below. The model also shows that posting four or more times about this movement is associated with a nearly ten-point increase in civic activity. A ten-point increase is the equivalent of participating in at least two activities very often that otherwise would not have occurred at all, and participating in two others at one level higher, or one activity at two levels higher. In 2018, though, the results indicate that those who posted at least two or three times about the MeToo movement did not have higher levels of civic activity than those who did not post at all.

We find stronger evidence that participating in protests related to the MeToo movement is connected with higher levels of civic engagement in 2020, when we expect that only those most strongly committed to this cause participated. In 2020, we found slight evidence that participating in protests two or three times is connected with an approximately four-point increase in civic engagement. This is the equivalent of participating in one activity very frequently that previously did not occur. Since we are testing a directional hypothesis, relying on the one-sided t-test is more appropriate (p = .041), rather than a two-sided test. What is more, we discovered that participating in protests four or more times is associated with an approximately 13-point increase in civic activity. This is equivalent to participating in three activities very frequently that otherwise would not have happened, plus one other activity at a higher level than what would otherwise have occurred.

Robustness Checks

To verify whether the results in Table 2.1 are model-dependent (Ho et al. 2007), we tested our models for robustness by removing one matching covariate at a time from each model. Then, we re-ran the matching routines with the remaining predictors in that model.[19] These results are contained in the online appendix. When we examine the models in those tables relative to those that we report here, 88% (or 44/50) of the models contained results that mirrored those reported in Table 2.1 for being a MeToo movement supporter. Thus, the robustness checks provide no evidence that those who self-identified as MeToo movement supporters were more likely to have been civically active.

When we query the models in Table 2.1 for posting about the MeToo movement, 66% (or 99/150) of the models in 2018 and 2020 contained results that are consistent with those that we report in Table 2.1. The 15 cases in 2018 that deviate from what we report largely involve the model for posting about the MeToo movement once relative to not at all. Even here, though, 73.33% (or 11/15) of the models for posting once about the MeToo movement relative to not at all contain statistically significant results when we use a one-tailed t-test, rather than a two-tailed t-test. Altogether, 94.20% of the models in 2018 are either identical in terms of signs and significance patterns to those contained in Table 2.1, or provide results that end up buttressing the argument and evidence that we provide related to posting about the MeToo movement.

In 2020, 26 of the 36 remaining cases (or 72.22%) of these cases are concentrated in the model that examines posting two or three times about the MeToo movement. What is more, 26 of the 27 model specifications (or 96.3%) for posting two or three times about the MeToo movement demonstrate results counter to those reported in Table 2.1. Thus, we cannot conclude that posting two or three times about the MeToo movement in 2020 is connected with any statistically significant change in civic engagement.

That said, eight of the remaining ten cases in 2020 are in the model for having posted four or more times about the MeToo movement. This requires context, as only 8 of the 27 (or 29.63%) model specifications provide a result that runs counter to that which we report in Table 2.1. Put differently, this result indicates that 70.37% (or 19/27) of the robustness checks are consistent with that which we report in Table 2.1 for posting about the MeToo movement. When these robustness checks are put together across years and model specifications, these checks provide evidence that supports hypothesis two: that posting once about the MeToo movement in 2018 and posting four times about the MeToo in 2020 (when offline civic engagement was costlier, due to the prevalence of Covid-19) is associated with higher levels of civic activity.

Upon inspecting the models in Table 2.1 for participating in protests related to the MeToo movement, we discover that 69.33% (or 104/150) of the possible specifications furnish results that are consistent with what we report in Table 2.1. Of the remaining 20 that are inconsistent with the results for protesting in 2020, 12 (or 60%) occur with respect to the model for participating in protests two or three times. This is not overly problematic, as the majority of specifications (13/27, or 55.56%) are consistent with what we report in this table for participating in protests two or three times. The remaining eight specifications that produce results that are inconsistent with what we report for protesting in 2020 are scattered throughout the remaining levels of participating in protests with no consistent pattern across them to report. Thus, we conclude that participating in protests related to the MeToo movement at least twice in 2020 is connected with higher levels of civic engagement.

However, the 2018 protesting results do not withstand the empirical scrutiny to which we subjected the 2020 results. To compound matters, most of these inconsistencies exist in the two places where Table 2.1 shows statistically significant results (for protesting once, or four or more times in 2018). Thus, while the results in Table 2.1 suggest that we observe a statistically significant, positive relationship between participating in protests in 2018 related to the MeToo movement and civic engagement, further analysis on the models in this table cast doubt on these findings. Given this situation, the most conservative option is to conclude that no statistically significant relationship existed between participating in protests related to the MeToo movement and civic engagement in 2018. The reason that we draw this conclusion despite the presence of statistically significant results in our table is that these results are not robust when we subject them to additional scrutiny.

Discussion and Conclusion

Although there is no link between mere support for the MeToo movement and higher levels of civic engagement, we have demonstrated that posting about a social movement whose primary goal is to eradicate sexual harassment and assault successfully draws young adults into the political process. In addition, participating in protests related to this movement at least twice in 2020 is connected with higher levels of offline civic activity. This is important because issues like those brought up by the MeToo movement strike at the core set of values that young adults hold such as diversity, inclusion, and women's rights (Rouse and Ross 2018; Parker, Graf, and Igielnik 2019). This discovery fits with the extant literature's finding that large-scale social movements can spur political participation (Andrews 1997; Baumgartner and Mahoney 2005; Braungart and Braungart 1990a; Chua 2015; Cowell-Meyers 2014; Gamson 1990). It is also consistent with the underlying literature that younger voters can civically engage in response to issues that directly affect them (Flavin and Griffin 2009; Rouse and Ross 2018; Verba and Brody 1970).

The link we demonstrate between posting about the MeToo movement and higher levels of civic engagement also speaks to the literature about slacktivism among younger voters. As online activism first emerged, articles began raising concerns that these new activities gave young adults the opportunity to feel good about themselves for taking low-cost actions that had no meaningful impact on the real world (see e.g., Morozov 2009; Robertson 2014). Yet, only limited support has emerged for the slacktivism hypothesis (Kwak et al. 2018). For example, some research has found that engaging in public acts of token support for a cause does little to increase individual's willingness to engage in more meaningful activities (Kristofferson, White, and Peloza 2014). Although posting messages in support of a cause have been criticized by some as merely token support, our results join the growing body of literature that calls the slacktivism hypothesis into question by showing a link between online expression and offline action (Boulianne 2015).

However, our results come with one caveat: we use cross-sectional data from both 2018 and 2020 to test our hypotheses. One possibility that can occur is that young people who were already engaged are also more likely to have posted about the MeToo movement or to have participated in protests related to that movement. Although matching helps us consider this possibility by comparing varying actions related to the movement by individuals who are otherwise similarly inclined to civic engagement, it does not eliminate this explanation.

To further address this, we also examined whether higher levels of offline civic activity made someone more apt to post or protest about MeToo. We used the same matching covariates in this chapter, but with the dependent variable being frequency of posting or protesting about the MeToo movement. Our primary treatment variable, then, is offline civic engagement. We operationalize our treatment variable using three levels: low offline civic activity (civic engagement score less than 12), medium offline civic activity (civic engagement score between 12 and 24, inclusive), and high offline civic activity (civic engagement score greater than 24). When we employ the same matching technique here used earlier in this chapter, we find that higher levels of offline civic activity are not connected with posting about the MeToo movement in 2018 as we found no statistically significant connection. In 2020, high levels of civic engagement are connected with an increased propensity to post about the MeToo movement ($p = .002$), but not with participating in protests related to this movement. Altogether, this suggests reverse causality is not an issue in most cases. Still, others can use longitudinal data on younger voters to further clarify the direction of the causal arrow by comparing levels of civic engagement at two time points and observing whether posting about the MeToo movement at the first time point produces higher civic activity levels at the second time point.

Future research might also examine what makes people decide to post or protest about MeToo, as we do not consider that question in our analysis. Traister (2018) suggests that this is because many women are angry about an array of issues ranging from sexual assault and harassment, public policies that harm many women, and the election of Donald Trump as president in 2016. Additional factors like internal and external efficacy, personal experiences of harassment or assault, and close connections to those who have these experiences might all shape the decision to post about MeToo as well. All of these can be found in the sentiments of activists when asked by reporters to share why they protested (Gotowitz 2017; Tate 2017; Burns and Attar 2018; Rosenblatt 2019). Yet, whatever leads individuals to post and protest about this movement, we have shown the choice to do so is associated with higher levels of civic engagement.

In the next chapter, we turn to young adult civic engagement and the nomination of two Supreme Court justices immediately prior to the 2018 and 2020 elections: Brett Kavanaugh and Amy Coney Barrett, respectively. Unlike social movements pushing for change throughout society, Supreme Court nominations offer a limited time window to try and influence Senators before a confirmation vote. Yet, Kavanaugh's confirmation hearings also involved allegations at the heart of the MeToo movement. Thus, this presented a concrete opportunity to influence government institutions within the backdrop of a larger social movement. In Chapter 3, we examine how young adults responded to this opportunity.

Notes

1 This distinction also has its critics. See, for example, D'Anieri, Ernst, and Kier (1990) who demonstrate several "old" movements' similarity to this characteristic of "new" movements.
2 McAdam and Tarrow (2010, 528) acknowledge that new online platforms can be used to help mobilize activism, but warn that

> [t]he cost of the greater extension of Internet-based diffusion may be to lose the sustaining quality that social trust offers to more direct diffusion among people who know each other. If true, the Internet may produce more easily triggered episodes of contentious politics – for example, in the electoral arena – at the cost of sustained social movements.

We are confident that this warning has not come to pass with respect to the MeToo movement, as this movement has sustained itself over a period of time, even though its primary mobilization form has occurred through the internet.
3 These generations have similar views on social issues (Parker, Graf, and Igielnik 2019).
4 We constrained the eligibility of participants in this survey to those whose location is in the United States and whose human interface task (HIT) approval rates are at least 95%. While we could not constrain by age here, we did so through the first question asking respondents whether they were between the ages of 18 and 25. If they responded no, then the survey ended.
5 These were the only questions in the survey about peer civic experiences. Some participants responded that they did not know for one or more of these questions. When building our index, we coded values for these variables as missing. Thus, no peer civic engagement score is present for those who answered "don't know" on a minimum of one of these questions.
6 This also acts as an indirect indicator with respect to mobilization, as people frequently act politically when others around them do so (see e.g., Gimpel, Lee, and Kamiski 2006).Yet, it is possible that mobilization efforts by those other than peers, like interest groups and political parties, also yield higher levels of participation (Rosenstone and Hansen 2002). There are no questions in this survey that allow us to directly account for the effects of mobilization on civic activity. That said, we do consider many other covariates that also affect mobilization as part of the matching routines in this analysis.
7 We employed a modified version of this variable for the models in which the treatment variable is posting about the MeToo movement, as we cannot have the treatment variable being essentially the same as an element of one of the matching covariates. More specifically, we removed posts about politics on social media from the online civic engagement index for this set of models because the treatment for the set of models examining the effects of posting about the MeToo movement is the extent to which one posted about that movement. We retained the remaining variables that comprise the online civic engagement index and created an additive index based on those (α = .81, 2018; α = .78, 2020).

8 Imbens and Rubin (2015, 16) state that any matching technique assumes that matching covariates are unaffected by treatment assignment. Thus, there should be no connection between any particular matching covariate and the assignment to treatment. Consequently, we exclude one variable from the set of matching covariates in this analysis: whether each respondent considers themselves as supporters of the MeToo movement. We exclude this because it is undoubtedly connected with our treatment variable: the extent to which one chooses to post about this movement. When we include this variable alongside the remaining matching covariates, the results for posting and participating in protests retain the same sign and significance patterns as we report here with two exceptions. First, posting twice about the MeToo movement is positive and statistically significant at the relatively loose .05, one-tailed standard (p=.092, two-tailed test, 2018; p = .089, two-tailed test, 2020). Second, protesting once related to the MeToo movement and posting four or more times related to that movement in 2020 is positive and statistically significant at the .05 level (p = .013, once; p = 3.542×10^{-13}, four or more times).

9 We asked an initial screening question that identified those who were between the ages of 18 and 25, and those who responded that they were not in this age range were excluded from further participation in the survey. When we performed the age computations based on the year and month that respondents selected, though, there were 49 respondents who stated that they were older than 25 in 2018. In the year-month calculation, there was usually about a six-month variance between the reported and actual age among those 49 respondents. Since we asked about both year and month of birth based on drop-down menus, it is possible that a substantial portion of these respondents misreported their year and/or month of birth in 2018 (see Gendall and Healey 2008). We have no reason to believe that this error is systematic and did not encounter the same concern in 2020. Thus, nonsystematic measurement error in an independent variable does not bias any conclusions in research studies (see King, Keohane, and Verba 1994).

10 It is possible that the results that we have obtained for the 2020 models were because we added additional independent variables to the model, relative to 2018. To check this possibility, we re-ran the 2020 models using the 2018 model covariates (excluding the variables related to Black Lives Matter and opinions about DACA), but substituting the Kavanaugh questions for Barrett questions. When we do this, the results largely mirror that which we report in this chapter with two exceptions. First, posting in 2020 is no longer statistically significant. Second, protesting four or more times is no longer significant. We retained the specifications in this chapter for 2020 as they are reported here because of the primacy that Black Lives Matter and issues of race had in 2020. These results are reported in Tables B1 and B2 in the Online Appendix.

11 Matching analyses are highly sensitive to even minor violations of these assumptions (Imbens and Rubin 2015).

12 If civic engagement was related to posting about the MeToo movement, then civic activity and posting about this movement would be highly correlated. To test whether this occurs, we correlated our dependent variable (civic engagement) and our treatment variables (supporting the MeToo movement, posting about it, and participating in protests related to it). This correlation is low enough given our number of observations for all variables (supporting the MeToo movement: $r = .044$ (2018), $r = .261$ (2020); posting: $r = .517$ (2018), $r = .651$ (2020); protests: $r = .640$ (2018), $r = .745$ (2020)) such that we can conclude that the first part of the SUTVA assumption is satisfied.

13 If we do not conduct our analysis in this manner, then we cannot satisfy SUTVA, as there would be alternative treatment forms (see Imbens and Rubin 2015, 10–13).
14 However, we do not generate a regression following the matching analysis (as Ho et al. 2007 advise), as Abadie and Spiess (2019) say that this is not appropriate when matching is performed with replacement as researchers obtain inaccurate estimates of their standard errors.
15 Because there are enough preexisting differences across several matching covariates in the protesting models in Table 2.1, we urge caution in interpreting the results from those models.
16 Consequently, this difference exists on what is ultimately a null finding. Thus, this is not problematic because we make no scientific claim about this model beyond the null finding that is produced.
17 These results require closer examination, as they initially indicate that there are no statistically significant differences in civic engagement between those who posted once relative to those who did not do so at all when we use a two-sided t-test (p=.064).
18 These increases are compared with those who reported never having posted about this movement.
19 One limitation of many matching analyses is that one can p-hack by changing the functional form of the matching routine to generate a set of results that confirms a researcher's theoretical expectations (Head et al. 2015).

References

Abadie, Alberto and Guido W. Imbens 2006. "Large Sample Properties of Matching Estimators for Average Treatment Effects." *Econometrica* 74(1): 235–267. https://doi.org/10.1111/j.1468-0262.2006.00655.x. Accessed online June 19, 2021.

Abadie, Alberto and Guido W. Imbens 2011. "Bias-Corrected Matching Estimators for Average Treatment Effects." *Journal of Business and Economic Statistics* 29(1): 1–11. https://doi.org/10.1198/jbes.2009.07333. Accessed online June 19, 2021.

Abadie, Alberto and Guido W. Imbens 2016. "Matching on the Estimated Propensity Score." *Econometrica* 84(2): 781–807. https://doi.org/10.3982/ECTA11293. Accessed online June 19, 2021.

Abadie, Alberto and Jann Spiess 2019. "Robust Post-Matching Inference." Forthcoming in the *Journal of the American Statistical Association*. https://doi.org/10.1080/01621459.2020.1840383. Accessed online June 19, 2021.

Abramowitz, Alan I. and Walter J. Stone 2006. "The Bush Effect: Polarization, Turnout, and Activism in the 2004 Presidential Election." *Presidential Studies Quarterly* 36(2): 141–154. https://doi.org/10.1111/j.1741-5705.2006.00295.x. Accessed online June 19, 2021.

Achen, Christopher H. and Larry M. Bartels 2016. *Democracy for Realists: Why Elections Do Not Produce Responsive Government*. Princeton, NJ: Princeton University Press.

Alamanzar, Nelson A. and Cedric Herring 2004. "Sacrificing for the Cause: Another Look at High-Risk/Cost Activism." *Race and Society* 7(2): 113–129. https://doi.org/10.1016/j.racsoc.2005.05.005. Accessed online June 19, 2021.

Alberici, Augusta Isabella and Patrizia Milesi 2016. "Online Discussion, Politicized Identity, and Collective Action." *Group Processes and Intergroup Relations* 19(1): 43–59. https://doi.org/10.1177/1368430215581430. Accessed online June 19, 2021.

Amenta, Edwin, Neal Caren, Elizabeth Chiarello, and Yang Su 2010. "The Political Consequences of Social Movements." *Annual Review of Sociology* 36(2010): 287–307. https://doi.org/10.1146/annurev-soc-070308-120029. Accessed online June 19, 2021.

Anderson, Monica and Skye Toor 2018. "How Social Media Users Have Discussed Sexual Harassment since #MeToo Went Viral." Pew Research Center. October 11. www.pewresearch.org/fact-tank/2018/10/11/how-social-media-users-have-discussed-sexual-harassment-since-metoo-went-viral/. Accessed online June 6, 2019.

Andrews, Kenneth T. 1997. "The Impacts of Social Movements on the Political Process: The Civil Rights Movement and Black Electoral Politics in Mississippi." *American Sociological Review* 62(5): 800–819.

Banaszak, Lee Ann 1996. *Why Movements Succeed or Fail: Opportunity, Culture and the Struggle for Women's Suffrage*. Princeton, NJ: Princeton University Press.

Banaszak, Lee Ann, Karen Beckwith, and Dieter Rucht (Eds.) 2003. *Women's Movements Facing the Reconfigured State*. New York, NY: Cambridge University Press.

Baumgartner, Frank R. and Christine Mahoney 2005. "Social Movements, the Rise of New Issues and the Public Agenda." In *Routing the Opposition: Social Movements, Public Policy, and Democracy*, David S. Meyer, Valerie Jenness, and Helen Ingram (Eds.). Minneapolis, MN: University of Minnesota Press.

Best, Samuel J. and Brian S. Krueger 2005. "Analyzing the Representativeness of Internet Political Participation." *Political Behavior* 27(2): 183–216. https://doi.org/10.1007/s11109-005-3242-y. Accessed online June 19, 2021.

Blackstone, Amy, Christopher Uggen, and Heather McLaughlin 2009. "Legal Consciousness and Responses to Sexual Harassment." *Law & Society Review* 43(3): 631–668. https://doi.org/10.1111/j.1540-5893.2009.00384.x. Accessed online June 19, 2021.

Bond, Robert M., Christopher J. Farriss, Jason J. Jones, Adam D. I. Kramer, Cameron Marlow, Jaime E. Settle, and James H. Fowler 2012. "A 61-Million-Person Experiment in Social Influence and Political Mobilization." *Nature* 489: 295–298.

Boulianne, Shelley 2015. "Social Media Use and Participation: A Meta-Analysis of Current Research." *Information, Communication & Society* 18(5): 524–538. https://doi.org/10.1080/1369118X.2015.1008542. Accessed online June 19, 2021.

Boulianne, Shelley 2019. "Revolution in the Making: Social Media Effects across the Globe." *Information, Communication and Society* 22(1): 39–54. https://doi.org/10.1080/1369118X.2017.1353641 Accessed online June 19, 2021.

Braungart, Richard G. and Margaret M. Braungart 1990a. "Youth Movements in the 1980s: A Global Perspective." *International Sociology* 5(2): 157–181. https://doi.org/10.1177/026858090005002004. Accessed online June 19, 2021.

Braungart, Richard G. and Margaret M. Braungart 1990b. "Generational Themes in the American Student Movements of the 1930s and 1960s." *Journal of Political and Military Sociology* 18(2): 79–121.

Burns, Asia Simone and Eslah Attar. 2018. "Women's March on Washington: 'We Are a Part of America, So We Need to Be Out Here.'" NPR. www.npr.org/2018/01/20/579441219/womens-march-on-washington-we-are-a-part-of-america-so-we-need-to-be-out-here. Accessed online January 8, 2021.

Cai, Weiyi and Scott Clement 2016. "What Americans Think about Feminism Today." *The Washington Post*. January 27. www.washingtonpost.com/graphics/national/feminism-project/poll/. Accessed online June 7, 2019.

Carlsen, Audrey, Maya Salam, Clair Cain Miller, Denise Lu, Ash Bgu, Jugal K. Patel, and Zach Wichter 2018. "#MeToo Brought Down 201 Powerful Men. Nearly Half of Their Replacements Are Women." *The New York Times*. October 29. www.nytimes.com/interactive/2018/10/23/us/metoo-replacements.html. Accessed online June 27, 2019.

Carmines, Edward G. and James A. Stimson 1989. *Issue Evolution: Race and the Transformation of American Politics*. Princeton, NJ: Princeton University Press.

Christakis, Nicholas A. and James H. Fowler 2009. *Connected: The Surprising Power of Our Social Networks and How They Shape Our Lives.* New York, NY: Little, Brown.

Chua, Lynette J. 2015. "The Vernacular Mobilization of Human Rights in Myanmar's Sexual Orientation and Gender Identity Movement." *Law and Society Review* 49(2): 299–332. https://doi.org/10.1111/lasr.12135. Accessed online June 19, 2021.

Converse, Phillip 1964. "The Nature of Belief Systems in Mass Publics." In *Ideology and Its Discontents,* David E. Apter (Ed.). New York, NY: Free Press of Glencoe.

Cowell-Meyers, Kimberly B. 2014. "The Social Movement as Political Party: The Northern Ireland Women's Coalition and the Campaign for Inclusion." *Perspectives on Politics* 12(1): 61–80. https://doi.org/10.1017/S153759271300371X. Accessed online June 19, 2021.

D'Agostino, Ralph B. 1998. "Propensity Score Methods for Bias Reduction in the Comparison of a Treatment to a Non-Randomized Control Group." *Statistics in Medicine* 17(9):2265–2281.https://doi.org/10.1002/(SICI)1097-0258(19981015)17:19<2265::AID-SIM918>3.0.CO;2-B. Accessed online June 19, 2021.

D'Anieri, Paul, Claire Ernst, and Elizabeth Kier 1990. "New Social Movements in Historical Perspective." *Comparative Politics* 22(4): 445–458.

Dalton, Russell J. 2015. *The Good Citizen: How a Younger Generation Is Reshaping American Politics.* 2nd Ed. Thousand Oaks, CA: CA Press.

Delli Carpini, Michael X. and Scott Keeter 1996. *What Americans Know about Politics and Why It Matters.* New Haven, CT: Yale University Press.

Diamond, Alexis and Jasjeet J. Sekhon 2013. "Genetic Matching for Estimating Causal Effects: A General Multivariate Matching Method for Achieving Balance in Observational Studies." *Review of Economics and Statistics* 95(3): 932–945. https://doi.org/10.1162/REST_a_00318. Accessed online June 19, 2021.

Eggers, Andrew C. and Jens Hainmueller 2009. "MPs for Sale? Returns to Office in Postwar British Politics." *American Political Science Review* 103(4): 513–533. https://doi.org/10.1017/S0003055409990190. Accessed online June 19, 2021.

Flavin, Patrick and John D. Griffin 2009. "Policy, Preferences, and Participation: Government's Impact on Democratic Citizenship." *Journal of Politics* 71(2): 544–559. https://doi.org/10.1017/S0022381609090458. Accessed online June 19, 2021.

Fording, Richard C. 2001. "The Political Response to Black Insurgency: A Critical Test of Competing Theories of the State." *American Political Science Review* 95(1): 115–130.

Gamson, William A. 1990. *The Strategy of Social Protest.* 2nd Ed. Belmont, CA: Wadsworth.

Garcia, Sandra E. 2017. "The Woman Who Created #MeToo Long before Hashtags." *The New York Times.* October 20. www.nytimes.com/2017/10/20/us/me-too-movement-tarana-burke.html. Accessed online June 6, 2019.

Gelman, Andrew and Jennifer Hill 2007. *Data Analysis Using Regression and Multilevel/Heiarchical Models.* New York: Cambridge University Press.

Gendall, Philip and Benjamin Healey 2008. "Asking the Age Question in Mail and Online Surveys." *International Journal of Market Research* 50(3): 309–317. https://doi.org/10.1177/147078530805000303. Accessed online June 19, 2021.

Gimpel, James G., Frances E. Lee, and Joshua Kaminski 2006. "The Political Geography of Campaign Contributions in American Politics." *Journal of Politics* 68(3): 626–639. https://doi.org/10.1111/j.1468-2508.2006.00450.x. Accessed online June 19, 2021.

Giugni, Marco, Doug McAdam, and Charles Tilly (Eds.) 1999. *How Social Movements Matter.* Minneapolis, MN: University of Minnesota Press.

Greene, William H. 2011. *Econometric Analysis.* 7th Ed. New York City, NY: Pearson Education.

Gutowitz, Jill. 2017. "10 Women and Teens Told Us Why They're Attending the Women's March." *Teen Vogue.* www.teenvogue.com/story/women-teens-why-attending-womens-march-on-washington. Accessed online January 8, 2021.

Hauck, Grace 2020. "Hundreds Gather for Women's March to Protest Trump, Barrett Nomination." *USA Today.* October 17. www.usatoday.com/story/news/nation/2020/10/17/womens-march-2020-protest-trump-amy-coney-barrett-nomination/3693810001. Accessed online November 24, 2020.

Head, Megan L., Luke Holman, Rob Lanfear, Andrew T. Kahn, and Michael D. Jennions 2015. "The Extent and Consequences of P-Hacking in Science." *Plos Biology* 13(3): e1002106. https://doi.org/10.1371/journal.pbio.1002106 Accessed online June 19, 2021.

Ho, Daniel E., Kosuke Imai, Gary King, and Elizabeth A. Stuart 2007. "Matching as Nonparametric Preprocessing for Reducing Model Dependence in Parametric Causal Inference." *Political Analysis* 15(3): 199–236. https://doi.org/10.1093/pan/mpl013. Accessed online June 19, 2021.

Imbens, Guido W. and Donald B. Rubin 2015. *Causal Inference for Statistics, Social, and Biomedical Sciences: An Introduction.* New York, NY: Cambridge University Press.

Johnson, Christen A. and K. T. Hawbaker 2019. "#MeToo: A Timeline of Events." *Chicago Tribune.* May 29. www.chicagotribune.com/lifestyles/ct-me-too-timeline-20171208/htmlstory.html. Accessed online June 6, 2019.

Kahne, Joseph and Benjamin Bowyer 2018. "The Political Significance of Social Media Activity and Social Networks." *Political Communication* 35(3): 470–493. https://doi.org/10.1080/10584609.2018.1426662. Accessed online June 19, 2021.

Kearl, Holly 2018. "The Facts behind the #metoo Movement: A National Study on Sexual Harassment and Assault." www.stopstreetharassment.org/wp-content/uploads/2018/01/Full-Report-2018-National-Study-on-Sexual-Harassment-and-Assault.pdf. Accessed online June 4, 2020.

Kelly, Cara and Aaron Hegarty 2018. "#MeToo Was a Culture Shock: But Changing Laws Will Take More than a Year." *USA Today.* October 4. www.usatoday.com/story/news/investigations/2018/10/04/metoo-me-too-sexual-assault-survivors-rights-bill/1074976002/. Accessed online June 27, 2019.

Kenski, Kate and Natalie Jomini Stroud 2006. "Connections between Internet Use and Political Efficacy, Knowledge, and Participation." *Journal of Broadcasting and Electronic Media* 50(2): 173–192. https://doi.org/10.1207/s15506878jobem5002_1. Accessed online June 19, 2021.

Kerbel, Matthew R. and Joel David Bloom 2005. "Blog for America and Civic Involvement." *The International Journal of Press/Politics* 10(4): 3–27. https://doi.org/10.1177/1081180X05281395. Accessed online June 19, 2021.

King, Gary, Christopher Lucas, and Richard A. Nielsen 2017. "The Balance-Sample Size Frontier in Matching Methods for Causal Inference." *American Journal of Political Science* 61(2): 473–489. https://doi.org/10.1111/ajps.12272.

King, Gary, Robert O. Keohane, and Sidney Verba 1994. *Designing Social Inquiry: Scientific Inference in Qualitative Research.* Princeton, NJ: Princeton University Press.

Kitschelt, Herbert 1993. "Social Movements, Political Parties, and Democratic Theory." *The Annals of the American Academy of Political and Social Science* 528(1): 13–29. https://doi.org/10.1177/0002716293528001002. Accessed online June 19, 2021.

Kristofferson, Kirk, Katerine White, and John Peloza 2014. "The Nature of Slacktivism: How the Social Observability of an Initial Act of Token Support Affects Subsequent Prosocial Action." *Journal of Consumer Research* 40: 1149–1166. https://doi.org/10.1086/674137. Accessed online June 19, 2021.

Kwak, Nojin, Daniel S. Lane, Brian E. Weeks, Dam Hee Kim, Slgi S. Lee, and Sarah Bachleda 2018. "Perceptions of Social Media for Politics: Testing the Slacktivism Hypothesis." *Human Communication Research* 44(2): 197–221. https://doi.org/10.1093/hcr/hqx008. Accessed online June 19, 2021.

Lewis, John 2005. "The Voting Rights Act: Ensuring Dignity and Democracy." *Human Rights* 32(2): 2–3, 7.

Ley, Barbara L. and Paul R. Brewer 2018. "Social Media, Networked Protest, and the March for Science." *Social Media and Society* 4(3): 1–12. https://doi.org/10.1177/2056305118793407. Accessed online June 19, 2021.

Loader, Brian D., Ariadne Vromen, and Michael A. Xenos 2014. "The Networked Young Citizen: Social Media, Political Participation and Civic Engagement." *Information, Communication and Society* 17(2): 143–150. https://doi.org/10.1080/1369118X.2013.871571. Accessed online June 19, 2021.

McAdam, Doug and Sidney Tarrow 2010. "Ballots and Barricades: On the Reciprocal Relationship between Elections and Social Movements." *Perspectives on Politics* 8(2): 529–542. https://doi.org/10.1017/S1537592710001234. Accessed online June 19, 2021.

Meyer, David S. 2007. *Politics of Protest: Social Movements in America*. New York, NY: Oxford University Press.

Meyer, David S., Valerie Jenness, and Helen Ingram (Eds.) 2005. *Routing the Opposition: Social Movements, Public Policy, and Democracy*. Minneapolis, MN: University of Minnesota Press.

Moffett, Kenneth W. and Laurie L. Rice 2018. "College Students and Online Political Expression in the 2016 Election." *Social Science Computer Review* 36(4): 422–439. https://doi.org/10.1177/0894439317721186. Accessed online June 19, 2021.

Nichols, Austin 2007. "Causal Inference with Observational Data." *The Stata Journal* 7(4): 507–541. https://doi.org/10.1177/1536867X0800700403. Accessed online June 19, 2021.

Nikolayenko, Olena 2007. "The Revolt of the Post-Soviet Generation: Youth Movements in Serbia, Georgia, and Ukraine." *Comparative Politics* 39(2): 169–188.

Milano, Alyssa 2017. "MeToo Tweet." https://twitter.com/alyssa_milano/status/919659438700670976?lang=en. Accessed online June 26, 2019.

Min, Song-Jae 2007. "Online vs. Face-to-Face Deliberation: Effects on Civic Engagement." *Journal of Computer-Mediated Communication* 12(4): 1369–1387. https://doi.org/10.1111/j.1083-6101.2007.00377.x. Accessed online June 19, 2021.

Moffett, Kenneth W. and Laurie L. Rice 2016. *Web 2.0 and the Political Mobilization of College Students*. Lanham, MD: Lexington Books.

Moffett, Kenneth W. and Laurie L. Rice 2018. "College Students and Online Political Expression in the 2016 Election." *Social Science Computer Review* 36(4): 422–439. https://doi.org/10.1177/0894439317721186. Accessed online June 19, 2021.

Morozov, Evgeny 2009. "The Brave New World of Slacktivism." *Foreign Policy*, May 19.

Olson, Mancur 1973. *The Logic of Collective Action: Public Goods and the Theory of Groups*. Cambridge, MA: Harvard University Press.

Opsahl, Robin 2018. "Here Are the 7 Congressmen Accused of Sexual Misconduct since #MeToo." *Roll Call*. April 27. www.rollcall.com/news/politics/heres-7-congressmen-accused-sexual-misconduct-since-metoo. Accessed online June 27, 2019.

Parker, Kim, Nikki Graf, and Ruth Igielnik 2019. "Generation Z Looks a Lot Like Millennials on Key Social and Political Issues." Pew Research Center. www.pewsocialtrends.org/2019/01/17/generation-z-looks-a-lot-like-millennials-on-key-social-and-political-issues/. Accessed online February 12, 2019.

Piven, Frances Fox and Richard A. Cloward 1977. *Poor People's Movements: Why They Succeed, How They Fail*. New York, NY: Pantheon Books.

Reny, Tyler T., Loren Collingwood and Ali A. Valenzuela 2019. "Vote Switching in the 2016 Election: How Racial and Immigration Attitudes, Not Economics, Explain Shifts in White Voting." *Public Opinion Quarterly* 83(1): 91–113. https://doi.org/10.1093/poq/nfz011. Accessed online June 19, 2021.

Robertson, Charlotte 2014. "Slacktivism: The Downfall of Millennials." Buzzsaw. www.buzzsawmag.org/2014/10/06/slacktivismwhy-this-generation-sucks/. Accessed online April 14, 2020.

Rosenblatt, Kalhan. 2019. "Passing the Mantle: Women's March Participants Find Inspiration in America's Youth." www.nbcnews.com/news/us-news/passing-mantle-women-s-march-participants-find-inspiration-america-s-n960596. Accessed online January 8, 2021.

Rosenstone, Steven J. and John Mark Hansen 2002. *Mobilization, Participation, and Democracy in America*. New York, NY: Pearson-Longman.

Ross, Ashley D. and Stella M. Rouse 2015. "Economic Uncertainty, Job Threat, and the Resiliency of the Millennial Generation's Attitudes toward Immigration." *Social Science Quarterly* 96(5): 1363–1379. https://doi.org/10.1111/ssqu.12168. Accessed online June 19, 2021.

Rouse, Stella M. and Ashley D. Ross 2018. *The Politics of Millennials: Political Beliefs and Policy Preferences of America's Most Diverse Generation*. Ann Arbor, MI: University of Michigan Press.

Ryan, Barbara 1992. *Feminism and the Women's Movement: Dynamics of Change in Social Movement Ideology and Activism*. New York, NY: Routledge.

Sekhon, Jasjeet S. 2011. "Multivariate and Propensity Score Matching Software with Automated Balance Optimization: The Matching Package for R." *Journal of Statistical Software* 42(7): 1–52.

Shah, Dhavan V., Nojin Kwak, and R. Lance Holbert 2001. "'Connecting' and 'Disconnecting' with Civic Life: Patterns of Internet Use and the Production of Social Capital." *Political Communication* 18(2): 141–162. https://doi.org/10.1080/105846001750322952. Accessed online June 19, 2021.

Shah, Dhavan V., Jaeho Cho, William P. Eveland, Jr., and Nojin Kwak 2005. "Information and Expression in a Digital Age: Modeling Internet Effects on Civic Participation." *Communication Research* 32(5): 531–565. https://doi.org/10.1177/0093650205279209. Accessed online June 19, 2021.

Shushok, Frank Jr. and Vera Kidd 2015. "Millennials in Higher Education: As Students Change, Much about Them Remains the Same." In *Positive Psychology on the College Campus*, John C. Wade, Lawrence I. Marks, and Roderick D. Hetzel (Eds.). New York, NY: Oxford University Press.

Smith, Aaron and Monica Anderson 2018. "Social Media Use in 2018," Pew Research Center. www.pewinternet.org/2018/03/01/social-media-use-in-2018/. Accessed online January 11, 2019.

Stewart, Abigail J., Isis H. Settles and Nicholas J. G. Winter 1998. "Women and the Social Movements of the 1960s: Activists, Engaged Observers, and Nonparticipants." *Political Psychology* 19(1): 63–94. https://doi.org/10.1111/0162-895X.00093. Accessed online June 19, 2021.

Stuart, Elizabeth A. 2010. "Matching Methods for Causal Inference: A Review and a Look Forward." *Statistical Science* 25(1): 1–21. https://doi.org/10.1214/09-STS313. Accessed online June 19, 2021.

Szymanski, Ann-Marie E. 2003. *Pathways to Prohibition: Radicals, Moderates, and Social Movement Outcomes.* Durham, NC: Duke University Press.

Tarrow, Sidney G. 1989. *Democracy and Disorder: Protest and Politics in Italy, 1965–1975.* New York, NY: Oxford University Press.

Tarrow, Sidney G. 2011. *Power in Movement: Social Movements and Contentious Politics.* 3rd Ed. New York, NY: Cambridge University Press.

Tate, Emily. 2017. "Beginning of a Movement." *Inside Higher Ed.* www.insidehighered.com/news/2017/01/23/tens-thousands-college-students-and-professors-march-washington. Accessed online January 8, 2021.

Tilly, Charles 1978. *From Mobilization to Revolution.* New York, NY: McGraw-Hill.

Towner, Terri L. 2013. "All Political Participation Is Socially Networked?: New Media and the 2012 Election." *Social Science Computer Review* 31(5): 527–541. https://doi.org/10.1177/0894439313489656. Accessed online June 19, 2021.

Towner, Terri L. and Caroline Lego Munoz 2018. "Baby Boom or Bust? The New Media Effect on Political Participation." *Journal of Political Marketing* 17(1): 32–61. https://doi.org/10.1080/15377857.2016.1153561. Accessed online June 19, 2021.

Traister, Rebecca 2018. *Good and Mad: The Revolutionary Power of Women's Anger.* New York, NY: Simon and Schuster.

van Stekelenburg, Jacquelien and Bert Klandermans. 2013. "The Social Psychology of Protest." *Current Sociology* 61(5–6): 886–905. https://doi.org/10.1177%2F0011392113479314. Accessed online June 19, 2021.

Verba, Sidney, Henry E. Brady, and Kay L. Schlozman 1995. *Voice and Equality: Civic Voluntarism in American Democracy.* Cambridge, MA: Harvard University Press.

Verba, Sidney and Richard A. Brody 1970. "Participation, Policy Preferences, and the War in Vietnam." *Public Opinion Quarterly* 34(3): 325–332. https://doi.org/10.1086/267809. Accessed online June 19, 2021.

Wahlstrom, Mattias and Magnus Wennerhag 2014. "Alone in the crowd: Lone protesters in Western European demonstrations." *International Sociology.* 29(6): 565–583. https://doi.org/10.1177/0268580914554117. Accessed online June 19, 2021.

Zukin, Cliff, Scott Keeter, Molly Andolina, Krista Jenkins, and Michael X. Delli Carpini 2006. *A New Engagement? Political Participation, Civic Life, & the Changing American Citizen.* New York, NY: Oxford University Press.

3
BRETT KAVANAUGH AND AMY CONEY BARRETT

How Controversial Supreme Court Nominations Provided Opportunities to Get Involved

Introduction

Supreme Court nomination battles may not seem the most obvious place to find political engagement among young adults. After all, compared to their elders, young adults have tended to be less knowledgeable about who serves on the Supreme Court (Kohut and Keeter 2010). Yet, the 2018 and 2020 elections, which drew record levels of voter turnout among young adults (CIRCLE 2018, 2020), were also preceded by controversial Supreme Court nominations. Both nominations shifted the ideology of the Court further to the right. Both nominations were made by then-President Donald Trump, whom young adults were far less likely to approve of than older Americans (*The Economist*/YouGov Poll 2020). For different reasons, both also generated high levels of controversy.

During a televised prime-time press conference on July 9, 2018, then-President Trump nominated Judge Brett Kavanaugh to replace retiring Justice Anthony Kennedy on the U.S. Supreme Court, declaring that "Judge Kavanaugh has impeccable credentials, unsurpassed qualifications, and a proven commitment to equal justice under the law" and that "this incredibly qualified nominee deserves a swift confirmation and robust bipartisan support" (Trump 2018). Although Kavanaugh was eventually confirmed, the process was neither swift nor bipartisan.

While there was little debate over Kavanaugh's qualifications, his views, along with the emergence of troubling allegations from his past, generated considerable controversy. On July 30, Senator Feinstein (D-CA) via Representative Eshoo (D-CA) received a letter from one of her constituents in which the constituent accused Kavanaugh of sexually assaulting her after a party when they were both in high school (Raju 2018). Consistent with that constituent's wishes, Senator Feinstein initially kept that letter confidential (Raju 2018). Kavanaugh's confirmation hearing began on September 4, with neither the public nor other senators knowing about the letter (Tatum 2018). After rumors of there being a letter that contained potentially incriminating evidence against Kavanaugh, this letter became public on September 12 (Tatum 2018).

Four days later, the letter's author became public: Dr. Christine Blasey Ford (Brown 2018). The MeToo movement and a Supreme Court nomination now intersected. The Senate Judiciary Committee suspended its scheduled vote on Kavanaugh's confirmation to decide how to proceed next. Meanwhile, two additional women, Julie Swetnick and Deborah Ramirez, accused Kavanaugh of sexual misconduct (Tatum 2018). On September 27, both Dr. Ford and Judge Kavanaugh testified before the Senate Judiciary Committee about the events on and surrounding the night outlined in the letter (Veslous, Brenson, and Abramson 2018). On September 28, the Senate Judiciary Committee voted the nomination out of committee on a party-line vote, but insisted that a brief FBI investigation of the allegations must occur before a vote by the entire Senate (Tatum 2018). The FBI released its findings to the Senate on October 4, and the Senate ultimately voted 50–48 on October 6 to confirm Kavanaugh's appointment to the Supreme Court (Tatum 2018).

This Supreme Court vacancy attracted more attention than many others both because of the controversy surrounding it and because a reliably conservative judge (Kavanaugh) replaced one who was comparatively more moderate (Kennedy) (Epstein et al. 2007). This made the stakes higher because the new median justice on the Court shifted rightward from Justice Kennedy to Chief Justice Roberts (Epstein et al. 2007). These stakes were not lost on the electorate, as the controversy surrounding Kavanaugh's nomination exacerbated preexisting polarization within the American public (Campbell 2018). Further, partisans on their respective sides of the aisle noted the stakes, as they used the controversy surrounding this nomination to mobilize differing segments of the electorate to vote and engage in other forms of civic activity during the 2018 midterm election cycle (Kim 2018).

Barrett's Nomination

Amy Coney Barrett's nomination to the Supreme Court, two years later, involved another high-stakes political battle and a different kind of controversy. Six weeks before the 2020 presidential election, Supreme Court Justice Ruth Bader Ginsburg succumbed to a long battle with pancreatic cancer on September 18 (Totenberg 2020a). On her deathbed, she told her granddaughter, "My most fervent wish is that I will not be replaced until a new president is installed" (Totenberg 2020a). Yet, on September 26, one day after she became the first woman to lay in state at the U.S. Capitol (Naylor 2020), then-President Trump nominated Amy Coney Barrett to replace her (The White House 2020). The replacement of a reliably liberal justice with a conservative one would cement a 6–3 conservative majority on the

Supreme Court. A further move to the right in the Court's median would likely have policy outcomes for years to come. Further, with a case on the Affordable Care Act on the Court's Fall 2020 docket, the impact of this change could potentially be both sweeping and immediate (Biskupic 2020). This alone guaranteed the nomination would be met with controversy.

Yet, more than policy was at stake. A nomination so close to a presidential election would undoubtedly be political, especially given the circumstances of the last Supreme Court vacancy that emerged in a president's last year in office. Conservative Supreme Court Justice Antonin Scalia died on February 13, 2016 (Totenberg 2016). It was then-President Obama's final year in office, with the 2016 presidential election still nearly nine months away. That week, Senate Majority Leader Mitch McConnell (R-KY) and Senate Judiciary Chairman Chuck Grassley (R-IA) co-authored an op-ed in the *Washington Post*, writing in part

> Given that we are in the midst of the presidential election process, we believe that the American people should seize the opportunity to weigh in on whom they trust to nominate the next person for a lifetime appointment to the Supreme Court. It is today the American people, rather than a lame-duck president whose priorities and policies they just rejected in the most-recent national election, who should be afforded the opportunity to replace Justice Scalia.
>
> *(McConnell and Grassley 2016)*

On March 16, 2016, after consulting with members of the Senate Judiciary Committee from both political parties, then-President Obama nominated Merrick Garland to replace Scalia (The White House 2016). Garland had a reputation as a moderate jurist, and political scientists estimated his ideology as center left (Bonica et al. 2016). If confirmed, he would have shifted the Court median to the left, but his estimated ideology was closer to the center than any sitting Supreme Court Justice nominated by a Democratic president (Bonica et al. 2016). The pick was meant to be conciliatory and described by some as the least political that then-President Obama could have made (Epps 2016). However, then-Majority Leader McConnell insisted that the nomination would not receive a vote from the Senate, and Republicans on the Senate Judiciary Committee refused to hold hearings on Garland's nomination (Elving 2018). In doing so, they claimed to be following what they termed "the Biden rule," a noncodified premise taken from a floor speech Senator Joe Biden gave in 1992 about a hypothetical Supreme Court vacancy that "…once the political season is under way, and it is, action on a Supreme Court nomination must be put off until after the election campaign is over" (Bradner 2020). They successfully held the vacancy open for nearly a year, giving newly elected then-President Trump the chance to nominate conservative Neil Gorsuch to the Supreme Court on January 31, 2017.

If McConnell and Grassley's logic and the "Biden rule" are applied to the vacancy created by Justice Ginsburg's death, the vacancy should not have been filled. Yet, the very night Ginsburg died, then-Republican Senate Majority Leader Mitch McConnell called then-President Trump, urging him to nominate Barrett (Taddonio 2020) and soon after her nomination was announced, then-Majority Leader McConnell insisted that she receive a Senate confirmation vote in 2020 (Daly 2020). Democrats quickly accused Republicans of blatant political hypocrisy (Daly 2020), and a majority of Americans thought the vacancy should not be filled until after the election (Langer 2020). To sidestep these concerns and avoid electoral backlash, Republican Senators, and especially those facing tight reelection battles, followed McConnell's lead and now claimed the "Biden rule" was limited to situations in which the Senate and presidency were controlled by opposite political parties (Barrett 2020; Daly 2020). Whatever the merits of their arguments in 2016 or in 2020, Republicans had the votes to block Garland's nomination and to confirm Barrett's. Barrett was confirmed to the Supreme Court 30 days after being nominated. The 52–48 vote was the first time a confirmed Supreme Court justice received no support from the minority party in a roll call confirmation vote in at least a century and a half (Mascaro 2020).

Young Adults and Opinions about Supreme Court Nominations

What is more, polls showed that levels of attention to both Kavanaugh's and Barrett's nominations and opinions about them varied dramatically by age. According to *The Economist*/YouGov Poll (2018) conducted on September 23–25, 2018, young adults were far less likely to report having both heard a lot about Kavanaugh's nomination and to have a very favorable opinion of it. Relative to their elders, young adults also were more likely to have a very unfavorable opinion of Kavanaugh, to see him as unqualified to serve on the Supreme Court, and to support an FBI investigation into the sexual assault allegations (*The Economist*/YouGov 2018). Similarly, according to *The Economist*/YouGov Poll (2020) conducted September 20–22, 2020, young adults were far less likely than older age groups to say that then-President Trump should fill the vacancy Justice Ginsburg left. In addition, while fewer young adults had opinions about Amy Coney Barrett compared to older age groups, young adults were less likely to think the Senate should vote to confirm her and substantially less likely than older age groups to have positive impressions of her (CNN/SSRS 2020). Thus, while it remains true that young adults are less familiar with Supreme Court Justices and nominees, young adults' opinions of both Kavanaugh and Barrett were less favorable than other age groups. This motivates the first research question addressed in this chapter: is opposition to their nominations connected with higher levels of civic engagement among younger voters? Then, regardless of young adults' specific opinions on each nomination, we examine whether those who care enough about each nomination to post or protest about it were more civically engaged than those who did not take these actions.

We use data from two Amazon mTurk surveys of young people between the ages of 18 and 25 in the United States taken on the days after the 2018 midterm election and the 2020 presidential election to test our hypotheses. We find no evidence that supports a link between opinions about either Kavanaugh's or Barrett's nominations and civic activity. However, we find evidence that those who posted about the nominations were more civically engaged than otherwise similar young adults. We also discover that those who protested the Kavanaugh nomination more than once were more civically engaged than otherwise similar young adults.

Supreme Court Nominations and Political Participation

Political scientists and pundits have long known that salient issues affect political participation (see e.g., Belanger and Meguid 2008; Converse 1964; Krosnick 1990; Lewis-Beck 1990). In particular, political issues can spur participation among certain segments of the public, known as issue publics, depending on the particular issue in question (Converse 1964). In addition, Krosnick (1990) notes that the American public looks as if it is structured into many smaller issue publics, and that citizens form preferences based on the issue positions that candidates take. However, not all issues are created equally, as issue ownership as it relates to vote choice occurs only when a voter perceives an issue as salient (Belanger and Meguid 2008). Issue-specific political activity pervades a wide range of salient issues among a diverse array of the electorate, including the economy (Lewis-Beck 1990), protracted wars (Verba and Brody 1970; Moffett, Rice, and Madupalli 2014), the tax cuts that occurred under then-President George W. Bush (Flavin and Griffin 2009), and the Affordable Care Act (Bennett 2012).

Supreme Court nominations can potentially mobilize; however, who sits on the Supreme Court does not always attract attention from the public (Kohut and Keeter 2010). Supreme Court appointments happen approximately once every two years (Shipan and Shannon 2003). Surveys show that public knowledge about who leads the Supreme Court is overall low relative to knowledge about other branches and domestic policies (Kohut and Keeter 2010). This lesser familiarity likely reflects the sparse coverage of the courts compared to other branches. A 2009 content analysis of coverage of the three branches of government on NBC found that the courts only garnered 6% of this coverage (Graber and Dunaway 2015, 211).

In this respect, it is not surprising that nominations for the Supreme Court receive much more attention from political institutions scholars than from those who study political behavior. Political institutions scholars have found that presidents use Supreme Court nominations to move the Court toward the president's ideal point (Cottrell, Shipan, and Anderson 2019) as part of the broader struggle over control of the federal courts between Congress and the president

(Krehbiel 2007). Depending on the preferences that Congress holds, this can generate considerable public attention, especially if a justice who holds one ideology replaces a justice who holds an opposing ideology (Epstein and Segal 2005), and if Congress is closely divided (Gibson and Caldeira 2009). In the modern era, judicial nominations for Supreme Court seats likely result in highly contentious confirmation battles precisely for these reasons (Maltese 1995).

These factors influence how the public evaluates Supreme Court nominees, as Gimpel and Wolpert (1996) find that Americans evaluate controversial Supreme Court nominees in the same general direction as they evaluate the president. In addition, Hutchings (2001) discovers that those groups who find particular Supreme Court nominations to be more salient, combined with political context, are more likely to pay attention to the confirmation battle and politically participate. Further, confirmation debates like those of Robert Bork, Clarence Thomas, Brett Kavanaugh, and Amy Coney Barrett grip the nation for extended periods (Caldeira and Smith 1996), with groups mobilizing for and against the nomination (Segal, Cameron, and Cover 1992). These groups offer competing frames through which to view the nominee (Gibson and Caldeira 2009), with opponents emphasizing "wrongdoing, a lack of qualifications, and ideological extremism" (Krutz, Fleisher, and Bond 1998), and supporters highlighting qualifications and judiciousness (Gibson and Caldeira 2009). Defeat of the nominee becomes more likely when opponents successfully make their frame dominant (Krutz, Fleisher, and Bond 1998).

To successfully defeat a nomination, opponents' charges must be seen as credible and worthy of defeating the nominee (Krutz, Fleisher, and Bond 1998). One example of this is found in the battle over the nomination of Robert Bork to the Supreme Court. Conservative and liberal interest groups devoted significant efforts to influencing public opinion about him, with opposing groups mobilizing more quickly than groups supporting the nomination (Caldeira and Wright 1998). Liberal groups spent far more on advertising to portray Bork as an unsuitable extremist than conservatives spent on pro-Bork advertising (Caldeira and Wright 1998). Nonetheless, both sides mobilized substantial constituent activity related to the nomination, with the ideological extremist frame winning out (Caldeira and Wright 1998). Consequently, conservatives mobilized more quickly to support Souter's and Thomas's nominations (Caldeira and Wright 1998).

Overall, Gibson and Caldeira (2009) find that Supreme Court nominations are subject to a positivity bias that stems from voters' institutional loyalty to the Supreme Court. Nominations are generally difficult to block, provided that the debate centers on judiciousness and the nominee is qualified (Gibson and Caldeira 2009). While Krutz, Fleisher, and Bond (1998) similarly suggest that nominations start from a presumption of success, when opponents raise allegations early in the process, offer meaningful reasons for opposition, and successfully expand the conflict by directing media attention to the allegations and engaging the public, the probability of confirmation drops. In particular, allegations of wrongdoing reduce the chances of confirmation by almost half (Krutz, Fleisher, and Bond 1998). Given this, Barrett's confirmation hearings, despite the political controversy, would have a greater presumption of success than Kavanaugh's because she faced no allegations of wrongdoing. While Kavanaugh was eventually confirmed despite the allegations levied against him, the vote was one of the narrowest in recent history.

Younger Voters, Supreme Court Nominations, and Civic Engagement

In Supreme Court confirmation battles, lobbying by opposing groups can be effective (Caldeira and Wright 1998). As part of these lobbying efforts, interest groups mobilize constituents to make phone calls, write letters, and engage in demonstrations to support or oppose nominees (Caldeira and Wright 1998). Interest groups also e-mail their supporters with requests to take specific actions for or against a nominee (Vining 2011). Vining (2011, 790) argues that "A Supreme Court vacancy is an opportunity to request mobilization because the confirmation process is highly salient, limited in duration, and allows only two outcomes – the confirmation of a new justice or failure of a nomination."

Participation may matter more when it involves Supreme Court nominations than in a typical policy debate, as confirmed nominees have lifetime appointments that assume good behavior. In addition, interest group lobbying influences senators' confirmation votes (Caldeira and Wright 1998). For instance, lobbying by opposition groups contributed to Bork's defeat and moderate levels of changes in mobilization could have changed the outcome of Thomas's confirmation vote (Caldeira and Wright 1998). Thus, interest groups have strong incentives to mobilize constituents to take actions to support or oppose Supreme Court nominations, and constituents have equally strong incentives to respond favorably to these requests for action. Unlike many policy debates, nominations offer individuals a clear opportunity to make a difference in a relatively short period – something that may be particularly attractive to young adults who are relatively new to the political process.

Young adults, due to their age, were likely to experience the impacts of Kavanaugh and Barrett on Supreme Court decisions for a longer time period. In addition, the current generation of young adults differs from their elders (Parker, Graf, and Igielnik 2019; Rouse and Ross 2018; Shushok and Kidd 2015). For instance, young adults utilize technology at far higher rates and tend to engage in online forms of civic activity frequently (Moffett and Rice 2016). In particular, Millennials and members of Generation Z are more liberal than preceding generations, particularly on social issues like gay marriage and racial equality (Parker, Graf, and Igielnik 2019; Ross and Rouse 2015; Rouse and Ross 2018). They support higher levels of diversity (Parker, Graf, and Igielnik 2019) and "expect progress toward equalization of genders to continue" (Shushok and

Kidd 2015, 38). One of the fundamental policy planks about which the struggle over Kavanaugh and Barrett's nominations endured was a basket of social issues, including the future of abortion, affirmative action, and Obamacare. In addition, because Kavanaugh's nomination involved allegations of sexual assault, this implicated a value that Millennials and Generation Z widely hold: gender equality.

Opposition to Kavanaugh and Barrett's Nominations and Civic Engagement

Thus, Kavanaugh and Barrett's nominations may encourage political participation among younger voters, especially if they see them as costly or threatening to their interests. Kahneman and Tversky (1979) demonstrate that individuals are more sensitive to losses than to gains, especially relative to the status quo (Tversky and Kahneman 1992). This differential response to losses and gains is known as prospect theory. Arnold (1990, 51) demonstrates this in his study of Congress, as he states that citizens "are far more likely to pursue traceability chains when they incur perceptible costs than when they reap an equal measure of benefits." He adds that one reason "is that costs produce more intense preferences than do benefits" (Arnold 1990, 51). As applied here, those who oppose Kavanaugh's or Barrett's nomination react to the costs that they may incur upon their confirmations to the Supreme Court since this would represent a loss compared to the status quo (i.e., the policy positions of Kennedy or Ginsburg). Thus, those who face potential policy losses in cases like this are more likely to act to prevent these losses than those who receive beneficial policy outcomes.

Therefore, those who viewed these nominations as a threat might have a greater incentive to participate than those who thought they would help advance their interests. After all, if most nominations begin with the presumption of success (Krutz, Fleisher, and Bond 1998; Gibson and Caldeira 2009), then there should be greater perceived need for action among those who want to stop a nomination. Supporters may discount action, telling themselves that the nominee will be confirmed, regardless of whether they do anything. Meanwhile, if opponents do not act, then confirmation is likely.

Moreover, political psychologists offer a concurring account for why participation may be greater among those who strongly opposed these nominations. Having the resources to participate only partially explains participation; motivation matters, too (Miller and Krosnick 2004). In particular, a perceived political threat can serve as a powerful motivator for political action (Marcus, MacKuen, and Neuman 2000; Miller and Krosnick 2004). Experimental research shows that policy change threats offer greater motivation for action than does the opportunity to bring about political change (Miller et al. 2016). The threat of policy change on an issue an individual finds important can be particularly motivating (Miller et al. 2016).

Groups that opposed Kavanaugh's and Barrett's nominations emphasized threats to abortion and other women's rights. In addition, Democrats emphasized Barrett's potential role in overturning the Affordable Care Act, otherwise known as Obamacare, a policy just over 60% of young adults supported (CNN/SSRS 2020). Thus, both Kavanaugh and Barrett represented policy change threats to many young voters, giving them incentive to actively oppose these nominations. For this reason, we expect there could be higher levels of civic engagement[1] among young voters who opposed these nominations to the Supreme Court. Yet, as we saw in the previous chapter, opinions alone do not necessarily produce action. Thus, while those who strongly opposed the Kavanaugh and Barrett nominations might be the most predisposed to act, strong opposition to their nominations alone may not be enough to boost other forms of civic engagement.

In addition, the allegations that emerged during Kavanaugh's confirmation hearings, amidst the backdrop of the MeToo movement, provided added urgency for young voters to take action to oppose his confirmation. This narrative of policy change threat combined with allegations of wrongdoing gave those opposed to Kavanaugh stronger reasons to participate compared to those motivated by the opportunity to bring policy change to the Court. This makes a comparison of reactions to the Kavanaugh and Barrett nominations particularly instructive. If heightened civic engagement is linked to opposing the Kavanaugh nomination but not Barrett's nomination, then Kavanaugh's intersection with the MeToo Movement might be driving this link. If, instead, opposition to both justices or Barrett alone is associated with higher levels of civic engagement, then it is more likely that this involvement was in fact driven by policy change threat.

Posting about Supreme Court Nominations and Civic Engagement

Actions are costly and individuals who care enough to act must know what actions to take that might help advance their views. While young adults are more likely to have recently taken a course in government or civics than older Americans, young adults have had less time to acquire political experience. Unlike older Americans, the Kavanaugh and Barrett nominations were most young adults' first highly contentious and controversial confirmation hearings. During the Kavanaugh hearings, interest groups mobilized individuals to contact elected officials, attend protests, and engage in other activities aimed at stopping or advancing his nomination. After Barrett's nomination, interest groups also began mobilizing individuals to pressure senators to support or oppose her confirmation (Walsh 2020).

Older Americans might already be on the contact lists of interest groups active in past highly contested Supreme Court nominations. However, young adults who did not publicly share their opinions about Kavanaugh's or Barrett's nominations had reduced chances of being subject to these mobilization attempts by interest groups. Posting about a nomination is a relatively low-cost way of making one's opinions about a nomination public. It indicates deeper care about the confirmation hearing outcome and some level of willingness to act, thus opening oneself up to mobilization attempts both from interest groups and from other likeminded individuals who may have more political experience. Because those who shared their views about Kavanaugh or Barrett online already showed some willingness to act on their views, they should also have a heightened probability of responding favorably to mobilization requests.

In addition, the link from posting about an issue to civic engagement can also occur more organically in the absence of interest group attempts at mobilization. Research has shown that individuals sharing concerns online increases feelings of efficacy and can help build online communities of concerned individuals who go on to engage in offline civic action (Ortiz and Osertag 2014). Thus, we expect that sharing one's views about the Kavanaugh or Barrett nomination online created multiple pathways to heightened levels of civic engagement.

Protesting about Supreme Court Nominations and Civic Engagement

In contrast to posting, protesting is a higher cost form of expressing one's view about a nomination. During the Kavanaugh confirmation hearings, protestors on both sides gathered in front of the Supreme Court to make their views known (Keneally 2018). Those opposing the nomination also took to Capitol Hill in protest. Protestors gathered outside the offices of Senator Susan Collins and Senator Jeff Flake before filling the rotunda of the Russell Senate Office Building, shouting "We Believe the Women" (Moyer 2018). Illustrating the very real risk of such protest, 128 of these protesters were arrested for engaging in unlawful demonstrations (Moyer 2018). They were willing to incur high costs, including arrests and the possibility of fines or jail time of up to 90 days (Code of the District of Columbia § 22–1307) to express their views. Yet, the protests were not limited to Washington, DC. Students at universities such as Yale, Harvard, University of Massachusetts, University of Wyoming, the University of Pittsburgh, the Claremont Colleges, Loyola University Chicago, Syracuse University, and the University of Vermont all held protests against Kavanaugh's nomination. While protests against Barrett's were more subdued, liberal interest groups began organizing rallies opposing her confirmation outside the Supreme Court within days of her nomination (Walsh 2020). These protests were also not limited to Washington, DC. For example, students at Notre Dame held dueling demonstrations, opposing and supporting her nomination (Gomez 2020) and University of Wisconsin-Milwaukee student Grace Quinn helped organize a protest at the Milwaukee County Courthouse (Torres 2020).

Individuals who care enough to protest are particularly ripe for additional mobilization attempts – they have already demonstrated willingness to act in costly ways and are more likely to be receptive to calls for additional action. Protests also provide opportunities for mobilization. For example, protests against the Kavanaugh nomination were supported by a range of groups including the Women's March and Planned Parenthood (Landers 2018) as well as the National Women's Law Center (Moyer 2018), the Center for Popular Democracy Action and Service Employees International Union 32BJ chapter in Washington, DC (Witt 2018). Leaders of many of these groups were active participants in these protests, providing opportunities for first-time protesters to meet group leaders (Moyer 2018; Witt 2018) and be recruited to join groups and engage in other activities. In addition, groups began coordinating actions with each other, giving preexisting group members who protested opportunities to build contacts with additional activists and organizations (Landers 2018). Even at protests at universities, student organizations joined together in coalitions protesting the nomination and to raise awareness about sexual assault (Darnell 2018).

All these face-to-face contacts built at protests are likely to result in receiving additional calls to action and the exposure to additional opportunities to get involved. Protesters should be especially likely to respond favorably to these since they have already demonstrated their willingness to take costly action in support of their views. The Women's March also mobilized against Barrett's nomination, holding a march that ended with text banking, although the Covid-era protest drew smaller crowds than previous Women's Marches (Hauck 2020). They were greeted by counterprotesters at the "I'm With Her!" rally organized by the Independent Women's Forum (Hauck 2020). We expect that those who participated in protests related to the Kavanaugh or Barrett nomination should be more civically engaged than those who chose not to protest, although we note that less participants for the Barrett protests may have meant less opportunities for mobilization than the Kavanaugh protests offered.

Data

To test our hypotheses, we performed separate online surveys via Amazon's Mechanical Turk (mTurk) platform on the day after each of the 2018 (November 7) and 2020 (November 4) general elections. The survey population was Americans between 18 and 25 years old – an age range that includes both older members of Generation Z and younger Millennials.[2] This platform allows members of the public to earn money for completing a multitude of tasks, including participating in survey research. A total of 1,010 participants completed the survey after we eliminated any incomplete responses in 2018.[3] Also, 969 participants completed the survey after eliminating any incomplete responses in 2020. Each participant was paid $1.50 for completing each survey in 2018 and 2020.

Dependent Variable

The dependent variable is the extent to which each respondent participated in civic and political activities away from the internet. Through separate questions, each person was asked about the frequency with which they have engaged in an array of activities including talking to people and explaining why they should vote for or against a specific candidate or party, attending political functions in support of a candidate or party, and making purchasing decisions based on a company's conduct or values. To create a single measure of political and civic activity, we summed the values for each of the 12 activities to produce a civic engagement index (α = .92, 2018; α = .95, 2020). The means of this index, 14.56 (2018) and 26.01 (2020), are quite low as this indicates an activity level equivalent to having done 4–6 of the 12 activities in this index very often. The standard deviations, 10.75 (2018) and 14.61 (2020), indicate substantial variance around this mean. Thus, we have captured both low and high participators alike in our survey. More precise descriptions of variable measurement and question wording for the dependent variable, treatment variables, and matching covariates can be found in the online appendix.

To test our theoretical expectations, we use a series of matching routines. This allows us to match respondents who are otherwise similar with respect to an array of variables known to affect participation levels. In turn, this provides the ability to isolate the separate effects of opinions about Supreme Court nominations (Kavanaugh in 2018, and Barrett in 2020), and posting or participating in protests related to these same nominations.

Treatment Variables

First, we test whether opinions about Supreme Court nominations (Kavanaugh in 2018, Barrett in 2020) influence civic activity. We asked each respondent whether they supported or opposed each respective nomination (Kavanaugh in 2018, Barrett in 2020) to the U.S. Supreme Court. Then, we followed up with those who supported (opposed) each nomination to gauge whether they had strongly or not strongly done so. We combined the responses to these questions to generate a five-point scale that ranged from strongly opposed to strongly supported.

Using separate sets of models, we test hypotheses two and three by calculating the effects of posting about Kavanaugh's nomination in 2018 and Barrett's nomination in 2020, or participating in protests related to each respective nomination, on civic engagement. Through separate questions, we asked each respondent about the extent to which they posted about each nomination or participated in protests related to it. The response options for each of these questions were never, once, two or three times, and four or more times.

Matching Covariates

We used two variables to investigate the effects of political engagement away from the internet. First, we asked each respondent about the extent to which they are interested in politics on a four-point scale that ranged from "Not at all interested" to "Very interested." Second, each respondent was asked three questions about the extent to which their friends engaged in a set of activities. We built an additive index based on the responses to these questions to examine the effects of peer civic activities on civic engagement ($\alpha = .63, 2018; \alpha = .58, 2020$).[4,5]

In addition, we used several variables to query the effects of political engagement using the internet. First, we asked each respondent how often they read blogs online about politics. Kerbel and Bloom (2005) and Moffett and Rice (2018) discover that blogs can act as outlets that foster enhanced civic activity, either online or offline. Second, each respondent was asked how frequently they read news on the internet about politics.

Third, we constructed an additive index of online civic activity consisting of five items, as several researchers have found a link between activities on social media and offline civic engagement (see e.g., Kahne and Bowyer 2018; Ley and Brewer 2018; Loader, Vromen, and Xenos 2014). Through separate questions, each respondent was asked about the extent to which they had relied on social media for news, posted about politics on social media, read social media feeds about politics, liked or shared posts about politics on social media, or read or watched posts about politics on social media, and we summed these to create an index of online civic activity ($\alpha = .84, 2018; \alpha = .83, 2020$).[6]

Fourth, each respondent was asked a set of questions about the extent to which they participated in protests related to gun control, immigration, the MeToo movement, Black Lives Matter (in 2020, but not in 2018), and about other issues. Fifth, each respondent was asked a series of questions about the extent to which they posted messages on social media about each of these issues.

We employed five variables to account for the effects of issue importance, as issues can sometimes prompt higher levels of political participation (Converse 1964; Carmines and Stimson 1989; Reny, Collingwood, and Valenzuela 2019). Using separate questions, we asked each respondent about the importance of congressional stances on immigration as well as gun control in influencing their vote choice.

We also asked each respondent about the extent to which they supported or opposed the family separation policy implementation under the Trump administration. We also asked about the extent to which they supported or opposed the DACA program in 2020, and whether they self-identified as a supporter of the Black Lives Matter movement in 2020.

Moreover, we employed several variables to account for the effects of personal characteristics on offline civic activity. First, we measure the extent to which each respondent strongly identifies with either the Republican or Democratic parties, as this attachment is associated with an array of other political activities (see e.g., Flavin and Griffin 2009; Verba, Brady, and Schlozman 1995). To do so, we computed a binary variable that is coded one for those who self-identified as having strong partisan attachments. Second, we examined the effects of ideology on civic engagement with a binary variable for liberals, as Achen and Bartels (2016) discover that self-identifying as either conservative or liberal shapes political participation. Third, we asked each respondent for their sex, and we coded this variable one for females, two for males, and three for those who self-identified in another category. Fourth, we acquired data on each respondent's age by asking each to report their month and year of birth. Then, we computed each respondent's age based on the month and year of the 2018 midterm election for the 2018 data, and the month and year of the 2020 general election for the 2020 data.[7] Fifth, we asked each respondent for their race and collapsed that information into a binary that is coded one for whites, and zero otherwise. Sixth, we asked each respondent for their level of education. Finally, we asked each respondent whether they approved or disapproved of the job that Donald Trump is doing as president, as presidential approval is connected with changes in participatory patterns (Abramowitz and Stone 2006).

Methods

To investigate whether both treatment variables are associated with civic engagement, we employ a matching analysis to compute the ATET. We choose a matching estimator for several reasons. First, nearly all regression-based techniques (including OLS) assume a linear relationship between the dependent and independent variables (see Greene 2011). Our theory posits a positive relationship between each of our treatment variables and civic activity, but makes no prediction about the remaining response options contained in any of the treatment variables. Consequently, the phenomenon that we examine is nonlinear by construction, and is ill suited to investigate using a method that assumes linearity (like OLS). Fortunately, matching analyses do not assume linearity, allow for a more flexible functional form, and have other statistical features that make them a more appropriate choice to test our hypotheses (Imbens and Rubin 2015).

Moreover, individuals have differing probabilities of holding varying opinions about Kavanaugh's (2018) or Barrett's (2020) nominations, or of posting or participating in protests with varying frequencies related to these nominations. OLS estimators presume treatment homogeneity, which is not likely to hold in the analyses. Individuals may have different treatment effects, particularly depending either on the opinion that they hold about each nomination, or the extent to which they posted about or participated in protests related to each nomination (see Abadie and Imbens 2011). Thus, the effects of opinions about each nomination vary depending on the particular opinion that one has about these nominations. For example, to the extent that opinions lead to action, we expect that those who strongly opposed Kavanaugh's nomination in 2018 or Barrett's in 2020 are apt to engage in offline civic activities more frequently than those who supported each nomination. Likewise, we anticipate that those who participated in protests related to each nomination or posted about this subject are more likely to have higher levels of offline civic engagement than those who neither participated in protests related to the nomination, or posted about this subject.

By construction, OLS-based estimators assume that we observe a linear, homogeneous relationship between opinions about the respective nominations (Kavanaugh in 2018, Barrett in 2020) and offline civic engagement. Matching-based approaches deal effectively with this issue because they assume neither linearity nor homogeneity (Imbens and Rubin 2015). Rather, matching-based approaches produce several treatment estimates depending on the level of treatment that a respondent received (Imbens and Rubin 2015). Thus, we can generate several, more accurate estimates of the effect that differing opinions about the respective nominations or that different levels of action had on civic engagement.

Moreover, OLS does not permit us to estimate what happens to civic activity in the absence of support of or opposition to the respective nominations (Kavanaugh in 2018, Barrett in 2020), or on the absence of having posted about or participated in protests related to either of these nominations (Nichols 2007). Matching analyses use the existing data to generate a dataset that includes observations that are as alike as possible, given the values of the remaining predictors (Stuart 2010). Thus, we can estimate what would have happened in the absence of support or opposition to each nomination, or in the absence of having posted about or protested related to a specific nomination (see Gelman and Hill 2007). Then, we can use this dataset to estimate the effects of a specific opinion about one of the nominations or a specified level of posting about or participating in protests related to that nomination on civic engagement. We iterate this procedure for each differing opinion about each nomination, or each level of posting about or participating in protests related to them. Finally, if we used OLS estimates to obtain the results, our results would likely be biased because any estimate of the treatment effect is conditioned on the values of the remaining independent variables. Consequently, OLS-based approaches do not compute ATETs.

Matching analyses handle each of these issues because they permit us to examine whether differing opinions about each particular nomination (Kavanaugh in 2018, Barrett in 2020), or posting about or participating in protests related to those nominations are associated with higher levels of civic engagement. By matching based on each of the predictor variables to make inferences, we can disentangle the effect of opinions about a particular nomination beyond individuals' other predispositions to participate. Similarly, we can unravel the effects of posting about or participating in protests related to each nomination beyond people's other inclinations to civically participate. Thus, doing so enables us to compare people with similar inclinations to civic activity who only vary in their opinions about a specific nomination, or who only vary in the extent to which they posted about or participated in protests related to that nomination. Moreover, matching allows us to calculate ATETs for each treatment level, and by doing so, to calculate more precise effect estimates with observational data.

Assumptions

Before performing our matching analyses, we must meet four assumptions. The validity of any matching analyses rests upon fulfilling these assumptions. First, we presume that all sets of treatment variables are binary. To make the first set of treatment variables binary, we generated a series of dichotomous variables for each response option, relative to neither supporting nor opposing the respective nomination (Kavanaugh in 2018, Barrett in 2020). These binaries are coded one for each of these categories, zero for neither supporting or opposing, and missing for those who declined to answer the question, and for the remaining scalar options. There are four binaries for strongly opposing, opposing, supporting, and strongly supporting this nomination. For instance, the binary for having strongly opposed a particular nomination is coded one for those who held that opinion, zero for neither supporting nor opposing this nomination, and missing for those who declined to answer the question, and for those who had opposed, supported, or strongly supported the nomination.

To force the second and third set of treatment variables (posting about and participating in protests related to Kavanaugh's nomination in 2018, or Barrett's nomination in 2020) to be binary, we generated a series of dichotomous variables for each response option, relative to never having posted about or participated in protests related to the respective nomination. These binaries are coded one for each of these categories, zero for never having posted about (or participated in protests related to) the specific nomination, and missing for those who declined to answer the question, and for the remaining scalar options. There are three binaries for posting once, posting two or three times, and for posting four or more times about the particular nomination. For instance, the binary for having posted once about a specific nomination is coded one for those who did so, zero for never having done so, and missing for those who declined to answer this question, and for those who reported having posted more than once. Similar binaries are created for each level of participating in protests related to a specific nomination. We expect positive signs for the ATET for all variables.

Second, we assume common support (or overlap), which means that it is possible that treated units may face an intervention that could have assigned them to the control group (see Imbens and Rubin 2015; King, Lucas, and Nielsen 2017). The data that we use meet this requirement because all respondents could have chosen not to have an opinion about either of the nominations, or not to post or protest about them.

Third, we must fulfill the SUTVA assumption, which means that "the potential outcomes for any unit do not vary with the treatments assigned to other units, and for each unit, there are no different forms or versions of each treatment level, which lead to different potential outcomes" (Imbens and Rubin 2015, 10). We have met the first part of this assumption because the possible outcomes for civic activity do not vary with the levels of opinions about either nomination, or with posting about or participating in protests related to them.[8]

The second aspect of this assumption is more intricate because we have different variations on the treatment variables. For our first treatment variable, the variations are strongly oppose, oppose, support, and strongly support. Our second treatment variable varies with respect to posting once, posting two or three times, and posting four or more times about the nomination. Moreover, our third treatment variable varies with respect to participating in protests once, participating in protests two or three times, and participating in protests four or more times about the nomination. Yet, we can compare the effects of having a directional opinion about a specific nomination to those who neither supported nor opposed this nomination. For instance, we can compare those who strongly opposed Kavanaugh's nomination to those who had neither supported nor opposed his nomination, if we exclude those who had opposed, supported, or strongly supported his nomination from that analysis.[9] We must perform an equivalent procedure to compare those who had opposed, supported, or strongly supported his or Barrett's nomination if we hope to execute a matching analysis without an alternative treatment.

Similarly, we can compare the effects of having posted (or participated in protests) with varying frequencies about a particular nomination relative to those who never did so. For example, we can compare those who posted (participated in protests) once about Barrett's nomination to those who never did so, provided that we exclude those who posted at all other frequencies from that analysis.[10] We have to perform an analogous procedure to compare those who had posted (participated in protests) two or three times, and those who posted (participated in protests) four or more times about her nomination if we hope to perform a matching analysis absent an alternative treatment. When we compute our ATETs in the manner prescribed above for all sets of models, we ultimately satisfy the SUTVA assumption because we have neither interference nor any hidden variations of the treatments (Imbens and Rubin, 2015, 10–11).

Finally, the treatment assignment must be conditionally independent of the outcome variable given a set of matching covariates (D'Agostino 1998, 2266). Thus, each respondent's assignment to treatment (i.e., opinion about Kavanaugh's or Barrett's nominations, posting about them, or participating in protests related to them) is unconnected with their level of civic engagement, given the values of the remaining explanatory variables. We observe greatly varied participatory levels with respect to civic activity, and the mean level of civic activity is relatively low (14.56, 2018; 26.01, 2020), given the minimum (0) and maximum values (48) possible with this index. Moreover, the activities that comprise offline civic activity do not cause an individual to be assigned to one or more treatment categories.

Matching Technique

Once we have met the statistical assumptions that underlie matching, we need to choose a method by which to execute this type of analysis. To perform our matching analyses, we use one-to-one genetic matching with replacement (Diamond and Sekhon 2013; Sekhon 2011). We incorporate a propensity score into the analysis, as knowing estimated values of this score meaningfully improves the accuracy of this method (Diamond and Sekhon 2013). Propensity score matching allows us to compare observations that are otherwise similar across other predictors, but have experienced different treatments. We perform our analysis with replacement, as matching discrepancies are reduced because we can use untreated units as a match multiple times (see Abadie and Imbens 2006).[11] To remove any bias that results due to the choice of the matching estimator without affecting the variance of that estimator, we employ a bias correction (Abadie and Imbens 2016).

Results

Before we discuss the results for our hypotheses regarding opinions about Supreme Court nominations and civic engagement, we need to analyze how similar the treatment and control groups are to one another (King, Lucas, and Nielsen 2017). If these groups are substantially dissimilar, then we cannot use matching to estimate ATETs. The imbalance statistics for the models in Tables 3.1 and 3.2 are contained in Tables A1 through A6 (for 2018) and Tables A7 through A12 (for 2020) in the online appendix. For 93.48% of all of the variables contained in the models in Table 3.1 in 2018 and for 98.15% of all the variables contained in this table in 2020, the KS tests are not significant at the .05 level after matching has occurred. For 86.96% of all of the variables contained in the models in the posting models in Table 3.2 in 2018, the KS tests are not significant at the .05 level after matching has occurred. In 2020, for 66.67% of all of the variables contained in the posting models in Table 3.2, the KS tests are not significant at the .05 level after matching has occurred. And, for 91.30% of all of the variables contained in the protesting models in Table 3.2 in 2018, the KS tests are not significant at the .05 level after matching has occurred. In the remaining 6 of 69 cases (or 8.70%), the KS test is significant. In 2020, for 64.20% of all of the variables contained in the protesting models in Table 3.2, the KS tests are not significant at the .05 level after matching has happened. In the remaining 29 of 81 cases (or 35.80%), the KS test is significant.

In the remaining cases where the KS test is significant, many of these involve one or more variables that we explore in later chapters. These include opinions about the family separation policy (in Chapter 5), posting about and participating in protests related to gun control (in Chapter 4), issue importance about immigration and family separation (in Chapter 5), and Black Lives Matter (in Chapter 6). In some cases, these also involve issues that we have already explored related to

TABLE 3.1 Opinions about Supreme Court Nominations and Civic Engagement

	2018 (Kavanaugh)				2020 (Barrett)			
	Strong Opposition	Opposition	Support	Strong Support	Strong Opposition	Opposition	Support	Strong Support
Effect on Offline Civic Engagement	1.762	-.937	1.479	1.979	3.166	9.609	1.483	.763
Abadie-Imbens Standard Error	1.172	1.779	2.532	1.762	1.928	3.582	4.835	1.684
95% Confidence Interval Lower Bound	-.545	-4.520	-3.628	-1.512	-.665	2.273	-8.458	-2.570
95% Confidence Interval Upper Bound	4.068	2.646	6.586	5.470	6.997	16.945	11.424	4.096
T-Statistic	1.504	-.527	.584	1.124	1.642	2.683	.307	.453
P-Value (two-tailed)	.133	.599	.559	.261	.101	.007	.759	.650
P-Value (one-tailed)	.067	.300	.280	.131	.051	.004	.380	.325
N	312	46	44	115	89	29	27	126

Notes: In each four-column set, the opinion about the nomination is compared with one who neither opposed nor supported the nomination. Second, the covariates on which the matching is based are described in the text. Third, the effects on offline civic engagement are the ATET. Finally, the matching results are from 1:1 genetic matching with post-matching bias adjustment. Thus, the N represents the matched number of observations.

TABLE 3.2 Civic Engagement, Posting, and Participating in Protests Related to Supreme Court Nominations

	Posting about Supreme Court Nominations						Protesting about Supreme Court Nominations					
	2018 (Kavanaugh)			2020 (Barrett)			2018 (Kavanaugh)			2020 (Barrett)		
	Once	Two or Three Times	Four or More Times	Once	Two or Three Times	Four or More Times	Once	Two or Three Times	Four or More Times	Once	Two or Three Times	Four or More Times
Effect on Offline Civic Engagement	3.120	5.443	6.677	5.250	-13.175	11.692	3.599	12.613	10.000	2.060	-.838	-20.906
Abadie-Imbens Standard Error	.992	1.776	2.961	2.989	5.606	4.386	7.744	4.408	4.608	2.305	2.569	59.672
95% Confidence Interval Lower Bound	1.150	1.921	.782	-.713	-26.309	2.938	-11.966	3.550	.277	-2.580	-5.955	-140.966
95% Confidence Interval Upper Bound	5.090	8.965	12.572	11.213	-2.041	20.446	19.164	21.676	19.723	6.700	4.279	99.154
T-Statistic	3.145	3.065	2.255	1.764	-2.350	2.666	.465	3.080	2.170	.894	-.326	-.350
P-Value (two-tailed)	.002	.002	.024	.079	.019	.008	.642	.002	.030	.371	.744	.726
P-Value (one-tailed)	.001	.001	.012	.040	.001	.004	.321	.001	.015	.186	.372	.363
N	93	103	78	69	92	68	50	27	18	47	76	48

Notes: In each three-column set, the number of times that one has posted or protested about the nomination is compared with one who has never done so about that subject. Second, the covariates on which the matching is based are described in the text. Third, the effects on offline civic engagement are the ATET. Finally, the matching results are from 1:1 genetic matching with post-matching bias adjustment. Thus, the N represents the matched number of observations.

the MeToo Movement (in Chapter 2). In addition, the remaining cases are sufficiently randomly distributed across the treatments with little systematic patterning across Tables 3.1 and 3.2. Consequently, we can be confident that we have reduced imbalance and have achieved sufficient balance across the model specifications in these tables. The matched groups have similar observable characteristics such that we can attribute any remaining differences across varying values of our treatment variables to the effects of those treatment variables, not to preexisting differences (Eggers and Hainmueller 2009).

In Table 3.1, we furnish our results from each of the matching routines for opinions about Supreme Court nominations. While the ATETs were highest for those with strong opinions in 2018, the results indicate no statistically significant relationship between opinions about Kavanaugh's nomination and civic engagement. Strong opposition did not produce significantly higher levels of civic engagement. Neither did support. In 2020, it appears that opposing Barrett's nomination is connected with higher levels of civic engagement. Upon further inspection, though, this result is not robust to empirical scrutiny. Altogether, the results provide clear evidence that no statistically significant relationship exists between opinions about Supreme Court nominations and civic activity. Regardless of one's opinion about either nomination, opinions alone were not enough to produce increased civic engagement.

In Table 3.2, we furnish results from each of the matching routines for posting and participating in protests. In 2018, the results show that posting about Kavanaugh's nomination at any level is associated with higher levels of civic engagement compared to having not posted at all about this nomination. More specifically, posting once about his nomination is connected with civic engagement scores that are approximately three points higher than those who had not posted about his nomination. A three-point increase is equivalent of having performed one activity frequently that previously was not performed at all, or performing up to three activities at one higher level. In addition, posting two or three more times, or four or more times were connected with civic engagement score increases of roughly five and seven points, respectively. A five-point increase is equivalent to having performed one activity very often that previously did not occur, plus participating in one other activity at a higher level. Also, a seven-point increase is equivalent to having performed one activity very often that previously was not performed at all and participating in two other activities at a higher frequency.

In 2020, the results provide less evidence that posting about Barrett's nomination is connected with higher levels of civic activity. When we use a one-tailed test (p = .040), we find that posting once about Barrett's nomination is connected with a five-point increase in civic engagement.[12] What is more, we find stronger evidence that posting four or more times about her nomination is connected with a nearly 12-point increase in civic engagement. This is the equivalent of having performed three activities very often that previously did not occur, or several other activities at greater frequency. However, we find a seemingly anomalous result: that posting two or three times about Barrett's nomination is negatively connected with civic activity. As we will see, this odd result is not robust to empirical scrutiny.

That said, though, the overall pattern of results across 2018 and 2020 provide evidence that confirms our second hypothesis: that posting about Supreme Court nominations is connected with higher levels of civic engagement. This result manifests most strongly with respect to posting about Kavanaugh's nomination, but also comes through with posting about Barrett's nomination. One reason for this is that Kavanaugh's nomination became one of the primary issues of the 2018 midterm elections. Senator McConnell (R-KY) stated in October 2018 that Kavanaugh's nomination and the subsequent controversy was "a great gift for us. The tactics have energized our base. I want to thank the mob, because they've done the one thing we were having trouble doing, which was energizing our base" (Kim 2018).

There was no such galvanizing that occurred with Barrett's nomination because three other political issues likely eclipsed it: the Covid-19 pandemic (which we discuss in the conclusion), issues of race and policing (which we discuss in Chapter 6), and Donald Trump being on the ballot in 2020 (which we will also investigate in the conclusion). In this respect, it makes sense why Kavanaugh's nomination had a more consistent effect with respect to posting compared to Barrett's. The Kavanaugh nomination's connection with the MeToo movement might also contribute to this distinction. However, since both nominations were election issues, this connection to electoral politics also helps explain why posting about both nominations was connected with higher levels of civic activity.

In 2018, the results show that participating in protests related to Kavanaugh's nomination more than once is associated with higher levels of civic engagement than having not participated in protests at all related to this nomination. More specifically, participating in protests two or three more times, or four or more times is connected with civic engagement score increases of roughly 13 and 10 points, respectively. A ten-point increase is equivalent to having performed two activities very often that previously did not occur, plus participating in at least one other activity at a higher level. Also, a 13-point increase is equivalent to having performed three activities very often that previously were not performed at all, and participating in one other activity at a higher frequency. This suggests that participating in protests had a strong mobilizing effect in 2018. There was no such strong mobilizing effect in 2020, as participating in protests about Barrett's nomination was not connected with changes in civic activity.

In this respect, the results provide clear evidence that supports our third hypothesis: that protesting about Kavanaugh's nomination is connected with higher levels of civic engagement. This evidence is not surprising because Kavanaugh's nomination spurred significant protests nationwide, while Barrett's did not. In addition, the circumstances under which Kavanaugh's nomination proceeded were more contentious than those under which Barrett's proceeded, because of the MeToo related allegations levied against him. In addition, Kavanaugh's nomination was one of the primary 2018 election issues, while Barrett's was not one of the prominent 2020 election issues. Further, Barrett's nomination occurred during a pandemic, when the need for social distancing hampered many forms of offline civic activity.

Robustness Checks

To verify whether the results in Tables 3.1 and 3.2 are model-dependent (Ho, King, and Stuart 2007), we tested our models for robustness by removing one matching covariate at a time from each model. Then, we re-ran the matching routines with the remaining predictors in each model.[13] These results are contained in the online appendix.[14] When we compare these robustness checks to what we report in Table 3.1, we find that 80.50% of the models contained results that mirror those contained in that table. In 2018, the remaining 13 cases occurred where the treatment was either strongly oppose or strongly support.[15] Even here, there appears to be no common, systematic set of variables across the categories of the treatment variable that drive the results.

However, 22 of the remaining 26 (or 84.62%) cases in 2020 where the results are not consistent with those that we report here occurred where the treatment was opposing Barrett's nomination, which is the one point where it appears that there is an affirmative finding. Further, 22 of 27 robustness checks for opposing Barrett's nomination furnish results that are not consistent with what we report in Table 3.1 in terms of the signs and significance patterns. In a situation like this, the most conservative approach is to conclude that there is no relationship between opinions about Barrett's nomination and civic activity in 2020 because the result for opposing is not robust. Moreover, the results for any other level of opinions about her nomination are not statistically significant.

When we query the robustness checks for the posting models in Table 3.2, we find that 82% (or 123/150) of the models contained results that mirrored those that we reported. The majority of the results that are inconsistent with what we report in Table 3.2 are concentrated on the models for posting two or three times about Barrett's nomination in 2020, as 14 of 27 (or 51.85%) of these disparate results occur here. What is more, a majority of the robustness checks results for posting two or three times about her nomination (14 out of 27, or 51.85%) show patterns that diverge from those furnished in Table 3.2. In situations like this, the best practice is to conclude that there is no relationship between posting two or three times about Barrett's nomination and civic engagement because the majority of robustness checks do not support one. When we examine the models in Table 3.2 for participating in protests related to Supreme Court nominations, 86.67% (or 130/150) furnished results that are similar to those contained in the table. The remainder of the models that deviate from this pattern are scattered across the models and have no systematic pattern connected to them.

Discussion and Conclusion

We have demonstrated that posting about Supreme Court nominations is associated with higher levels of political participation among young adults. We also find that participating in protests related to Kavanaugh's nomination is associated with heightened participation among young adults, an age group in which some previous research may indicate such results would be unlikely. The relationship between civic activity and posting and protesting about Supreme Court nominations was at its strongest in 2018. In particular, posting at any level about Kavanaugh's nomination was associated with gains in civic engagement. Further, those who posted more frequently about this nomination had even higher levels of civic engagement. Yet, the size of these increases is not strictly linear from one level of posting to the next. These differences in effect size across different levels of posting provide support for using matching rather than OLS, which presumes linearity.

Many researchers note that young adults are typically less knowledgeable than their elders about politics, especially when it comes to knowledge of current public figures (Delli Carpini and Keeter 1996, 146). This age gap extends to the Supreme Court, with 21% of 18–29-year-olds able to correctly identify the Chief Justice of the Supreme Court compared to 25% of 30–49-year-olds and 34% of those 50 and older (Kohut and Keeter 2010). Further stacking the deck against the likelihood of a Supreme Court nomination generating heightened participation among young adults, this age group also typically participates less in politics in general (Rouse and Ross 2018), especially when it comes to traditional forms of participation (Zukin et al. 2006). Altogether, this seemingly suggests that few young adults would be likely to act as the result of a Supreme Court nomination.

Yet, some issues have successfully drawn young adults to participate, especially those that collide with core principles, like women's rights and diversity, that this cohort of young adults holds dear (Rouse and Ross 2018; Parker, Graf, and Igielnik 2019). While we did not find that opinions about Supreme Court nominations were associated with heightened levels of civic engagement, nonetheless, young adults were more likely to hold very unfavorable views of Kavanaugh than other age groups and far less likely to hold very favorable views of him than other age groups (*The Economist*/YouGov 2018).

This tendency among young adults is reflected in our data as well. The number of cases in Table 3.1 indicates that among young adults who had an opinion about the Kavanaugh nomination, they were far more likely to hold a strong opinion than a not strong opinion. In addition, the size of the strong opposition group is 2.7 times the size of the strong support group. Young adult opinions were heavily skewed against Kavanaugh's nomination. It stands to reason then that among those who posted about the Kavanaugh nomination and those who protested about it, opinions were also heavily skewed against the nomination. This pattern fits with the idea of prospect theory. Those who take action about an issue are more likely to act in this fashion in opposition to that issue than to support it, as people exhibit greater sensitivity to potential losses relative to potential gains (Kahneman and Tversky 1979).

When viewed through this lens, our findings are not surprising. They fit with the extant literature that younger voters are more civically engaged in response to issues that directly concern them (Rouse and Ross 2018), like protracted war (Moffett, Rice, and Madupalli 2014; Verba and Brody 1970). More broadly, our finding fits nicely with the literature that connects political issues like the economy (Lewis-Beck 1990), the tax cuts that occurred under then-President George W. Bush (Flavin and Griffin 2009), and the Affordable Care Act (Bennett 2012) to higher levels of political activity. Supreme Court nominations are another issue that can spark political activity, as they have recently become more contentious (Caldeira and Smith 1996) and produce high levels of concentrated interest group activity aimed at mobilizing constituents and influencing confirmation votes (Krutz, Fleisher, and Bond 1998; Vining 2011).

However, opinions alone do not guarantee action. Rather, it is young adults who *acted* to advance their opinion – either via posting or protest – that had heightened levels of civic engagement. This supports our argument that both posting and protesting provide pathways for additional mobilization. Young adults seem particularly prone to engage in these activities. The link we identify between posting about Supreme Court nominations and civic engagement adds further to the evidence against the slacktivism hypothesis. Sharing views online about the Supreme Court nominations was more than just cheap talk or symbolic action because it led to engaging in other activities. In addition, Millennials and Gen Z are more likely to believe that protesting an issue will bring about the most political change than non-Millennials (Rouse and Ross 2018). It remains to be seen whether they are right about this. Yet, we have shown in this chapter that their proclivity toward protesting leads to branching out into other forms of civic activity as well. Our results clearly indicate that when young adults posted about Supreme Court nominations or protested to express their views about Kavanaugh's nomination, they became more likely to engage in other forms of civic activity.

Yet, our findings come with one potential concern: those with higher levels of civic engagement may be more likely to post about or participate in protests related to Supreme Court nominations. To examine this possibility, we re-ran our matching routines in Table 3.2 with the same matching covariates that exist for the models in both tables. Our treatment variable, then, is a three-level indicator for civic engagement measured at low (civic engagement score less than or equal to 12), medium (civic engagement score greater than 12, but less than or equal to 24), and high levels (civic engagement score exceeding 24). Our dependent variables are posting about it and protesting about it.

In 2018, the results from these reverse causality checks indicate that posting about Kavanaugh's nomination is not a function of civic engagement. Those with medium or low levels of civic engagement are not more likely to have posted about his nomination. Similarly, participating in protests related to his nomination is not a function of civic engagement. Those with medium or low levels of civic engagement are not more likely to have participated in protests related to his nomination. Altogether, these results indicate that higher levels of civic engagement did not cause young people to post about or participate in protests related to Kavanaugh's nomination.

In 2020, though, those with higher levels of civic engagement were more likely to have both protested about and posted about Amy Coney Barrett's nomination. Barrett's nomination was less salient relative to Kavanaugh's, as opposition to or support for her was based more on ideological grounds and the timing of her nomination rather than personal scandal. On the contrary, opposition to or support for Kavanaugh's nomination was less about the timing of his nomination. It was partly about ideology but also was significantly influenced by a significant personal scandal that implicated other values that young voters hold, like support for gender equality (see Rouse and Ross 2018). When viewed in this way, it makes sense that civic engagement is connected with higher levels of posting and protesting under Barrett's nomination, rather than with Kavanaugh's. For this reason, we cannot rule out reverse causality for Barrett's nomination, but can do so for Kavanaugh's nomination. Other less political reasons drove opinions about Kavanaugh's nomination compared to Barrett's.

We also examined whether the 2020 results are a function of adding four additional variables to the matching routines in this chapter: support for Black Lives Matter, posting about Black Lives Matter, participating in protests related to Black Lives Matter, or opinions about the DACA program. To verify whether this occurred, we re-ran the models using the covariates in the 2018 models while substituting any Kavanaugh questions for Barrett ones using 2020 data. The results are consistent with what we report in Tables 3.1 and 3.2, and, especially, with how we interpret those results. The results are available in Tables B1 through B3 in the online appendix. Thus, we can eliminate any concern that the results are an artifact of a different model specification entirely.

Supreme Court nominations offer a clear opportunity to get involved with a limited timespan to try and make a difference. Adults of all ages and on both sides of these nominations became involved. Yet, taking advantage of these opportunities, especially by posting about the nominations, yielded higher civic engagement rates among young adults. In the next chapter, we turn to an issue where young adults dominated the headlines in 2018 – the debate over gun control. Their involvement was sparked by a specific tragedy, yet, as they got involved, they tried to make a difference in a policy debate that has raged for far longer than their lifetimes. Did their involvement on this issue also produce higher civic engagement rates?

Notes

1. We use this term to refer to a broad range of political and civic activity, as described in the following section and in Chapter 1.
2. These generations have similar views on social issues (Parker, Graf, and Igielnik 2019).
3. We constrained the eligibility of participants in this survey to those whose location is in the United States and whose human interface task (HIT) approval rates are at least 95%. Although we could not constrain by age here, we did so through the first question asking respondents whether they were between the ages of 18 and 25. If they responded no, then the survey ended.
4. These were the only questions in the survey about peer civic experiences. Some respondents responded that they did not know for one or more of these questions. When building our index, we coded values for these variables as missing. Thus, no peer civic engagement score is present for those who answered "don't know" on a minimum of one of these questions.
5. This also acts as an indirect indicator with respect to mobilization, as people frequently act politically when others around them do so (see e.g., Gimpel, Lee, and Kamiski 2006). Yet, it is possible that mobilization efforts by those other than peers, like interest groups and political parties, also yield higher levels of participation (Rosenstone and Hansen 2002). There are no questions in this survey that allow us to directly account for the effects of mobilization on civic activity. That said, we do consider many other covariates that also affect mobilization as part of the matching routines in this analysis.
6. We employed a modified version of this variable for the models in which the treatment variable is posting about Kavanaugh's nomination in 2018 (or Barrett's nomination in 2020), as we cannot have the treatment variable being essentially the same as an element of one of the matching covariates. More specifically, we removed postings about politics on social media from the online civic engagement index for this set of models because the treatment for the set of models examining the effects of posting about Kavanaugh's nomination in 2018 (or Barrett's nomination in 2020) is the extent to which one posted about that nomination. We retained the remaining variables that comprise the online civic engagement index and created an additive index based on those ($\alpha = .81$, 2018; $\alpha = .78$, 2020).
7. We asked an initial screening question that identified those who were between the ages of 18 and 25, and those who responded that they were not in this age range were excluded from further participation in the survey. When we performed the age computations based on the year and month that respondents selected, though, there were 49 respondents who stated that they were older than 25 in 2018. In the year-month calculation, there was usually about a six-month variance between the reported and actual age among those 49 respondents. Since we asked about both year and month of birth based on drop-down menus, it is possible that a substantial portion of these respondents misreported their year and/or month of birth in 2018 (see Gendall and Healey 2008). We have no reason to believe that this error is systematic and did not encounter the same concern in 2020. Thus, nonsystematic measurement error in an independent variable does not bias any conclusions in research studies (see King, Keohane, and Verba 1994).
8. If civic engagement were related to opinions about Kavanaugh's nomination, then civic activity and opinions about his nomination would be highly correlated. To test whether this happens, we correlated our dependent variable (offline civic activity)

and our treatment variables. The correlations are .096 (opinions about Kavanaugh's nomination) and .393 (opinions about Barrett's nomination); .572 (2018) and .688 (2020) for posting about the respective Supreme Court nominations; and .608 (2018) and .753 (2020) for participating in protests related to the respective Supreme Court nominations. These correlations are sufficiently low such that we can conclude that the first part of the SUTVA assumption is satisfied.
9 If we do not conduct our analysis in this manner, then we would be unable to satisfy SUTVA, as there would be alternative treatment forms (see Imbens and Rubin 2015, 10–13).
10 If we do not conduct our analysis in this way, then we cannot satisfy SUTVA, as alternative treatment forms would exist (see Imbens and Rubin 2015, 10–13).
11 However, we do not perform a regression following the matching analysis (as Ho et al. 2007 recommend), as Abadie and Spiess (2019) state that this is inappropriate when matching is done with replacement as researchers obtain inaccurate standard error estimates.
12 A one-tailed test is more appropriate to use in this instance since we are testing a directional hypothesis.
13 One limitation of many matching analyses is that one can p-hack by varying the functional form of the matching algorithm to produce a set of results that coincidentally confirms a researcher's hypotheses (Head et al. 2015).
14 The online appendix for these and the other models in this chapter is available at www.kenmoffett.net/research.
15 One limitation of many matching analyses is that one can p-hack by varying the functional form of the matching algorithm to produce a set of results that coincidentally confirms a researcher's hypotheses (Head et al. 2015).

References

Abadie, Alberto and Guido W. Imbens 2006. "Large Sample Properties of Matching Estimators for Average Treatment Effects." *Econometrica* 74(1): 235–267. https://doi.org/10.1111/j.1468-0262.2006.00655.x. Accessed online June 19, 2021.

Abadie, Alberto and Guido W. Imbens 2011. "Bias-Corrected Matching Estimators for Average Treatment Effects." *Journal of Business and Economic Statistics* 29(1): 1–11. https://doi.org/10.1198/jbes.2009.07333. Accessed online June 19, 2021.

Abadie, Alberto and Guido W. Imbens 2016. "Matching on the Estimated Propensity Score." *Econometrica* 84(2): 781–807. https://doi.org/10.3982/ECTA11293. Accessed online June 19, 2021.

Abadie, Alberto and Jann Spiess 2019. "Robust Post-Matching Inference." Forthcoming in the *Journal of the American Statistical Association*. https://doi.org/10.1080/01621459.2020.1840383. Accessed online June 19, 2021.

Abramowitz, Alan I. and Walter J. Stone 2006. "The Bush Effect: Polarization, Turnout, and Activism in the 2004 Presidential Election." *Presidential Studies Quarterly* 36(2): 141–154. https://doi.org/10.1111/j.1741-5705.2006.00295.x. Accessed online June 19, 2021.

Achen, Christopher H. and Larry M. Bartels 2016. *Democracy for Realists: Why Elections Do Not Produce Responsive Government*. Princeton, NJ: Princeton University Press.

Arnold, R. Douglas 1990. *The Logic of Congressional Action*. New Haven, CT: Yale University Press.

Barrett, Maura 2020. "Collins and Ernst Split on Barrett Confirmation in Tough Re-Election Bids." NBC News. October 25. www.nbcnews.com/politics/2020-election/collins-ernst-split-barrett-confirmation-tough-re-election-bids-n1244710. Accessed online November 24, 2020.

Belanger, Eric and Bonnie M. Meguid 2008. "Issue Salience, Issue Ownership, and Issue-Based Vote Choice." *Electoral Studies* 27(3): 477–491. https://doi.org/10.1016/j.electstud.2008.01.001. Accessed online June 19, 2021.

Bennett, W. Lance 2012. "The Personalization of Politics: Political Identity, Social Media, and the Changing Patterns of Participation." *The ANNALS of the American Academy of Political and Social Science* 644(1): 20–39. https://doi.org/10.1177/0002716212451428. Accessed online June 19, 2021.

Biskupic, Joan 2020. "What Amy Coney Barrett Could Mean for Obamacare." CNN. October 12. www.cnn.com/2020/10/10/politics/affordable-care-act-amy-coney-barrett-obamacare/index.html. Accessed online November 24, 2020.

Bonica, Adam, Adam Chilton, Jacob Goldin, Kyle Rozema, and Maya Sen 2016. "New Data Show How Liberal Merrick Garland Really Is." *The Monkey Cage*. March 30. www.washingtonpost.com/news/monkey-cage/wp/2016/03/30/new-data-show-how-liberal-merrick-garland-really-is/. Accessed online November 24, 2020.

Bradner, Eric. 2020. "Here's What Happened When Senate Republicans Refused to Vote on Merrick Garland's Supreme Court Nomination." CNN. www.cnn.com/2020/09/18/politics/merrick-garland-senate-republicans-timeline/index.html. Accessed online November 24, 2020.

Brown, Emma 2018. "California Professor, Writer of Confidential Brett Kavanaugh Letter, Speaks Out about Her Allegation of Sexual Assault." www.washingtonpost.com/investigations/california-professor-writer-of-confidential-brett-kavanaugh-letter-speaks-out-about-her-allegation-of-sexual-assault/2018/09/16/46982194-b846-11e8-94eb-3bd52dfe917b_story.html?noredirect=on&utm_term=.d88f4f587cf0. Accessed online February 5, 2019.

Caldeira, Gregory A. and Charles E. Smith 1996. "Campaigning for the Supreme Court: The Dynamics of Public Opinion on the Thomas Nomination." *Journal of Politics* 58(3): 655–681. https://doi.org/10.2307/2960437 Accessed online June 19, 2021.

Caldeira, Gregory A. and John R. Wright. 1998. "Lobbying for Justice: Organized Interests Supreme Court Nominations, and United States Senate." *American Journal of Political Science* 42(2): 499–523.

Campbell, James D. 2018. *Polarized: Making Sense of a Divided America*. Princeton: Princeton University Press.

Carmines, Edward G. and James A. Stimson 1989. *Issue Evolution: Race and the Transformation of American Politics*. Princeton, NJ: Princeton University Press.

CIRCLE 2018. "Election Night 2018: Historically High Youth Turnout, Support for Democrats." November 7. https://circle.tufts.edu/latest-research/election-night-2018-historically-high-youth-turnout-support-democrats. Accessed online November 24, 2020.

CIRCLE 2020. "Youth Voter Turnout Increased in 2020." November 18. https://circle.tufts.edu/latest-research/election-week-2020#youth-voter-turnout-increased-in-2020. Accessed online November 24, 2020.

CNN/SSRS 2020. October 1–4. http://cdn.cnn.com/cnn/2020/images/10/07/rel12c.-.scotus,.aca.pdf. Accessed online November 24, 2020.

Code of the District of Columbia. § 22–1307. "Crowding, Obstructing, or Incommoding." https://code.dccouncil.us/dc/council/code/sections/22-1307.html. Accessed online January 12, 2021.

Converse, Phillip 1964. "The Nature of Belief Systems in Mass Publics." In *Ideology and Its Discontents,* David E. Apter (Ed.). New York, NY: Free Press of Glencoe.

Cottrell, David, Charles R. Shipan, and Richard J. Anderson 2019. "The Power to Appoint: Presidential Nominations and Change on the Supreme Court." *Journal of Politics* 81(3): 1057–1068. https://doi.org/10.1086/703382. Accessed online June 19, 2021.

D'Agostino, Ralph B. 1998. "Propensity Score Methods for Bias Reduction in the Comparison of a Treatment to a Non-Randomized Control Group." *Statistics in Medicine* 17(9): 2265–2281. https://doi.org/10.1002/(SICI)1097-0258(19981015)17:19<2265::AID-SIM918>3.0.CO;2-B. Accessed online June 19, 2021.

Daly, Matthew. 2020. "Who's a Hypocrite? GOP, Dems Debate Past Comments on Court." AP. September 21. https://apnews.com/article/election-2020-ruth-bader-ginsburg-merrick-garland-elections-us-supreme-court-bb9932748b199f793cb2ccbefa713a5f. Accessed online November 24, 2020.

Darnell, Casey. 2018. "SU Students Plan Thursday Walkout to Protest Kavanaugh, Sexual Assault." http://dailyorange.com/2018/10/su-students-plan-thursday-walkout-protest-kavanaugh-sexual-assault/. Accessed online January 8, 2021.

Delli Carpini, Michael X. and Scott Keeter 1996. *What Americans Know about Politics and Why It Matters.* New Haven, CT: Yale University Press.

Diamond, Alexis and Jasjeet J. Sekhon 2013. "Genetic Matching for Estimating Causal Effects: A General Multivariate Matching Method for Achieving Balance in Observational Studies." *Review of Economics and Statistics* 95(3): 932–945. https://doi.org/10.1162/REST_a_00318. Accessed online June 19, 2021.

Eggers, Andrew C. and Jens Hainmueller 2009. "MPs for Sale? Returns to Office in Postwar British Politics." *American Political Science Review* 103(4): 513–533. https://doi.org/10.1017/S0003055409990190. Accessed online June 19, 2021.

Elving, Ron 2018. "What Happened with Merrick Garland in 2016 and Why It Matters Now." NPR. June 29. www.npr.org/2018/06/29/624467256/what-happened-with-merrick-garland-in-2016-and-why-it-matters-now. Accessed online November 24, 2020.

Epps, Garrett 2016. "Merrick Garland Is a Great Pick; That May Not Matter." *The Atlantic.* March 16. www.theatlantic.com/politics/archive/2016/03/merrick-garland-is-a-great-choice-that-may-not-matter/474093. Accessed online November 24, 2020.

Epstein, Lee and Jeffrey A. Segal 2005. *Advice and Consent: The Politics of Judicial Appointments.* New York, NY: Oxford University Press.

Epstein, Lee, Andrew D. Martin, Kevin M. Quinn, and Chad Westerland 2007. "The Judicial Common Space." *The Journal of Law, Economics, and Organization* 23(1): 303–325. https://doi.org/10.1093/jleo/ewm024. Accessed online June 19, 2021.

Flavin, Patrick and John D. Griffin 2009. "Policy, Preferences, and Participation: Government's Impact on Democratic Citizenship." *Journal of Politics* 71(2): 544–559. https://doi.org/10.1017/S0022381609090458. Accessed online June 19, 2021.

Gelman, Andrew and Jennifer Hill 2007. *Data Analysis Using Regression and Multilevel/Hierarchical Models.* New York, NY: Cambridge University Press.

Gendall, Philip and Benjamin Healey 2008. "Asking the Age Question in Mail and Online Surveys." *International Journal of Market Research* 50(3): 309–317. https://doi.org/10.1177/147078530805000303. Accessed online June 19, 2021.

Gibson, James L. and Gregory A. Caldeira 2009. "Confirmation Politics and the Legitimacy of the U.S. Supreme Court: Institutional Loyalty, Positivity Bias, and the

Alito Nomination." *American Journal of Political Science* 53(1): 139–155. https://doi.org/10.1111/j.1540-5907.2008.00362.x. Accessed online June 19, 2021.

Gimpel, James G., Frances E. Lee, and Joshua Kaminski 2006. "The Political Geography of Campaign Contributions in American Politics." *Journal of Politics* 68(3): 626–639. https://doi.org/10.1111/j.1468-2508.2006.00450.x. Accessed online June 19, 2021.

Gimpel, James G. and Robin W. Wolpert 1996. "Opinion-Holding and Public Attitudes toward Controversial Supreme Court Nominees." *Political Research Quarterly* 49(1): 163–176. https://doi.org/10.1177/106591299604900110. Accessed online June 19, 2021.

Gomez, Dessi. 2020. "Dueling Demonstrations at Notre Dame Offer Different Messages on Amy Coney Barrett." *South Bend Tribune*. www.southbendtribune.com/news/local/dueling-demonstrations-at-notre-dame-offer-different-messages-on-amy-coney-barrett/article_56afe1ce-1a3d-11eb-a170-835d190fa7fa.html. Accessed online January 8, 2021.

Graber, Doris A. and Johanna Dunaway 2015. *Mass Media and American Politics*. 9th Ed. Thousand Oaks, CA: CQ Press.

Greene, William H. 2011. *Econometric Analysis*. 7th Ed. New York, NY: Pearson Education.

Hauck, Grace 2020. "Hundreds Gather for Women's March to Protest Trump, Barrett Nomination." *USA Today*. October 17. www.usatoday.com/story/news/nation/2020/10/17/womens-march-2020-protest-trump-amy-coney-barrett-nomination/3693810001. Accessed online November 24, 2020.

Head, Megan L., Luke Holman, Rob Lanfear, Andrew T. Kahn, and Michael D. Jennions 2015. "The Extent and Consequences of P-Hacking in Science." *Plos Biology* 13(3): e1002106. https://doi.org/10.1371/journal.pbio.1002106. Accessed online June 19, 2021.

Ho, Daniel E., Kosuke Imai, Gary King, and Elizabeth A. Stuart 2007. "Matching as Nonparametric Preprocessing for Reducing Model Dependence in Parametric Causal Inference." *Political Analysis* 15(3): 199–236. https://doi.org/10.1093/pan/mpl013. Accessed online June 19, 2021.

Hutchings, Vincent L. 2001. "Political Context, Issue Salience, and Selective Attentiveness: Constituent Knowledge of the Clarence Thomas Confirmation Vote." *Journal of Politics* 63(3): 846–868. https://doi.org/10.1111/0022-3816.00090. Accessed online June 19, 2021.

Imbens, Guido W. and Donald B. Rubin 2015. *Causal Inference for Statistics, Social, and Biomedical Sciences: An Introduction*. New York, NY: Cambridge University Press. Kaheneman, Daniel and Amos Tversky 1979. "Prospect Theory: An Analysis of Decision under Risk." *Econometrica* 47(2): 263–292.

Kahne, Joseph and Benjamin Bowyer 2018. "The Political Significance of Social Media Activity and Social Networks." *Political Communication* 35(3): 470–493.

Keneally, Meghan 2018. "Ahead of Crucial Kavanaugh Vote, Hundreds of Protesters Rally in Front of Supreme Court." ABC News. October 4. https://abcnews.go.com/Politics/ahead-crucial-kavanaugh-vote-hundreds-protesters-rally-front/story?id=58281986. Accessed online January 28, 2020.

Kerbel, Matthew R. and Joel David Bloom 2005. "Blog for America and Civic Involvement." *The International Journal of Press/Politics* 10(4): 3–27. https://doi.org/10.1177/1081180X05281395. Accessed online June 19, 2021.

Kim, Seung Min 2018. "McConnell Calls Opposition to Kavanaugh a 'Great Political Gift' to Republicans." *The Washington Post*. October 6. www.washingtonpost.com/politics/mcconnell-calls-opposition-to-kavanaugh-a-great-political-gift-to-republicans/2018/10/06/761b8610-c988-11e8-9158-09630a6d8725_story.html?utm_term=.ad75d3a6363d. Accessed online February 2, 2019.

King, Gary, Christopher Lucas, and Richard A. Nielsen 2017. "The Balance-Sample Size Frontier in Matching Methods for Causal Inference." *American Journal of Political Science* 61(2): 473–489. https://doi.org/10.1111/ajps.12272. Accessed online June 19, 2021.

King, Gary, Robert O. Keohane, and Sidney Verba 1994. *Designing Social Inquiry: Scientific Inference in Qualitative Research*. Princeton, NJ: Princeton University Press.

Kohut, Andrew and Scott Keeter 2010. "Political Knowledge Update: Well Known: Twitter; Little Known: John Roberts." http://assets.pewresearch.org/wp-content/uploads/sites/. Accessed online June 19, 2021.

Krehbiel, Keith 2007. "Supreme Court Appointments as a Move-the-Median Game." *American Journal of Political Science* 51(2): 231–240. https://doi.org/10.1111/j.1540-5907.2007.00247.x. Accessed online June 19, 2021.

Krosnick, Jon A. 1990. "Government Policy and Citizen Passion: A Study of Issue Publics in Contemporary America." *Political Behavior* 12(1): 69–92. https://doi.org/10.1007/BF00992332. Accessed online June 19, 2021.

Krutz, Glen S., Richard Fleisher, and Jon R. Bond 1998. "From Abe Fortas to Zöe Baird: Why Some Presidential Nominations Fail in the Senate." *American Political Science Review* 92(4): 871–881. https://doi.org/10.2307/2586309. Accessed online June 19, 2021.

Landers, Elizabeth 2018. "Meet the Protesters Interrupting Brett Kavanaugh's Confirmation Hearing." CNN. September 5, 2018. www.cnn.com/2018/09/05/politics/kavanaugh-hearing-protests/index.html. Accessed online January 28, 2020.

Langer, Gary 2020. "Majority Says Wait on the SCOTUS Seat; 6 in 10 Favor Upholding Roe: POLL." ABC News. October 12. https://abcnews.go.com/Politics/majority-wait-scotus-seat-10-favor-upholding-roe/story?id=73528313. Accessed online November 24, 2020.

Lewis-Beck, Michael S. 1990. *Economics and Elections: The Major Western Democracies*. Ann Arbor, MI: University of Michigan Press.

Ley, Barbara L. and Paul R. Brewer 2018. "Social Media, Networked Protest, and the March for Science." *Social Media and Society* 4(3): 1–12. https://doi.org/10.1177/2056305118793407. Accessed online June 19, 2021.

Loader, Brian D., Ariadne Vromen, and Michael A. Xenos 2014. "The Networked Young Citizen: Social Media, Political Participation and Civic Engagement." *Information, Communication and Society* 17(2): 143–150. https://doi.org/10.1080/1369118X.2013.871571. Accessed online June 19, 2021.

Maltese, John Anthony 1995. *The Selling of Supreme Court Nominees*. Baltimore, MD: Johns Hopkins University Press.

Marcus, George E., Michael MacKuen, and W. Russell Neuman 2000. *Affective Intelligence and Political Judgment*. Chicago, IL: University of Chicago Press.

Mascaro, Lisa 2020. "Barrett Confirmed as Supreme Court Justice in Partisan Vote." AP. October 26. https://apnews.com/article/82a02a618343c98b80ca2b6bf9eafe07. Accessed online November 24, 2020.

McConnell, Mitch and Chuck Grassley 2016. "McConnell and Grassley: Democrats Shouldn't Rob Voters of Chance to Replace Scalia." *The Washington Post*. February 18. www.washingtonpost.com/opinions/mcconnell-and-grassley-democrats-shouldnt-rob-voters-of-chance-to-replace-scalia/2016/02/18/e5ae9bdc-d68a-11e5-be55-2cc3c1e4b76b_story.html. Accessed online November 24, 2020.

Miller, Joanne M. and Jon A. Krosnick 2004. "Threat as a Motivator of Political Activism: A Field Experiment." *Political Psychology* 25(4): 507–523. https://doi.org/10.1111/j.1467-9221.2004.00384.x. Accessed online June 19, 2021.

Miller, Joanne M., Jon A. Krosnick, Allyson Hollbrook, Alexander Tahk, and Laura Dionne 2016. "The Impact of Policy Change Threat on Financial Contributions to Interest Groups." In *Political Psychology: New Explorations*. Jon A. Krosnick, I-Chant A. Chiang, and Tobias H. Stark (Eds.). New York, NY: Taylor & Francis.

Moffett, Kenneth W. and Laurie L. Rice 2016. *Web 2.0 and the Political Mobilization of College Students*. Lanham, MD: Lexington Books.

Moffett, Kenneth W. and Laurie L. Rice 2018. "College Students and Online Political Expression in the 2016 Election." *Social Science Computer Review* 36(4): 422–439. https://doi.org/10.1177/0894439317721186. Accessed online June 19, 2021.

Moffett, Kenneth W., Laurie L. Rice, and Ramana Madupalli 2014. "Young Voters and War: The Iraq War as a Catalyst for Political Participation." *Social Science Quarterly* 95(5): 1419–1443. https://doi.org/10.1111/ssqu.12116. Accessed online June 19, 2021.

Moyer, Justin Wm 2018. "128 Arrested after Anti-Kavanaugh Protest." *The Washington Post*. September 24. www.washingtonpost.com/dc-md-va/2018/09/24/arrested-after-anti-kavanaugh-protest-capitol-hill/. Accessed online April 15, 2020.

Naylor, Brian. 2020. "Ginsburg, Champion of Gender Equality, Becomes 1st Woman to Lie in State." NPR. September 25. www.npr.org/sections/death-of-ruth-bader-ginsburg/2020/09/25/916526420/justice-ginsburg-lies-in-state-at-u-s-capitol. Accessed online November 24, 2020.

Nichols, Austin 2007. "Causal Inference with Observational Data." *The Stata Journal* 7(4): 507–541. https://doi.org/10.1177/1536867X0800700403. Accessed online June 19, 2021.

Ortiz, David G. and Stephen F. Ostertag 2014. "Katrina Bloggers and the Development of Collective Civic Action: The Web as a Virtual Mobilizing Structure." *Sociological Perspectives* 57(1): 52–78. https://doi.org/10.1177/0731121413517558. Accessed online June 19, 2021.

Parker, Kim, Nikki Graf, and Ruth Igielnik 2019. "Generation Z Looks a Lot Like Millennials on Key Social and Political Issues." Pew Research Center www.pewsocialtrends.org/2019/01/17/generation-z-looks-a-lot-like-millennials-on-key-social-and-political-issues/. Accessed online February 12, 2019.

Raju, Many 2018. "Why Dianne Feinstein Waited to Take the Brett Kavanaugh Allegations to the FBI." www.cnn.com/2018/09/17/politics/dianne-feinstein-brett-kavanaugh-allegations/index.html. Accessed online February 5, 2019.

Reny, Tyler T.; Loren Collingwood and Ali A. Valenzuela 2019. "Vote Switching in the 2016 Election: How Racial and Immigration Attitudes, Not Economics, Explain Shifts in White Voting." *Public Opinion Quarterly* 83(1): 91–113. https://doi.org/10.1093/poq/nfz011. Accessed online June 19, 2021.

Rosenstone, Steven J. and John Mark Hansen 2002. *Mobilization, Participation, and Democracy in America*. New York, NY: Pearson-Longman.

Ross, Ashley D. and Stella M. Rouse 2015. "Economic Uncertainty, Job Threat, and the Resiliency of the Millennial Generation's Attitudes toward Immigration." *Social Science Quarterly* 96(5): 1363–1379. https://doi.org/10.1111/ssqu.12168. Accessed online June 19, 2021.

Rouse, Stella M. and Ashley D. Ross 2018. *The Politics of Millennials: Political Beliefs and Policy Preferences of America's Most Diverse Generation*. Ann Arbor, MI: University of Michigan Press.

Segal, Jeffrey A., Charles M. Cameron, and Albert D. Cover 1992. "A Spatial Model of Roll Call Voting: Senators, Constituents, Presidents, and Interest Groups in Supreme Court Nominations." *American Journal of Political Science* 36(1): 96–121.

Sekhon, Jasjeet S. 2011. "Multivariate and Propensity Score Matching Software with Automated Balance Optimization: The Matching Package for R." *Journal of Statistical Software* 42(7): 1–52.

Shipan, Charles R. and Megan L. Shannon 2003. "Delaying Justice(s): A Duration Analysis of Supreme Court Nominations." *American Journal of Political Science* 47(4): 654–668. https://doi.org/10.1111/1540-5907.00046. Accessed online June 19, 2021.

Shushok, Frank Jr. and Vera Kidd 2015. "Millennials in Higher Education: As Students Change, Much about Them Remains the Same." In *Positive Psychology on the College Campus*, John C. Wade, Lawrence I. Marks, and Roderick D. Hetzel (Eds.). New York, NY: Oxford University Press.

Stuart, Elizabeth A. 2010. "Matching Methods for Causal Inference: A Review and a Look Forward." *Statistical Science* 25(1): 1–21. https://doi.org/10.1214/09-STS313. Accessed online June 19, 2021.

Taddonio, Patrice 2020. "On Night of Ginsburg's Death, McConnell Pushed Trump to Nominate Amy Coney Barrett." November 24. www.pbs.org/wgbh/frontline/article/on-night-of-ginsburgs-death-mcconnell-pushed-trump-to-nominate-amy-coney-barrett/. Accessed online November 24, 2020.

Tatum, Sophia 2018. "Brett Kavanaugh's Nomination: A Timeline." www.cnn.com/interactive/2018/10/politics/timeline-kavanaugh/. Accessed online February 5, 2019.

The Economist/YouGov Poll 2018. September 23–25.

The Economist/YouGov Poll 2020. September 20–22. https://docs.cdn.yougov.com/b8ow3q7r1e/econTabReport.pdf. Accessed online November 24, 2020.

Torres, Ricardo. 2020. "'I Just Felt that I Needed to Do Something': Protesters Oppose Barrett's Nomination to Supreme Court." *Milwaukee Journal Sentinel*. www.jsonline.com/story/news/local/milwaukee/2020/10/17/protesters-oppose-amy-coney-barretts-nomination-supreme-court/3697205001/. Accessed online November 24, 2020.

Totenberg, Nina 2016. "Justice Antonin Scalia, Known for Biting Dissents, Dies at 79." NPR. February 13. www.npr.org/2016/02/13/140647230/justice-antonin-scalia-known-for-biting-dissents-dies-at-79. Accessed online November 24, 2020.

Totenberg, Nina 2020a. "Justice Ruth Bader Ginsburg, Champion of Gender Equality Dies at 87." NPR. September 18. www.npr.org/2020/09/18/100306972/justice-ruth-bader-ginsburg-champion-of-gender-equality-dies-at-87. Accessed online November 24, 2020.

Trump, Donald J. 2018. "Remarks by President Trump Announcing Judge Brett M. Kavanaugh as the Nominee for Associate Justice of the Supreme Court of the United States." www.whitehouse.gov/briefings-statements/remarks-president-trump-announcing-judge-brett-m-kavanaugh-nominee-associate-justice-supreme-court-united-states/. Accessed online February 12, 2019.

Tversky, Amos and Daniel Kahneman 1992. "Advances in Prospect Theory: Cumulative Representation of Uncertainty." *Journal of Risk and Uncertainty* 5(4): 297–323. https://doi.org/10.1007/BF00122574. Accessed online June 19, 2021.

Verba, Sidney and Richard A. Brody 1970. "Participation, Policy Preferences, and the War in Vietnam." *Public Opinion Quarterly* 34(3): 325–332. https://doi.org/10.1086/267809. Accessed online June 19, 2021.

Verba, Sidney, Henry E. Brady, and Kay L. Schlozman 1995. *Voice and Equality: Civic Voluntarism in American Democracy*. Cambridge, MA: Harvard University Press.

Veslous, Abby, Tessa Berenson, and Alana Abramson 2018. "Brett Kavanaugh Said His Reputation Has Been 'Permanently Destroyed.' The Latest on his Senate Testimony."

http://time.com/5408177/brett-kavanaugh-christine-blasey-ford-testimony/. Accessed online February 5, 2019.

Vining, Richard L., Jr. 2011. "Grassroots Mobilization in the Digital Age: Interest Group Response to Supreme Court Nominees." *Political Research Quarterly* 64(4): 790–802. https://doi.org/10.1177/1065912910373550. Accessed online June 19, 2021.

Walsh, Deidre 2020. "What Amy Coney Barrett's Supreme Court Nomination Means for the 2020 Election." NPR. September 27. www.npr.org/2020/09/27/917303199/what-amy-coney-barretts-supreme-court-nomination-means-for-the-2020-election. Accessed online November 24, 2020.

White House 2016. "Remarks by the President Announcing Judge Merrick Garland as his Nominee to the Supreme Court." March 16. https://obamawhitehouse.archives.gov/the-press-office/2016/03/16/remarks-president-announcing-judge-merrick-garland-his-nominee-supreme. Accessed online November 24, 2020.

White House 2020. "President Donald J. Trump Announces Intent to Nominate Judge Amy Coney Barrett to the Supreme Court of the United States." September 26. www.whitehouse.gov/presidential-actions/president-donald-j-trump-announces-intent-nominate-judge-amy-coney-barrett-supreme-court-united-states/. Accessed online November 24, 2020.

Witt, Emily 2018. "How the Kavanaugh Nomination Has Intensified the Feminist Protest Movement." *The New Yorker*. www.newyorker.com/news/news-desk/how-the-kavanaugh-nomination-has-intensified-the-feminist-protest-movement. Accessed online April 15, 2020.

Zukin, Cliff, Scott Keeter, Molly Andolina, Krista Jenkins, and Michael X. Delli Carpini 2006. *A New Engagement? Political Participation, Civic Life, & the Changing American Citizen*. New York, NY: Oxford University Press.

4

SCHOOL SHOOTINGS

How Gun Violence Encouraged Civic Involvement

Introduction

The tragic mass shooting in Parkland, Florida, in 2018 bore similarities to previous school shootings. In retrospect, the warning signs were clear. Nikolas Cruz battled depression and other mental illnesses throughout his life and was fascinated with firearms and other weapons (Sanchez 2018). In fact, he had showed firearms to a former classmate, stored a semiautomatic rifle in a lockbox in his room, and had at one point introduced himself as a "school shooter" (Sanchez 2018). He had been expelled from his high school for disciplinary reasons (Chuck, Johnson, and Siemaszko 2018). Then, on February 14, 2018, Nikolas Cruz was dropped off at his former high school, Marjory Stoneman Douglas, by an Uber driver, and he possessed a .223 caliber AR-15 and multiple magazines in a case (Chuck, Johnson and Siemaszko 2018; Sanchez 2018). After he entered the school building, he activated a fire alarm and began opening fire on his former classmates (Sanchez 2018). He roamed the first and second floor hallways before fleeing down a stairwell. By the time he was caught a short time later, Cruz had murdered 17 people and wounded 14 (Chuck, Johnson and Siemaszko 2018).

Survivors of this mass shooting recounted their experiences on social media in real time as they occurred. Those survivors shared video, pictures, text, and other forms of media to the entire world. Among them was David Hogg, who became a prominent fixture on cable news in the days that followed, sharing about his experience, and calling for change (Alter 2018). Then, in the days after the shooting in Parkland, Florida, several survivors including Cameron Kasky, Jaclyn Corin, and Alex Wind created #NeverAgain and formed an organization devoted to enacting stricter gun control laws (Andone 2018). Social media posts played a prominent role in this movement, and information spread virally. One survivor turned activist, Emma Gonzales, went from no Twitter account to having more followers than the National Rifle Association (NRA) in less than two weeks (Alter 2018).

Together, these and other young activists organized a demonstration, March for Our Lives, on March 24, 2018, in Washington, DC, to advocate for stricter gun control laws (Andone 2018). As Kasky was interviewed about the group's plans, he stated: "My message for the people in office is, you're either with us or against us. We are losing our lives while the adults are playing around" (Andone 2018). Meanwhile, Hogg told journalists: "We're going to show these politicians that we're coming for them" (Alter 2018). Their organization took their fight to Tallahassee, Florida, where they pushed the Florida state legislature and governor to enact more stringent firearms regulations. Their fight in Florida was successful, as then-Governor Rick Scott (R-FL) signed a new gun control measure into law (National Public Radio 2018). This measure increased the legal age for firearms purchases to 21, enacted a three-day waiting period between the time that a firearm is purchased to when it is acquired, created a "red flag" initiative that allows for courts to seize firearms from those who are suspected of being a danger to themselves or others, and allowed school districts to arm nonteachers to protect children (National Public Radio 2018). This bill was passed by a Republican-controlled legislature and signed into law by a Republican governor.

This incident illustrates both the saliency of gun control to Generation Z and Millennials and the potential power that both this saliency and this generation have to produce legal changes. School shootings uniquely affect this generation, as there were only three years between 1998 and 2018 where there were no casualties from active shooter incidents in elementary and secondary schools (Center for Homeland Defense and Security 2018). In response to this threat, active shooter drills in schools have become commonplace, companies market bulletproof backpacks, and students wonder whether their school might be next.

As we saw in Chapter 3, threats – both real and perceived – can powerfully motivate action. Yet, the threat considered in this chapter runs far deeper than the threat of potential policy changes brought about by a new member's shift in the ideology of the Supreme Court. The threat of mass shootings is a matter of life and death and is not spread equally among all segments of society. A study of active shooter incidents between 2000 and 2013 found that educational institutions were the second most common type of location for these incidents, and that school shootings resulted in some of the highest casualty counts (Blair and Schweit 2014). Thus, young adults live under a disproportionate threat of falling victim to a mass shooter.

Here, we consider how the threat of mass shootings may have helped mobilize young adults. We begin with a deeper look at the nature of the threat and introduce how media coverage of issues can help focus public attention and lead to action. Then, we introduce what the research says about both how fear of gun violence mobilizes action and how threats to the self-interest of particular age groups or other segments of society can propel political action. We discuss how this research applies to the mobilization seen on this issue in 2018 and compare it to previous movements against gun violence. We then examine participation rates by levels of concern about gun violence and test whether speaking up about gun control online or participating in protests about it helped broaden the civic engagement of young adults.

The Threat of Mass Shootings

While deeply tragic, the likelihood of being killed in a mass shooting incident at school is far lower than being a victim of a homicide. Panel A of Figure 4.1 shows the total numbers per year of homicides at school with a victim between the ages of 5 and 18 (dotted line) and homicides overall with a victim between the ages of 5 and 18 (solid line). Homicides at school make up only a tiny fraction of total homicides of those aged 5–18. The large gap between the two lines in the figure suggests that school is not the most dangerous place for young people. However, it may well feel that way.

As Panel B of Figure 4.1 shows, 2018 marked the worst year in two decades for both the total number of active shooter incidents in schools and the total numbers injured or killed as a result. The deadliest among them was the February 14 shooting at Marjory Stoneman Douglas High School that resulted in 17 victims (Alter 2018). Yet, just three weeks earlier an active shooter incident in Marshall County, Kentucky, resulted in 2 dead, 14 shot, and 4 injured in other ways(Wolfson 2019). The school year concluded with a shooting at Santa Fe High School that resulted in 10 dead and another 13 injured (Deutch 2019). Thus, while the likelihood of being killed in a mass shooting at school remained small compared to the likelihood of being a victim of a homicide elsewhere, the threat of mass shootings at schools loomed larger in 2018 than before.

Active shooter incidents also draw significant media attention. Figure 4.2 shows the percentage of all cable news channel coverage, measured in 15 second blocks, referring to school shootings from January 2010[1] through 2020. The spikes in coverage tend to coincide with the occurrence of school shootings. In contrast, similar searches of the GDELT Television Explorer database for coverage of "child homicide" or "youth homicide" (not shown) never go beyond .041% of total airtime in a month. Fox News devoted the highest overall percentage of their airtime to stories that included the words child and homicide, but the average percentage of their coverage devoted to these words was a mere .0014. In contrast, the average percentage of coverage over this timespan that includes the word school and shooting was .0415 for CNN, .0323 for Fox News, and .027 for MSNBC. These averages are not solely driven by a few spikes in coverage. In 19% of the months in this time period, the total percentage of coverage devoted to school shootings is higher than the highest spike for child homicide. School shootings generate more media attention.

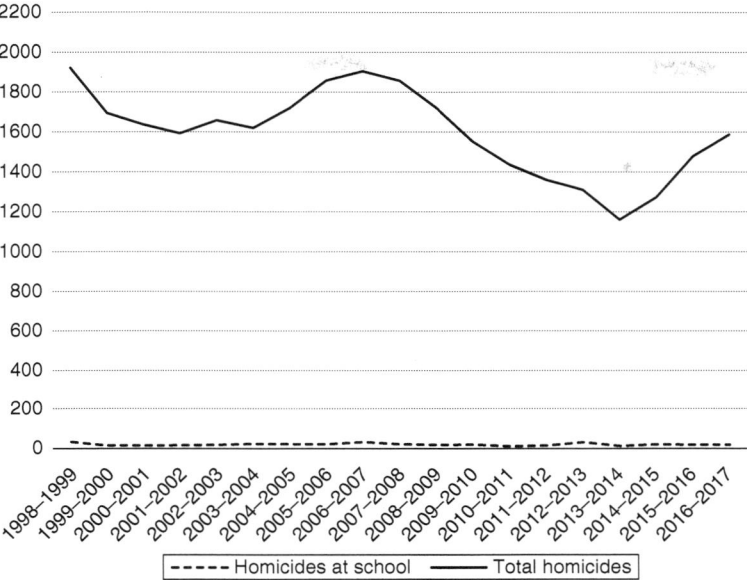

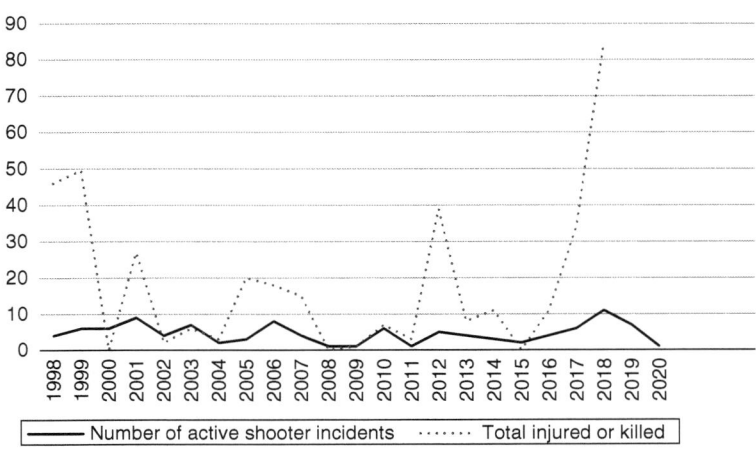

FIGURE 4.1 Threats to School Aged Children.

(a) Homicides of Those Aged 5–18.
Source: *Indicators of School Crime and Safety: 2018* and *Indicators of School Crime and Safety: 2019*.

(b) Active Shooter Incidents and Casualties Resulting from Them in Schools, K-12.
Source: Center for Homeland Defense and Security. www.chds.us/ssdb/category/active-shooter/.

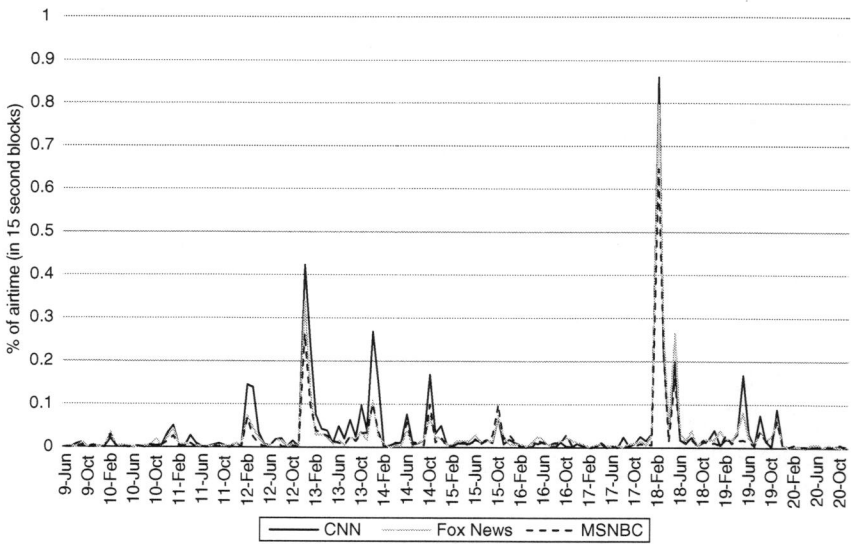

FIGURE 4.2 Media Coverage of School Shootings.
Source: GDELT Television Explorer Database.

Some school shootings generate more media attention than others, though. As Figure 4.2 shows, CNN, Fox News, and MSNBC devoted twice as much of their airtime to school shootings in early 2018, a time period that included the mass shooter incident at Marjory Stoneman Douglas High School, than they did at their previous highpoint in late 2012, around the time of the mass shooter incident at Sandy Hook Elementary School in Newtown, Connecticut. Together, these school shootings resulted in a far greater percentage of media coverage than others.

Thus, while the number of school shootings has not varied dramatically over the past two decades, and the numbers injured or killed pales in comparison to homicides of those ages 18 and under, Figures 4.1 and 4.2 suggest four environmental changes that made mobilization on this issue more likely in 2018. First, after nearly a decade of decline, the numbers of child homicides had increased for several years in a row leading up to 2018. Second, 2018 set a record for the highest number of school shootings in the period 1998–2018 (two more than the previous high). Third, school shootings in 2018 were more deadly than in previous years. And, finally, school shootings received a massive amount of media coverage in 2018 compared to what they had previously.

Media Coverage and Issue Importance

Research shows that high levels of media coverage of issues prime people to consider those issues important. This is often referred to as agenda setting.[2] For example, in experimental settings, viewers exposed to stories about defense readiness or pollution saw those issues as more important (Iyengar, Peters, and Kinder 1982). Just one news story a day for a week on topics like arms control, civil rights, and unemployment makes viewers significantly more likely to name the problem as one of the most serious ones facing the nation (Iyengar and Kinder 1987). Television coverage of energy, inflation, and unemployment responds to real world changes in these conditions and media coverage of energy and inflation help drive levels of public concern about these topics (Behr and Iyengar 1985). Some posit a recency effect is responsible – when asked what are the most important issues facing the nation, people will be more likely to respond with what they have heard about recently because this information is most accessible in their minds (Zaller and Feldman 1992).

People are especially likely to be swayed by news coverage that an issue is important if that content provokes negative emotions (Miller 2007). In particular, coverage of crime that causes people to feel sad or afraid makes them more likely to see crime as an important national issue (Miller 2007). School shootings and lone-wolf terrorist shootings receive a disproportionately high proportion of the coverage the media devotes to mass shootings (Silva and Capellan 2019) and media coverage of school shootings increases fear (Burns and Crawford 1999). This suggests that the high level of media coverage of mass shootings at schools in 2018 would contribute to increasing public concern about this issue.

Media Framing, Public Opinion, and Participation

The frames the media employ to cover an issue also help shape public opinion about it (Iyengar 1996; Chong and Druckman 2007). A brief look at how the media has covered previous mass shootings at schools proves instructive. In 1999, two students at Columbine High School in Littleton, Colorado, killed 13 and injured more than 20. As time passed, the mass shooting at Columbine was increasingly framed not as a local event but as one with national significance (Chyi and McCombs 2004). This trend of covering school shootings as a locally experienced symptom of a larger, national problem is also present in coverage of other mass shootings in schools (Muschert and Carr 2006). This tendency to use a national significance frame makes people more likely to see it as an issue that needs addressing. However, the mass shooting at Columbine High School served as only a "blurry focusing event" because it had limited impact on public policy outcomes (Birkland and Lawrence 2009).

While the media tends to portray school shootings as a symptom of a larger national problem instead of an isolated local event, media coverage of mass shootings is also more likely to blame mental illness as a cause than guns (McGinty et al. 2014). After the Columbine attack, the public only briefly increased its support for stricter gun laws (Birkland and Lawrence 2009) before returning to its previous levels. Support for stricter gun laws also briefly increased after the Sandy Hook shooting but there was no reduction in polarization over gun policy before it reverted to the mean (Wozniak 2017). This is consistent with the dynamics of mass shootings, as public support for gun control increases in the immediate aftermath and then reduces to approximately the level that it was before (Blackman and Baird 2014). Alternatively, the public has been very supportive of potential measures that would make it harder for the mentally ill to obtain guns. In 2017, surveys showed that large majorities of both gun owners and non–gun owners supported universal background checks and restrictions on the ability of the mentally ill to get and keep guns (Barry et al. 2018).

Yet, young adults tend to pay less attention to traditional news sources (Mindich 2004) and favor online or social media sources instead (Sveningsson 2015). This might make them less likely to be influenced by news coverage. However, there is good reason to think the content on social media will reflect that on traditional news. A study comparing online news media coverage of mass shootings with tweets about mass shootings found that the frames employed in news coverage of mass shootings influence the frames used in tweets about mass shootings but frames used on Twitter also help shape news coverage (Guggenheim et al. 2015).

Media coverage of some issues can help spark action. For example, annual variations in the levels of media coverage devoted to the health risks of smoking are associated with changes in levels of those quitting smoking (Pierce and Gilpin 2001). News media can also provide mobilizing information that encourages collective action (Nicodemus 2004; Hoffman 2006). Both effects were present after the coverage of a shooting at a daycare in 1999.

The shooting at Marjory Stoneman Douglas High School was not the first time media coverage of a mass shooting helped spawn a movement. Donna Dees launched the Million Mom March after she watched media coverage of preschoolers being led to safety after a shooting at a daycare at a Jewish Community Center in August of 1999 (Wallack, Winett, and Nettekoven 2003). This was one of several high-profile mass shootings in the late 1990s, occurring just months after the shooting in Columbine. Moms came together, mobilized to protect the nation's children from gun violence. Dees' background as a publicist came in handy and her plan for a march in Washington, DC, drew extensive news coverage (Wallack, Winett, and Nettekoven 2003). The first Million Mom March in 2000 drew crowds estimated between 200,000 and 750,000 in Washington, DC, and smaller crowds attended marches in 70 other American cities (Wallack, Winett, and Nettekoven 2003).

The movement received assistance from several organizations already formed to prevent gun violence and drew in many who had little to no experience with political activity (Wallack, Winett, and Nettekoven 2003). Electronic communications, still relatively new at the time, facilitated relationships between these new political activists that "helped to make what might have been an intimidating activity – flying to Washington, DC, to participate in a large, politically-charged social protest – into an exciting venture with like-minded friends" (Wallack, Winett, and Nettekoven 2003, 371). Wallack, Winett, and Nettekoven (2003) reference "stories of Moms who set aside their own doubts to become first-time public speakers, talk to journalists and appear on camera, seek private meetings with legislators, become computer savvy, and participate in the crush of large crowds" (370). Like Dees, many of the women who participated were driven by the realization that what they had seen on television could have easily been their own children.

Threat, Shared Grievances, and Collective Action

Like the mothers in the Million Mom March, particular threats can mobilize specific groups (Simmons 2014). Snow and Soule (2010) suggest that shared grievances can be severe enough that they provoke collective action. Perhaps among the most severe shared grievances are those that threaten a group's way of life or the lives of the group or the lives of those they care about. In her study of grassroots advocacy against gun violence, Frattaroli (2003) found that survivors of gun violence and friends and family members of those killed played an important role in the movement against gun violence.

As the Million Mom March example shows, when issues disproportionately affect a particular segment of society, that group pays more attention to it and may be mobilized to act. There are many other issues on which a shared threat provokes action. For example, Social Security is an issue that uniquely affects a specific age group – those past retirement age. As a result, senior citizens pay close attention when elected officials consider changes to Social Security (Campbell 2003). Yet, not all senior citizens are equally affected. Those with lower levels of income depend more on Social Security income to survive. Campbell (2002) found that among seniors, lower income levels are associated with greater rates of contacting elected officials about Social Security. Those with the most to lose have the highest incentive to act. Threats to self-interest can act as a driver of participation among young adults, too. For example, student loan recipients with lower incomes were more likely to contact elected officials about student loan programs (Ozemy 2012).

However, Nadeau, Niemi, and Amato (1995) find that threat or anxiety only causes people to see an issue as important if they have some hope that this threat can successfully be averted. According to them, "When there is hopelessness, no amount of threat stimulates greater interest and learning. It is only when there is hope that anxiety alters people's views" (Nadeau, Niemi, and Amato 1995, 569). The moms who marched in 2000 and the young adults who organized under the rallying cry #NeverAgain after the Parkland shooting in 2018 shared a belief that change was possible.

Placing #NeverAgain in Context

Efforts to reduce and prevent gun violence have been ongoing for decades. These efforts had seen some success at the state level. For example, Wallack, Winett, and Lee's (2005) study of the work of the Youth Violence Prevention Initiative's

Policy and Public Education Program in California to reduce youth gun violence acknowledged the role of focusing events and identified four other key factors to their success: clear policy goals, strategic issue framing, identifying and creating political opportunities, and mobilizing resources. Yet, the movement faced challenges, too. One of these was a lack of diversity within the movement (Frattaroli 2003; Wallack, Winett, and Nettekoven 2003). Other challenges included generating a credible risk and what Frattaroli (2003) termed the "need for a roar." According to Frattaroli (2003, 339), "Publicizing the human toll of gun violence, calling forth public outrage, and showing that individuals' actions can affect policy are central to building the movement." In the sections that follow, we address how these factors apply to #NeverAgain.

Fifteen years before the shooting in Parkland, Florida, that helped launch a movement against gun violence led by young adults, Frattaroli (2003) found that youth participation in the movement against gun violence was growing. As this happened, organizations and long-term activists began to see youth as potentially valuable partners (Frattaroli 2003). This may have helped make it more likely that the movement launched in 2018 would be supported by existing organizations, as the Million Mom March was before it (Wallack, Winett, and Nettekoven 2003).

The Parkland Shooting as a "Focusing Event"

Focusing events, because they happen suddenly, allow newer voices and politically disadvantaged groups the opportunity to successfully frame policy debates (Birkland 1998). According to Birkland (1998), characteristics of focusing events include happening suddenly, harming a distinct community, gaining the public's attention, and unveiling the possibility of additional future adverse effects if nothing is done. Mass shootings at schools all fulfill these characteristics but they have not all launched movements against gun violence. The "need for a roar" in the movement identified by Frattaroli (2003) was not fulfilled until after the shooting at Marjory Stoneman Douglas High School. When survivors spoke to the news media in the days that followed, they didn't just talk about the fear, terror, and loss they had experienced as survivors, they expressed outrage and calls for change (Alter 2018). One survivor told the media,

> If you looked around this closet and saw everybody just hiding together, you would know that this shouldn't be happening anymore and that it doesn't deserve to happen to anyone, and no amount of money should make it more easily accessible to get guns.
>
> *(Hogg and Hogg 2018, 95)*

This tragedy, which received massive media coverage, triggered a roar that was heard nationwide.

Credible Risk, Strategic Framing, and Mobilization

Credible risk was not hard to establish. School shootings had been on the rise, as were the number of casualties from them. The 2017–2018 school year was averaging one major mass shooting event a month and numerous other more isolated shooting incidents. A majority of students between the ages of 13 and 17 reported being worried that a school shooting would happen at their school (Graf 2018). Homicide rates of those under the age of 18 increased, too. Many students were fearful for their lives. This perceived shared threat to existence, even if severely overestimated, and the collective grievance that politicians hadn't done anything to help protect them, provided powerful grounds for mobilization. Tired of living under threat, students across the country quickly mobilized around survivors' online rallying cry #NeverAgain (Yee and Blinder 2018). This cry expressed a belief that they could make a difference, something Nadeau, Niemi, and Amato (1995) found was key for stimulating interest and attention to an issue.

In contrast to some of the previous gun violence prevention movements (see e.g., Merry 2020), there was some diversity among the movement leaders. The initial small group of leaders from Marjory Stoneman Douglas High School also sought to involve additional diverse voices and criticized the media when they were left out of their coverage (Willingham and Gallagher 2018). They sought to expand those involved, with David Hogg writing, "If people only listen when privileged white kids get killed – and even then, only when the number of dead kids is high enough to make the news – we're never going to fix this problem" (Hogg and Hogg 2018, 231). This approach helped both mobilize a broader coalition and expand the movement to be one about reducing all forms of gun violence and not just mass shootings at schools. In this respect, this approach counters a commonly seen trend in which both gun control and gun rights groups distort the issue of gun violence by emphasizing atypical actors and venues in the policy discussion (see Merry 2020).

Clear Policy Goals

The movement's leaders developed an 11-point strategy to reduce gun violence. Their policy goals included demanding universal background checks, red flag laws, an assault weapons ban, and funding for intervention programs and gun violence research, and they sought to use their vote and their voices to help achieve these (Hogg and Hogg 2018). We will return to assessing the effectiveness of the movement in mobilizing to achieve these policy goals in the second half of the book. For now, we focus on its ability to mobilize at the individual level.

Concern for School Shootings and Getting Involved

Purely threat or anxiety-based explanations of activity would suggest that those more concerned about school shootings would participate more. Figure 4.3 shows

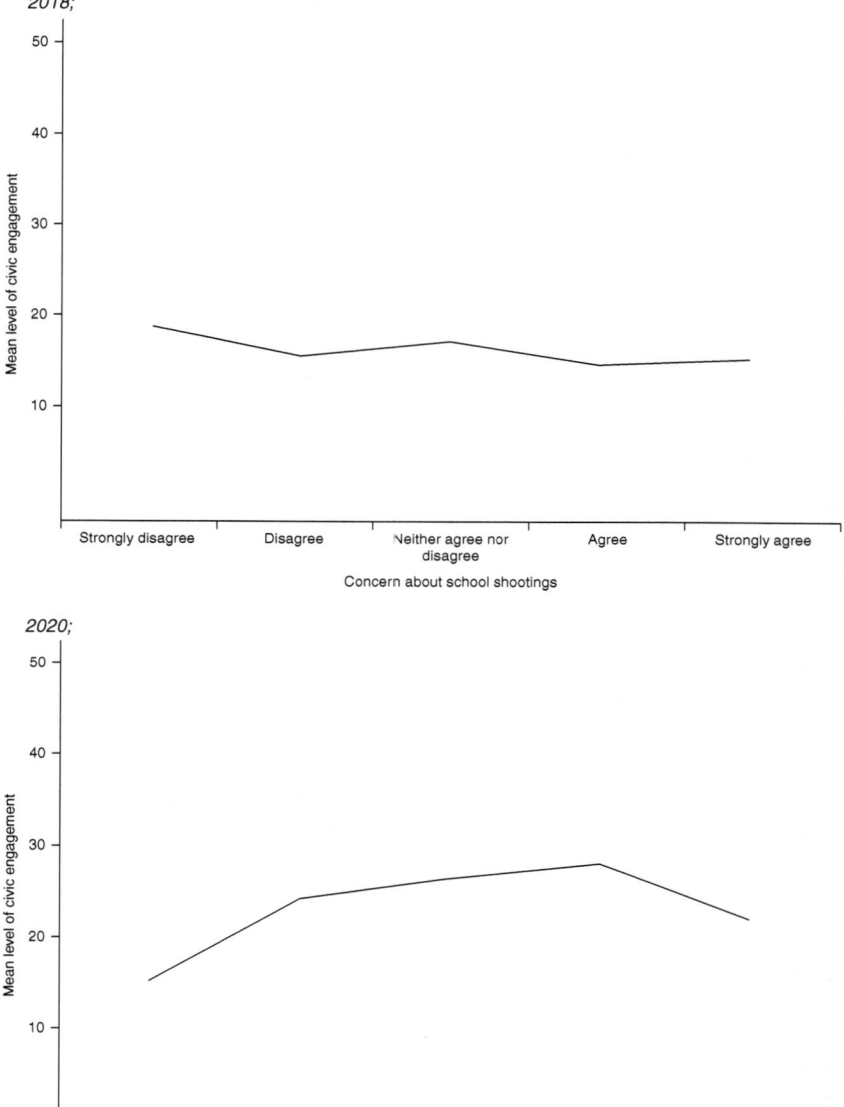

FIGURE 4.3 Mean Civic Engagement Levels by Concern about School Shootings.

the mean level of civic engagement among individuals in our survey with each level of concern about school shootings in both 2018 and 2020. It does not lend much support to an anxiety-based explanation. Levels of civic engagement do not vary dramatically by level of concern about school shootings in 2018 and, in fact, mean civic engagement levels are highest among those that strongly disagree that they are concerned about school shootings. In 2020, though, levels of civic engagement generally increase with levels of concern about school shootings, with a peak for those who agree, but not strongly agree that they are concerned about school shootings. This pattern in 2020 is more consistent with mobilizing in response to perceived threat. Nonetheless, these patterns do not entirely rule out the threat-based explanation in 2018. After all, our survey is of those between the ages of 18 and 25. It is possible we would see more significant differences across levels of concern and higher participation rates among those concerned about school shootings if our survey had focused on those still in high school.

Posting and Protesting about Gun Control and Civic Engagement

Individuals can post about gun control or other political issues for a variety of reasons, including hoping for change. Posting one's views online carries costs (Moffett and Rice 2018) so those who engage in it must think it has some value. This willingness to incur these costs may also indicate a higher probability of willingness to participate in other, more costly ways. This suggests that those who post more about gun control will have higher levels of civic engagement, all else equal. Yet, this is not the only reason we expect there to be a link between posting about gun control and civic engagement.

Social movements allow individuals to become part of something bigger than themselves. Even though the internet was still in its infancy during the first Million Mom March against gun violence, Wallack, Winett, and Nettekoven (2003) identified its importance in organizing and in facilitating "lateral connections" that encouraged participation in the movement. Similar patterns occurred with #NeverAgain. As people shared their views online, they became connected to others with similar opinions. Shared opinions can become important building blocks for friendships. In addition, young adults with friends who are more engaged often become more engaged themselves (Moffett and Rice 2016). Thus, taking the first step of sharing one's views online helps connect one to a community with similar views, who become likely to share opportunities to get involved with each other and encourage each other to take them.

As a first test of whether #NeverAgain helped expand the participation rates of young adults, we examine whether those who posted online about gun control in 2018 had higher rates of civic engagement.[3] The movement was quite popular among young adults that year, so posting should be relatively commonplace. We expect that those who post online about gun control will engage in higher levels of civic engagement than otherwise similar young adults who choose not to post about this issue. We also expect that any increase seen in civic engagement will be most pronounced among those who post at high rates. Posting four or more times about gun control not only expresses stronger commitment to advancing this cause, it heightens the likelihood of becoming connected to others with similar commitments and increases the chances of responding favorably to invitations to participate in other ways.

In addition to posting online, protest was a key part of this movement. School walkouts took place across the nation on multiple dates (Alter 2018; Taylor 2018). Students who chose to do so faced the potential risk of disciplinary consequences. The March for Our Lives demonstration on March 24, 2018, in Washington, DC, was costly in other ways. It attracted hundreds of thousands of participants and smaller protests took place in cities across the country (Jamison et al. 2018). Those who participated made the decision to forego other activities and some incurred significant travel costs as well. While the organizers of the march received help from celebrities, these protests, too, were youth driven (Jamison et al. 2018). This might make exposure to other more politically experienced groups and individuals less likely than at protests on other issues, decreasing the likelihood of other forms of mobilization. Still, those willing to incur the costs of protesting show high willingness to act about this issue. The experience of joining together in a protest with other young people might boost efficacy and heighten interest in other forms of civic activity. Thus, we also investigate whether those who participated in these protests in 2018 were otherwise more civically engaged than those who chose not to protest on this issue.

Yet, some of the same factors that fueled the movement in 2018 were missing in 2020. Most notably, the "need for a roar" was abated by the Covid-19 pandemic. With many schools switching to all virtual or hybrid learning for portions of the 2019–2020 and 2020–2021 school years, there were fewer opportunities for school shootings to occur. This temporarily alleviated the risks faced by students. As seen in Panel B of Figure 4.1, the number of school shootings involving active shooters dropped dramatically. Accordingly, news coverage of this issue dropped significantly, too, as seen in Figure 4.2. Searches of the GDELT Television Explorer database show that the amount of news coverage on CNN that mentioned school shootings in 2018 was 56 times higher than the amount of coverage that contained the words school shooting in 2020. Thus, the impetus for action waned. Only the most committed to the cause would be likely to post or protest in this environment and the movement's ability to spread would be significantly hampered. In a timespan when this subject had moved off center stage, the movement was unlikely to draw in new participants.

Thus, those who did post in 2020 had been likely doing so since 2018. If so, they should have already been drawn in to engage in other ways. Thus, we would not necessarily expect to see additional increases in their civic engagement. In addition, posting online remained a safe form of activity during the Covid-19 pandemic as many forms of offline civic engagement now carried potential health risks. However, those who protest in 2020 not only show strong commitment to a cause, but also demonstrate a willingness to take potentially costly and risky actions in the midst of a pandemic. We note that some of the activities in our offline civic engagement measure not only became riskier but were also made much more difficult during a time of social distancing and especially during stay at home orders. As a result, in general, we expect stronger effects in 2018 than in 2020. However, we also anticipate that those who show a strong willingness to protest despite the health risks in 2020, may also be more willing to engage in other offline forms of civic engagement perhaps standing in the gap left by those whose underlying health conditions or age put them at heightened risk.

Data

To test our hypotheses, we performed online surveys on November 7, 2018, and November 4, 2020, of Americans between 18 and 25 years old – an age range that includes both younger Millennials and older members of Generation Z.[4] We used Amazon's Mechanical Turk (mTurk) platform to carry out this survey, a website that allows members of the public to earn money for completing many kinds of tasks, including participating in survey research. Each participant was paid $1.50 for completing the survey. A total of 1,010 participants completed the survey in 2018 and 969 completed it in 2020 after we removed any incomplete responses.[5]

Dependent Variable

The dependent variable is the extent to which each respondent participated in civic and political activities away from the internet. Through separate questions, each person was asked about the frequency with which they have engaged in an array of activities such as talking to people and explaining why they should vote for or against a specific candidate or party, attending political functions in support of a candidate or party, and making purchasing decisions based on a company's conduct or values. To create a single measure of political and civic activity, we summed the values for each of the 12 activities to produce an index that was based on answers to this set of questions (α = .92, 2018; α = .95, 2020). The means of this index, 14.56 (2018) and 26.01 (2020), are quite low as this indicates an activity level equivalent to having done 4–6 of the 12 activities in this index very often. The standard deviations, 10.75 (2018) and 14.61 (2020), indicate substantial variance around this mean. Thus, we have captured both low and high participators in our surveys. The question wording and precise operationalization of each treatment variable, matching covariate, and the dependent variable can be found in the online appendix. Then, to test our theoretical expectations, we use a series of matching routines.[6]

Treatment Variables

To test our hypotheses, we compute the effects of posting about gun control and participating in protests related to this issue on civic engagement. Using separate questions, we asked each respondent about the extent to which they posted about gun control, or participated in protests related to this issue. The response options were never, posted once, posted two or three times, and posted four or more times.

Matching Covariates

We used two variables to investigate the effects of political engagement apart from the internet. First, we asked each respondent about the extent to which they are interested in politics on a four-point scale that ranged from four points for "Very interested" to zero points for "Not at all interested." Second, each respondent was asked three questions about the extent to which their friends engaged in a set of activities. We built an additive index based on the responses to these questions to examine the effects of peer civic activities on civic engagement ($\alpha = .63$, 2018; $\alpha = .58$, 2020).[7,8]

In addition, we used several variables to investigate the effects of political engagement using the internet. First, we asked each respondent how often they read blogs online about politics. Kerbel and Bloom (2005) and Moffett and Rice (2018) discover that blogs can act as outlets that foster enhanced civic activity, either online or offline. Second, each respondent was asked how frequently they read news on the internet about politics.

Third, we constructed an additive index of online civic activity consisting of five items, as several researchers have unearthed a link between activities on social media and offline civic engagement (see e.g., Kahne and Bowyer 2018; Ley and Brewer 2018; Loader, Vromen, and Xenos 2014). Through separate questions, we asked each respondent about the extent to which they had relied on social media for news, posted about politics on social media, read social media feeds about politics, liked or shared posts about politics on social media, or read or watched posts about politics on social media and created an additive index of online civic activity ($\alpha = .84$, 2018; $\alpha = .83$, 2020).[9]

Fourth, each respondent was asked a series of questions about the extent to which they posted messages on social media about Supreme Court nominations (Barrett in 2020, Kavanaugh in 2018), immigration, the MeToo movement, Black Lives Matter (in 2020 only), and about other issues. Fifth, each respondent was asked a set of questions about the extent to which they participated in protests related to Supreme Court nominations (Kavanaugh in 2018, Barrett in 2020), immigration, the MeToo movement, Black Lives Matter (in 2020, but not in 2018), and about other issues.

We employed four variables to account for the effects of issue importance, as issues can sometimes facilitate higher levels of political participation (Converse

1964; Carmines and Stimson 1989; Reny, Collingwood, and Valenzuela 2019). We asked each respondent about the importance of congressional stances on immigration in influencing their vote choice. Second, we asked each respondent about the extent to which they supported or opposed the family separation policy implementation under the Trump administration. Third, we asked each respondent about the extent to which they supported or opposed the DACA program in 2020, but not in 2018. Fourth, we asked each respondent whether they self-identified as a supporter of the Black Lives Matter movement (in 2020, but not in 2018).

What is more, we used several variables to consider the effects of personal characteristics on offline civic activity. First, we asked respondents about their partisanship and created a binary variable for strong partisanship, as this attachment is associated with an array of other political activities (see e.g., Flavin and Griffin 2009; Verba, Brady, and Schlozman 1995). Second, we examined the effects of ideology on civic engagement and created a binary for liberals as Achen and Bartels (2016) discover that ideological identification shapes political participation.

Third, we asked each respondent for their sex, and we coded this variable one for females, two for males, and three for those who self-identified in another category. Fourth, we acquired data on each respondent's age by asking each to report their month and year of birth. Then, we computed each respondent's age based on the month and year of the 2018 midterm election for the 2018 data, and on the month and year of the 2020 general election for the 2020 data.[10] Fifth, we asked each respondent for their race and collapsed that information into a binary that is coded one for whites, and zero otherwise. Sixth, we asked each respondent for their level of education.

Finally, we used three variables to control for the effects of underlying political attitudes, as these can affect participation patterns. First, we asked each respondent whether they approved or disapproved of the job that Donald Trump is doing as president, as presidential approval is connected with changes in participatory patterns (Abramowitz and Stone 2006). Second, we asked each respondent whether they self-identified as a supporter of the MeToo movement.[11] Third, we asked each respondent about their opinions about Brett Kavanaugh's nomination in 2018 and Amy Coney Barrett's nomination in 2020 using a five-point scale that ranged from strongly opposed to strongly supported.

Methods

To investigate whether both treatment variables are connected with offline civic activity, we use a matching analysis to compute the ATET. We choose a matching estimator for several reasons. First, most regression-based techniques (including OLS) assume that there exists a linear relationship between the dependent and independent variables (see Greene 2011). Our theory posits a positive relationship between both treatment variables and civic engagement, but makes no prediction about the remaining response options contained in either treatment variable. Thus, the phenomenon that we examine is nonlinear by construction, and is ill suited to investigate using a method that assumes linearity (like OLS). Fortunately, matching analyses do not assume linearity, allow for a more flexible functional form, and have many other statistical properties that make them a more appropriate choice to test the hypotheses in this chapter (Imbens and Rubin 2015).

What is more, individuals have differing probabilities of posting about gun control, or participating in protests related to that issue. OLS estimators presume treatment homogeneity, which is unlikely to hold in this analysis. It is likely that individuals have different treatment effects, particularly depending on the extent to which they posted about gun control or participated in protests related to it (see Abadie and Imbens 2011). Thus, the effects of participating in protests related to gun control or posting about it vary depending on the frequency with which one has participated in protests related to this topic or posted about it. For instance, those who posted more frequently about gun control may be more apt to engage in offline civic activities more frequently than one who has never posted about this subject. In a similar vein, those who participated in protests related to gun control more frequently may engage in higher levels of offline civic engagement more frequently than one who has never participated in protests related to this issue.

By construction, OLS-based estimators assume that we observe a linear, homogeneous relationship between posting about this topic, or participating in protests related to it and offline civic engagement. Matching-based approaches deal effectively with this issue because they assume neither linearity nor homogeneity (Imbens and Rubin 2015). Rather, matching-based approaches produce several treatment estimates depending on the level of treatment that a respondent received (Imbens and Rubin 2015). Thus, we can generate several, more accurate estimates of the effect that differing levels of posting or protesting about gun control had on offline civic engagement.

Moreover, OLS does not permit us to estimate what happens to offline civic activity in the absence of posting about gun control or participating in protests related to it (Nichols 2007). Matching analyses use the existing data to generate a dataset that includes observations that are as alike as possible, given the values of the remaining predictors (Stuart 2010). Thus, we can estimate what would have happened had particular respondents not posted about gun control or participated in protests related to it (see Gelman and Hill 2007). Then, we can use this dataset to estimate the effects of differing frequencies of posting about gun control or participating in protests related to it. We iterate this procedure for each level of posting about that topic or participating in protests related to it. Finally, if we used OLS estimates to obtain the results, our results would likely be biased because any estimate of the treatment effect is conditioned on the values of the remaining independent variables. Consequently, OLS-based approaches do not compute ATETs.

Matching analyses contend well with each of these issues because they let us examine whether differing levels of posting about gun control or participating in protests related to it are connected with higher levels of civic engagement. By matching based on each of the predictors to make inferences, we can disentangle the effects of posting about this issue (or participating in protests related to it) beyond people's other inclinations to civically participate. Thus, doing so enables us to compare people with similar inclinations to civic activity who only vary in the extent to which they posted about or participated in protests related to this topic. Moreover, matching allows us to calculate ATETs for each treatment level, and by doing so, to calculate more precise effect estimates with observational data.

Assumptions

Before performing our matching analyses, we must meet four assumptions. The validity of any matching analyses hinges on satisfying these assumptions. First, we presume that both sets of treatment variables are binary. To make our first treatment variable binary, we generated a series of dichotomous variables for each response option, relative to never having posted about gun control. These binaries are coded one for each of these categories, zero for never having posted about this issue, and missing for those who declined to answer the question, and for the remaining scalar options. There are three binaries for posting once, posting two or three times, and for having posted four or more times about this issue. For instance, the binary for having posted once about this issue is coded one for those who did so, zero for never having done so, and missing for those who declined to answer this question, and for those who reported having posted more than once. We follow an analogous procedure for having participated in protests related to gun control, as that variable is measured in the same manner. We expect positive signs for all ATETs that we estimate in this chapter.

Second, we assume common support (or overlap), which means that it is possible that treated units may face an intervention that could have assigned them to the control group (see Imbens and Rubin 2015; King, Lucas, and Nielsen 2017). The data that we use meet this requirement because all respondents could have chosen not to post about gun control or participate in protests related to this issue.

Third, we must fulfill the SUTVA assumption, which means that "the potential outcomes for any unit do not vary with the treatments assigned to other units, and for each unit, there are no different forms or versions of each treatment level, which lead to different potential outcomes" (Imbens and Rubin 2015, 10). We have met the first part of this assumption because the possible outcomes for civic activity do not vary with the levels of posting about gun control, or with participating in protests related to this issue.[12]

The second aspect of this assumption is more intricate because we have different variations on our treatment variable, as variations exist with respect to posting once, posting two or three times, and posting four or more times about gun control. Yet, we can compare the effects of having posted with varying frequencies about this issue relative to those who never did so. For example, we can compare those who posted once about this issue to those who never did so, provided that we exclude those who posted at all other frequencies from that analysis.[13] We have to perform an analogous procedure to compare those who had posted two or three times, and those who posted four or more times about this issue if we hope to perform a matching analysis without an alternative treatment. We perform a substantially similar procedure with respect to our other treatment variable, participating in protests related to gun control, as we measure it using the same scale as our posting measure. When we compute our ATETs in this manner, we ultimately satisfy the SUTVA assumption because we have neither interference, nor any hidden variations of the treatments (Imbens and Rubin 2015, 10–11).

Finally, the treatment assignment must be conditionally independent of the outcome variable given a set of matching covariates (D'Agostino 1998, 2266). Thus, each respondent's assignment to treatment (i.e., posting about gun control or participating in protests related to it) is unconnected with their level of civic engagement, given the values of the remaining explanatory variables. We observe substantial variance in participatory levels with respect to civic activity, and the mean level of civic activity is relatively low (14.56, 2018; 26.01, 2020), given the minimum (0) and maximum values (48) possible with this index. Moreover, the activities that comprise offline civic activity do not cause an individual to be assigned to one or more treatment categories.

Matching Technique

Once we have met the statistical assumptions that underlie matching, we need to select a method by which to perform this type of analysis. To perform our matching analyses, we use one-to-one genetic matching with replacement (Diamond and Sekhon 2013; Sekhon 2011). We incorporate a propensity score into the analysis, as knowing estimated values of this score meaningfully improves the accuracy of this method (Diamond and Sekhon 2013). Propensity score matching allows us to compare observations that are otherwise similar across other predictors, but have experienced different treatments. We perform our analysis with replacement, as matching discrepancies are reduced because we can use untreated units as a match multiple times (see Abadie and Imbens 2006).[14] To remove any bias that results due to the choice of the matching estimator without affecting the variance of that estimator, we employ a bias correction (Abadie and Imbens 2016).

Results

Before we discuss the results, we need to examine how similar the control and treatment groups are to one another (King, Lucas, and Nielsen 2017). If these groups are substantially dissimilar, then we cannot use matching to estimate ATETs. The imbalance statistics for the models in Table 4.1 is contained in Tables A1 through A8 in the online appendix. For 86.11% (or 124/144) of the variables

TABLE 4.1 Civic Engagement and Posting and Protesting about Gun Control

	Posting about Gun Control						Protesting about Gun Control					
	2018			2020			2018			2020		
	Once	Two or Three Times	Four or More Times	Once	Two or Three Times	Four or More Times	Once	Two or Three Times	Four or More Times	Once	Two or Three Times	Four or More Times
Effect on Offline Civic Engagement	4.538	2.404	6.184	1.059	-9.134	3.548	-.098	-2.075	-3.427	2.752	3.472	5.521
Abadie–Imbens Standard Error	1.686	1.616	3.397	2.930	11.402	2.478	1.958	3.481	4.972	6.902	2.940	3.056
95% Confidence Interval Lower Bound	1.190	-.792	-.593	-4.822	-31.756	-1.398	-4.012	-9.121	-13.714	-11.093	-2.376	-.664
95% Confidence Interval Upper Bound	7.886	5.600	12.961	6.940	13.488	8.494	3.816	4.971	6.860	16.597	9.320	11.706
T-Statistic	2.691	1.488	1.820	.361	-.801	1.432	-.050	-.596	-.689	.399	1.181	1.807
P-Value (two-tailed test)	.007	.137	.069	.718	.423	.152	.960	.551	.491	.690	.238	.071
P-Value (one-tailed test)	.004	.069	.035	.359	.212	.076	.480	.276	.246	.345	.119	.036
N	95	135	69	53	102	68	63	39	24	54	83	39

Notes: In each three-column set, the number of times that one has posted or protested about gun control is compared with one who has never done so about that subject. Second, the covariates on which the matching is based are described in the text. Third, the effects on offline civic engagement are the ATET. Finally, the matching results are from 1:1 genetic matching with post-matching bias adjustment. Thus, the N represents the matched number of observations.

contained in the models in Table 4.1 in 2018, the KS tests are not significant at the .05 level after matching has occurred. In 2020, 65.47% (or 110/168) of the variables contained in the models in this same table feature KS tests that are not significant at the .05 level after matching has happened.

In 2018, 14 of the remaining 20 cases where the KS tests are significant involve issues that we explore in other chapters. Also, in 2020, 32 of the remaining 48 cases where KS tests are significant also involve issues that we explore elsewhere. In both 2018 and 2020, these issues include the MeToo Movement (Chapter 2), Supreme Court nominations (Chapter 3), immigration and family separation (Chapter 5), and Black Lives Matter (Chapter 6, 2020). The remaining cases are randomly distributed across the differing models and have no systematic component that underlies them. Altogether, we can be confident that we have substantially reduced imbalance across the model specifications. The matched groups have similar enough observable characteristics such that we can attribute any remaining differences across levels of posting about gun control to the effects of posting, not to preexisting differences (Eggers and Hainmueller 2009). Similarly, we can attribute any remaining differences across levels of participating in protests about gun control to the effects of participating in protests, not to preexisting differences.

We provide the results from the matching routines in Table 4.1. The results indicate that there is no statistically significant relationship between any level of participating in protests about gun control and subsequent civic engagement in 2018 and at most levels in 2020, too. The 2020 results, when examined using a one-tailed test of statistical significance (p = .036) rather than a two-tailed test, indicate that participating in protests related to gun control four or more times is connected with a nearly six-point increase in civic engagement.[15] A six-point increase in civic engagement is the equivalent of participating in one additional activity very often that otherwise would not have happened, and two activities at one higher level than what would have otherwise occurred.

The results for the posting models require a more intricate analysis. On the one hand, the results indicate no statistically significant connection between posting about gun control and civic activity in 2020 at any level. However, the results in 2018 point to what appears to be a statistically significant relationship between posting once about gun control and higher levels of civic activity. When we use a one-tailed test of statistical significance to examine the results for posting four or more times about gun control in 2018 (p = .035), the results indicate that there are statistically significant differences in civic engagement between those who posted four or more times relative to those who did not do so at all.[16] More specifically, those who posted four or more times about gun control had civic activity scores that were approximately six points higher. A six-point increase is the equivalent of participating in one activity very often that otherwise would not have occurred, *and* two activities at one level higher, or one activity at two levels higher.[17]

We must verify whether the results that we obtained are model dependent by removing one matching covariate at a time from the models (Ho et al. 2007). Then, we re-ran the matching routines with the remaining predictors.[18] These results are contained in the online appendix for both 2018 and 2020. When we examine the posting models relative to what we report here, 81.41% (or 127/156) of the specifications contain results that are consistent with what we report here.

In 2018, the remaining cases occur across the models, but are particularly concentrated when examining the connection between posting once about gun control and civic engagement. When we query this relationship, 13 out of 24 models (or 54.17%) of the models contain results that contradict what appears to be an affirmative finding for posting once about gun control from Table 4.1. Thus, the results from the model for having posted once about gun control should be interpreted skeptically and conservatively. When we utilize such an interpretation, we cannot safely conclude there is a statistically significant relationship between posting once about gun control and civic engagement, but we can conclude that a statistically significant relationship exists between posting four or more times about gun control and civic activity. We also performed a similar set of robustness checks for the protesting models contained in Table 4.1. Of these, 97.43% (or 152/156) contain results that are consistent with what we report in the table for protesting. The four remaining results are scattered throughout the models with no systematic pattern. Thus, we are highly confident in the results that we have obtained for protesting.

Conclusion

In sum, we find some evidence that posting about gun control in 2018 led to higher levels of civic engagement, but not in 2020. More specifically, we found that posting four or more times about gun control in 2018 relates to higher levels of civic activity. This, once again, contrasts strongly with the slacktivism charge levied at young adults. Young adults are not just hiding behind their screens trying to bring about change. Our results suggest that posting views online about gun control at high levels also leads to higher levels of civic and political activity, both online and offline. Yet, in 2020, when the impetus for action had waned, the movement was crowded out by other, more salient issues, and offline civic activity became more difficult due to the Covid-19 pandemic, posting about gun control no longer expanded into other forms of civic engagement.

Protesting about gun control did not increase civic engagement levels among young adults in 2018, when protesting about this issue was commonplace, but did so in 2020 among those who protested four or more times. In 2018 this could suggest that young adults were so focused on this issue that they had yet to branch into other forms of civic engagement. This might also be because there were even more salient and recent issues that drove participation among most young people during that election cycle: Brett Kavanaugh's nomination (which happened just before the 2018 midterm election) and the emergence of the MeToo movement. These are somewhat tied together, as the issues surrounding Kavanaugh's nomination struck at the core of several of the issues around which the MeToo movement organized. This issue pattern is somewhat consistent with the extant political science literature, as issues are frequently viewed as short-term effects (see e.g., Campbell et al. 1960) that may affect particular elections but rarely exert long-term effects.

Moreover, scholars who research gun control have consistently found that mass shootings increase support for gun control immediately after they have occurred (Blackman and Baird 2014; Newman and Hartman 2019). In addition, these higher levels of support hold more strongly in those places that are in proximity to one or more mass shootings (Newman and Hartman 2019). Yet, these increases in support for gun control evaporate relatively quickly after they emerge, as other issues crowd out gun control (Blackman and Baird 2014).

In addition, the #Never Again movement was one primarily involving high school students. Yet, our surveys, with their focus on 18–25-year-olds, leave out many high school students. Thus, in 2018 many of those most active in the movement were not eligible to participate. Since those who had already graduated high school played a much less prominent role in this movement early on, it is not surprising that we did not find much evidence that views and actions on this issue increased civic engagement more broadly beyond those who posted four or more times about this issue in 2018.

By 2020, more of those most active in the movement in 2018 would be old enough to participate in our survey. We found that those who participated in protests four or more times about gun control in 2020 had higher levels of civic engagement. These young adults showed a sustained commitment to this cause, even at a time it had waned in salience for others. In addition, these young adults showed a willingness to take costly action to advance their cause multiple times. As the pandemic worsened, they appeared undeterred by the possibility of health risks. If they were willing to participate in protests where social distance can be difficult, it should perhaps come as no surprise that they were also willing to engage in other forms of offline civic engagement, despite any health risks they now carried due to the pandemic.

We found little to no evidence that those only minimally involved in the movement, posting or protesting less than three times, had higher rates of civic engagement. However, that is not to say that this movement had no meaningful effects beyond the frequent posters in 2018 and the frequent protestors in 2020. We will explore those effects further in the second half of this book. Meanwhile, in the next chapter, we examine whether views and actions about another salient issue in 2018 and 2020, immigration, yielded higher levels of civic engagement. It is to that task that we turn.

Notes

1 Year 2010 is the first complete year for which this data is available.
2 See Kosicki (1993) for a review of this literature.
3 While our focus in this chapter is on #NeverAgain, movements can also spawn countermovements. By looking at posts about gun control, we test whether posting about this issue, regardless of the substance of the posts, helps increase civic engagement. Many of the same explanations for how the #NeverAgain movement for gun control increased civic engagement could also be applied to those countermobilizing against gun control. For example, some gun owners might feel threatened by talk of gun control. And, when they post their views online, that also helps facilitate connections to like-minded individuals who may encourage their participation.
4 These generations have similar views on social issues (Parker, Graf, and Igielnik 2019).
5 We constrained the eligibility of participants in this survey to those with HIT approval rates of at least 95% and whose location is in the United States. While we were unable to constrain by age here, we did so through the first question asking respondents whether they were between the ages of 18 and 25. If they responded no, then the survey ended.
6 The online appendix contains the complete wording for each of the questions for the mTurk sample, along with a more extensive discussion of the variables that we used.
7 These were the only questions in the survey about peer civic experiences. Some participants responded that they did not know for one or more of these questions. When constructing our index, we coded values for these variables as missing. Consequently, no peer civic engagement score is present for those who answered "don't know" on a minimum of one of these questions.
8 This also acts as an indirect indicator with respect to mobilization, as people frequently act politically when others around them do so (see e.g., Gimpel, Lee, and Kamiski 2006). Yet, it is possible that mobilization efforts by those other than peers, like interest groups and political parties, also yield higher levels of participation (Rosenstone and Hansen 2002). There are no questions in this survey that allow us to directly account for the effects of mobilization on civic activity. That said, we do consider many other covariates that also affect mobilization as part of the matching routines in this analysis.
9 We employed a modified version of this variable for the models in which the treatment variable is posting about gun control, as we cannot have the treatment variable being essentially the same as an element of one of the matching covariates. More specifically, we removed posting about politics on social media from the online civic engagement index for this set of models because the treatment for the set of models examining the effects of posting about gun control is the extent to which one posted about this issue. We retained the remaining variables that comprise the online civic engagement index and created an additive index based on those (α = .81, 2018; α =.78, 2020).
10 We asked an initial screening question that identified those who were between the ages of 18 and 25, and those who responded that they were not in this age range were excluded from further participation in the survey. When we performed the age computations based on the year and month that respondents selected, though, there were 49 respondents who stated that they were older than 25 in 2018. In the year-month calculation, there was usually about a six-month variance between the reported and actual age among those 49 respondents. Since we asked about both year and month of birth based on drop-down menus, it is possible that a substantial portion of

these respondents misreported their year and/or month of birth in 2018 (see Gendall and Healey 2008). We have no reason to believe that this error is systematic, and did not encounter the same concern in 2020. Thus, nonsystematic measurement error in an independent variable does not bias any conclusions in research studies (see King, Keohane, and Verba 1994).
11 Imbens and Rubin (2015, 16) state that any matching technique assumes that matching covariates are unaffected by treatment assignment. Thus, there should be no connection between any particular matching covariate and the assignment to treatment. Consequently, we exclude one variable from the set of matching covariates in this analysis: posting about gun control, as this variable acts as the treatment.
12 If civic engagement were related to posting about gun control, then civic activity and posting about this issue would be highly correlated. To test whether this happens, we correlated our dependent variable (offline civic activity) and out treatment variables (posting about gun control and participating in protests related to gun control). The correlations are .497 and .600 in 2018, and .633 and .752 in 2020, respectively. These correlations are low enough such that we can conclude that the first part of the SUTVA assumption is satisfied.
13 If we do not conduct our analysis in this manner, then we cannot satisfy SUTVA, as there would be alternative treatment forms (see Imbens and Rubin 2015, 10–13).
14 However, we do not perform a regression following the matching analysis (as Ho et al. 2007 recommend), as Abadie and Spiess (2019) state that this is inappropriate when matching is done with replacement as researchers obtain inaccurate standard error estimates.
15 In cases like this, a one-tailed significance test is more appropriate than a two-sided test because we are testing a directional hypothesis. Standard conventions of significance testing and reporting require that we report two-tailed statistical tests for matching analyses, and we follow those in the tables.
16 When this occurs, a one-tailed significance test is more appropriate to analyze than a two-sided one because we are testing a directional hypothesis. Nonetheless, we follow the standard conventions of significance testing and reporting those results for the matching analyses in our tables.
17 These increases are compared with those who reported never having posted about this movement.
18 One limitation of many matching analyses is that one can p-hack by changing the functional form of the matching routine to generate a set of results that confirms a researcher's theoretical expectations (Head et al. 2015).

References

Abadie, Alberto and Guido W. Imbens 2006. "Large Sample Properties of Matching Estimators for Average Treatment Effects." *Econometrica* 74(1): 235–267. https://doi.org/10.1111/j.1468-0262.2006.00655.x. Accessed online June 19, 2021.

Abadie, Alberto and Guido W. Imbens 2011. "Bias-Corrected Matching Estimators for Average Treatment Effects." *Journal of Business and Economic Statistics* 29(1): 1–11. https://doi.org/10.1198/jbes.2009.07333. Accessed online June 19, 2021.

Abadie, Alberto and Guido W. Imbens 2016. "Matching on the Estimated Propensity Score." *Econometrica* 84(2): 781–807. https://doi.org/10.3982/ECTA11293. Accessed online June 19, 2021.

Abadie, Alberto and Jann Spiess 2019. "Robust Post-Matching Inference." Forthcoming in the *Journal of the American Statistical Association*. https://doi.org/10.1080/01621459.2020.1840383. Accessed online June 19, 2021.

Abramowitz, Alan I. and Walter J. Stone 2006. "The Bush Effect: Polarization, Turnout, and Activism in the 2004 Presidential Election." *Presidential Studies Quarterly* 36(2): 141–154. https://doi.org/10.1111/j.1741-5705.2006.00295.x. Accessed online June 19, 2021.

Achen, Christopher H. and Larry M. Bartels 2016. *Democracy for Realists: Why Elections Do Not Produce Responsive Government*. Princeton, NJ: Princeton University Press.

Alter, Charlotte 2018. "The School Shooting Generation Has Had Enough." *Time* March 22. https://time.com/longform/never-again-movement/. Accessed online January 30, 2020.

Andone, Dakin 2018. "What You Should Know about the March for Our Lives." www.cnn.com/2018/03/21/us/march-for-our-lives-explainer/index.html. Accessed online December 13, 2019.

Barry, Colleen L., Daniel W. Webster, Elizabeth Stone, Cassandra K. Crifasi, Jon S. Veride, and Emma E. McGinty 2018. "Public Support for Gun Violence Prevention Policies among Gun Owners and Non-Gun Owners in 2017." *American Journal of Public Health* 108(7): 878–881. https://doi.org/10.2105/AJPH.2018.304432. Accessed online June 19, 2021.

Behr, Roy L. and Shanto Iyengar 1985. "Television News, Real-World Cues, and Changes in the Public Agenda." *Public Opinion Quarterly* 49(1): 38–57. https://doi.org/10.1086/268900. Accessed online June 19, 2021.

Birkland, Thomas A. 1998. "Focusing Events, Mobilization, and Agenda Setting." *Journal of Public Policy* 18(1): 53–74. https://doi.org/10.1017/S0143814X98000038. Accessed online June 19, 2021.

Birkland, Thomas A. and Regina G. Lawrence 2009. "Media Framing and Policy Change after Columbine." *American Behavioral Scientist* 52(10): 1405–1425. https://doi.org/10.1177/0002764209332555. Accessed online June 19, 2021.

Blackman, Josh and Shelby Baird 2014. "The Shooting Cycle." *Connecticut Law Review* 46(4): 1513–1579.

Blair, J. Pete and Katherine W. Schweit 2014. *A Study of Active Shooter Incidents in the United States between 2000 and 2013*. Texas State University and U.S. Department of Justice. Washington, DC: Federal Bureau of Investigation. www.fbi.gov/file-repository/active-shooter-study-2000-2013-1.pdf/view. Accessed online October 4, 2019.

Burns, Ronald and Charles Crawford 1999. "School Shootings, the Media, and Public Fear: Ingredients for a Moral Panic." *Crime, Law and Social Change* 32(2): 147–168. https://doi.org/10.1023/A:1008338323953. Accessed online June 19, 2021.

Campbell, Andrea L. 2002. "Self-Interest, Social Security, and the Distinctive Participation Patterns of Senior Citizens." *American Political Science Review* 96(3): 565–574. https://doi.org/10.1017/S0003055402000333. Accessed online June 19, 2021.

Campbell, Andrea. L. 2003. "Participatory Reactions to Policy Threats: Senior Citizens and the Defense of Social Security and Medicare." *Political Behavior* 25(1): 29–49. https://doi.org/10.1023/A:1022900327448. Accessed online June 19, 2021.

Campbell, Angus, Philip E. Converse, Warren E. Miller, and Donald E. Stokes 1960. *The American Voter Unabridged Edition*. Chicago, IL: University of Chicago Press.

Carmines, Edward G. and James A. Stimson 1989. *Issue Evolution: Race and the Transformation of American Politics*. Princeton, NJ: Princeton University Press.

Center for Homeland Defense and Security 2018. "CHDS K-12 School Shooting Database." www.chds.us/ssdb. Accessed online December 13, 2019.

Chong, Dennis and James N. Druckman 2007. "A Theory of Framing and Opinion Formation in Competitive Elite Environments." *Journal of Communication* 57(1): 99–118. https://doi.org/10.1111/j.1460-2466.2006.00331.x. Accessed online June 19, 2021.

Chuck, Elizabeth, Alex Johnson, and Corky Siemaszko 2018. "17 Killed in Mass Shooting at High School in Parkland, Florida." www.nbcnews.com/news/us-news/police-respond-shooting-parkland-florida-high-school-n848101. Accessed online December 13, 2019.

Chyi, Hsiang Iris and Maxwell McCombs 2004. "Media Salience and the Process of Framing: Coverage of the Columbine School Shootings." *Journalism and Mass Communication Quarterly* 81(1): 22–35. https://doi.org/10.1177/107769900408100103. Accessed online June 19, 2021.

Converse, Phillip 1964. "The Nature of Belief Systems in Mass Publics." In *Ideology and Its Discontents,* David E. Apter (Ed.). New York, NY: Free Press of Glencoe.

D'Agostino, Ralph B. 1998. "Propensity Score Methods for Bias Reduction in the Comparison of a Treatment to a Non-Randomized Control Group." *Statistics in Medicine* 17(9): 2265–2281. https://doi.org/10.1002/(SICI)1097-0258(19981015)17:19<2265::AID-SIM918>3.0.CO;2-B. Accessed online June 19, 2021.

Deutch, Gabby. 2019. "The School Shooting America Forgot." *The Atlantic.* www.theatlantic.com/education/archive/2019/05/santa-fe-texas-school-shooting-america-forgot/589552/. Accessed online December 13, 2019.

Diamond, Alexis and Jasjeet J. Sekhon 2013. "Genetic Matching for Estimating Causal Effects: A General Multivariate Matching Method for Achieving Balance in Observational Studies." *Review of Economics and Statistics* 95(3): 932–945. https://doi.org/10.1162/REST_a_00318. Accessed online June 19, 2021.

Eggers, Andrew C. and Jens Hainmueller 2009. "MPs for Sale? Returns to Office in Postwar British Politics." *American Political Science Review* 103(4): 513–533. https://doi.org/10.1017/S0003055409990190. Accessed online June 19, 2021.

Flavin, Patrick and John D. Griffin 2009. "Policy, Preferences, and Participation: Government's Impact on Democratic Citizenship." *Journal of Politics* 71(2): 544–559. https://doi.org/10.1017/S0022381609090458. Accessed online June 19, 2021.

Frattaroli, Shannon 2003. "Grassroots Advocacy for Gun Violence Prevention: A Status Report on Mobilizing a Movement." *Journal of Public Health Policy* 24(3–4): 332–354. https://doi.org/10.2307/3343381. Accessed online June 19, 2021.

Gelman, Andrew and Jennifer Hill 2007. *Data Analysis Using Regression and Multilevel/Hierarchical Models.* New York: Cambridge University Press.

Gendall, Philip and Benjamin Healey 2008. "Asking the Age Question in Mail and Online Surveys." *International Journal of Market Research* 50(3): 309–317. https://doi.org/10.1177/147078530805000303. Accessed online June 19, 2021.

Gimpel, James G., Frances E. Lee, and Joshua Kaminski 2006. "The Political Geography of Campaign Contributions in American Politics." *Journal of Politics* 68(3): 626–639. https://doi.org/10.1111/j.1468-2508.2006.00450.x. Accessed online June 19, 2021.

Graf, Nikki 2018. "A Majority of U.S. Teens Fear a Shooting Could Happen at Their School, and Most Parents Share Their Concern." Pew Research Center. www.pewresearch.org/fact-tank/2018/04/18/a-majority-of-u-s-teens-fear-a-shooting-could-happen-at-their-school-and-most-parents-share-their-concern/. Accessed online October 7, 2019.

Greene, William H. 2011. *Econometric Analysis.* 7th Ed. New York City, NY: Pearson Education.

Guggenheim, Lauren, S., Mo Jang, Soo Young Bae, and W. Russell Neuman 2015. "The Dynamics of Issue Frame Competition in Traditional and Social Media." *The Annals of the American Academy of Political and Social Science* 659(1): 207–224. https://doi.org/10.1177/0002716215570549. Accessed online June 19, 2021.

Head, Megan L., Luke Holman, Rob Lanfear, Andrew T. Kahn, and Michael D. Jennions 2015. "The Extent and Consequences of P-Hacking in Science." *Plos Biology* 13(3): e1002106. https://doi.org/10.1371/journal.pbio.1002106. Accessed online June 19, 2021.

Ho, Daniel E., Kosuke Imai, Gary King, and Elizabeth A. Stuart 2007. "Matching as Nonparametric Preprocessing for Reducing Model Dependence in Parametric Causal Inference." *Political Analysis* 15(3): 199–236. https://doi.org/10.1093/pan/mpl013. Accessed online June 19, 2021.

Hoffman, Lindsay H. 2006. "Is Internet Content Different After All? A Content Analysis of Mobilizing Information in Online and Print Newspapers." *Journalism and Mass Communication Quarterly* 83(1): 58–76. https://doi.org/10.1177/107769900608300105. Accessed online June 19, 2021.

Hogg, David and Lauren Hogg 2018. *#NeverAgain: A New Generation Draws the Line*. New York, NY: Random House.

Imbens, Guido W. and Donald B. Rubin 2015. *Causal Inference for Statistics, Social, and Biomedical Sciences: An Introduction*. New York, NY: Cambridge University Press.

Iyengar, Shanto 1996. "Framing Responsibility for Political Issues." *Annals of the American Academy of Political and Social Science* 546(1): 59–70. https://doi.org/10.1177/0002716296546001006. Accessed online June 19, 2021.

Iyengar, Shanto and Donald R. Kinder 1987. *News that Matters: Television and American Opinion*. Chicago, IL: University of Chicago Press.

Iyengar, Shanto, Mark D. Peters, and Donald R. Kinder 1982. "Experimental Demonstrations of the 'Not-So-Minimal' Consequences of Television News Programs." *American Political Science Review* 76(4): 848–858. https://doi.org/10.1017/S000305540018966X. Accessed online June 19, 2021.

Jamison, Peter, Joe Heim, Lori Aratani, and Marissa J. Lang 2018. "'Never Again!' Students Demand Action against Gun Violence in Nation's Capital." *The Washington Post*. March 24. www.washingtonpost.com/local/march-for-our-lives-huge-crowds-gather-for-rally-against-gun-violence-in-nations-capital/2018/03/24/4121b100-2f7d-11e8-b0b0-f706877db618_story.html. Accessed online January 30, 2020.

Kahne, Joseph and Benjamin Bowyer 2018. "The Political Significance of Social Media Activity and Social Networks." *Political Communication* 35(3): 470–493.

Kerbel, Matthew R. and Joel David Bloom 2005. "Blog for America and Civic Involvement." *The International Journal of Press/Politics* 10(4): 3–27. https://doi.org/10.1177/1081180X05281395. Accessed online June 19, 2021.

King, Gary, Christopher Lucas, and Richard A. Nielsen 2017. "The Balance-Sample Size Frontier in Matching Methods for Causal Inference." *American Journal of Political Science* 61(2): 473–489. https://doi.org/10.1111/ajps.12272. Accessed online June 19, 2021.

King, Gary, Robert O. Keohane, and Sidney Verba 1994. *Designing Social Inquiry: Scientific Inference in Qualitative Research*. Princeton, NJ: Princeton University Press.

Kosicki, Gerald M. 1993. "Problems and Opportunities in Agenda-Setting Research." *Journal of Communication* 43(2): 100–127. https://doi.org/10.1111/j.1460-2466.1993.tb01265.x. Accessed online June 19, 2021.

Ley, Barbara L. and Paul R. Brewer 2018. "Social Media, Networked Protest, and the March for Science." *Social Media and Society* 4(3): 1–12. https://doi.org/10.1177/2056305118793407. Accessed online June 19, 2021.

Loader, Brian D., Ariadne Vromen, and Michael A. Xenos 2014. "The Networked Young Citizen: Social Media, Political Participation and Civic Engagement." *Information, Communication and Society* 17(2): 143–150. https://doi.org/10.1080/1369118X.2013.871571. Accessed online June 19, 2021.

McGinty, Emma E., Daniel W. Webster, Marian Jarlenski, and Colleen L. Barry 2014. "News Media Framing of Serious Mental Illness and Gun Violence in the United States, 1997–2012." *American Journal of Public Health* 104(3): 406–413. https://doi.org/10.2105/AJPH.2013.301557. Accessed online June 19, 2021.

Merry, Melissa K. 2020. *Warped Narratives: Distortion in the Framing of Gun Policy*. Ann Arbor, MI: University of Michigan Press.

Miller, Joanne M. 2007. "Examining the Mediators of Agenda Setting: A New Experimental Paradigm Reveals the Role of Emotions." *Political Psychology* 28(6): 689–717. https://doi.org/10.1111/j.1467-9221.2007.00600.x. Accessed online June 19, 2021.

Mindich, David T. Z. 2004. *Tuned Out: Why Americans Under 40 Don't Follow the News*. New York, NY: Oxford University Press.

Moffett, Kenneth W. and Laurie L. Rice 2016. *Web 2.0 and the Political Mobilization of College Students*. Lanham, MD: Lexington Books.

Moffett, Kenneth W. and Laurie L. Rice 2018. "College Students and Online Political Expression in the 2016 Election." *Social Science Computer Review* 36(4): 422–439. https://doi.org/10.1177/0894439317721186. Accessed online June 19, 2021.

Muschert, Glenn W. and Dawn Carr 2006. "Media Salience and Frame Changing across Events: Coverage of Nine School Shootings, 1997–2001." *Journalism and Mass Communication Quarterly* 83(2): 747–766. https://doi.org/10.1177/107769900608300402. Accessed online June 19, 2021.

Nadeau, Richard, Richard G. Niemi, and Timothy Amato 1995. "Emotions, Issue Importance, and Political Learning." *American Journal of Political Science* 39(3): 558–574.

National Public Radio 2018. "Florida Governor Signs Package of New Gun Restrictions." www.npr.org/sections/thetwo-way/2018/03/09/592393010/florida-gov-rick-scott-signs-gun-package. Accessed online December 13, 2019.

Newman, Benjamin J. and Todd K. Hartman 2019. "Mass Shootings and Public Support for Gun Control." *British Journal of Political Science* 49(4): 1527–1553. https://doi.org/10.1017/S0007123417000333. Accessed online June 19, 2021.

Nichols, Austin 2007. "Causal Inference with Observational Data." *The Stata Journal* 7(4): 507–541. https://doi.org/10.1177/1536867X0800700403. Accessed online June 19, 2021.

Nicodemus, Diane M. 2004. "Mobilizing Information: Local News and the Formation of a Viable Political Community." *Political Communication* 21(2): 161–176. https://doi.org/10.1080/10584600490443868. Accessed online June 19, 2021.

Ozymy, Joshua. 2012. "The Poverty of Participation: Self-Interest, Student Loans, and Student Activism." *Political Behavior* 34(1): 103–116. https://doi.org/10.1007/sl1109-010-9154-5. Accessed online June 19, 2021.

Parker, Kim, Nikki Graf, and Ruth Igielnik 2019. "Generation Z Looks a Lot Like Millennials on Key Social and Political Issues." Pew Research Center www.pewsocialtrends.org/2019/01/17/generation-z-looks-a-lot-like-millennials-on-key-social-and-political-issues/. Accessed online February 12, 2019.

Pierce, John P. and Elizabeth A. Gilpin 2001. "News Media Coverage of Smoking and Health Is Associated with Changes in Population Rates of Smoking Cessation but Not Initiation." *Tobacco Control* 10(2): 145–153. http://dx.doi.org/10.1136/tc.10.2.145. Accessed online June 19, 2021.

Reny, Tyler T., Loren Collingwood, and Ali A. Valenzuela 2019. "Vote Switching in the 2016 Election: How Racial and Immigration Attitudes, Not Economics, Explain Shifts in White Voting." *Public Opinion Quarterly* 83(1): 91–113. https://doi.org/10.1093/poq/nfz011. Accessed online June 19, 2021.

Rosenstone, Steven J. and John Mark Hansen 2002. *Mobilization, Participation, and Democracy in America*. New York, NY: Pearson-Longman.

Sanchez, Ray 2018. "'My School Is Being Shot Up': The Massacre at Marjory Stoneman Douglas, Moment by Moment." www.cnn.com/2018/02/18/us/parkland-florida-school-shooting-accounts/index.html. Accessed online December 13, 2019.

Sekhon, Jasjeet S. 2011. "Multivariate and Propensity Score Matching Software with Automated Balance Optimization: The Matching Package for R." *Journal of Statistical Software* 42(7): 1–52.

Silva, Jason R. and Joel A. Capellan 2019. "A Comparative Analysis of Media Coverage of Mass Public Shootings: Examining Rampage, Disgruntled, Employee, School, and Lone-Wolf Terrorist Shootings in the United States." *Criminal Justice Policy Review* 30(9): 1312–1341. https://doi.org/10.1177/0887403418786556. Accessed online June 19, 2021.

Simmons, Erica. 2014. "Grievances Do Matter in Mobilization." *Theory and Society*. 43(5): 513–546. https://doi.org/10.1007/s11186-014-9231-6. Accessed online June 19, 2021.

Snow, David A. and Sarah A. Soule 2010. *A Primer on Social Movements*. New York, NY: W. W. Norton.

Stuart, Elizabeth A. 2010. "Matching Methods for Causal Inference: A Review and a Look Forward." *Statistical Science* 25(1): 1–21. https://doi.org/10.1214/09-STS313. Accessed online June 19, 2021.

Sveningsson, Malin 2015. "'It's Only a Pastime, Really': Young People's Experiences of Social Media as a Source of News about Public Affairs." *Social Media + Society* 1(2):. https://doi.org/10.1177/2056305115604855. Accessed online June 19, 2021.

Taylor, Alan. 2018. "Photos: Teenagers Demand 'Never Again' in an Age of Mass Shootings." *The Atlantic*. www.theatlantic.com/photo/2018/02/florida-gun-control-protests-photos/553883/. Accessed online January 30, 2020.

Verba, Sidney, Henry E. Brady, and Kay L. Schlozman 1995. *Voice and Equality: Civic Voluntarism in American Democracy*. Cambridge, MA: Harvard University Press.

Wallack, Lawrence, Liana Winett, and Amy Lee. 2005. "Successful Public Policy Change in California: Firearms and Youth Resources." *Journal of Public Health Policy* 26(2): 206–226. https://doi.org/10.1057/palgrave.jphp.3200022. Accessed online June 19, 2021.

Wallack, Lawrence, Liana Winett, and Linda Nettekoven 2003. "The Million Mom March: Engaging the Public on Gun Policy." *Journal of Public Health Policy* 24(3/4): 355–379. https://doi.org/10.2307/3343382. Accessed online June 19, 2021.

Willingham, A. J. and Dianne Gallagher 2018. "David Hogg Says Voices from Diverse Communities Need to Be a Focus If the #NeverAgain Movement Is to Succeed." CNN. www.cnn.com/2018/04/20/us/david-hogg-national-school-walkout-reaction-trnd/index.html. Accessed online October 7, 2019.

Wolfson, Andrew 2019. "A Year Later: Marshall County High School Shooting and the Prosecution." *Courier Journal*. www.courier-journal.com/story/news/crime/2019/01/17/marshall-county-high-school-kentucky-shooting-a-year-later/2593728002/. Accessed online October 4, 2019

Wozniak, Kevin H. 2017. "Public Opinion about Gun Control Post Sandy-Hook." *Criminal Justice Policy Review* 28(3): 255–278. https://doi.org/10.1177/0887403415577192. Accessed online June 19, 2021.

Yee, Vivian and Alan Blinder 2018. "National School Walkout: Thousands Protest Against Gun Violence across the U.S." *The New York Times.* www.nytimes.com/2018/03/14/us/school-Walkout. Accessed online August 9, 2019.

Zaller, John and Stanley Feldman 1992. "A Simple Theory of the Survey Response: Answering Questions versus Revealing Preferences." *American Journal of Political Science* 36(3): 579–616.

5
IMMIGRATION AND FAMILY SEPARATION

When Political Expression Fails to Expand Participation

Introduction

Although the United States is a nation of immigrants, most major influxes of immigrants from a particular country or region trigger an anti-immigrant backlash (Arnold 2011). This backlash often centers on perceived threats to American jobs, economic well-being, safety, or way of life (Simon and Alexander 1993). While in earlier generations immigrants from nations such as Ireland, Italy, and China faced significant prejudice, in recent years, this backlash has focused on immigrants from Mexico and Central America (Tichenor 2015).

Policy changes in the 1960s and 1970s, including an end to guest worker programs and strict limits on the number of people from Mexico and Central America who could legally migrate to the United States, made legal immigration to the United States from these nations increasingly difficult (Brick, Challinor, and Rosenblum 2011; Tichenor 2015). Yet, beginning in the 1970s, the United States also saw a significant and rapid increase in the number of immigrants from Mexico and Central America (Brick, Challinor, and Rosenblum 2011) fleeing various challenges including significant economic and political instability, civil wars, violence from warring cartels, extreme poverty, food insecurity, and natural disasters. With limited legal pathways available to them, individuals from Mexico, El Salvador, Guatemala, and Honduras made up an estimated 70% of the unauthorized immigrant population living in the United States in 2015 (Department of Homeland Security 2018). Like other waves of immigrants who came before them, they were seen by some current Americans as a threat to economic well-being and safety.

Donald Trump (2015) capitalized on these perceived threats when announcing his run for the presidency on June 16, 2015, when he stated:

DOI: 10.4324/9781003168898-6

> When Mexico sends its people, they're not sending their best. They're not sending you. They're not sending you. They're sending people that have lots of problems, and they're bringing those problems with us. They're bringing drugs. They're bringing crime. They're rapists. And some, I assume, are good people. But I speak to border guards and they tell us what we're getting. And it only makes common sense. It only makes common sense. They're sending us not the right people. It's coming from more than Mexico. It's coming from all over South and Latin America, and it's coming probably – probably – from the Middle East. But we don't know. Because we have no protection and we have no competence, we don't know what's happening. And it's got to stop and it's got to stop fast.

This emphasis helped successfully draw into his campaign coalition those who felt threatened by this latest wave of immigration and the changing demographics of the American public. As a candidate and then as president, Donald Trump proposed measures to stop the flow of unauthorized immigrants across the United States' southern border. Among these were building a wall on the U.S.-Mexico border, separating children from their parents if caught crossing the border illegally, and attempting to end DACA, a program through which young adults, brought by their parents to the United States illegally as children, could apply to stay in the United States for renewable two-year periods. Strongly supported by some, these measures, and especially the policy of family separation, also provoked significant backlash among those who viewed his policies as contrary to American values.

In this chapter, we consider how these differing views about immigration might shape political participation. We begin with an overview of young adult views on immigration, a border wall, family separation policies, and the DACA program. We then explore why strong support and strong opposition to family separation and the DACA program may lead to greater participation. As we have seen in previous chapters, threats – real or perceived – can motivate action, but opinions alone rarely translate into heightened civic engagement. However, both those who strongly supported family separation and those who strongly opposed it enough to post or protest about it are likely to be more civically engaged, but for different reasons. Perceived threats to self-interest and anxiety over immigration is one potential motivator of heightened participation levels. Group identification, empathy, and threats to core values is another. We draw on relevant academic literature to develop each potential pathway to higher levels of civic engagement. We then test whether speaking up about immigration policies online or through participating in protests increased young adults' levels of civic engagement.

Young Adults and Views on Immigration

A month before the 2018 midterm election, 65% of registered voters said immigration would be very important to their vote (Pew Research Center 2018b). Like

Americans as a whole, our survey shows that those aged 18–25 saw immigration as an important issue. Around 67% of our respondents either agreed or strongly agreed that they were concerned about the issue of immigration. In addition, a little under 60% of our respondents saw this issue as important or very important in the 2018 election.

Yet, also like Americans as a whole, our surveys suggest some deep divisions among young adults over specific immigration policies, especially when it comes to the border wall that then-President Trump proposed along the southern border of the United States. In 2018, 50.8% of our respondents strongly opposed a wall along the southern border while 23.5% strongly supported it. Meanwhile, just over 14% were in the middle, saying they neither supported it nor opposed it. Only about 10% expressed an opinion that was not strong and these were nearly evenly split between support of the wall and opposition to the wall. Clearly, the border wall was a polarizing issue among young adults, with extreme opinions far more likely than those in the middle. Figure 5.1 compares these results to those of a Gallup Poll of American adults taken in January 2019. Although some of the differences could be influenced by the time gap between the two surveys and the variations in question wording, the results suggest that young adults were both more likely to hold strong opinions on this issue and more likely to strongly oppose the wall than adults as a whole.

Another measure employed by the Trump administration to attempt to stop unauthorized immigration was to implement a zero-tolerance policy that separated more than 2,800 families crossing illegally, criminally charging the adults, and placing them in detention centers while putting children in separate facilities under the custody of Health and Human Services (Jervis and Gomez 2019). Even when families themselves chose to temporarily separate as some members

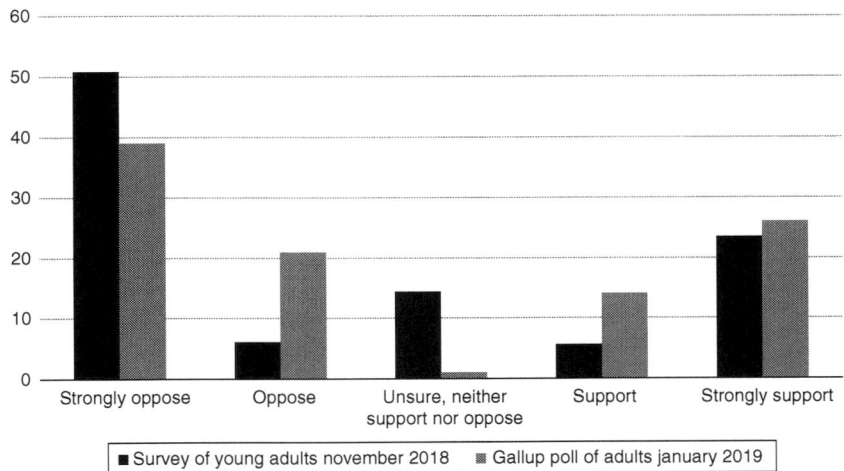

FIGURE 5.1 Opinions about a Border Wall.

immigrate while others stayed behind, this separation was found to produce negative consequences including social and emotional isolation (Martin 2017), depression (Letiecq et al. 2014), and even trauma (Rees et al. 2013). Forced separation might be expected to heighten these negative outcomes.

After public outcry, the policy officially ended in June 2018, although a limited number of family separations continued thereafter (Jervis and Gomez 2019). Nearly 63% of the respondents in our survey of young adults at the time of the 2018 midterm election expressed some level of opposition to this policy. This is about the same percentage reported in national polls at the time the policy was in full force. Specifically, 44.6% of young adult respondents strongly disapproved of the Trump administration policy of family separation, 18.3% disapproved of it, 14.8% neither approved nor disapproved, 14.8% approved, and 7.5% strongly approved. This suggests the most common stance among young adults was strong opposition while the least common opinion was strong approval.

In 2020, the importance of immigration was crowded out for many voters by more pressing issues like Covid-19 and the economy. Roughly two months before the 2020 election, 52% of Americans said immigration would be very important to their vote, a drop of 13% points from 2018 (Pew Research Center 2018b, 2020a). Our survey shows young adults were even less likely to see immigration as important in 2020, with just under 44% of respondents saying immigration was important or very important to their vote. Accordingly, immigration policy was not a major focus area in presidential debates and then-President Trump's border wall received far less attention in 2020 than it did in 2018.

Yet, the Trump administration's family separation policy returned to the news with just two weeks to go until the 2020 presidential election, as news reports emerged that 545 children, some of them under the age of five, remained separated from their parents despite the policy's end two years prior (Dickerson 2020). This provided an opportunity for views on this issue to spark last-minute electoral engagement. Yet our survey results suggest strong opposition to this policy shrunk substantially among young adults compared to 2018. While the percentage of young adults strongly opposed to the policy remained more than double of that who strongly supported it, overall more of our survey respondents expressed some level of support for the policy than those who expressed some level of opposition. This shift in opinion suggests lowered likelihood that this issue would spark widespread engagement among young adults in 2020.

Deferred Action for Childhood Arrivals

A more likely place to find young adult immigration-related engagement in 2020 may be over the status of the DACA policy. When then-President Trump first tried to end this Obama administration policy in 2017, young adults engaged in protests and participated in walkouts (Preston 2017; Stein 2017). Many young adults did so on behalf of themselves, and their peers threatened with deportation to a country they barely remembered. After all, two-thirds of those who would face potential deportation if the Obama administration's DACA policy ended were under the age of 25 (Lopez and Krogstad 2017), making young adults far more likely to have a friend who is a DACA recipient than members of other age groups.

Rather than end the policy immediately, then-Attorney General Jeff Sessions, announced in September 2017 that DACA was illegal and would be ended in six months, in order to give Congress time to find a solution (Hackman 2020). However, DACA recipients found redress in the Courts rather than from Congress. In January 2018, a federal district court ruled that the Trump administration must continue to accept DACA renewal applications, shielding DACA recipients, at least temporarily, from deportation, while the case made its way up to the Supreme Court (Hackman 2020). With the program temporarily spared, attention to this issue became less widespread. A search of the GDELT Television Explorer database for mentions of DACA, the results of which are displayed in Figure 5.2, shows that coverage dropped significantly after this ruling and spent much of 2019 at very low levels until the Supreme Court took up oral arguments in November. Media coverage of DACA returned to low levels until the anticipated Supreme Court decision neared in June 2020. As it returned to the spotlight, so, too, did activism among young adults.

When the Supreme Court rejected the Trump administration's rescinding of the program as "arbitrary and capricious," a small group of socially distanced young adult activists held up a celebratory sign on the steps of the Supreme Court (Totenberg

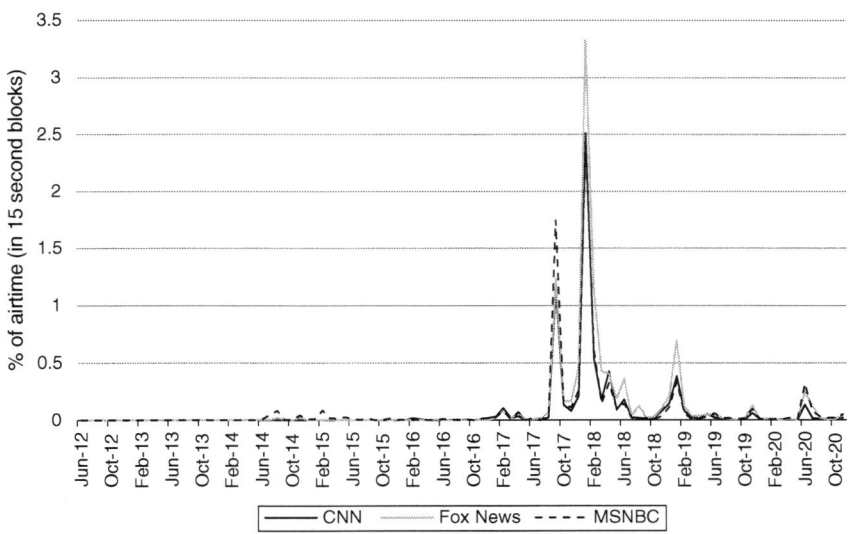

FIGURE 5.2 Media Coverage of DACA.
Source: GDELT Television Explorer Database.

2020b). They were not alone in their support of the ruling. In November 2020, 41.4% of young adults surveyed expressed support and 21.8% expressed strong support for the Supreme Court's decision that kept DACA intact, with just over two-thirds also expressing some level of support for the DACA program. Meanwhile, less than 14% of the young adults we surveyed expressed some level of opposition to the Court's decision and only 10% expressed some degree of opposition to the DACA program itself. In comparison, at the time of the Supreme Court decision, 40% of voters said they strongly supported the Supreme Court's DACA decision, 15% somewhat supported it, 12% somewhat opposed it, and 16% strongly opposed it (Easley 2020). While these surveys occurred several months apart, the difference in results suggests young adults may be far less likely than Americans across age groups to oppose the Court's decision that kept the program intact.

One reason for young adults' stronger support may be because young adults, given the age range of DACA recipients, are far more likely to know one of the more than 600,000 young people who benefit from this program. And, in the 2020 election, DACA recipients and those seeking DACA status urged their citizen peers to be their voice. For example, then 22-year-old college senior at University of Massachusetts, Boston, Estefany Pineda, was nervously refreshing her computer for news of the Supreme Court's decision and was relieved when she learned it meant she would be able to stay in the United States and complete her degree (Dooling, Atkins, and Larkin 2020). Then 20-year-old Luis Rodriguez, a community college student in the Chicago area, was hoping to apply for the DACA program for the first time, and registering people to vote in the 2020 election, telling reporters that while he could not vote, "every person that I get registered to vote is a vote for me, basically" (Malagon 2020). Similarly, then 18-year-old Daniele Chavira, a student at Grand Canyon University in Phoenix, worked phone banks to encourage voter registration among young people, stating, "Do it for someone who is struggling to fit in at college and trying to figure out if they are going to be here within the next four years" (Ishmael 2020).

Opinions about Immigration and Participation

While young adults were more likely to oppose Trump administration immigration policies than support them, there was division over these policies. Strong opinions about some policies are linked to greater participation levels (Flavin and Griffin 2009). This might suggest that the 52% with strong opinions about family separation in 2018, the 28% with strong opinions about family separation in 2020, and the nearly 28% with strong opinions about the DACA program in 2020 would be more civically engaged than their peers without strong opinions about these policies. On other policies, clear policy winners (those who supported the policy and thought it worked) and policy losers (those who opposed the policy and thought it ended up making things worse) increased their participation levels (Flavin and Griffin 2009). Though we did not measure young adults' perceptions of these policies, it suggests young adults on both sides of these issues might engage in heightened levels of activity.

Meanwhile, other research suggests that strong opposition to policies, such as young adults' opposition to the Iraq War, is associated with heightened civic engagement (Moffett, Rice, and Madupalli 2014). Thus, on at least some issues, increased participation is only seen among those who strongly oppose policies, not among those who strongly support them. If immigration policies are among these, then we would expect higher civic engagement levels among the 44.6% of young adult respondents who strongly disapproved of the Trump administration policy of family separation in 2018, the 19.4% who strongly opposed family separation in 2020, and the mere 3.4% of young adult respondents who strongly opposed the DACA program in 2020 compared to their peers with other opinions about these policies.

While previous research suggests both those who strongly opposed tough immigration policies and those who strongly favored them might be more likely to participate, the motivations behind this heightened engagement are distinct. We begin with what the literature says about those motivated by anxiety or fear over immigration and then contrast that with what the literature says about those motivated by group identification, empathy, or threats to values.

Immigration, Anxiety, Threats to Self-Interest, and Participation

People notice growth in immigrant communities more so than their current levels (Newman and Velez 2014), and immigrants from Mexico and Central America have increased substantially since the 1970s (Brick, Challinor, and Rosenblum 2011). While some welcome immigrants with open arms, others see them as potential threats. One reason for such variation in support stems from the way a policy is framed in the media or by politicians. For example, between 2007 and 2011, most major news outlets were more likely to describe plans that would allow undocumented immigrants to obtain legal status as "amnesty" than as a "path to citizenship," with the former frame significantly reducing support for such a policy (Merolla, Ramakrishnan, and Haynes 2013a). Another stems from prejudice. Ethnic stereotypes and racial hostility have been found to shape views on immigration policy (Citrin et al. 2001). Yet another reason is rooted in self-interest.

In recent years, undocumented immigrants have been commonly portrayed as both security threats and as threats to American jobs and economic well-being (Tichenor 2015). This threat-based narrative can trigger self-interest concerns and produce anxiety. Negative views about immigrants are associated with support for decreasing welfare programs and spending (Garand, XU, and Davis 2017). Even among Hispanic-Americans, those who see illegal immigrants as threats to their economic well-being are more likely to support policies that would decrease immigration (Hood, Morris, and Shirkey 1997). Meanwhile, when immigration is framed as a threat to security, people are more likely to see immigration as an important issue that needs to be addressed (Lahav and Courtemanche 2012).

Perceived threats such as these can trigger anxiety (Marcus, Neuman, and MacKuen 2000) and cause people to look for additional information about the cause of their anxiety (Valentino et al. 2008). However, information searches are often subject to confirmation bias, a tendency to seek out and pay attention to that information that helps confirm preexisting beliefs (Nickerson 1998). While anxiety can sometimes lead to openness to new information (Valentino et al. 2008), when there are waves of new immigrants, there is rarely a shortage of elite rhetoric or media coverage that emphasizes these immigrants as threats (Simon and Alexander 1993). Even coverage of immigration reform proposals may be more likely to take an anti-immigration stance. Content analysis of immigration reform coverage on English language national television news found that the coverage typically struck a neutral tone, but negative coverage far outweighed positive coverage of immigration (Abrajano and Singh 2009).

Thus, those prone to see immigrants as threats will be heavily exposed to information that helps reinforce their views and may gravitate to politicians that speak to these threats. For example, Republicans have used concern about immigration to pull some white voters away from the Democratic party, especially in states where Latinx populations are rapidly growing but not yet large enough where their countermobilization would likely sway election outcomes (Hajnal and Rivera 2014; Reny 2017).

Experimental research suggests exposure to stories about the cost of immigration also produces increased anxiety, worry, and anger, but only when the immigrants are portrayed as Latinx, not when they are portrayed as European (Brader, Valentino, and Suhay 2008). Then-President Trump's announcement speech, quoted earlier, tapped into this anxiety. This can be a powerful campaign strategy as research has found that during elections, when campaigns can trigger strong emotions like anxiety or anger, they heighten political participation (Marcus, MacKuen, and Neuman 2000; Valentino et al. 2011; Weber 2013). In addition, negative stories about Latinx immigrants can mobilize opposition to immigration, making individuals more likely to choose to send a message to Congress that immigration should be reduced (Brader, Valentino, and Suhay 2008). Thus, those concerned about immigration because they see it as a threat may be more likely to be more civically engaged.

Immigration, Group Identification and Empathy, Core Values, and Participation

In contrast, some people are concerned about immigration because of the way current policies treat immigrants. One source of this concern is group identification and empathy. For example, naturalized Latinx Americans are more likely to feel threatened by anti-immigrant sentiment and policy, even though they themselves are not undocumented, and these threatened individuals pay more attention to politics (Pantoja and Segura 2003). Identifying with a threatened group can also heighten involvement. Media coverage about immigration has been found to help mobilize Latinx political participation (Merolla et al. 2013b). Having friends who are immigrants is also associated with support for more liberal immigration policies (Knoll 2009). In addition, exposure to more positive coverage of immigration may lead to more positive views of immigrants. For example, Spanish language coverage of immigration reform proposals in 2004 was more positive toward immigrants and those who watched had more favorable views of them and of policies aimed at helping them (Abrajano and Singh 2009). Together, this research suggests that those who identify with immigrants, whether because of shared ethnic heritage, friendship with those with immigrant experiences, or the empathy sparked by positive media coverage, might be more likely to act to oppose anti-immigrant policies.

Another source of concern over the way current policies treat immigrants is the threat the treatment of undocumented immigrants may pose to core values. While those who self-identify as liberal are more likely to support multiculturalism (Citrin et al. 2001), views about immigration cross typical ideological and partisan lines. For example, a greater frequency of attending religious services, typically associated with more conservative viewpoints and support for the Republican party, is also associated with support for more liberal immigration policies (Knoll 2009). Among members of Judeo-Christian faiths, this may stem from core religious texts' emphasis on loving the stranger and the alien from other lands[1] or from the policy cues offered from the pulpit (Knoll 2009).

Values have been found to help shape behaviors, including activism (Miles 2015). If one views separating families crossing the border illegally as a threat to their deeply held values, they may be more likely to take action to oppose this policy. Similarly, if one views deporting young adults brought to this country illegally as young children back to countries of which they may have little to no memory, as threatening core values, they should be more likely to act to oppose deportations. In addition, both social identification with a group and altruistic concerns can generate heightened political participation (Fowler and Kam 2007). Thus, those concerned about immigration because they care about how immigrants are treated may also be more likely to be civically engaged.

Concern about Immigration and Getting Involved

Immigration is a complex issue that can trigger a variety of individual responses, ranging from strong opposition to strong support. In the previous sections, we established why opinions about immigration might help motivate people to participate. As a first test of this, we examined the mean level of civic engagement among individuals in our surveys with each level of concern about immigration during 2018 and 2020. In 2018, civic engagement was not necessarily clearly related to a specific stance on immigration. In 2020, however, mean civic engagement levels do increase with higher levels of concern about immigration. Both high anxiety about immigration or identification with the plight of immigrants might lead people to say they are concerned about immigration. Alternatively, some might say they are not concerned about immigration because they empathize with immigrants.

In addition to the level of concern about immigration, specific views on the policies of family separation or DACA might spark increased civic engagement. Since the literature offers competing explanations, we test whether those with strong opinions – both for and against – are associated with increased levels of engagement. Yet, as we saw in previous chapters, opinions alone do not guarantee action. Another way of measuring concern is to examine those concerned enough about immigration and family separation to post messages online about these topics or to engage in protests related to them. In the next sections, we consider how posting messages and protesting about immigration and family separation might result in higher levels of civic engagement.

Posting about Immigration and Family Separation and Civic Engagement

As we saw earlier in this chapter, 63% of the young adults in our survey expressed some level of opposition to family separation in 2018, with 44.6% of young adult respondents strongly disapproving of the Trump administration policy of family separation and 18.3% disapproving but not strongly. These individuals might post about immigration and family separation because they see this policy as a threat to core values or because they identify or empathize with the families separated at the border. Conversely, 22.3% expressed some level of support for the family separation policy, with 7.5% strongly approving and 14.8% approving but not strongly. These individuals might post about immigration and family separation because they see this policy as a way of stopping the perceived threat that immigration poses to their self-interest and reducing the anxiety they feel about immigration. Similarly, young adults who opposed DACA, though few in number, might post about this policy out of perceived threat or anxiety while the larger numbers who supported DACA might post about this policy because of the empathy they feel for their peers potentially threatened with deportation if the program were ended.

Regardless of an individual's views about this topic or the motivation behind them, posting them involves making them public to at least some degree. As we have argued in previous chapters, public commitment to a cause might lead to invitations to participate in other ways and heightened pressure to respond favorably to such invitations. For example, in addition to immigration-focused groups like United We Dream, a variety of groups with broader issue focuses acted to oppose the family separation policy including the American Civil Liberties Union (ACLU), Amnesty International USA, Human Rights Watch, and the National

Organization for Women (McCausland, Guadalupe, and Rosenblatt 2018; Joint Letter 2018).

When an individual posts online opposing family separation, they may become more likely to see pleas from these organizations related to family separation in their feeds or in online ads. If young adults see these and develop connections with organizations that encourage activism in a variety of ways on a variety of issues, then posting about immigration and family separation might serve as a pathway to heightened civic engagement more broadly. Yet, because the family separation policy was officially ended in June of 2018 after public protest that month (Jervis and Gomez 2019) and only returned to public attention weeks before the 2020 election due to news reports about government failures to reunite some children with their parents, this policy concern was settled more quickly than some of the other issues we have examined which remain ongoing. The limited timespan of controversy before the policy was successfully ended might limit the ability of posting about family separation to facilitate connections with organizations and individuals calling for additional actions compared to other policy debates with longer time horizons. If so, posting on this issue might not have the same positive impacts on civic engagement that we have seen on other issues.

However, even if connections to organizations failed to materialize, increases in efficacy might still produce a link between posting and heightened civic engagement. Political uses of social media such as posting one's views online increases efficacy, a precursor to online political participation (Yang and DeHart 2016) and heightened political participation more broadly (Gil de Zúñiga, Jung, and Valenzuela 2012). In addition, researchers found that on the issues of the Iraq War and Bush tax cuts, policy winners had increased levels of both efficacy and political participation (Flavin and Griffin 2009). When family separation ended in 2018, those who opposed the policy became policy winners. This policy win on the issue of family separation in 2018 might substantially boost efficacy among those who opposed the policy and in turn lead to heightened levels of civic engagement. Meanwhile, the news about the failure to reunite some of the separated children with their parents in 2020 might have increased dissatisfaction among those who opposed family separation and lead to increased civic engagement, similar to what Flavin and Griffin (2009) found occurred among policy losers on the issues of the Iraq War and the Bush tax cuts.

Thus, we hypothesize several potential causal pathways between posting about immigration and family separation and civic engagement, one via the connections that come through making one's views known online and the others via changes in efficacy or changes in dissatisfaction, depending on one's views of the policy. While we do not test these directly, if one or more is present, we should see a link between posting about immigration and family separation and heightened civic engagement. Thus, we explore whether being concerned enough about immigration and family separation to post a message about it in 2018 or 2020 (whether in support or opposition) results in higher levels of civic engagement.

Protesting about Immigration and Family Separation and Civic Engagement

Participating in a protest about immigration or family separation represents a far costlier commitment to this cause. Protests are likely to draw in those with particularly strong opinions and given both the distribution of young adult opinion on this issue and the makeup of protests regarding family separation policies, most young adults who joined in protests were likely to be strongly opposed to the policy of family separation. Publicly joining together to raise voices in protest against this policy might help boost efficacy, as people become connected to a larger movement and can see how their voices raised together made a difference. High political efficacy is a strong predictor of political participation (Pollock 1983), so if the efficacy link holds here, those who protested about immigration and family separation should engage in higher levels of civic and political activity.

In addition, those who protest have opportunities to meet others with similar views and commitment levels and become connected with additional organizations as well. For example, at one of the Families Belong Together protests against family separation on June 15 in Boston that brought together first-time protestors and seasoned activists, city council member and congressional candidate Ayanna Pressley noted to a reporter that:

> I am seeing many of the same people in multiple spaces in the resistance. The same people that are here today affirming that immigrant rights are human rights, I also saw testifying at the State House for criminal justice reform, I also saw at the women's march, I also see advocating for trans rights.
>
> *(Nierenberg 2018)*

This suggests activism can be contagious and lead to networks of activists across multiple issues.

Organized interest groups may help fuel this. For example, the over 600 "Families Belong Together" protests scattered across the country on June 30, 2018 seeking to reunite separated families, received funding and organizational support from groups like the ACLU and MoveOn.org as well as a variety of faith-based organizations (McCausland, Guadalupe, and Rosenblatt 2018). The new personal and organizational contacts protestors develop at protest events might actively encourage other forms of participation. If so, then participating in a protest on this issue might serve as a pathway to heightened levels of civic engagement more broadly, as protestors have already demonstrated their willingness to act.

Data

To test these hypotheses, we executed separate online surveys via Amazon's Mechanical Turk (mTurk) platform on the day after each of the 2018 (November

7) and 2020 (November 4) general elections. The survey population was Americans between 18 and 25 years old – an age range that includes both younger Millennials and older members of Generation Z.[2] This platform allows members of the public to earn money for completing an array of tasks, including participating in survey research. A total of 1,010 participants completed the survey after we eliminated any incomplete responses in 2018.[3] Also, 969 participants completed the survey after eliminating any incomplete responses in 2020. Each participant was paid $1.50 for completing each survey in 2018 and 2020.

Dependent Variable

The dependent variable is the extent to which each respondent participated in civic and political activities away from the internet. Through separate questions, each person was asked about the frequency of their engagement in an array of activities including making purchasing decisions based on a company's conduct or values, talking to people and explaining why they should vote for or against a specific candidate or party, and attending political functions in support of a candidate or party. To create a single measure of political and civic activity, we added the values for each of the 12 activities to produce an index that was based on answers to this set of questions ($\alpha = .92$, 2018; $\alpha = .95$, 2020). The means of this civic engagement index ($M = 14.56$, 2018; $M = 26.01$, 2020) are comparatively low as this indicates an activity level comparable to having done 4 of the 12 activities in this index very often in 2018, and 6 of the 12 activities in this index occurring very often in 2020. The standard deviations ($SD = 10.75$, 2018; $SD = 14.61$, 2020) indicate substantial variance around this mean. In this way, we have captured a range of participation levels in our survey.

To test our theoretical expectations, we employ a series of matching routines. This statistical technique allows us to match respondents who are similar with respect to a variety of variables known to influence participation levels and isolate the separate effects of our treatment variables on civic engagement. The online appendix contains the complete wording for each of the questions for the mTurk surveys in 2018 and 2020, along with additional information about the measurement of each variable that we used.

Treatment Variables

We use four treatment variables to test our hypotheses. To determine the effects of opinions about the Trump administration's implementation of the immigration and family separation policy, we asked each respondent about the extent to which they approved or disapproved of this policy implementation in both 2018 and 2020. Second, we asked each participant about the extent to which they approved or disapproved of the DACA program in 2020, but not in 2018. Both questions were measured on a five-point scale that ranged from strongly opposed to strongly supported.

To test our remaining hypotheses, we compute the effects of posting about immigration and family separation and participating in protests related to this issue on civic engagement. Using separate questions, we asked each respondent about the extent to which they posted about immigration or family separation, or participated in protests related to this issue in both 2018 and 2020. The response options were never, posted once, posted two or three times, and posted four or more times.

Matching Covariates

We used two variables to query the effects of political engagement away from the internet. First, we asked each respondent about the extent to which they are interested in politics on a four-point scale that ranged from four points for "Very interested" to zero points for "Not at all interested." Second, each respondent was asked three questions about the extent to which their friends engaged in a set of activities. From these responses we created an additive index of peer civic activities ($\alpha = .63$, 2018; $\alpha = .58$, 2020).[4,5]

In addition, we used several variables to investigate the effects of political engagement using the internet. First, each respondent was asked how frequently they read news on the internet about politics. Second, we asked each respondent how often they read blogs online about politics. Kerbel and Bloom (2005) and Moffett and Rice (2018) find that blogs can act as outlets that foster enhanced civic activity, either online or offline.

Third, we constructed an additive index of online civic activity composed of five items, as several researchers have unearthed a link between activities on social media and offline civic engagement (see e.g., Kahne and Bowyer 2018; Ley and Brewer 2018; Loader, Vromen, and Xenos 2014). We asked each respondent about the extent to which they had relied on social media for news, posted about politics on social media, read social media feeds about politics, liked or shared posts about politics on social media, or read or watched posts about politics on social media and summed the values of these responses ($\alpha = .84$, 2018; $\alpha = .83$, 2020).[6]

Fourth, each respondent was asked a series of questions about the extent to which they posted messages on social media about Supreme Court nominations (Kavanaugh in 2018, Barrett in 2020), gun control, the MeToo movement, Black Lives Matter (in 2020, but not in 2018), and about other issues. Fifth, each respondent was asked a set of questions about the extent to which they participated in protests related to Supreme Court nominations (Kavanaugh in 2018, Barrett in 2020), Black Lives Matter (in 2020, but not in 2018), gun control, the MeToo movement, and about other issues.

We considered the effects of issue importance, as issues can sometimes facilitate higher levels of political participation (Converse 1964; Carmines and Stimson 1989; Reny, Collingwood, and Valenzuela 2019) by asking each respondent about the importance of congressional stances on gun control in influencing their vote choice.

Moreover, we employed many variables to account for the effects of personal characteristics on offline civic activity. First, we examined the effects of ideology on civic engagement, as Achen and Bartels (2016) discover that self-identifying as either conservative or liberal shapes political participation. Respondents who identified as moderate, something else, or did not know were then asked whether that person self-identified as a conservative or liberal if they had to choose. We then created a binary for liberals.

Second, we measured the strength of partisan attachment and created a binary for strong partisans, as this attachment is associated with an array of other political activities (see e.g., Flavin and Griffin 2009; Verba, Brady, and Schlozman 1995). Third, we asked each respondent for their sex, and we coded this variable one for females, two for males, and three for those who self-identified in another category. Fourth, we acquired data on each respondent's age by asking each to report their month and year of birth. Then, we computed each respondent's age based on the month and year of the 2018 midterm election for 2018 and the 2020 presidential election for 2020.[7] Fifth, we asked each respondent for their race and collapsed that information into a binary that is coded one for whites and zero otherwise. Sixth, we asked each respondent for their level of education.

What is more, we used four variables to control for the effects of underlying political attitudes, as these can affect participation patterns. First, we asked each respondent whether they approved or disapproved of the job that Donald Trump is doing as president, as presidential approval is associated with changes in participatory patterns (Abramowitz and Stone 2006).[8] Second, we asked each respondent separate questions about whether they self-identified as a supporter of the MeToo movement, and whether they self-identified as a Black Lives Matter supporter.[9,10] Finally, we asked each respondent about their opinions about Brett Kavanaugh's nomination in 2018 and Amy Coney Barrett's nomination in 2020 using a five-point scale that ranged from strongly opposed to strongly supported.

Methods

To investigate whether both treatment variables are connected with offline civic activity, we use a matching analysis to compute the ATET. We use a matching estimator for several reasons. First, a lot of regression-based techniques (including OLS) assume that there exists a linear relationship between the predictor and response variables (see Greene 2011). Our theory posits a positive relationship between the treatment variables and civic engagement, but makes no prediction about the remaining response options contained in any treatment variable. Thus, the phenomenon that we examine is nonlinear by construction and is not appropriate to investigate using a method that assumes linearity (like OLS).

Fortunately, matching analyses do not assume linearity, allow for a more flexible functional form, and have several other statistical attributes that make them a more appropriate choice to test the hypotheses in this chapter (Imbens and Rubin 2015).

In addition, individuals have differing likelihoods of posting about immigration or family separation, participating in protests related to that issue, holding varying opinions about Trump's implementation of the immigration and family separation policy, or holding varying opinions about the DACA program. OLS estimators presume treatment homogeneity, which is unlikely to hold in any of these analyses. It is likely that individuals have different treatment effects, particularly depending on the extent to which they posted about immigration or family separation or participated in protests related to it, depending on the opinion that they hold about Trump's implementation of the family separation and immigration policy, or depending on the opinion that they have about the DACA program (see Abadie and Imbens 2011).

Thus, the effects of participating in protests related to immigration or family separation or posting about it vary depending on the frequency with which one has participated in protests related to this topic or posted about it. For instance, those who posted more frequently about family separation or immigration may be more apt to engage in offline civic activities more frequently than one who has never posted about this subject. In a similar vein, those who participated in protests related to family separation or immigration more frequently may tend to engage in higher levels of offline civic engagement more frequently than one who has never participated in protests related to this issue. In addition, to the extent that opinions lead to action, we expect that those who have strong opinions about either Trump's implementation of the immigration and family separation policy or the DACA program are apt to engage in offline civic activities more frequently than those who lack strong opinions.

By construction, OLS-based estimators assume that we observe a linear, homogeneous relationship between posting about immigration or family separation, participating in protests related to it, opinions about Trump's implementation of the family separation policy, or opinions about the DACA program and offline civic engagement. Matching-based approaches deal effectively with this issue because they assume neither homogeneity nor linearity (Imbens and Rubin 2015). Rather, matching-based approaches yield several treatment estimates depending on the level of treatment that a respondent received (Imbens and Rubin 2015). Thus, we can generate several, more accurate estimates of the effect that each level of each treatment level had on civic engagement.

Moreover, OLS does not permit us to estimate what happens to offline civic activity in the absence of posting about immigration or family separation, participating in protests related to it, opinions about Trump's implementation of the family separation policy, or opinions about the DACA program (Nichols 2007). Matching analyses use the existing data to generate a dataset that includes observations that are as alike as possible, given the values of the remaining predictors (Stuart 2010). Thus, we can estimate what would have happened had specific respondents not posted about family separation or immigration, participated in protests related to it, or held opinions about Trump's implementation of the family separation policy, or opinions about the DACA program (see Gelman and Hill 2007). Then, we can use this dataset to estimate the effects of differing frequencies of posting about immigration or family separation, participating in protests related to it, opinions about Trump's implementation of the family separation policy, or opinions about the DACA program. We iterate this procedure for each level of each of the three treatment variables. Finally, if we used OLS estimates to obtain the results, our results are highly likely to be biased because any estimate of the treatment effect is conditioned on the values of the remaining independent variables. Consequently, OLS-based approaches do not compute ATETs.

Matching analyses contend well with each of these issues because they let us examine whether differing levels of posting about immigration or family separation, participating in protests related to it, opinions about Trump's implementation of the family separation policy, or opinions about the DACA program are connected with higher levels of civic engagement. By matching based on each of the predictors to make inferences, we can disentangle the effects of posting about this issue (or participating in protests related to it), opinions about Trump's implementation of the family separation policy, or opinions about the DACA program beyond people's other inclinations to civically participate. Doing so enables us to compare people with similar inclinations to civic activity who only vary in their opinions about Trump's implementation of the immigration or family separation policy, opinions about the DACA program, or the extent to which they posted about or participated in protests related to this topic. Moreover, matching allows us to calculate ATETs for each treatment level, and by doing so, to calculate more precise effect estimates with observational data.

Assumptions

Before performing our matching analyses, we must meet four assumptions. The validity of any matching analyses hinges on satisfying these assumptions. First, we presume that both sets of treatment variables are binary. To make our first treatment variable binary, we generated a series of dichotomous variables for each response option, relative to never having posted about immigration and family separation. These binaries are coded one for each of these categories, zero for never having posted about this issue, and missing for those who declined to answer the question, and for the remaining scalar options. There are three binaries for posting once, posting two or three times, and for having posted four or more times about this issue. For instance, the binary for having posted once about this issue is coded one for those who did so, zero for never having done so, and missing for those who declined to answer this question, and for those who reported having posted more than once. We follow an analogous procedure for having participated in protests related to immigration and family separation, as that variable is measured in the same manner.

To make the final sets of treatment variables binary, we generated a series of dichotomous variables for each response option, relative to neither supporting nor opposing then-President Trump's implementation of the family separation policy. Separately, we generated a series of binaries for each response option, relative to neither supporting nor opposing the DACA program. These binaries are coded one for each of these categories, zero for neither supporting or opposing, and missing for those who declined to answer each question, and for the remaining scalar options. For instance, there are four binaries for strongly opposing, opposing, supporting, and strongly supporting Trump's implementation of the immigration and family separation policy. The binary for having strongly opposed Trump's implementation of the immigration and family separation policy is coded one for those who held that opinion, zero for neither supporting nor opposing that policy implementation, and missing for those who declined to answer this question, and for those who had opposed, supported, or strongly supported that policy implementation. We perform an analogous implementation for varying opinions about the DACA program. We expect positive signs for all ATETs that we estimate in this chapter.

Second, we assume common support (or overlap), which means that it is possible that treated units may face an intervention that could have assigned them to the control group (see Imbens and Rubin 2015; King, Lucas, and Nielsen 2017). The data that we use meet this requirement because all respondents could have chosen not to post about immigration and family separation, participate in protests related to this issue, or alternatively, not to have an opinion about this policy implementation.

Third, we must fulfill the SUTVA assumption, which means that "the potential outcomes for any unit do not vary with the treatments assigned to other units, and for each unit, there are no different forms or versions of each treatment level, which lead to different potential outcomes" (Imbens and Rubin 2015, 10). We have met the first part of this assumption because the possible outcomes for civic activity do not vary with the levels of posting about immigration or family separation, with participating in protests related to this issue, with opinions about Trump's implementation of the immigration and family separation policy, or with opinions about the DACA program.[11]

The second aspect of this assumption is more intricate because we have different variations on our treatment variable, as variations exist with respect to posting once, posting two or three times, and posting four or more times about immigration or family separation. Yet, we can compare the effects of having posted with varying frequencies about this issue relative to those who never did so. For example, we can compare those who posted once about this issue to those who never did so, provided that we exclude those who posted at all other frequencies from that analysis.[12] We have to perform an analogous procedure to compare those who had posted two or three times and those who posted four or more times about this issue if we hope to perform a matching analysis without an alternative treatment. We perform a substantially similar procedure with respect to our other treatment variable, participating in protests related to immigration or family separation, as we measure it using the same scale as our posting measure. When we compute our ATETs in this manner, we ultimately satisfy the SUTVA assumption because we have neither interference nor any hidden variations of the treatments (Imbens and Rubin 2015, 10–11).

For our remaining treatment variables, though, the variations are slightly different: strongly oppose, oppose, support, and strongly support. Nonetheless, we can compare the effects of having a directional opinion about Trump's implementation of the immigration and family separation policy to those who neither disapproved nor approved of this policy implementation, or about the DACA program. We must perform an equivalent procedure to compare those who had opposed, supported, or strongly supported this policy implementation or the DACA program if we hope to execute a matching analysis without an alternative treatment.

Finally, the treatment assignment must be conditionally independent of the outcome variable given a set of matching covariates (D'Agostino 1998, 2266). Thus, each respondent's assignment to treatment (i.e., posting about immigration and family separation, participating in protests related to it, opinions about Trump's implementation of the immigration and family separation policy, or opinions about the DACA program) is unconnected with their level of civic engagement, given the values of the remaining explanatory variables. We observe greatly varied participatory levels with respect to civic activity, and the mean level of civic activity is fairly low (14.56, 2018; 26.01, 2020), given the minimum (0) and maximum values (48) possible with this index. Moreover, the activities that comprise offline civic activity do not cause an individual to be assigned to one or more treatment categories.

Matching Technique

Once we have met the statistical assumptions that underlie matching, we must select a method by which to perform this type of analysis. To perform our matching analyses, we use one-to-one genetic matching with replacement (Diamond and Sekhon 2013; Sekhon 2011). We incorporate a propensity score into the analysis, as knowing estimated values of this score meaningfully improves the accuracy of this method (Diamond and Sekhon 2013). Propensity score matching allows us to compare observations that are otherwise similar across other predictors, but have experienced different treatments. We perform our analysis with replacement, as matching discrepancies are reduced because we can use untreated units as a match multiple times (see Abadie and Imbens 2006).[13] To remove any bias that results

146 Posting, Protesting, and Civic Engagement

due to the choice of the matching estimator without affecting the variance of that estimator, we employ a bias correction (Abadie and Imbens 2016).

Results

Before we discuss the results, we must analyze how similar the treatment and control groups are to one another (King, Lucas, and Nielsen 2017). If these groups are substantially dissimilar, then we cannot use matching to estimate ATETs. The imbalance statistics for the models in Tables 5.1 and 5.2 are contained in Tables A1 through A14 in the online appendix. In 2018, for 86.83% (or 196/226) of all of the variables contained in the models in Table 5.1 and 5.2, the KS tests are not significant at the .05 level after matching has occurred. And, 19 of the remaining 30 cases where the KS tests are significant involve issues that were explored in other chapters, including the MeToo Movement (Chapter 2), Brett Kavanaugh's nomination (Chapter 3), and gun control (Chapter 4). The remaining 11 cases are randomly distributed across the differing models and have no systematic component that underlies them.

In 2020, for 74.56% (or 269/356) of the variables contained in the models in Tables 5.1 and 5.2, the KS tests are not significant at the .05 level after matching has happened. About 36 of the remaining 87 cases where the KS tests are significant involve issues that we examined in other chapters, including the MeToo movement (Chapter 2), Amy Coney Barrett's nomination (Chapter 3), gun control (Chapter 4), and Black Lives Matter (Chapter 6). Thus, we can be confident that we have substantially reduced imbalance across the model specifications. The matched groups have similar enough observable characteristics such that we can attribute any remaining differences across levels of posting about immigration and family separation to the effects of posting, not to preexisting differences. Similarly, we can attribute any remaining differences across levels of participating in protests about immigration and family separation to the effects of participating in protests, not to preexisting differences. Also, we can attribute any remaining differences across varying opinions about Trump's implementation of immigration and family separation policies to the effects of that policy implementation, not to preexisting differences. Finally, we can attribute any differences that remain across varying opinions about the DACA program to the effects of those opinions, not to previously existing differences.

We provide the results from the matching routines in Tables 5.1 and 5.2. The results for protesting in Table 5.1 indicate that there is no statistically significant relationship between any level of participating in protests related to immigration or family separation in either 2018 or 2020 and civic engagement. Further, the results in Table 5.2 indicate that there is no statistically significant connection between opinions about the DACA program and civic engagement in 2020.

In addition, the results from Table 5.1 demonstrate that there was no statistically significant relationship between posting about immigration and family separation

TABLE 5.1 Civic Engagement and Posting and Protesting about Immigration and Family Separation

	Posting about Immigration and Family Separation						Protesting about Immigration and Family Separation					
	2018			2020			2018			2020		
	Once	Two or Three Times	Four or More Times	Once	Two or Three Times	Four or More Times	Once	Two or Three Times	Four or More Times	Once	Two or Three Times	Four or More Times
Effect on Offline Civic Engagement	-.896	2.200	-1.531	2.494	3.056	30.571	.476	1.822	5.150	-2.164	1.465	3.272
Abadie-Imbens Standard Error	1.473	2.133	2.421	3.873	13.479	5.802	2.772	4.611	4.160	2.756	1.976	2.064
95% Confidence Interval Lower Bound	-3.820	-2.032	-6.344	-5.240	-23.673	19.008	-5.118	-7.506	-3.557	-7.682	-2.469	-.893
95% Confidence Interval Upper Bound	2.028	6.432	3.282	10.228	29.785	42.134	6.070	11.150	13.857	3.353	5.399	7.437
T-Statistic	-.608	1.032	-.632	.644	.227	5.269	.172	.395	1.238	-.777	.742	1.585
P-Value (two-tailed)	.543	.302	.527	.520	.821	1.373×10^{-7}	.864	.693	.216	.437	.458	.113
P-Value (one-tailed)	.272	.151	.264	.260	.411	6.865×10^{-9}	.432	.347	.108	.219	.229	.057
N	97	102	86	66	105	75	43	40	20	58	79	43

Notes: In each three-column set, the number of times that one has posted or protested about immigration and family separation is compared with one who has never done so about that subject. Second, the covariates on which the matching is based are described in the text. Third, the effects on offline civic engagement are the ATET. Finally, the matching results are from 1:1 genetic matching with post-matching bias adjustment. Thus, the N represents the matched number of observations.

TABLE 5.2 Civic Engagement and Opinions about Family Separation and DACA

	Opinions about Family Separation								Opinions about DACA			
	2018				2020				2020			
	Strong Opposition	Opposition	Support	Strong Support	Strong Opposition	Opposition	Support	Strong Support	Strong Opposition	Opposition	Support	Strong Support
Effect on Offline Civic Engagement	-4.235	2.245	.882	.866	-14.275	9.955	.158	1.029	-1.000	-3.943	-.463	.516
Abadie-Imbens Standard Error	2.159	1.719	2.181	2.418	4.709	5.476	1.688	3.440	3.064	4.457	1.704	1.740
95% Confidence Interval Lower Bound	-8.484	-1.616	-3.467	-4.026	-23.608	-.964	-3.181	-5.989	-7.465	-13.071	-3.828	-2.931
95% Confidence Interval Upper Bound	.014	5.650	5.231	5.758	-4.942	20.874	3.497	8.047	5.465	5.185	2.902	3.963
T-Statistic	-1.961	1.307	.404	.358	-3.031	1.818	.094	.299	-.277	-.863	-.272	.296
P-Value (two-tailed)	.050	.191	.686	.720	.002	.061	.925	.765	.781	.388	.786	.767
P-value (one-tailed)	.025	.096	.343	.360	.001	.031	.463	.383	.391	.194	.393	.384
N	284	116	72	40	109	72	133	32	18	29	163	114

Notes: In each four-column set, the opinion about Family separation or DACA is compared with one who neither supported nor opposed the policy. Second, the covariates on which the matching is based are described in the text. Third, the effects on offline civic engagement are the ATET. Finally, the matching results are from 1:1 genetic matching with post-matching bias adjustment. Thus, the N represents the matched number of observations and civic activity in 2018. Moreover, the results from Table 5.1 in 2020 indicate that there is a statistically significant relationship between posting four or more times about immigration and family separation and civic engagement. Those who posted four or more times about this subject are connected with an approximately 31-point increase in civic engagement. This is the equivalent of participating in seven activities very often that otherwise would have occurred, plus three other activities at one level higher.

The results for views on immigration and family separation shown in Table 5.2 are more intricate. In 2018, the results point to what appears to be a statistically significant relationship between strongly opposing then-President Trump's implementation of the immigration and family separation policy and higher levels of civic engagement. More specifically, strongly opposing Trump's implementation of the family separation and immigration policy may be associated with a more than four-point *decrease* in civic activity. This is the equivalent of not performing one activity at all that previously would have happened very often, or not performing multiple activities that would have been performed at some level.

In 2020, the results indicate a statistically significant relationship between opposition to Trump's implementation of the immigration and family separation policy and civic engagement. More specifically, strong opposition to Trump's implementation of the immigration and family separation policy is connected to a 14-point decrease in civic engagement. This is the equivalent of not participating in three activities that otherwise would have happened very often and two activities at lesser levels than otherwise would have happened. Further, opposition to Trump's implementation of the immigration and family separation policy is associated with a ten-point increase in civic activity, when we use a one-sided test of statistical significance ($p = .031$).[14] This is equivalent to participating very often in two activities that otherwise would not have happened, and two other activities at higher levels than otherwise would have occurred. If the results for strong opposition in both 2018 and 2020 withstand closer empirical examination, this would provide evidence that directly counters the theoretical expectation in this chapter.

To provide this empirical scrutiny for the results in this section, we need to verify whether those results that we have obtained are model dependent by removing one matching covariate at a time from each of the models (Ho et al. 2007). Then, we re-ran the matching routines with the remaining predictors in each model.[15] When we examine the models in those tables relative to what we report here, 80.92% (or 471/582) of the models contained results that mirrored those that we report in Tables 5.1 and 5.2. The complete set of robustness checks is available in the online appendix.

In 2018, the remaining cases are concentrated when examining the relationship between strongly opposing Trump's implementation of the family separation and immigration policy and civic engagement. When we more closely examine this relationship, 18 out of 22 (or 81.82%) of the models contain results that contradict what appears to be a finding against our theoretical expectations in Table 5.2. Thus, the results from the model for having strongly opposed Trump's implementation of the immigration and family separation policy should be interpreted skeptically and conservatively. When we utilize this interpretation, we cannot conclude that a statistically significant relationship exists between strongly opposing then-President Trump's implementation of the family separation policy in 2018 and civic engagement.[16]

A more involved story, however, emerges when we examine the results from posting in Table 5.1 in 2020, where only 46.15% (or 36/78) of the models contained results that mirror those that we report in the table. In addition, 29 of the 42 results (or 69.04%) that diverge from what is contained in the table involve models for posting three times or less about immigration or family separation. Since the models that we report contain null results with these frequencies in 2020, the most conservative practice is to conclude that no relationship exists with respect to posting three or fewer times. However, a slim majority (14/27, or 51.85%) of the models in the checks and in Table 5.1 for posting four or more times in 2020 contains results that are consistent with what we report here. Thus, we can conclude, albeit not particularly strongly, that posting four or more times about immigration or family separation in 2020 is connected with higher levels of civic engagement.

Conclusion

We find limited evidence that posting about immigration or family separation in 2020 is connected with any change in civic activity. Only those who posted four or more times, suggesting a strong commitment to this cause, exhibited significantly higher levels of civic engagement. In addition, we find mixed evidence that opposition to the Trump administration's implementation of the family separation policy in 2020 is connected with changes in civic activity. On the one hand, strong opposition is associated with lower levels of civic engagement, yet opposition is connected with increases in civic activity. At first glance, it seems puzzling why strong opposition would be associated with significantly lower levels of civic engagement while opposition would be associated with significantly higher levels of civic engagement. One factor that may help explain this is that up until two weeks before the presidential election, it appeared that the family separation policy had been successfully ended. Before that point, there would not have been a perceived need to take any action related to a defunct policy.

Yet, as news reports emerged that 545 children remained separated from their parents two years after the policy's end (Dickerson 2020), suddenly the need for action reemerged. Why did those strongly opposed to the policy respond differently from those opposed to the policy? One potential answer may lie in a theory introduced in the previous chapter involving the necessity of having hope to act in response to a perceived threat (Nadeau, Niemi, and Amato 1995). One reason

Immigration and Family Separation   151

for young adults being against family separation is the threat it poses to core values. Those who strongly opposed family separation may have been more likely to lose hope by the news that so many children remained separated from their parents. The distressing news may have further discouraged them from being involved in the last two weeks before the election. Yet, it is possible that those opposed but not strongly so retained hope that change was possible and chose to engage in additional civic activity.

Moreover, protesting about immigration and family separation in both 2018 and 2020 and opinions about the DACA program are not connected with increases in civic activity. We note that this does not necessarily indicate that young adult participation related to these causes did not matter, a topic we visit in Part II of this book. In most cases, though, it appears that participation on this issue failed to extend young adult civic engagement more broadly construed.

Three issues may contribute to the null findings in this chapter. First, there were more salient and recent issues that drove participation among most young people in 2018: the emergence of the MeToo movement in early 2018 and Brett Kavanaugh's nomination. Similarly, there were more salient issues in 2020, like Black Lives Matter among young voters. Second, compared to the MeToo movement and Supreme Court nominations, policy battles over immigration and family separation, as well as over gun violence, brought together narrower issue-specific coalitions. While the coalition opposing immigration and family separation was broader than the one involving gun violence, it was still not nearly as broad as the coalitions that form for and against Supreme Court nominations. These narrower coalitions may be more successful at issue-specific mobilization than they are at broadening participation. Meanwhile, issues that bring together members of diverse interest groups with their own normally distinct agendas, like Supreme Court nominations and the MeToo movement, might be more effective at helping expand civic engagement across issues while also encouraging issue-specific mobilization. Third, the family separation policy was ended in response to public protest in June 2018 and it was not until two weeks before the 2020 election that the policy returned to the news. The policy's quick official end left only a very limited time window when additional action was needed in 2018 and 2020, limiting the opportunities for action on this issue, whether through posting or protesting, to spill over into other forms of civic engagement. In the next chapter, we examine another phenomenon: the reemergence of Black Lives Matter in 2020 in light of the protests that occurred surrounding race and policing in America.

Notes

1 For a sampling of Bible verses on this topic, see: https://sojo.net/22-bible-verses-welcoming-immigrants.
2 These generations have similar views on social issues (Parker, Graf, and Igielnik 2019).

3 We constrained the eligibility of participants in this survey to those whose location is in the United States and whose HIT approval rates are at least 95%. While we could not constrain by age here, we did so through the first question asking respondents whether they were between the ages of 18 and 25. If they responded no, then the survey ended.
4 These were the only questions in the survey about peer civic experiences. Some participants responded that they did not know for one or more of these questions. When constructing our index, we coded values for these variables as missing. Consequently, no peer civic engagement score is present for those who answered "don't know" on a minimum of one of these questions.
5 This also acts as an indirect indicator with respect to mobilization, as people frequently act politically when others around them do so (see e.g., Gimpel, Lee, and Kamiski 2006). Yet, it is possible that mobilization efforts by those other than peers, like interest groups and political parties, also yield higher levels of participation (Rosenstone and Hansen 2002). There are no questions in this survey that allow us to directly account for the effects of mobilization on civic activity. That said, we do consider many other covariates that also affect mobilization as part of the matching routines in this analysis.
6 We employed an adapted version of this variable for the models in which the treatment variable is posting about immigration and family separation, as we cannot have the treatment variable being essentially the same as an element of one of the matching covariates. More specifically, we removed posting about politics on social media from the online civic engagement index for this set of models because the treatment for the set of models examining the effects of posting about gun control is the extent to which one posted about this issue. We retained the remaining variables that comprise the online civic engagement index and created an additive index based on those (α = .81).
7 We asked an initial screening question that identified those who were between the ages of 18 and 25, and those who responded that they were not were excluded from the survey. When we performed the age computations based on the month and year that respondents identified, though, there were 49 respondents who reported that they were older than 25. In the month-year calculation, there was typically about a six-month variance between the reported and actual age among those 49 respondents. Since we asked about both month and year of birth based on drop-down menus, it is possible that a significant portion of these respondents misreported their month and/or year of birth (see Gendall and Healey 2008). There is no reason to believe that this error is systematic. Accordingly, nonsystematic measurement error in an independent variable does not bias any conclusions in research studies (see King, Keohane, and Verba 1994).
8 We omitted this variable in the models for opinions about the family separation policy shown in Table 5.2, as the question wording for this query mentions then-President Trump explicitly. We cannot simultaneously match on a variable (presidential approval) of which a component is contained in the variable on which we perform matching (opinions about Trump's implementation of the immigration and family separation policy). If we did so, we would violate one of the main assumptions of the matching technique (see Imbens and Rubin 2015 for more details).
9 The question about self-identifying as a Black Lives Matter supporter was asked in 2020, but not in 2018.
10 Imbens and Rubin (2015, 16) state that any matching technique assumes that matching covariates are unaffected by treatment assignment. Thus, there should be

no connection between any particular matching covariate and the assignment to treatment. Consequently, we exclude one variable from the set of matching covariates in this analysis: posting about immigration, as this variable acts as the treatment.
11 If civic engagement were related to posting about or participating in protests related to immigration and family separation or with opinions about then-President Trump's implementation of the immigration and family separation policy, then civic activity and these treatment variables would be highly correlated. To test whether this happens, we correlated our dependent variable (offline civic activity) and both treatment variables (posting about immigration and family separation and participating in protests related to immigration and family separation). The correlations are .501 and .640, respectively. Further, the correlation between opinions about then-President Trump's implementation of immigration and family separation policy and civic engagement is .056. These correlations are low enough such that we can conclude that the first part of the SUTVA assumption is satisfied.
12 If we do not conduct our analysis in this manner, then we cannot satisfy SUTVA, as there would be alternative treatment forms (see Imbens and Rubin 2015, 10–13).
13 However, we do not perform a regression following the matching analysis (as Ho et al. 2007 recommend), as Abadie and Spiess (2019) state that this is inappropriate when matching is done with replacement as researchers obtain inaccurate standard error estimates.
14 One-tailed tests of statistical significance are more appropriate to use when testing directional hypotheses.
15 One limitation of many matching analyses is that one can p-hack by changing the functional form of the matching routine to generate a set of results that confirms a researcher's theoretical expectations (Head et al. 2015).
16 The models in Tables 5.1 and 5.2 do not have any issues with respect to robustness. When we remove one matching covariate at a time and re-run the remaining variables in our matching routines, 94.20% (or 130/138) of the models contain results that run the same direction in terms of the signs and significance patterns that we report in this chapter.

References

Abadie, Alberto and Guido W. Imbens 2006. "Large Sample Properties of Matching Estimators for Average Treatment Effects." *Econometrica* 74(1): 235–267. https://doi.org/10.1111/j.1468-0262.2006.00655.x. Accessed online June 19, 2021.

Abadie, Alberto and Guido W. Imbens 2011. "Bias-Corrected Matching Estimators for Average Treatment Effects." *Journal of Business and Economic Statistics* 29(1): 1–11. https://doi.org/10.1198/jbes.2009.07333. Accessed online June 19, 2021.

Abadie, Alberto and Guido W. Imbens 2016. "Matching on the Estimated Propensity Score." *Econometrica* 84(2): 781–807. https://doi.org/10.3982/ECTA11293. Accessed online June 19, 2021.

Abadie, Alberto and Jann Spiess 2019. "Robust Post-Matching Inference." Forthcoming in the *Journal of the American Statistical Association*. https://doi.org/10.1080/01621459.2020.1840383. Accessed online June 19, 2021.

Abrajano, Marisa and Simran Singh 2009. "Examining the Link between Issue Attitudes and News Source: The Case of Latinos and Immigration Reform." *Political Behavior* 31(1): 1–30. https://doi.org/10.1007/s11109-008-9067-8. Accessed online June 19, 2021.

Abramowitz, Alan I. and Walter J. Stone 2006. "The Bush Effect: Polarization, Turnout, and Activism in the 2004 Presidential Election." *Presidential Studies Quarterly* 36(2): 141–154. https://doi.org/10.1111/j.1741-5705.2006.00295.x. Accessed online June 19, 2021.

Achen, Christopher H. and Larry M. Bartels 2016. *Democracy for Realists: Why Elections Do Not Produce Responsive Government*. Princeton, NJ: Princeton University Press.

Arnold, Kathleen R. (Ed.) 2011. *Anti-immigration in the United States: A Historical Encyclopedia*. Santa Barbara, CA: Greenwood.

Brader, Ted, Nicholas A. Valentino, and Elizabeth Suhay 2008. "What Triggers Public Opposition to Immigration? Anxiety, Group Cues, and Immigration Threat." *American Journal of Political Science* 52(4): 959–978. https://doi.org/10.1111/j.1540-5907.2008.00353.x. Accessed online June 19, 2021.

Brick, Kate, A. E. Challinor, and Marc R. Rosenblum 2011. *Mexican and Central American Immigrants in the United States*. Washington, DC: Migration Policy Institute.

Carmines, Edward G. and James A. Stimson 1989. *Issue Evolution: Race and the Transformation of American Politics*. Princeton, NJ: Princeton University Press.

Citrin, Jack, David O. Sears, Christopher Muste, and Cara Wong 2001. "Multiculturalism in American Public Opinion." *British Journal of Political Science* 31(2): 247–275. https://doi.org/10.1017/S0007123401000102. Accessed online June 19, 2021.

Converse, Phillip 1964. "The Nature of Belief Systems in Mass Publics." In *Ideology and Its Discontents*, David E. Apter (Ed.). New York, NY: Free Press of Glencoe.

D'Agostino, Ralph B. 1998. "Propensity Score Methods for Bias Reduction in the Comparison of a Treatment to a Non-Randomized Control Group." *Statistics in Medicine* 17(9): 2265–2281. https://doi.org/10.1002/(SICI)1097-0258(19981015)17:19<2265::AID-SIM918>3.0.CO;2-B. Accessed online June 19, 2021.

Department of Homeland Security Office of Immigration Statistics 2018. "Population Estimates: Illegal Alien Population Residing in the United States."

Diamond, Alexis and Jasjeet J. Sekhon 2013. "Genetic Matching for Estimating Causal Effects: A General Multivariate Matching Method for Achieving Balance in Observational Studies." *Review of Economics and Statistics* 95(3): 932–945. https://doi.org/10.1162/REST_a_00318. Accessed online June 19, 2021.

Dickerson, Caitlin. 2020. "Parents of 545 Children Separated at the Border Cannot Be Found." *The New York Times*. www.nytimes.com/2020/10/21/us/migrant-children-separated.html. Accessed online December 21, 2020.

Dooling, Shannon, Kimberly Atkins, and Max Larkin 2020. "DACA Recipients, Advocates and Mass. Politicos Rejoice Over SCOTUS Ruling." WBUR News. www.wbur.org/news/2020/06/18/daca-recipients-immigration-advocates-and-mass-politicos-rejoice-scotus-ruling-call-for-greater-protections. Accessed online February 8, 2021.

Easley, Cameron. 2020. "Most Voters Support Supreme Court Decisions on DACA, Workplace Discrimination." *Morning Consult*. https://morningconsult.com/2020/06/24/voters-daca-workplace-supreme-court-poll/. Accessed online January 12, 2021.

Flavin, Patrick and John D. Griffin 2009. "Policy, Preferences, and Participation: Government's Impact on Democratic Citizenship." *Journal of Politics* 71(2): 544–559. https://doi.org/10.1017/S0022381609090458. Accessed online June 19, 2021.

Fowler, James H. and Cindy D. Kam 2007 "Beyond the Self: Social Identity, Altruism and Political Participation." *Journal of Politics* 69(3): 813–827. https://doi.org/10.1111/j.1468-2508.2007.00577.x. Accessed online June 19, 2021.

Garand, James C., Ping Xu, and Belinda C. Davis 2017. "Immigration Attitudes and Support for the Welfare State in the American Mass Public." *American Journal of*

Political Science 61(1): 146–162. https://doi.org/10.1111/ajps.12233. Accessed online June 19, 2021.

Gelman, Andrew and Jennifer Hill 2007. *Data Analysis Using Regression and Multilevel/Heiarchical Models*. New York: Cambridge University Press.

Gendall, Philip and Benjamin Healey 2008. "Asking the Age Question in Mail and Online Surveys." *International Journal of Market Research* 50(3): 309–317. https://doi.org/10.1177/147078530805000303. Accessed online June 19, 2021.

Gil de Zúñiga, Homero, Nakwon Jung, and S. Sebastian Valenzuela 2012. "Social Media Use for News and Individuals' Social Capital, Civic Engagement and Political Participation." *Journal of Computer-Mediated Communication*. 17(3): 319–336. https://doi.org/10.1111/j.1083-6101.2012.01574.x. Accessed online June 19, 2021.

Gimpel, James G., Frances E. Lee, and Joshua Kaminski 2006. "The Political Geography of Campaign Contributions in American Politics." *Journal of Politics* 68(3): 626–639. https://doi.org/10.1111/j.1468-2508.2006.00450.x. Accessed online June 19, 2021.

Greene, William H. 2011. *Econometric Analysis*. 7th Ed. New York City, NY: Pearson Education.

Hackman, Michelle. 2020. "Texas Challenges Legality of DACA in Latest Bid to End the Program." *The Wall Street Journal*. www.wsj.com/articles/texas-challenges-legality-of-daca-in-latest-bid-to-end-the-program-11608575254. Accessed online December 22, 2020.

Hajnal, Zoltan and Michael U. Rivera 2014. "Immigration, Latinos, and White Partisan Politics: The New Democratic Defection." *American Journal of Political Science* 58(4): 773–789. https://doi.org/10.1111/ajps.12101. Accessed online June 19, 2021.

Head, Megan L., Luke Holman, Rob Lanfear, Andrew T. Kahn, and Michael D. Jennions 2015. "The Extent and Consequences of P-Hacking in Science." *Plos Biology* 13(3): e1002106. https://doi.org/10.1371/journal.pbio.1002106. Accessed online June 19, 2021.

Ho, Daniel E., Kosuke Imai, Gary King, and Elizabeth A. Stuart 2007. "Matching as Nonparametric Preprocessing for Reducing Model Dependence in Parametric Causal Inference." *Political Analysis* 15(3): 199–236. https://doi.org/10.1093/pan/mpl013. Accessed online June 19, 2021.

Hood III, M.V., Irwin L. Morris, and Kurt A. Shirkey 1997. "'!Quedate o Vente!': Uncovering the Determinants of Hispanic Public Opinion toward Immigration." *Political Research Quarterly* 50(3): 627–647. https://doi.org/10.1177/106591299705000307. Accessed online June 19, 2021.

Imbens, Guido W. and Donald B. Rubin 2015. *Causal Inference for Statistics, Social, and Biomedical Sciences: An Introduction*. New York, NY: Cambridge University Press.

Ishmael, Aiyana 2020. "Noncitizens Can't Vote, so They're Urging People to Vote for Them." Teen Vogue. www.teenvogue.com/story/daca-green-card-2020-election. Accessed online February 8, 2021.

Jervis, Rick and Alan Gomez 2019. "Trump Administration Has Separated Hundreds of Children from Their Migrant Families since 2018." *USA Today*. www.usatoday.com/story/news/nation/2019/05/02/border-family-separations-trump-administration-border-patrol/3563990002/. Accessed online October 23, 2019.

Joint Letter to the U.S. Senate Committee on Homeland Security and Governmental Affairs. September 14, 2018.

Kahne, Joseph and Benjamin Bowyer 2018. "The Political Significance of Social Media Activity and Social Networks." *Political Communication* 35(3): 470–493. https://doi.org/10.1080/10584609.2018.1426662. Accessed online June 19, 2021.

Kerbel, Matthew R. and Joel David Bloom 2005. "Blog for America and Civic Involvement." *The International Journal of Press/Politics* 10(4): 3–27. https://doi.org/10.1177/1081180X05281395. Accessed online June 19, 2021.

King, Gary, Christopher Lucas, and Richard A. Nielsen 2017. "The Balance-Sample Size Frontier in Matching Methods for Causal Inference." *American Journal of Political Science* 61(2): 473–489. https://doi.org/10.1111/ajps.12272. Accessed online June 19, 2021.

King, Gary, Robert O. Keohane, and Sidney Verba 1994. *Designing Social Inquiry: Scientific Inference in Qualitative Research.* Princeton, NJ: Princeton University Press.

Knoll, Benjamin R. 2009. "'And Who Is My Neighbor?' Religion and Immigration Policy Attitudes." *Journal for the Scientific Study of Religion* 48(2): 313–331. https://doi.org/10.1111/j.1468-5906.2009.01449.x. Accessed online June 19, 2021.

Lahav, Gallya and Marie Courtemanche 2012. "The Ideological Effects of Framing Threat on Immigration and Civil Liberties." *Political Behavior* 34(3): 477–505. https://doi.org/10.1007/s11109-011-9171-z. Accessed online June 19, 2021.

Letiecq, Bethany L., Joseph G. Grzywacz, Katie M. Gray, and Yanet M. Eudave 2014. "Depression among Mexican Men on the Migration Frontier: The Role of Family Separation and Other Structural and Situational Stressors." *Journal of Immigrant Minority Health* 16(6): 1193–1200. https://doi.org/10.1007/s10903-013-9918-1. Accessed online June 19, 2021.

Ley, Barbara L. and Paul R. Brewer 2018. "Social Media, Networked Protest, and the March for Science." *Social Media and Society* 4(3): 1–12. https://doi.org/10.1177/2056305118793407. Accessed online June 19, 2021.

Loader, Brian D., Ariadne Vromen, and Michael A. Xenos 2014. "The Networked Young Citizen: Social Media, Political Participation and Civic Engagement." *Information, Communication and Society* 17(2): 143–150. https://doi.org/10.1080/1369118X.2013.871571. Accessed online June 19, 2021.

Lopez, Gustavo and Jens Manuel Krogstad 2017. "Key Facts about Unauthorized Immigrants Enrolled in DACA." Pew Research Center. www.pewresearch.org/fact-tank/2017/09/25/key-facts-about-unauthorized-immigrants-enrolled-in-daca. Accessed online June 9, 2020.

Malagon, Elvia 2020. "Shut Out of DACA Protections, Immigrant Youth in Chicago Area Face Uncertain Future." *Chicago Sun Times.* https://chicago.suntimes.com/2020/10/27/21528805/immigration-daca-supreme-court-trump-youth-limbo. Accessed online February 8, 2021.

Marcus, George E., Michael MacKuen, and W. Russell Neuman 2000. *Affective Intelligence and Political Judgment.* Chicago, IL: University of Chicago Press.

Martin, Beth 2017. "Experiences of Family Separation for Adults Who Immigrate Alone: Lessons for Social Work Practice and Research." *Canadian Social Work Review/Revue Canadienne de service social* 34(2): 253–273.

McCausland, Phil, Patricia Guadalupe, and Kalhan Rosenblatt 2018. "Thousands across U.S. Join 'Keep Families Together' March to Protest Family Separation." NBC News. www.nbcnews.com/news/us-news/thousands-across-u-s-join-keep-families-together-march-protest-n888006. Accessed online August 21, 2019.

Merolla, Jennifer L., S. Karthick Ramakrishnan, and Chris Haynes 2013a. "'Illegal,' 'Undocumented,' or 'Unauthorized': Equivalency Frames, Issue Frames, and Public Opinion on Immigration." *Perspectives on Politics* 11(3): 789–807. https://doi.org/10.1017/S1537592713002077. Accessed online June 19, 2021.

Merolla, Jennifer L., Adrian D. Pantoja, Ivy A. M. Cargile, and Juana Mora 2013b. "From Coverage to Action: The Immigration Debate and Its Effects on Participation." *Political Research Quarterly* 66(2): 322–335. https://doi.org/10.1177/1065912912443313. Accessed online June 19, 2021.

Miles, Andrew 2015. "The (Re)genesis of Values: Examining the Importance of Values for Action." *American Sociological Review* 80(4): 680–704. https://doi.org/10.1177/0003122415591800. Accessed online June 19, 2021.

Moffett, Kenneth W. and Laurie L. Rice 2018. "College Students and Online Political Expression in the 2016 Election." *Social Science Computer Review* 36(4): 422–439. https://doi.org/10.1177/0894439317721186. Accessed online June 19, 2021.

Moffett, Kenneth W., Laurie L. Rice, and Ramana Madupalli 2014. "Young Voters and War: the Iraq War as a Catalyst for Political Participation." *Social Science Quarterly* 95(5): 1419–1443. https://doi.org/10.1111/ssqu.12116. Accessed online June 19, 2021.

Nadeau, Richard, Richard G. Niemi, and Timothy Amato 1995. "Emotions, Issue Importance, and Political Learning." *American Journal of Political Science* 39(3): 558–574.

Newman, Benjamin J. and Yamil Velez 2014. "Group Size versus Change? Assessing Americans' Perception of Local Immigration." *Political Research Quarterly* 67(2): 293–303. https://doi.org/10.1177/1065912913517303. Accessed online June 19, 2021.

Nichols, Austin 2007. "Causal Inference with Observational Data." *The Stata Journal* 7(4): 507–541. https://doi.org/10.1177/1536867X0800700403. Accessed online June 19, 2021.

Nickerson, Raymond S. 1998. "Confirmation Bias: A Ubiquitous Phenomenon in Many Guises." *Review of General Psychology* 2(2): 175–220. https://doi.org/10.1037/1089-2680.2.2.175. Accessed online June 19, 2021.

Nierenberg, Amelia. 2018. "Grass-Roots Rally Draws Crowds Protesting Separation of Immigrant Families." *The Boston Globe.* www3.bostonglobe.com/metro/2018/06/14/grass-roots-rally-draws-crowds-protesting-separation-immigrant-families/Yfs1d1puVsc8FTTGEYpN2M/story.html?arc404=true. Accessed online December 22, 2020.

Pantoja, Adrian D. and Gary M. Segura. 2003. "Fear and Loathing in California: Contextual Threat and Political Sophistication among Latino Voters." *Political Behavior* 25(3): 265–286. https://doi.org/10.1023/A:1025119724207. Accessed online June 19, 2021.

Parker, Kim, Nikki Graf, and Ruth Igielnik 2019. "Generation Z Looks a Lot Like Millennials on Key Social and Political Issues" Pew Research Center. www.pewsocialtrends.org/2019/01/17/generation-z-looks-a-lot-like-millennials-on-key-social-and-political-issues/. Accessed online February 12, 2019.

Pew Research Center 2018b. "Voter Enthusiasm at Record High in Nationalized Midterm Environment." www.people-press.org/2018/09/26/voter-enthusiasm-at-record-high-in-nationalized-midterm-environment/. Accessed online March 11, 2019.

Pew Research Center 2020a. "Election 2020: Voters Are Highly Engaged, but Nearly Half Expect to Have Difficulties Voting." www.pewresearch.org/politics/2020/08/13/important-issues-in-the-2020-election/. Accessed online December 21, 2020.

Pollock, Philip H. III 1983. "The Participatory Consequences of Internal and External Political Efficacy: A Research Note." *Western Political Quarterly* 36(3): 400–409. https://doi.org/10.1177/106591298303600306. Accessed online June 19, 2021.

Preston, Julia 2017. "How the Dreamers Learned to Play Politics." *Politico*. www.politico.com/magazine/story/2017/09/09/dreamers-daca-learned-to-play-politics-215588. Accessed online August 21, 2019.

Rees, Susan, Derrick M. Silove, Kuowei Tay, and Moses Kareth 2013. "Human Rights Trauma and the Mental Health of West Papuan Refugees Resettled in Australia." *Medical Journal of Australia* 199(4): 280–283. https://doi.org/10.5694/mja12.11651. Accessed online June 19, 2021.

Reny, Tyler T. 2017. "Demographic Change, Latino Countermobilization, and the Politics of Immigration in U.S. Senate Campaigns." *Political Research Quarterly* 70(4): 735–748. https://doi.org/10.1177/1065912917713155. Accessed online June 19, 2021.

Reny, Tyler T., Loren Collingwood, and Ali A. Valenzuela 2019. "Vote Switching in the 2016 Election: How Racial and Immigration Attitudes, Not Economics, Explain Shifts in White Voting." *Public Opinion Quarterly* 83(1): 91–113. https://doi.org/10.1093/poq/nfz011. Accessed online June 19, 2021.

Rosenstone, Steven J. and John Mark Hansen 2002. *Mobilization, Participation, and Democracy in America*. New York, NY: Pearson-Longman.

Sekhon, Jasjeet S. 2011. "Multivariate and Propensity Score Matching Software with Automated Balance Optimization: The Matching Package for R." *Journal of Statistical Software* 42(7): 1–52.

Simon, Rita, and Susan Alexander 1993. *The Ambivalent Welcome: Print Media, Public Opinion, and Immigration*. Westport, CT: Praeger.

Stein, Perry 2017. "'Undocumented, Unafraid.': DACA Recipients Storm the U.S. Capitol." *The Washington Post*. www.washingtonpost.com/local/undocumented-unafraid-daca-recipients-storm-the-us-capitol-for-their-cause/2017/11/09/4d9ae0bc-c558-11e7-aae0-cb18a8c29c65_story.html. Accessed online August 21, 2019.

Stuart, Elizabeth A. 2010. "Matching Methods for Causal Inference: A Review and a Look Forward." *Statistical Science* 25(1): 1–21. https://doi.org/10.1214/09-STS313. Accessed online June 19, 2021.

Tichenor, Daniel 2015. "The Political Dynamics of Unauthorized Immigration: Conflict, Change, and Agency in Time." *Polity* 47(3): 283–301. https://doi.org/10.1057/pol.2015.11. Accessed online June 19, 2021.

Totenberg, Nina 2020b. "Supreme Court Rules for DREAMers, Against Trump." NPR. June 18. www.npr.org/2020/06/18/829858289/supreme-court-upholds-daca-in-blow-totrump-administration. Accessed online December 22, 2020.

Trump, Donald J. 2015 "Here's Donald Trump's Presidential Announcement Speech." *Time*. https://time.com/3923128/donald-trump-announcement-speech/. Accessed online October 21, 2019.

Valentino, Nicholas A., Vincent L. Hutchings, Antoine J. Banks, and Anne K. Davis 2008. "Is a Worried Citizen a Good Citizen? Emotions, Political Information Seeking, and Learning via the Internet." *Political Psychology* 29(2): 247–273. https://doi.org/10.1111/j.1467-9221.2008.00625.x. Accessed online June 19, 2021.

Valentino, Nicholas A., Ted Brader, Eric W. Groenendyk, Krysha Gregorowicz, and Vincent L. Hutchings 2011. "Election Night's Alright for Fighting: The Role of Emotions in Political Participation." *Journal of Politics* 73(1): 156–170. https://doi.org/10.1017/S0022381610000939. Accessed online June 19, 2021.

Verba, Sidney, Henry E. Brady, and Kay L. Schlozman 1995. *Voice and Equality: Civic Voluntarism in American Democracy*. Cambridge, MA: Harvard University Press.

Weber, Christopher 2013. "Emotions, Campaigns, and Political Participation." *Political Research Quarterly* 66(2): 414–428. https://doi.org/10.1177/1065912912449697. Accessed online June 19, 2021.

Yang, Hongwei "Chris" and Jean L. DeHart. 2016. "Social Media Use and Online Political Participation among College Students during the US Election 2012." *Social Media + Society*, 2(1): https://doi.org/10.1177/2056305115623802. Accessed online June 19, 2021.

6
BLACK LIVES MATTER
How a Surging Movement Engaged Young People in 2020

Introduction

The Black Lives Matter movement was launched in 2013. George Zimmerman had just been acquitted on second degree murder and manslaughter charges for the shooting death of Florida teenager Trayvon Martin by an all-female jury that concluded Zimmerman had acted in self-defense (Alcindor 2013). Labor organizer Alicia Garza pulled out her phone as the news came in to see what people were posting on Facebook (Guynn 2015). Disappointed by the racism she saw in the responses and thinking how Martin could have instead been her younger brother, Garza posted several messages that she called "a love letter to black people" (Guynn 2015; Cobb 2016). Among her posts were the words "I continue to be surprised at how little black lives matter. And I will continue that. stop giving up on black life." And "black people. I love you. I love us. Our lives matter" (Cobb 2016). One of her friends, whom she had met years earlier at an organizers' conference, Patrisse Cullors, saw her post and added #BlackLivesMatter, inviting Black people to join them in a movement, while another organizer friend, Opal Tometi, offered to help build spaces on Facebook and Twitter where activists in the movement they just launched could connect (Cobb 2016). Together, these three Millennials gave words to a movement and created an online organizational platform where the nascent movement could grow.

The founders of Black Lives Matter intentionally created a horizontal structure that made it easy for people to participate. Alicia Garza told reporters:

> We want to make sure there is the broadest participation possible in this new iteration of a Black freedom movement... We can't afford to just follow one voice. We have so many different experiences that are rich and complex. We

DOI: 10.4324/9781003168898-7

need to bring all of those experiences to the table in order to achieve the solutions we desire.

(Guynn 2015)

Yet this meant individuals and even organized chapters under the umbrella Black Lives Matter did not always match the principles of the movement's founders such as LGBTQ rights and gender identity activism (Chase 2018). Chase (2018, 1109) noted:

> The fact that these principles often are not addressed in the media's coverage of Black Lives Matter is likely the product of individuals appropriating the movement's rallying cry, without first seeking to understand the movement. But also, a movement that intentionally avoids any centralized leadership will have this kind of fluctuation and evolution of values over time.

While this allowed the movement to diverge from what its founders envisioned at times, the lack of centralized leadership also provided opportunities for young adults to exert leadership in a nascent movement. In the remainder of this chapter, we explore whether young adult support for and participation in the Black Lives

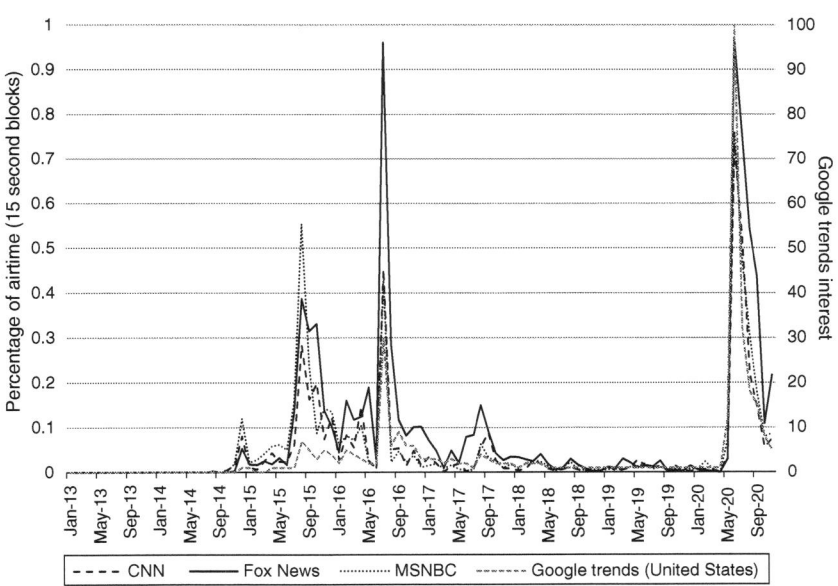

FIGURE 6.1 Media and Public Attention to Black Lives Matter, 2013–Election Day 2020.

Source: GDELT Television Explorer Database and Google Trends.

Matter movement helped expand the civic engagement of young adults as the civil rights movement did decades prior.

Media and Public Attention to Black Lives Matter

As Figure 6.1 shows, the movement initially struggled to gain the attention of traditional media or the public. That changed in the summer of 2014, when two more deaths of unarmed black men, this time at the hands of police, captured media and public attention. On July 17, 2014, Eric Garner died from a chokehold by police officer Daniel Pantaleo after officers suspected Garner of selling untaxed cigarettes (Associated Press 2019a). An observer's cell phone video caught some of Garner's last words – "I can't breathe" – and this became a rallying cry at the protests that followed (Associated Press 2019a). While the medical examiner ruled Garner's death a homicide on August 1, 2014, Pantaleo was not charged in his death in either state or federal court and it took just over five years for New York Police Department disciplinary action to result in his firing (Associated Press 2019a).

On August 9, 2014, as Michael Brown and a friend were walking down the middle of Canfield Drive in Ferguson, Missouri, a confrontation ensued between police officer Darren Wilson and Brown that culminated in Wilson shooting and killing Brown, an 18-year-old unarmed black teenager (Associated Press 2019b). Wilson claimed Brown struck him in the face, that Brown tried to grab his gun and several shots were fired in the scuffle, that Brown then ran away with Wilson pursuing, and when Wilson told Brown to get on the ground, Brown instead charged at him, at which point Wilson fired again multiple times (BBC 2015). A grand jury presented with testimony and evidence determined there was not sufficient evidence to bring charges against Wilson (BBC 2015), and a subsequent reinvestigation of his death years later also yielded no charges against former officer Wilson (Romero 2020). Brown's death, and the fact that his body lay in the hot summer street for four hours, triggered outrage and became a flashpoint for pent up anger over police brutality and systemic racism. Black Lives Matter was displayed on signs at the protests that ensued and became a rallying cry of protestors in Ferguson and across the United States (Luibrand 2015). The hashtag #BlackLivesMatter made a resurgence, too, spiking with each death, the subsequent protests, and with the announcements that the officers responsible for the deaths of Garner and of Brown would not be charged (Freelon, McIlwain, and Clark 2016).

Figure 6.1 shows the percentage of airtime in 15 second blocks devoted to "Black Lives Matter" between 2013 and Election Day 2020 on CNN, Fox News, and MSNBC, along with Google Trends data for Black Lives Matter during the same period. This figure indicates that media coverage of Black Lives Matter was largely absent until the month Michael Brown was killed. By the following year, though, both media attention and public interest, as measured by Google Trends Interest had grown substantially. The 2015 spikes in attention, also evident on

Twitter, coincide with the shooting death of Walter Scott and the fatal injuries sustained by Freddie Gray in the back of a police transport van (Freelon, McIlwain, and Clark 2016). Then, in July 2016 when Alton Sterling and Philando Castile were shot and killed by police, media, and public attention nearly doubled over its 2015 peak. Similar trends can be seen in the use of #BlackLivesMatter on Twitter that month (Anderson 2016).

Yet, like other social movements before it, Black Lives Matter soon sparked backlash. Some read the phrase black lives matter as stating *only* black lives matter or black lives matter *more* when instead the movement might more accurately be described as fighting for the recognition that black lives matter *too*. This misunderstanding led some to emphasize "all lives matter" instead. For example, McDonald (2016) points out how Mike Huckabee invoked Martin Luther King, Jr. in his 2015 argument against the Black Lives Matter movement. Huckabee stated:

> When I hear people scream, 'black lives matter,' I think, 'Of course they do.' But all lives matter. It's not that any life matters more than another. That's the whole message think Dr. King tried to present and I think he'd be appalled with the notion that we're elevating some lives above others.
>
> *(McDonald 2016, 143–144)*

Yet, McDonald (2016) argues that "…the phrase 'black lives matter' intends to draw attention to social injustices that relegate black lives to the status of second-class citizens, not claim that black lives are more important than other lives" (144), an argument that echoes that made by Black Lives Matter movement leaders as well (Luibrand 2015). The media and large segments of the public soon lost interest. By the beginning of 2018, media attention to Black Lives Matter declined substantially, as did Google searches. The issues Black Lives Matter raised were crowded out by other topics in the 2018 midterm elections and it wasn't until May 2020 that Black Lives Matter returned to center stage.

A Resurgent Black Lives Matter

Our primary focus in this chapter involves the impact of the movement's resurgence and amplification in 2020 after the death of George Floyd under police officer Derek Chauvin's knee. In May 2020, three cell phone videos in relatively quick succession, following the shooting death of Breonna Taylor by police in her apartment on March 13, 2020, exposed how little black lives seemed to matter to some Americans. The first was a video of Ahmaud Arbery, chased down and killed while jogging.

Ahmaud Arbery was shot and killed on February 23, 2020, but the video of his death did not emerge until several months later. The 25-year-old black man was out jogging, according to his family, but Gregory McMichael and his son

Travis McMichael claimed they thought he was a burglar (Griffith 2020). The father and son, along with neighbor William Bryan, attempted to block him with their vehicles, with Travis McMichael exiting a vehicle with his shotgun (Griffith 2020). McMichael claimed Arbery attacked him and he fired his weapon in self-defense, shooting and killing Arbery, and a series of prosecutors seemingly accepted the account and declined to pursue charges against those involved (Griffith 2020). As calls for justice for both Breonna Taylor and Ahmaud Arbery were ongoing, on May 5, 2020, a video of the shooting of Arbery emerged online that called the McMichaels' account into question (Griffith 2020). A young black man had been killed but those involved in his death walked free, sending the signal that his life and death did not matter. That same day protesters gathered (many of them taking social distancing precautions) to call for justice for Ahmaud Arbery (Burke 2020).

Online calls for justice for Ahmaud Arbery mounted, too, with runners taking to social media on May 8, which would have been Arbery's 26th birthday, running 2.23 miles and posting their run with the hashtags #runwithmaud and #IrunwithMaud (Burke 2020). The protests and online calls for justice helped lead to the Georgia Bureau of Investigation taking over the case and making arrests, with Gregory McMichael, Travis McMichael, and William Bryan indicted on murder charges in June 2020 (Waldrop, Henry, and Barajas 2020). Although the defendants had insisted they were not motivated by race, at a preliminary hearing in early June, investigators testified there were police reports that Travis McMichael had used a racial slur after killing Arbery, that he had a history of using racial slurs, and that body camera footage showed the sticker of a Confederate flag on the toolbox of McMichael's truck (McLaughlin 2020). Afterward, protestors outside the courthouse chanted, "All lives matter when black lives matter" (McLaughlin 2020).

As calls for justice increased for Ahmaud Arbery, the video of another incident in which a black man's life was minimized spread virally. On May 25, 2020, Christian Cooper, a black man birdwatching in Central Park in New York City, asked Amy Cooper, a white woman walking her dog unleashed in a protected nature area where leashes are required, to leash her dog (Pereira and Katersky 2020). Instead, she threatened to call the police on him and Cooper responded by using his cell phone to begin filming her. She is filmed saying, "I'm taking a picture and calling the cops. I'm going to tell them there's an African American man threatening my life" (Pereira and Katersky 2020). She soon followed through on this threat, calling police, emphasizing the race of the man, and claiming "he is recording me and threatening myself and my dog" (Pereira and Katersky 2020; Ransom 2020) along with "I'm being threatened by a man in the Ramble. Please send the cops immediately!" (Vera and Ly 2020). While Amy Cooper later apologized for the encounter (Stump 2020), the video suggested her own convenience was more important to her than the black man's life. News of this incident, and the accompanying video, spread quickly and provoked discussions about a broader pattern of white people making false reports about black people, as a false call such as this could have easily ended in tragedy (Ransom 2020).

Then, on the night of May 25, 2020, an employee at Cup Foods in Minneapolis called police to report that George Floyd had paid with a suspicious-looking 20-dollar bill (Li 2020). Responding officers Thomas Lane and J. A. Kueng found Floyd in the driver's seat of a vehicle around the corner. As officers attempted to place Floyd in a squad car, he said he was claustrophobic and fell to the ground as police officers Tou Thao and Derek Chauvin arrived on scene (Li 2020). Chauvin placed his left knee on Floyd's head and neck as Floyd remained handcuffed, face down on the pavement (Li 2020). A crowd gathered and some, with cell phones in hand, began filming. Video captured by Darnella Frazier showed Floyd repeatedly pleading "Please. Please. I can't breathe, officer…I cannot breathe. I cannot breathe" (Dakss 2020). The growing crowd witnessing it pled with Chauvin to stop, but even after the crowd warned that he was not responsive, Lane asked if Floyd should be moved on his side, and Kueng warned he could not find a pulse, Chauvin kept his knee in place. Charging documents for Chauvin later stated Chauvin had kept his knee on Floyd's neck for two minutes and 43 seconds after Floyd lost consciousness (Li 2020). An ambulance arrived and transported Floyd to a hospital where he was pronounced dead (Cohen 2020). Floyd's cries of "I can't breathe" as he died echoed those of Eric Garner almost six years earlier.

These deeply disturbing videos were viewed on millions of cell phone and television screens. Some Americans were working from home due to safer at home orders while others had become unemployed. Restaurants, gyms, movie theaters, and other entertainment venues in many states remained closed to prevent the spread of Covid-19. With fewer distractions than usual to occupy Americans' time, these videos were hard to miss. The free time most Americans had on hand also may have helped dedicate more time to protest (Gerbaudo 2020). Most Americans had spent several months social distancing due to Covid-19, but they quickly took to the streets in protest. The Crowd Counting Consortium was still processing data on the protests against racial injustice that occurred in June 2020 at the time of the writing of this book, and as of January 11, 2021, they had already recorded more than 6,500 distinct antiracism protests in June 2020 involving a minimum of 1.7 million participants (Crowd Counting Consortium 2021).

Millions of Americans awakened to the presence of racial injustice in the United States. This awakening fits with Havercroft and Owens' (2016, 754) conception of soul dawning:

> So long as the white majority in the United States is soul blind to the suffering and brutality that black Americans face not just in the U.S. criminal justice system but in American social and political life more generally, the police order that finds its expression in this suffering and brutality will remain in place even if the particular forms and locations of the individual and institutional expression of soul blindness may change. It is important

to be clear here that we are not claiming that changing laws, allocations of resources, and the ways that systems operate are not important. On the contrary, these may be crucial to cultivating conditions that support the widespread emergence of soul-dawning, a social awakening to the reality of racial injustice.

Prior to the incidents in May of 2020 that helped cut through this soul blindness, many white Americans had been insulated from the treatment of black Americans, due in part to the persistent effects of discriminatory policies put in place many decades prior. Practices such as redlining and racially restrictive housing covenants helped keep communities racially segregated and the impact of these practices still linger in housing patterns today (see e.g., Theising 2003). While the Fair Housing Act prohibited discrimination in housing based on race, 40 years later many suburbs remained segregated (Larkin 2007). Racially segregated housing patterns can help contribute to racially segregated schools, workplaces, and churches, resulting in some white Americans having little interaction with black Americans. Such isolation can help facilitate soul blindness. It makes it easy for ethnocentrism to shape perceptions, leading to stereotypes (Sumner 1906; Kam and Kinder 2012) and in some cases the development of racial resentment, which serves as a powerful predictor of white opinion on policies related to race (Kinder and Sanders 1996; Kinder and Winter 2001; Tuch and Hughes 2011).

Insulated from black Americans, many white Americans assumed that black Americans' experiences with police officers were like their own interactions with police officers and that because they did not see evidence of racism in their everyday lives, black Americans no longer experienced racism. For example, in 2015, almost three quarters of white Americans thought race was unrelated to police decisions to use deadly force while more than three in five black Americans reported that they or a family member had been treated unfairly by police on the basis of race (Luibrand 2015). Statistics show that despite many white Americans' perceptions, African American males face a disproportionately high risk of being killed by police use of force. Edwards, Lee, and Esposito (2019) estimate that black men face a 1 in 1,000 lifetime risk of being killed by police; this is roughly 2.5 times the risk faced by white males and the risk is highest before the age of 30. The rate of black males between the ages of 25 and 29 killed by law enforcement ranges between 2.8 and 4.1 per 100,000, the rate for Native American males of the same age ranges between 1.5 and 2.8 per 100,000, the rate for Latinos in that age group ranges between 1.4 and 2.2 per 100,000 while the rate for white males between the ages of 25 and 29 ranges between 0.9 and 1.4 per 100,000 (Edwards, Lee, and Esposito 2019).

Yet, as the poll referenced above shows, many white Americans were oblivious to this racial disparity in police use of deadly force. The three cell phone videos in relatively rapid succession in May 2020 broke through this soul blindness for many white Americans, some of whom began to confront their own white privilege for the first time. An examination of public opinion data on Black Lives Matter shows evidence of such a social awakening.

Public Opinion on Black Lives Matter

Pew Research Center polls show that public opinion about Black Lives Matter shifted significantly between 2016 and 2020, but it also varied dramatically by race, partisan affiliation, and age. In 2016, 65% of Black Americans expressed some level of support for the Black Lives Matter movement while 12% expressed some level of opposition (Pew Research Center 2016). In 2020, the percentage of Black Americans expressing support for the movement increased to 87 (Thomas and Horowitz 2020). Meanwhile, only 40% of white Americans expressed support for the Black Lives Matter movement in 2016 (Pew Research Center 2016) and this increased to 60% in June of 2020 before falling to 45% in September of 2020 (Thomas and Horowitz 2020). To understand why this soul dawning seems short lived requires looking at public opinion and partisanship.

Steep partisan divisions exist in white Americans' opinions about Black Lives Matter. In 2016, among those white Americans who had heard of Black Lives Matter, 64% of Democrats and only 20% of Republicans expressed some level of support for Black Lives Matter. In June of 2020, just weeks after Floyd's death, 92% of Democrats or those who lean toward the Democratic Party expressed support for Black Lives Matter and in September of 2020 their support remained nearly steady at 88% (Thomas and Horowitz 2020). However, among white Republicans and those who lean toward the Republican Party, support for Black Lives Matter was at 37% in June but dropped by more than half to only 16% by September 2020 (Thomas and Horowitz 2020).

This partisan difference in views on Black Lives Matter may stem partly from partisan differences in news sources. In November 2019, six in ten Republicans reported they had turned to Fox News in the past week (Gramlich 2020) and 93% of those who rely on Fox News as their main political news source identify as Republican or lean Republican (Grieco 2020). As Figure 6.1 shows, Fox News devoted far more coverage to Black Lives Matter than did other major cable news channels. According to the GDELT Television Explorer database, by far, the most attention devoted on Fox to Black Lives Matter came from Hannity, followed by the O'Reilly Factor and Tucker Carlson Tonight. Fox News viewers were not only far more likely to hear about Black Lives Matter than viewers of other major cable networks, they were more likely to hear critical comments about this movement. Searches of the GDELT Television Explorer Database shows they devoted far more coverage to the words "loot" and "riot" during this period than other networks, with some guests referring to the movement as "Marxist" and "anarchist."[1] Some comments by Fox hosts instilled fear and yielded significant public outcry. For example, Tucker Carlson told his viewers on June 8, 2020, "This may be a lot of things, this moment we're living through, but it is definitely not about black lives.

Remember that when they come for you, and at this rate, they will," never clearly identifying who "they" were and leaving it to viewers to infer (Chiu 2020). The negative coverage, combined with President Trump's criticism of the movement, likely explains the sharp erosion of white Republican support between June and September 2020.

In addition to the steep partisan divisions, there are also sharp differences in opinion about Black Lives Matter based on age. In 2016, 60% of White Americans between the ages of 18 and 29 expressed some level of support for Black Lives Matter, compared to 46% of those between the ages of 30 and 49, 37% of those between the ages of 50 and 64, and only 26% among those over the age of 65 (Pew Research Center 2016). A similar CBS News Poll in June of 2020 provides differences in opinion by age and by race but not by both age and race together. It shows 72% of Americans between the ages of 18 and 29 expressed some level of support for the Black Lives Matter movement, compared to 61% of Americans between 30 and 49, 55% of Americans between the ages of 45 and 64, and 54% of Americans over the age of 65 (CBS News Poll 2020). Clearly, young adults are more supportive of Black Lives Matter than other age groups. This is not solely because young adults are more Democratic or that young Americans' are more Democratic because they are more racially diverse than previous generations (Medenica 2018). In our November 2020 survey of young adults, 78% of respondents identified as a supporter of the Black Lives Matter movement, including 75% of white respondents, 83% of white Democrat respondents, and 65% of white Republican respondents. While there are still some differences in opinion based on race and party among young Americans, unlike other age groups, our survey indicates a large majority of young Americans, regardless of race or partisan affiliation, support Black Lives Matter.

It should come as no surprise, then, that young adults led the way in many of the Black Lives Matter protests in the summer of 2020. For example, 18-year-old Haylee Gaines helped organize protests in Edwardsville, IL, and told reporters "… now being of age, I just wanted my voice to be heard, and not only for me but for all of us" (Baalman 2020). And, 21-year-old Adriana Aquarius, who organized protests in Bend, Oregon, and other central Oregon towns, urged others, "Now is our moment. Let us use our voice" (Gajahan 2020). These are not isolated incidents. From George Floyd's death through June 18, 2020 there were more than 1,700 protests about police killings of black people (Haseman et al. 2020) and many of these were organized by young people. Young adults' strong support for Black Lives Matter coupled with their social media savvy led young adults to organize protests throughout the country. For example, Amanda Quinonez, aged 18 and a freshman at University of California San Diego, said she Googled "how to organize a protest" before posting on June 2 about meeting the next day at El Centro Lions Park in La Habra, California, for a protest and had about 200 show up (Walker 2020). Likewise, Jamel Burney and Jessie Selph, both aged 23, used Facebook to organize a protest in their hometown of Olean, New York, that drew over 300 people in a town with a population of less than 14,000 (Gajahan 2020). Did supporting the Black Lives Matter Movement, posting about it, or protesting about it lead to higher levels of civic engagement?

Support for Black Lives Matter and Civic Engagement

While young adults supported Black Lives Matter at relatively high levels, support for an idea is not always sufficient to produce action in support of it. We have seen this in previous chapters for other movements such as Me Too. This was also evident in the civil rights movement. The black church has long "…communicated the revolutionary message of equality before God," yet not all ministers and their congregants were active during the civil rights movement (Calhoun-Brown 2000). People have different propensities for action that can be influenced by their level of grievance (Opp 1988), their own resources as well as those devoted to group mobilization (Brady, Verba, and Schlozman 1995; Jenkins 1983), and the frames or messages employed and how those resonate with the culture of the organizations to which one belongs (Tarrow 1992; Calhoun-Brown 2000). Whether one takes action to advance one's views can also be influenced by the costs of collective action, the number of political organizations to which one belongs, whether or not one belongs to privileged social groups, and one's level of trust in political institutions, among other factors (DiGrazia 2014). Taken together, this might suggest we would not automatically see a link between identifying as a supporter of Black Lives Matter and higher civic engagement levels.

However, there are at least some occasions when support for a movement, even if no action is taken at the time, produces a lifelong impact on civic engagement. Specifically, a follow-up study of young engaged observers[2] of the women's movement, the civil rights movement, and the anti-Vietnam War movements found that they were more likely to belong to political and community organizations later in life (Stewart, Settles, and Winter 1998). Supporting a protest movement can produce short-term gains in political activity, too. Gillion (2020) finds that the level of support for Black Lives Matter protest among both those who are liberal and those who are black was associated with higher probabilities of voting in 2016, while views about Black Lives Matter was not associated with whether members of other racial or ideological groups voted. With young adults particularly likely to support Black Lives Matter in 2020, it is important to examine whether support for Black Lives Matter and civic engagement are positively linked.

Posting about Black Lives Matter and Civic Engagement

If young adults are going to act on their views, one of the easiest and most familiar ways for young adults to do so is to express their political views online (Moffett and Rice 2016, 2018). About 75% of our survey respondents reported some level of posting on social media about Black Lives Matter. Was posting associated with higher levels of civic engagement?

We expect a link between posting about Black Lives Matter and civic engagement for similar reasons advanced in prior chapters for other issues. Posting has been found to boost efficacy which in turn makes other forms of civic engagement more likely (de Zuniga, Jung, and Valenzuela 2012; Yang and DeHart 2016). However, given the virulent backlash that also exists against this movement (Gillion 2020), some young adults who posted online might have their views greeted with ridicule or vitriol. Some of these young adults, with lesser commitment to the cause, might be discouraged from taking additional action by this experience. However, those with stronger commitment, as evidenced by posting multiple times, have demonstrated that if they experienced this backlash, they were not dissuaded by it. Thus, those who post multiple times may be more likely to exhibit heightened levels of civic engagement.

In addition, sharing views online helps those with similar viewpoints find each other. While sharing views online might invite pushback, it can also help foster online communities that make plans to engage together in offline civic activity (Ortiz and Ostertag 2014). By scrolling through social media feeds, preexisting acquaintances may discover they have a shared passion for an issue like Black Lives Matter. This may lead to discussions on civic engagement and what they might do together to advance a cause. Publicly posting one's views also allows people with similar views who lack prior direct ties to each other to find each other through mutual contacts and expand their social network. Although the civil rights movement of the 1950s and 1960s existed long before the creation of online social networks, McAdam's (1986) study of participation in the Freedom Summer found that positive social pressure from individuals' social networks helped draw them to take low cost actions to advance civil rights. Similarly, when young adults post online about Black Lives Matter, their online social networks may encourage them to act in other ways to advance the cause, increasing their civic engagement in the process.

Protesting about Black Lives Matter and Civic Engagement

While the black church helped provide organizational resources to support protests during the civil rights movement in the 1960s, social media use by young adults around #BlackLivesMatter did so for Black Lives Matter protests in 2020. For example, Ryan Staples, a recent high school graduate from O'Fallon, Missouri, a predominantly white suburb, organized a Black Lives Matter protest with two of his friends by announcing it on social media. Staples told reporters, "I had no idea that 1,500 plus people were going to come and throw their support behind us" (Grimsley 2020). Among those who joined the protest was O'Fallon Police Chief Tim Clothier, who locked arms with Staples and marched side by side, a white police officer, and a young black man, an experience which Staples told reporters made him feel empowered and believe that change is possible (Grimsley 2020). Positive experiences like these at Black Lives Matter protests should make young adults more likely to engage in other forms of civic activity.

Other Black Lives Matter protests were organized by young adults who knew each other from previous activism. In Howard County Maryland, two 19-year-olds who knew each other previously from their participation in a March for Our Lives march started sending texts to others they thought might be interested in planning a Black Lives Matter march after the death of George Floyd (Faguy 2020). This can be seen as an example of network ties helping gather people to participate in social movements (DiGrazia 2014). The two young women created a planning group of 17 young adults who went on to create a presence for what they called HoCo for Justice on Facebook, Instagram, and Twitter, with their Instagram page reaching 2,000 followers in just two days (Faguy 2020). The protest was large and well organized with 100 trained marshals who guided people and helped maintain social distancing (Faguy 2020). One of the organizers, 20-year-old Sara Wunete, told reporters, "As for us being young, utilizing social media because of how quick it can get to people, that's why we were able to make something like this happen in four days" (Faguy 2020). Though not every community had protests as well planned as the one in Howard County, many of the protests across the United States had similar beginnings with young adults reaching out to friends and posting announcements for a Black Lives Matter protest in their community on social media.

Why were so many young adults willing to take this step? Another of the HoCo for Justice organizers, 21-year-old Ibukun Sokoya, told reporters, "Our generation is a lot of things, but one thing we are not is fearful. We are not scared to push the limits. We are not scared to take risks." If so, then the efficacy developed at protests, like Staples described, combined with the new contacts built organizing and participating in protests, should help lead to higher civic engagement levels. After all, the forms of civic engagement we explore carry far less risk than participating in protests.

Data

To test our hypotheses, we performed online surveys on November 7, 2018, and November 4, 2020, of Americans between 18 and 25 years old – an age range that captures both younger Millennials and older members of Generation Z.[3] To execute this survey, we used Amazon's Mechanical Turk (mTurk) platform, a website that allows members of the public to earn money for completing an array of tasks, including participating in survey research. Each participant was paid $1.50 for completing the survey. A total of 969 participants completed the survey after we removed any incomplete responses.[4]

Dependent Variable

The dependent variable is the extent to which each individual participated in civic and political activities away from the internet. Through separate questions, each respondent was asked about the frequency with which they have engaged in an array of activities that ranged from "never" having done so to having done each of them "very often" using a five-point scale. These activities included talking to people and explaining why they should vote for or against a specific candidate or party, attending political functions in support of a candidate or party, and making purchasing decisions based on a company's conduct or values. To create a single measure of political and civic engagement, we added the values for each of the 12 activities to produce an index that was based on answers to this set of questions ($\alpha = .92$, 2018; $\alpha = .95$, 2020). The means of this index, 14.56 (2018) and 26.01 (2020), are low as this indicates an activity level equivalent to having done 4–6 of the 12 activities in this index very often. The standard deviations, 10.75 (2018) and 14.61 (2020), indicate substantial variance around this mean. Thus, we have captured both low and high participators in our surveys. To test our theoretical expectations, we use a series of matching routines.[5]

Treatment Variables

To test our hypotheses, we compute the effects of supporting Black Lives Matter, posting about Black Lives Matter, and participating in protests related to this issue on civic engagement. We asked each participant whether they self-identified as a supporter of Black Lives Matter. Using separate questions, we also asked each respondent about the extent to which they posted about Black Lives Matter, or participated in protests related to this movement. The response options were never, once, two or three times, and four or more times.

Matching Covariates

We used two variables to investigate the effects of political engagement away from the internet. First, we asked each respondent about the extent to which they are interested in politics on a four-point scale that ranged from four points for "Very interested" to zero points for "Not at all interested." Second, each respondent was asked three questions about the extent to which their friends engaged in a set of activities and we built an additive index based on the responses ($\alpha = .63$, 2018; $\alpha = .58$, 2020).[6,7]

In addition, we used many variables to investigate the effects of political engagement using the internet. First, we asked each respondent how often they read blogs online about politics. Kerbel and Bloom (2005) and Moffett and Rice (2018) discover that blogs can act as outlets that foster enhanced civic activity, either online or offline. Second, each respondent was asked how frequently they read news on the internet about politics.

Third, we created an additive index of online civic activity consisting of five items, as several researchers have unearthed a link between activities on social media and offline civic engagement (see e.g., Kahne and Bowyer 2018; Ley and Brewer 2018; Loader, Vromen, and Xenos 2014). Through separate questions, we asked each respondent about the extent to which they had relied on social media for news, posted about politics on social media, read social media feeds about politics, liked or shared posts about politics on social media, or read or watched posts about politics on social media, and summed these responses to create an index of online civic activity ($\alpha = .84, 2018; \alpha = .83, 2020$).[8]

Fourth, each respondent was asked a series of questions about the extent to which they posted messages on social media about Supreme Court nominations (Kavanaugh in 2018, Barrett in 2020), immigration, the MeToo movement, gun control, and about other issues. Fifth, each respondent was asked a set of questions about the extent to which they participated in protests related to Supreme Court nominations (Kavanaugh in 2018, Barrett in 2020), immigration, the MeToo movement, gun control, and about other issues.

We used four variables to account for the effects of issue importance, as issues can sometimes facilitate higher levels of political participation (Converse 1964; Carmines and Stimson 1989; Reny, Collingwood, and Valenzuela 2019). We asked each respondent about the importance of congressional stances on immigration in influencing their vote choice. Second, we asked each respondent about the extent to which they supported or opposed the family separation policy implementation under the Trump administration. Third, we asked each respondent about the extent to which they supported or opposed the DACA program in 2020, but not in 2018.

What is more, we used several variables to consider the effects of personal characteristics on offline civic activity. First, we created a measure of strong partisanship, as this attachment is associated with an array of other political activities (see e.g., Flavin and Griffin 2009; Verba, Brady, and Schlozman 1995). Second, we examined the effects of ideology on civic engagement, as Achen and Bartels (2016) discover that self-identifying as either conservative or liberal shapes political participation. By asking those who identified as moderate, something else, or did not know, a follow-up question about whether that person self-identified as a conservative or liberal if they had to choose, we were able to create a binary variable for liberals.

Third, we asked each respondent for their sex, and we coded this variable one for females, two for males, and three for those who self-identified in another category. Fourth, we acquired data on each respondent's age by asking each to report their month and year of birth. Then, we computed each respondent's age based on the month and year of the 2018 midterm election for the 2018 data, and the month and year of the 2020 general election for the 2020 data.[9] Fifth, we asked each respondent for their race and collapsed that information into a binary that is coded one for whites and zero otherwise. Sixth, we asked each respondent for their level of education.

Finally, we used three variables to control for the effects of underlying political attitudes, as these can affect participation patterns. First, we asked each respondent whether they approved or disapproved of the job that Donald Trump is doing as president, as presidential approval is associated with changes in participatory patterns (Abramowitz and Stone 2006). Second, we asked each respondent whether they self-identified as a supporter of the MeToo movement.[10] Third, we asked each respondent about their opinions about Brett Kavanaugh's nomination in 2018 and Amy Coney Barrett's nomination in 2020.

Methods

To investigate whether our treatment variables are associated with offline civic activity, we use a matching analysis to compute the ATET. We choose a matching estimator for several reasons. First, nearly all regression-based techniques (including OLS) assume that there exists a linear relationship between the dependent and independent variables (see Greene 2011). Our theory advances a positive relationship between our treatment variables and civic engagement, but makes no prediction about the treatment effects at each level of supporting Black Lives Matter, posting about, or participating in protests related to this movement beyond a positive sign on each of them. Thus, the phenomenon that we examine is likely to be nonlinear and is ill suited to investigate using a method that assumes linearity (like OLS). Fortunately, matching analyses do not assume linearity, allow for a more flexible functional form and have many other statistical properties that make them a better choice to test our hypothesis (Imbens and Rubin 2015).

What is more, individuals have differing probabilities of supporting Black Lives Matter, posting about it or participating in protests related to it with varying frequencies. OLS estimators presume treatment homogeneity, which is unlikely to hold. Individuals likely have different treatment effects, particularly depending on their support for this movement, or the frequency with which they have posted about or participated in protests related to this movement (see Abadie and Imbens 2011). Thus, the effects of supporting this movement, posting about, or participating in protests related to Black Lives Matter may vary depending on the frequency with which one has posted about it. By construction, OLS-based estimators assume that we observe a linear, homogeneous relationship between supporting, posting about and participating in protests related to this movement, and offline civic activity. Matching-based approaches deal effectively with this issue because they assume neither linearity nor homogeneity (Imbens and Rubin 2015). Rather, matching-based approaches produce several treatment estimates depending on the level of treatment that a respondent received (Imbens and Rubin 2015). Thus, we can generate several, more accurate estimates of the effect that supporting, posting about, or participating in protests related to this movement had on offline civic engagement.

Moreover, OLS does not permit us to estimate what happens to offline civic activity in the absence of either self-identifying as a supporter of Black Lives Matter, posting about it, or participating in protests related to it (Nichols 2007). Matching analyses use the existing data to generate a dataset that includes observations that are as similar as possible, given the values of the remaining predictors (Stuart 2010). Thus, we can estimate what would have happened in the absence of supporting this movement, posting about it, or participating in protests related to it (see Gelman and Hill 2007). Then, we can use this dataset to estimate the effects of a specific level of supporting, posting, or participating in protests on offline civic activity. We iterate this procedure for each differing level of posting or participating in protests, relative to not having posted or participated in protests at all, or not having supported this movement. Finally, if we used OLS estimates to obtain the results, our results would likely be biased because any estimate of the treatment effect is conditioned on the values of the remaining independent variables. Consequently, OLS-based approaches do not compute ATETs.

Matching analyses manage each of these issues because they let us examine whether differing levels of supporting, posting about, or participating in protests related to Black Lives Matter are associated with higher levels of civic engagement. By matching based on each of the predictor variables to make inferences, we can separate the effect of posting about or participating in protests related to this movement beyond individuals' other predispositions to participate. Thus, doing so enables us to compare people with similar inclinations to civic activity who only vary in their frequency of supporting, posting about, or participating in protests related to this movement. Moreover, matching allows us to calculate ATETs for each treatment level, and by doing so, to calculate more precise effect sizes with observational data.

Assumptions

Before performing our matching analyses, we must fulfill four assumptions. The validity of any matching analyses hinges on satisfying these assumptions.[11] First, we presume that each treatment variable is binary. The first treatment variable, supporting Black Lives Matter, is already binary. The other treatment variables, posting about and participating in protests related to Black Lives Matter, are not. To make the posting variable binary, we generated a series of dichotomous variables for each response option, relative to never having posted about Black Lives Matter. Similarly, we made the participating in protests variable binary by creating a series of binary variables for each response option, relative to never having participated in protests related to Black Lives Matter. These binaries are coded one for each of these categories, zero for never having participated in the respective activity (e.g., posting or participating in protests), and missing for those who declined to answer the question, and for the remaining scalar options.

There are three binaries for posting once, posting two or three times, and for having posted four or more times. For instance, the binary for having posted once about this movement is coded one for those who did so, zero for never having done so, and missing for those who declined to answer this question, and for those who reported having posted more than once. Similarly, there are three dichotomous variables for participating in protests once, participating in protests twice or three times, and for having participated in protests four or more times. For example, the binary for having participated in protests once related to this movement is coded one for those who did so, zero for never having done so, and missing for those who decided not to answer this question, and for those who reported having participated in protests at higher frequencies. We expect positive signs for the ATET for each variable.

Second, we assume common support (or overlap), which means that it is possible that treated units may face an intervention that could have assigned them to the control group (see Imbens and Rubin 2015; King, Lucas, and Nielsen 2017). The data that we use meet this requirement because all respondents could have chosen not to post about or participate in protests related to this movement, or not to support it.

Third, we must fulfill the SUTVA assumption, which means that "the potential outcomes for any unit do not vary with the treatments assigned to other units, and for each unit, there are no different forms or versions of each treatment level, which lead to different potential outcomes" (Imbens and Rubin 2015, 10). We have met the first part of this assumption because the possible outcomes for civic activity do not vary with the levels of having posted about or participated in protests related to this movement, or with having been a Black Lives Matter supporter.[12]

The second aspect of this assumption is more complex because we have different variations on two of our treatment variables (posting about or participating in protests related to Black Lives Matter): once, two or three times, and four or more times about this movement. Yet, we can compare the effects of having posted with varying frequencies about this movement relative to those who never did so. For example, we can compare those who posted once about this movement to those who never did so, provided that we exclude those who posted at all other frequencies from that analysis.[13] Similarly, we can compare the effects of having participated in protests with varying frequencies related to this movement relative to those who never did so. We must perform an equivalent procedure to compare those who had posted or participated in protests two or three times, and those who did so four or more times about this movement if we hope to execute a matching analysis without an alternative treatment. When we compute our ATETs in this manner, we ultimately satisfy the SUTVA assumption because we have neither interference nor any hidden variations of the treatments (Imbens and Rubin, 2015, 10–11).

Finally, the treatment assignment must be conditionally independent of the outcome variable given a set of matching covariates (D'Agostino 1998, 2266). Thus, each respondent's assignment to either treatment (i.e., posting about Black Lives Matter, participating in protests related to this movement, or self-identifying as a supporter) is unconnected with their level of civic engagement, given the values of the remaining explanatory variables. We observe greatly varied participatory levels with respect to civic activity, and the mean level of civic activity is fairly low (M = 14.56, 2018; M = 26.01, 2020), given the minimum (0) and maximum values (48) possible with this index. Moreover, the activities that comprise offline civic activity do not cause an individual to be assigned to one or more treatment categories.

Matching Technique

To perform our matching analyses, we use one-to-one genetic matching with replacement (Diamond and Sekhon 2013; Sekhon 2011). We incorporate a propensity score into the analysis, as knowing estimated values of this score meaningfully improves the accuracy of this method (Diamond and Sekhon 2013). Propensity score matching allows us to compare observations that are otherwise similar across other predictors, but have experienced different treatments. We perform our analysis with replacement, as matching discrepancies are reduced because we can use untreated units as a match multiple times (see Abadie and Imbens 2006).[14] To remove any bias that results due to the choice of the matching estimator without affecting the variance of that estimator, we employ a bias correction (Abadie and Imbens 2016).

Results

Before analyzing the results testing a link between each of our treatment variables and higher levels of civic engagement, we need to investigate how similar the control and treatment groups are to one another (King, Lucas, and Nielsen 2017). If these groups substantially differ, then we cannot use matching to estimate effect size. The imbalance statistics for these models are available in Tables A1 through A5 in the online appendix. For 70.92% (139/196) of the variables contained in the models in Table 6.1, the KS tests are not significant at the .05 level after matching has occurred. Of the remaining 57 cases where the KS tests are statistically significant, 32 of them (or 56.14%) involve issues that we examine elsewhere in this volume, including the MeToo movement (in Chapter 2), Supreme Court nominations (Chapter 3), gun control (Chapter 4), and immigration and family separation, including opinions about the DACA program (Chapter 5). The

TABLE 6.1 Civic Engagement and Black Lives Matter

Effect on Offline Civic Engagement	Supporting Black Lives Matter	Posting about Black Lives Matter			Participating in Protests Related to Black Lives Matter		
	Model	Once	Two or Three Times	Four or More Times	Once	Two or Three Times	Four or More Times
Effect on Offline Civic Engagement	-.009	18.868	16.903	6.153	4.994	8.850	7.747
Abadie–Imbens Standard Error	2.364	12.471	8.380	2.298	2.646	5.816	2.650
95% Confidence Interval Lower Bound	-4.661	-43.735	.269	1.589	-.317	-2.712	2.452
95% Confidence Interval Upper Bound	4.643	5.999	33.537	10.717	10.305	20.412	13.042
T-Statistic	-.004	-1.513	2.017	2.677	1.888	1.522	2.924
P-Value (two-tailed)	.997	.130	.044	.007	.059	.128	.003
P-Value (one-tailed)	.499	.065	.022	.004	.030	.064	.002
N	286	71	96	95	53	86	64

Notes: In each two-column set, the number of times that one has posted about or participated in protests related to Black Lives Matter is compared with one who has never posted about or participated in protests related to that movement. Second, the covariates on which the matching is based are described in the text. Third, the effects on offline civic engagement are the ATET. Finally, the matching results are from 1:1 genetic matching with post-matching bias adjustment. Thus, the N represents the matched number of observations remaining 25 cases are randomly distributed across the varying models such that one cannot discern any systematic component that underlies them.

Thus, we are confident that we have substantially reduced imbalance across the model specifications. The matched groups have similar enough observable characteristics such that we can attribute any remaining differences across levels of posting about Black Lives Matter to the effects of posting, not to preexisting differences. Similarly, we can attribute any remaining differences across levels of participating in protests related to Black Lives Matter to the effects of participating in protests, not to preexisting differences. Also, we can attribute any remaining differences across support for Black Lives Matter to the effects of supporting that movement.

In Table 6.1, we provide the results from our matching routines. The results indicate that there is no statistically significant difference in civic engagement by virtue of having supported Black Lives Matter. This reaffirms an insight that we have gained through other chapters: that support for a particular cause does not automatically mobilize young people. Moreover, the results about posting seemingly indicate that posting about Black Lives Matter is connected with higher levels of civic activity, as posting two or more times about this movement shows what appears to be a statistically significant connection. However, neither of these results for posting is robust when we remove one matching covariate at a time from the models.

Conversely, the results about participating in protests related to Black Lives Matter are slightly more promising than what we have seen with respect to self-identifying as a Black Lives Matter supporter or posting about this movement. On the one hand, participating in protests two or three times is not connected to any statistically significant increases in civic engagement. However, participating in protests four or more times related to Black Lives Matter is connected with higher levels of civic activity, as we observe a nearly eight-point increase in civic engagement. This increase is the equivalent of participating in two activities very often that otherwise would not have happened, or participating in several activities at higher frequencies than would have occurred in the absence of participating in protests four or more times. In addition, participating in protests once appears to be associated with an increase in civic engagement when we use a one-tailed test of statistical significance. This increase, though, is not robust when we examine it using a one-tailed significance test and remove one matching covariate at a time from the model.

Robustness Checks

To verify whether the results in this chapter are model dependent (Ho et al. 2007), we tested our models for robustness by removing one matching covariate at a time from each model. Then, we re-ran the matching routines with the remaining predictors in each model.[15] When we examine those models relative to what we report here, 100% (or 28/28) of the models contained results that mirrored those that we report here for self-identifying as Black Lives Matter supporters.[16]

When we examine the models for posting compared to what we report here, only 48.80% (or 41/84) of the models contain results that are consistent with what we report here. Of the 43 models where the results diverge from what we report here, 42 (or 97.67%) of them are centered on the specifications for posting two or more times about Black Lives Matter. In slightly different terms, 75% (or 42/56) of the robustness checks for posting two or more times about Black Lives Matter provides results that diverge from what is contained in Table 6.1. In situations like this, we cannot conclude that posting two or more times about Black Lives Matter is connected with any statistically significant change in civic activity among young people.

When we examine the connection between participating in protests and civic engagement, 22 out of 28 specifications (or 78.57%) when we remove one variable at a time from the model for participating in protests two or three times furnish results that are inconsistent with what we report here. Moreover, 22 out of 28 possible model specifications (or 78.57%) for participating in protests once contain results that are not consistent with what we report here when we use this same one-tailed test. Thus, we cannot conclude that participating in protests related to Black Lives Matter three or fewer times is connected with a statistically significant change in civic activity. Fortunately, the results are more robust when we examine participating in protests four or more times, as 15 out of 29 results, including the one that is reported here (or 51.72%) run in a direction that is consistent with this conclusion.[17] Consequently, we can conclude that there is some evidence that participating in Black Lives Matter protests is connected with higher levels of civic activity.

Discussion and Conclusion

At first glance, the results in Table 6.1 suggest that most levels of posting and protesting related to Black Lives Matter produce gains in civic engagement. Yet, we discovered that only the link between protesting four or more times about Black Lives Matter in 2020 and higher levels of civic engagement is robust across a majority of specifications. One possible reason for this set of results is that the primary recipient of the protests was the public, not entirely elected officials. If true, then the protests achieved their primary objective: to mobilize the public.[18]

Thus, while we do not completely rule out the possibility that posting about Black Lives Matter or protesting at lower levels about it can help expand civic engagement, there is not consistent evidence in favor of these effects. In addition, we found no evidence that just being a supporter of Black Lives Matter was enough to expand young adults' civic engagement. Young adults may have led the way in planning Black Lives Matter protests across the nation in 2020, but only commitment strong enough to protest four or more times was linked with higher levels of civic engagement. That is not to say posting about Black Lives Matter did not have other impacts. The prevalence of young adults using social media to organize protests related to Black Lives Matter suggests there may well be a link between posting about Black Lives Matter and protesting about it, something we do not examine directly here. Yet, this would be consistent with Ortiz and Ostertag's (2014) discovery that posting views online can lead to the development of supportive online communities who decide to take offline action together to advance their views.

Our findings linking high levels of protesting about Black Lives Matter and heightened levels of civic engagement is consistent with what we found for the other social movements we examined in 2020. At a time when both protest and most other forms of offline engagement were made costlier than usual due to the Covid-19 pandemic, it took strong willingness to bear the costs of protest in this environment in order to see any spread from protesting as part of these movements to other forms of civic or political activity. This complements others' findings that the decision to take action to support one's views can be influenced by the costs of collective action (DiGrazia 2014).

While at first glance the paucity of significant, robust results linking support for or involvement in the Black Lives Matter movement in 2020 and higher levels of civic engagement aside from that for protesting four or more times might suggest that young adults' involvement in Black Lives Matter had little broader impact, collectively, these results also do not foreclose the possibility that being active with respect to Black Lives Matter is connected with contacting elected government officials. We investigate this possibility further in Chapters 7 and 8, where we examine whether posting and participating in protests related to varying issues, including Black Lives Matter, is associated with a higher propensity to contact elected government officials.

Notes

1 The loose, horizontal organizational structure of Black Lives Matter accommodates a wide range of views within the movement (Chase 2018). However, by tying Black Lives Matter as a whole to the views of those individuals within it with extreme viewpoints, those who opposed it were able to successfully reduce support among some Republicans for advancing the basic premise of the movement that is shared by all of its members, that black lives matter.
2 This is a term used to refer to those who supported a movement and followed it closely but did not take action to support it.
3 These generations have similar views on social issues (Parker, Graf, and Igielnik 2019).
4 We constrained the eligibility of participants in this survey to those with HIT approval rates of at least 95% and whose location is in the United States. While we were unable to constrain by age here, we did so through the first question asking respondents whether they were between the ages of 18 and 25. If they responded no, then the survey ended.

5 The online appendix contains the complete wording for each of the questions for the mTurk sample, along with a more extensive discussion of the variables that we used and their measurement.
6 These were the only questions in the survey about peer civic experiences. Some participants responded that they did not know for one or more of these questions. When constructing our index, we coded values for these variables as missing. Consequently, no peer civic engagement score is present for those who answered "don't know" on a minimum of one of these questions.
7 This also acts as an indirect indicator with respect to mobilization, as people frequently act politically when others around them do so (see e.g., Gimpel, Lee, and Kamiski 2006). Yet, it is possible that mobilization efforts by those other than peers, like interest groups and political parties, also yield higher levels of participation (Rosenstone and Hansen 2002). There are no questions in this survey that allow us to directly account for the effects of mobilization on civic activity. That said, we do consider many other covariates that also affect mobilization as part of the matching routines in this analysis.
8 We employed an adapted version of this variable for the models in which the treatment variable is posting about Black Lives Matter, as we cannot have the treatment variable being essentially the same as an element of one of the matching covariates. More specifically, we removed posted about politics on social media from the online civic engagement index for this set of models because the treatment for the set of models examining the effects of posting about Black Lives Matter is the extent to which one posted about this issue. We retained the remaining variables that comprise the online civic engagement index and created an additive index based on those (α = .81, 2018; α =.78, 2020).
9 We asked an initial screening question that identified those who were between the ages of 18 and 25, and those who responded that they were not in this age range were excluded from further participation in the survey. When we performed the age computations based on the year and month that respondents selected, though, there were 49 respondents who stated that they were older than 25 in 2018. In the year-month calculation, there was usually about a six-month variance between the reported and actual age among those 49 respondents. Since we asked about both year and month of birth based on drop-down menus, it is possible that a substantial portion of these respondents misreported their year and/or month of birth in 2018 (see Gendall and Healey 2008). We have no reason to believe that this error is systematic, and did not encounter the same concern in 2020. Thus, nonsystematic measurement error in an independent variable does not bias any conclusions in research studies (see King, Keohane, and Verba 1994).
10 Imbens and Rubin (2015, 16) state that any matching technique assumes that matching covariates are unaffected by treatment assignment. Thus, there should be no connection between any particular matching covariate and the assignment to treatment. Consequently, we exclude one variable from the set of matching covariates in this analysis: posting about Black Lives Matter, as this variable acts as the treatment.
11 Matching analyses are highly sensitive to even minor violations of these assumptions (Imbens and Rubin 2015).
12 If civic engagement were related to posting about Black Lives Matter, then civic activity and posting about this movement would be highly correlated. To test whether this occurs, we correlated our dependent variable (offline civic activity) and our treatment variables (supporting Black Lives Matter, posting about it, and participating in protests related to it). This correlation is low enough given our number of observations for all

variables (supporting Black Lives Matter: r = .309; posting: r = .517; protests: r =.728) such that we can conclude that the first part of the SUTVA assumption is satisfied.
13 If we do not conduct our analysis in this manner, then we cannot satisfy SUTVA, as there would be alternative treatment forms (see Imbens and Rubin 2015, 10–13).
14 However, we do not generate a regression following the matching analysis (as Ho et al. 2007 advise), as Abadie and Spiess (2019) say that this is not appropriate when matching is performed with replacement as researchers obtain inaccurate estimates of their standard errors.
15 One limitation of many matching analyses is that one can p-hack by changing the functional form of the matching routine to generate a set of results that confirms a researcher's theoretical expectations (Head et al. 2015).
16 The online appendix is available at www.kenmoffett.net/research.
17 Because this is a bare majority of results, one should exercise some caution in making strong, definitive conclusions.
18 We thank Melissa Michelson for this insight.

References

Abadie, Alberto and Guido W. Imbens 2006. "Large Sample Properties of Matching Estimators for Average Treatment Effects." *Econometrica* 74(1): 235–267. https://doi.org/10.1111/j.1468-0262.2006.00655.x. Accessed online June 19, 2021.

Abadie, Alberto and Guido W. Imbens 2011. "Bias-Corrected Matching Estimators for Average Treatment Effects." *Journal of Business and Economic Statistics* 29(1): 1–11. https://doi.org/10.1198/jbes.2009.07333. Accessed online June 19, 2021.

Abadie, Alberto and Guido W. Imbens 2016. "Matching on the Estimated Propensity Score." *Econometrica* 84(2): 781–807. https://doi.org/10.3982/ECTA11293. Accessed online June 19, 2021.

Abadie, Alberto and Jann Spiess 2019. "Robust Post-Matching Inference." Forthcoming in the *Journal of the American Statistical Association*. https://doi.org/10.1080/01621459.2020.1840383. Accessed online June 19, 2021.

Abramowitz, Alan I. and Walter J. Stone 2006. "The Bush Effect: Polarization, Turnout, and Activism in the 2004 Presidential Election." *Presidential Studies Quarterly* 36(2): 141–154. https://doi.org/10.1111/j.1741-5705.2006.00295.x. Accessed online June 19, 2021.

Achen, Christopher H. and Larry M. Bartels 2016. *Democracy for Realists: Why Elections Do Not Produce Responsive Government*. Princeton, NJ: Princeton University Press.

Alcindor, Yamiche. 2013. "George Zimmerman Found Not Guilty." *USA Today*. www.usatoday.com/story/news/nation/2013/07/13/george-zimmerman-found-not-guilty/2514163/. Accessed online January 12, 2021.

Anderson, Monica. 2016. "Major Recent Events Bring #BlackLivesMatter Back to the Forefront as the Tone Shifts Overnight." Pew Research Center. www.pewresearch.org/internet/2016/08/15/major-recent-events-bring-blacklivesmatter-back-to-the-forefront-as-the-tone-shifts-overnight/. Accessed online January 12, 2021.

Associated Press 2019a. "From Eric Garner's Death to Firing of NYPD Officer: A Timeline of Key Events." *USA Today*. www.usatoday.com/story/news/2019/08/20/eric-garner-timeline-chokehold-death-daniel-pantaleo-fired/2059708001/. Accessed online January 12, 2021.

Associated Press 2019b. "Timeline of Events in Shooting of Michael Brown." https://apnews.com/article/9aa32033692547699a3b61da8fd1fc62. Accessed online January 12, 2021.

Baalman, Jesse 2020. "Teenagers Lead Noviolent Black Lives Matter Protests across the Metro East." *St. Louis Magazine*. www.stlmag.com/news/teenagers-lead-peaceful-black-lives-matter-protests-across-t. Accessed online February 8, 2021.

BBC. 2015. "Ferguson Unrest: From Shooting to Nationwide Protests." BBC. www.bbc.com/news/world-us-canada-30193354. Accessed online January 12, 2021.

Brady, Henry E., Sidney Verba, and Kay Lehman Schlozman 1995. "Beyond SES: A Resource Model of Political Participation." *American Political Science Review* 89(2): 271–294. https://doi.org/10.2307/2082425. Accessed online June 19, 2021.

Burke, Minyvonne 2020. "Video Appears to Show Georgia Man Shot While Jogging; Lawyers Call for Arrests." NBC News. www.nbcnews.com/news/nbcblk/video-appears-show-georgia-man-shot-while-jogging-lawyers-call-n120130. Accessed online May 22, 2020.

Calhoun-Brown, Allison. 2000. "Upon This Rock: The Black Church, Nonviolence, and the Civil Rights Movement." *Political Science and Politics* 33(2): 168–174. https://doi.org/10.2307/420886. Accessed online June 19, 2021.

Carmines, Edward G. and James A. Stimson 1989. *Issue Evolution: Race and the Transformation of American Politics*. Princeton, NJ: Princeton University Press.

CBS News Poll. June 23–26, 2020. https://drive.google.com/file/d/1l0XruPxbVV8mBoT0mpmeLk4AmbnkIGeH/view. Accessed online January 12, 2021.

Chase, Garrett 2018. "The Early History of the Black Lives Matter Movement, and the Implications Thereof." *Nevada Law Review Journal* 18(3): 1091–1112.

Chiu, Allyson 2020. "Tucker Carlson says, George Floyd Protests Are 'Not Really about Black Lives' Prompting Backlash." *The Washington Post*. www.washingtonpost.com/nation/2020/06/09/fox-black-lives-carlson/. Accessed online January 12, 2021.

Cobb, Jelani 2016. "The Matter of Black Lives." *The New Yorker*. www.newyorker.com/magazine/2016/03/14/where-is-black-lives-matter-headed. Accessed online January 12, 2021.

Cohen, Li 2020. "George Floyd's Death Sparks Large Protests, Confrontations with Police." CBS News. www.cbsnews.com/news/george-floyds-death-massive-protests-minneapolis/. Accessed online January 12, 2021.

Converse, Phillip 1964. "The Nature of Belief Systems in Mass Publics." In *Ideology and Its Discontents*, David E. Apter (Ed.). New York, NY: Free Press of Glencoe.

Crowd Counting Consortium 2021. https://sites.google.com/view/crowdcountingconsortium/home. Accessed online December 17, 2019.

D'Agostino, Ralph B. 1998. "Propensity Score Methods for Bias Reduction in the Comparison of a Treatment to a Non-Randomized Control Group." *Statistics in Medicine* 17(9): 2265–2281. https://doi.org/10.1002/(SICI)1097-0258(19981015)17:19<2265::AID-SIM918>3.0.CO;2-B. Accessed online June 19, 2021.

Dakss, Brian 2020. "Video Shows Minneapolis Cop with Knee on Neck of Motionless, Moaning Man Who Later Died." CBS News. www.cbsnews.com/news/minneapolis-police-george-floyd-died-officer-kneeling-neck-arrest/. Accessed online June 9, 2020.

Diamond, Alexis and Jasjeet J. Sekhon 2013. "Genetic Matching for Estimating Causal Effects: A General Multivariate Matching Method for Achieving Balance in Observational Studies." *Review of Economics and Statistics* 95(3): 932–945. https://doi.org/10.1162/REST_a_00318. Accessed online June 19, 2021.

DiGrazia, Joseph. 2014. "Individual Protest Participation in the United States." *Social Science Quarterly* 95(1): 111–131. https://doi.org/10.1111/ssqu.12048. Accessed online June 19, 2021.

Edwards, Frank, Hedwig Lee, and Michael Espisito 2019. "Risk of Being Killed by Police Use of Force in the United States by Age, Race-Ethnicity, and Sex." *Proceedings of the National Academy of Sciences of the United States of America* 116(34): 16793–16798. https://doi.org/10.1073/pnas.1821204116. Accessed online June 19, 2021.

Faguy, Ana 2020. "Youth-Led Group behind Columbia's Black Lives Matter Protests Discusses What It Takes to Organize in 2020." *Baltimore Sun*. www.baltimoresun.com/maryland/howard/cng-ho-youth-organizing-protests-20200605-gwfdwqdxmfaapkymmq2pvc27km-story.html. Accessed online June 9, 2020.

Flavin, Patrick and John D. Griffin 2009. "Policy, Preferences, and Participation: Government's Impact on Democratic Citizenship." *Journal of Politics* 71(2): 544–559. https://doi.org/10.1017/S0022381609090458. Accessed online June 19, 2021.

Freelon, Dean, Charlton D. McIlwain, and Meredith D. Clark. 2016. "Beyond the Hashtags: #Ferguson, #Blacklivesmatter, and the Online Struggle for Offline Justice." *Center for Media and Social Impact*. https://cmsimpact.org/wp-content/uploads/2016/03/beyond_the_hashtags_2016.pdf. Accessed online January 12, 2021.

Gajanan, Mahita 2020. "Protests Are Being Held in Small Cities and Towns across the U.S. – and Young People Are Leading the Charge." *Time*. https://time.com/5847228/george-floyd-nationwide-protests. Accessed online February 8, 2021.

Gelman, Andrew and Jennifer Hill 2007. *Data Analysis Using Regression and Multilevel/Heiarchical Models*. New York, NY: Cambridge University Press.

Gendall, Philip and Benjamin Healey 2008. "Asking the Age Question in Mail and Online Surveys." *International Journal of Market Research* 50(3): 309–317. https://doi.org/10.1177/147078530805000303. Accessed online June 19, 2021.

Gerbaudo, Paolo. 2020. "The Pandemic Crowd: Protest in the Time of Covid-19." *Journal of International Affairs* 73(2): 61–75.

Gil de Zúñiga, Homero, Nakwon Jung, and Sebastian Valenzuela 2012. "Social Media Use for News and Individuals' Social Capital, Civic Engagement and Political Participation." *Journal of Computer-Mediated Communication*. 17(3): 319–336. https://doi.org/10.1111/j.1083-6101.2012.01574.x. Accessed online June 19, 2021.

Gillion, Daniel Q. 2020. *The Loud Minority: Why Protests Matter in American Democracy*. Princeton, NJ: Princeton University Press.

Gimpel, James G., Frances E. Lee, and Joshua Kaminski 2006. "The Political Geography of Campaign Contributions in American Politics." *Journal of Politics* 68(3): 626–639. https://doi.org/10.1111/j.1468-2508.2006.00450.x. Accessed online June 19, 2021.

Gramlich, John. 2020. "5 Facts about Fox News." Pew Research Center. www.pewresearch.org/fact-tank/2020/04/08/five-facts-about-fox-news/. Accessed online January 12, 2021.

Greene, William H. 2011. *Econometric Analysis*. 7th Ed. New York, NY: Pearson Education.

Grieco, Elizabeth. 2020. "Americans' Main Sources for Political News Vary by Party and Age." Pew Research Center. www.pewresearch.org/fact-tank/2020/04/01/americans-main-sources-for-political-news-vary-by-party-and-age/. Accessed online January 12, 2021.

Griffith, Janelle. 2020. "Ahmaud Arbery Shooting: A Timeline of the Case." NBC News. www.nbcnews.com/news/us-news/ahmaud-arbery-shooting-timeline-case-n1204306. Accessed online January 12, 2021.

Grimsley, Brooke 2020. "Ft. Zumwalt West Grad Lead Peaceful Protest: 'It's Truly a Blessing to Bring People Together." KMOV News. www.kmov.com/news/ft-zumwalt-west-grad-leads-peaceful-protest-its-truly-a-blessing-to-bring-people-together/article_98d194b2-a913-11ea-8482-0387620ff5d0.html. Accessed online June 9, 2020.

Guynn, Jessica. 2015. "Meet the Woman Who Coined #BlackLivesMatter." *USA Today*. www.usatoday.com/story/tech/2015/03/04/alicia-garza-black-lives-matter/24341593/. Accessed online January 12, 2021.

Haseman, Janie, Karina Zeiets, Mitchell Thorson, Carlie Process, George Petras, and Shawn J. Sullivan 2020. "Tracking Protests across the USA in the Wake of George Floyd's Death." *USA Today*. www.usatoday.com/in-depth/graphics/2020/06/03/map-protests-wake-george-floyds-death/5310149002. Accessed online February 8, 2021.

Havercroft, Jonathan and David Owen. 2016. "Soul-Blindness, Police Orders and Black Lives Matter." *Political Theory* 44(6): 739–763. https://doi.org/10.1177/0090591716657857. Accessed online June 19, 2021.

Head, Megan L., Luke Holman, Rob Lanfear, Andrew T. Kahn, and Michael D. Jennions 2015. "The Extent and Consequences of P-Hacking in Science." *Plos Biology* 13(3): e1002106. https://doi.org/10.1371/journal.pbio.1002106. Accessed online June 19, 2021.

Ho, Daniel E., Kosuke Imai, Gary King, and Elizabeth A. Stuart 2007. "Matching as Nonparametric Preprocessing for Reducing Model Dependence in Parametric Causal Inference." *Political Analysis* 15(3): 199–236. https://doi.org/10.1093/pan/mpl013. Accessed online June 19, 2021.

Imbens, Guido W. and Donald B. Rubin 2015. *Causal Inference for Statistics, Social, and Biomedical Sciences: An Introduction*. New York, NY: Cambridge University Press.

Jenkins, J. Craig. 1983. "Resource Mobilization: Theory and Study of Social Movements." *Annual Review of Sociology* 9(1983): 527–553. https://doi.org/10.1146/annurev.so.09.080183.002523. Accessed online June 19, 2021.

Kahne, Joseph and Benjamin Bowyer 2018. "The Political Significance of Social Media Activity and Social Networks." *Political Communication* 35(3): 470–493. https://doi.org/10.1080/10584609.2018.1426662. Accessed online June 19, 2021.

Kam, Cindy D. and Donald R. Kinder. 2012. "Ethnocentrism as a Short-Term Force in the 2008 Presidential Election." *American Journal of Political Science* 56(2): 326–340. https://doi.org/10.1111/j.1540-5907.2011.00564.x. Accessed online June 19, 2021.

Kerbel, Matthew R. and Joel David Bloom 2005. "Blog for America and Civic Involvement." *The International Journal of Press/Politics* 10(4): 3–27. https://doi.org/10.1177/1081180X05281395. Accessed online June 19, 2021.

Kinder, Donald R. and Lynn M. Sanders. 1996. *Divided by Color: Racial Politics and Democratic Ideals*. Chicago, IL: University of Chicago Press.

Kinder, Donald R. and Nicholas Winter. 2001. "Exploring the Racial Divide: Blacks, Whites, and Opinion on National Policy." *American Journal of Political Science* 45(2): 439–456.

King, Gary, Christopher Lucas, and Richard A. Nielsen 2017. "The Balance-Sample Size Frontier in Matching Methods for Causal Inference." *American Journal of Political Science* 61(2): 473–489. https://doi.org/10.1111/ajps.12272. Accessed online June 19, 2021.

King, Gary, Robert O. Keohane, and Sidney Verba 1994. *Designing Social Inquiry: Scientific Inference in Qualitative Research*. Princeton, NJ: Princeton University Press.

Larkin, Brian Patrick. 2007. "The Forty-Year 'First Step': The Fair Housing Act as an Incomplete Tool for Suburban Integration." *Columbia Law Review* 107(7): 1617–1654.

Ley, Barbara L. and Paul R. Brewer 2018. "Social Media, Networked Protest, and the March for Science." *Social Media and Society* 4(3): 1–12. https://doi.org/10.1177/2056305118793407. Accessed online June 19, 2021.

Li, David K. 2020. "George Floyd Told Police He Was Struggling to Breathe before an Officer Put a Knee on His Neck." NBC News. www.nbcnews.com/news/us-news/george-floyd-told-police-he-was-struggling-breathe-officer-put-n1218556. Accessed online January 12, 2021.

Loader, Brian D., Ariadne Vromen, and Michael A. Xenos 2014. "The Networked Young Citizen: Social Media, Political Participation and Civic Engagement." *Information, Communication and Society* 17(2): 143–150. https://doi.org/10.1080/1369118X.2013.871571. Accessed online June 19, 2021.

Luibrand, Shannon. 2015. "How a Death in Ferguson Sparked a Movement in America." CBS News. www.cbsnews.com/news/how-the-black-lives-matter-movement-changed-america-one-year-later/. Accessed online January 12, 2021.

McAdam, Doug 1986. "Recruitment to High-Risk Activism: The Case of Freedom Summer." *American Journal of Sociology* 92(1): 64–90. https://doi.org/10.1086/228463. Accessed online June 19, 2021.

McDonald, Jermaine M. 2016. "Ferguson and Baltimore according to Dr. King: How Competing Interpretations of King's Legacy Frame the Public Discourse on Black Lives Matter." *Journal of the Society of Christian Ethics* 36(2): 141–158. https://doi.org/10.1353/sce.2016.0035. Accessed online June 19, 2021.

McLaughlin, Eliott C. 2020. "Ahmaud Arbery Was Hit with a Truck before He Died and His Killer Allegedly Used a Racial Slur, Investigator Testifies." CNN. www.cnn.com/2020/06/04/us/mcmichaels-hearing-ahmaud-arbery/index.html. Accessed online January 12, 2021.

Medenica, Vladimir Enrique. 2018. "Millennials and Race in the 2016 Election." *Journal of Race, Ethnicity and Politics* 3(1): 55–76. https://doi.org/10.1017/rep.2017.33. Accessed online June 19, 2021.

Moffett, Kenneth W. and Laurie L. Rice 2016. *Web 2.0 and the Political Mobilization of College Students*. Lanham, MD: Lexington Books.

Moffett, Kenneth W. and Laurie L. Rice 2018. "College Students and Online Political Expression in the 2016 Election." *Social Science Computer Review* 36(4): 422–439. https://doi.org/10.1177/0894439317721186. Accessed online June 19, 2021.

Nichols, Austin 2007. "Causal Inference with Observational Data." *The Stata Journal* 7(4): 507–541. https://doi.org/10.1177/1536867X0800700403. Accessed online June 19, 2021.

Opp, Karl-Dieter. 1988. "Grievances and Participation in Social Movements." *American Sociological Review* 53(6): 853–864.

Ortiz, David G. and Stephen F. Ostertag 2014. "Katrina Bloggers and the Development of Collective Civic Action: The Web as a Virtual Mobilizing Structure." *Sociological Perspectives* 57 (1): 52–78. https://doi.org/10.1177/0731121413517558. Accessed online June 19, 2021.

Parker, Kim, Nikki Graf, and Ruth Igielnik 2019. "Generation Z Looks a Lot Like Millennials on Key Social and Political Issues." Pew Research Center www.pewsocialtrends.org/2019/01/17/generation-z-looks-a-lot-like-millennials-on-key-social-and-political-issues/. Accessed online February 12, 2019.

Pereira, Ivan and Aaron Katersky. 2020. "Amy Cooper Charged in Central Park False Report against Black Bird Watcher." ABC News. https://abcnews.go.com/US/amy-cooper-charged-central-park-false-report-christian/story?id=71635157. Accessed online January 12, 2021.

Pew Research Center 2016. "On Views of Race and Inequality, Blacks and Whites Are Worlds Apart." June 27. www.pewsocialtrends.org/2016/06/27/on-views-of-race-and-inequality-blacks-and-whites-are-worlds-apart/. Accessed online January 12, 2021.

Ransom, Jan 2020. "Amy Cooper Faces Charges after Calling Police on Black Bird-Watcher." *The New York Times*. www.nytimes.com/2020/07/06/nyregion/amy-cooper-false-report-charge.html. Accessed online January 12, 2021.

Reny, Tyler T., Loren Collingwood, and Ali A. Valenzuela 2019. "Vote Switching in the 2016 Election: How Racial and Immigration Attitudes, Not Economics, Explain Shifts in White Voting." *Public Opinion Quarterly* 83(1): 91–113. https://doi.org/10.1093/poq/nfz011. Accessed online June 19, 2021.

Romero, Dennis 2020. "No Charges for Officer Who Shot Michael Brown in Ferguson, Missouri, after Follow-Up Probe." NBC News. July 30. www.nbcnews.com/news/us-news/no-charges-officer-who-shot-michael-brown-ferguson-missouri-after-n1235382. Accessed February 2, 2021.

Rosenstone, Steven J. and John Mark Hansen 2002. *Mobilization, Participation, and Democracy in America*. New York, NY: Pearson-Longman.

Sekhon, Jasjeet S. 2011. "Multivariate and Propensity Score Matching Software with Automated Balance Optimization: The Matching Package for R." *Journal of Statistical Software* 42(7): 1–52.

Stewart, Abigail J., Isis H. Settles, and Nicholas J. G. Winter 1998. "Women and the Social Movements of the 1960s: Activists, Engaged Observers, and Nonparticipants." *Political Psychology* 19(1): 63–94. https://doi.org/10.1111/0162-895X.00093. Accessed online June 19, 2021.

Stuart, Elizabeth A. 2010. "Matching Methods for Causal Inference: A Review and a Look Forward." *Statistical Science* 25(1): 1–21 https://doi.org/10.1214/09-STS313. Accessed online June 19, 2021.

Stump, Scott 2020. "Woman Speaks Out after viral Central Park Confrontation with Man Sparks Outrage." *Today*. www.today.com/news/amy-cooper-woman-viral-central-park-confrontation-video-apologizes-t182412. Accessed online February 8, 2021.

Sunmer, William Graham 1906. *Folkways*. Boston: Ginn.

Tarrow, Sidney 1992. "Mentalities, Political Cultures and Collective Action Frames: Constructing Meanings through Action." In *Frontiers in Social Movement Theory*, Aldon Morris and Carol McClurg Mueller (Eds.). New Haven, CT: Yale University Press.

Theising, Andrew J. 2003. *Made in the USA: East St. Louis*. St. Louis, MO: Virginia.

Thomas, Deja and Juliana Menasce Horowitz. 2020. "Support for Black Lives Matter Has Decreased since June but Remains Strong among Black Americans." Pew Research Center. www.pewresearch.org/fact-tank/2020/09/16/support-for-black-lives-matter-has-decreased-since-june-but-remains-strong-among-black-americans/. Accessed online January 12, 2021.

Tuch, Steven A. and Michael Hughes. 2011. "Whites' Racial Policy Attitudes in the Twenty-First Century: The Continuing Significance of Racial Resentment." *The Annals of the American Academy of Political and Social Science* 634(1): 134–153. https://doi.org/10.1177/0002716210390288. Accessed online June 19, 2021.

Vera, Amir and Laura Ly. 2020. "White Woman Who Called Police on a Black Man Bird-Watching in Central Park Has Been Fired." www.cnn.com/2020/05/26/us/central-park-video-dog-video-african-american-trnd/index.html. Accessed online January 12, 2021.

Verba, Sidney, Henry E. Brady, and Kay L. Schlozman 1995. *Voice and Equality: Civic Voluntarism in American Democracy*. Cambridge, MA: Harvard University Press.

Waldrop, Theresa, Erica Henry, and Angela Barajas. 2020. "Three Men Indicted in the Death of Ahmaud Arbery." CNN. www.cnn.com/2020/06/24/us/ahmaud-arbery-grand-jury-indictment/index.html. Accessed online January 12, 2021.

Walker, Theresa. 2020. "When Black Lives Matter to Everyone: A New Generation Leads Call for Change, Sparked by the Killing of George Floyd." *The Orange County Register.* www.ocregister.com/2020/06/05/when-black-lives-matter-to-everyone-a-new-generation-leads-call-for-change-sparked-by-the-killing-of-george-floyd. Accessed online June 9, 2020.

Yang, Hongwei "Chris" and Jean L. DeHart. 2016. "Social Media Use and Online Political Participation among College Students during the US Election 2012." *Social Media + Society* 2(1): https://doi.org/10.1177/2056305115623802. Accessed online June 19, 2021.

PART II
Moving from the Outside in

The Link between Posting and Protesting and Contacting Elected Officials

7
MESSAGES RECEIVED?

Examining the Link between Young Adults Posting Political Views Online and Sharing Views with Elected Officials

Introduction

Some view posting views about politics negatively, pointing to the development of online echo chambers, where people communicate only with those who share their views, reinforcing the strength of these views, and making it hard to understand any side to an issue but their own (Jacobson, Myung, and Johnson 2016; Del Vicario et al. 2016). Other research suggests that while people tend to seek and share similar viewpoints (Bakshy, Messing, and Adamic 2015), this echo chamber characterization of people's online habits is overstated (Iyengar and Hahn 2009; Lawrence, Sides, and Farrell 2010; Flaxman, Goel, and Rao 2016; Dubois and Grant 2018). The social networks of people who rarely discuss politics accommodate a variety of hidden political viewpoints.

However, as presidential elections approach, they provide a shock to the system, causing previously hidden viewpoints to reveal themselves. Suddenly, social media feeds become full of political posts, and people discover some of their friends have sharply different political views than their own. In the run-up to the 2016 election, 37% of social media users reported feeling worn out by political posts and discussions online, while only 20% reported they liked seeing it (Duggan and Smith 2016). In this same survey, 59% found online discussions with whom they disagree stressful and frustrating and nearly two-thirds said they yield discoveries that they have less in common politically than they thought (Duggan and Smith 2016). This sometimes even leads to decisions to unfriend or block those on social media with different political views; 17% of Americans reported having done so because of the 2016 election (Dann 2016). This was magnified in the lead-up to the 2020 election, with 55% of social media users reporting feeling "worn out" by political posts on social media and only 15% saying they like seeing this content (Anderson and Auxier 2020). Further, 70% of social media users reported finding talking about politics on social media with people they disagree with stressful and frustrating, and 72% said these discussions lead to discoveries they have less in common politically than they thought (Anderson and Auxier 2020).

Others refer to posting one's views online dismissively as slacktivism, which Lexico (2020) defines as "the practice of supporting a political or social cause by means such as social media or online petitions, characterized as involving very little effort or commitment." Proponents of this characterization argue sharing one's views online carries little cost and produces little to no consequence, allowing someone to feel good about themselves for doing what amounts to nothing. In Part I, though, we found some evidence that contradicts this slacktivism complaint and showed that posting one's political views online can have positive consequences. Posting about the MeToo Movement, Supreme Court nominations, gun control, and immigration and family separation are connected with higher levels of civic engagement. This supports a growing line of research that online political expression boosts civic engagement (Shah et al. 2005; Yamamoto, Kushin, and Dalisay 2013; Boulianne 2019; Moffett and Rice 2016, 2018).

In this chapter, we explore whether the messages young adults post online also make their way to elected officials. To begin, we discuss how patterns of posting online about politics and contacting elected officials differ dramatically by age. We then review the literature on responsiveness and on contacting elected officials. We discuss posting online as messages to elected officials and develop a theory of why posting online should lead to contacting elected officials. Then, to test this link we explore whether posting about politics makes people more likely to contact elected officials. Then, we turn to whether posting about each of the specific issues explored in Part I helps make young adults more likely to contact elected officials about those issues. The results suggest young adults' participation patterns may be changing in ways that make them more likely to be heard.

Generational Patterns of Posting and Contacting

Voting is not the only political activity whose rates vary dramatically by age. When it comes to a variety of types of activities that Zukin et al. (2006) characterize as public voice they noted that young adults "…are not especially reluctant to voice their opinions, compared with older people" (77). However, they found one exception: older generations reported contacting elected officials at roughly twice the rate of Millennials (Zukin et al. 2006). Figure 7.1 shows that, whether online or offline, young adults contacted elected officials at substantially lower rates than older age groups.

Young adults seeking change instead are more likely to post political messages online. For example, a study of undergraduate communications students found

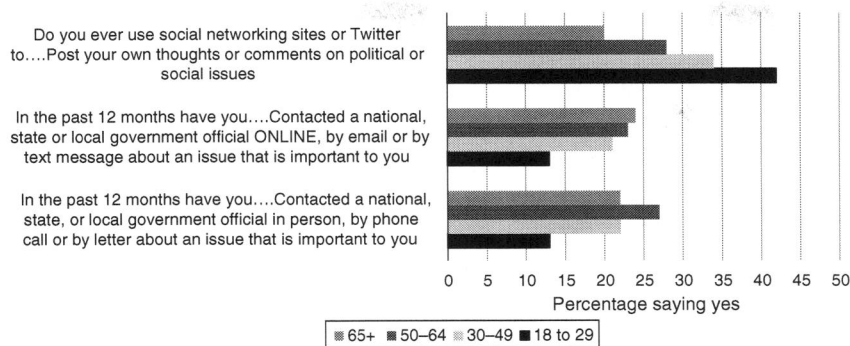

FIGURE 7.1 Posting and Contacting Elected Officials by Age in 2012.
Source: Pew Research Center's Internet & American Life Project Civic Engagement Tracking Survey July 16, 2012–August 7, 2012.

nearly three-quarters reported expressing opinions about social issues on social media (Seelig 2018). Those under age 29 were significantly more likely than older age groups to share their thoughts on issues, encourage others to act, and share many forms of political material online (Rainie et al. 2012). As seen in Figure 7.1, those aged 18–29 were also more likely to post their views about political or social issues on social networking sites. These patterns raise an important question: do young adults express their views in ways likely to reach the eyes and ears of elected officials?

The Responsiveness of Elected Officials

Theories vary about how responsive elected officials should be to public opinion. Democratic elitism argues that citizens are generally incapable of understanding the complexities of policy and instead elect officials who will know better. It sees elected officials as trustees who should use their own best judgment in making decisions.[1] If most elected officials saw their role in this way, generation gaps in contacting elected officials would have minimal consequences for the relative representation of their views.

Other theories of democratic representation instead see elected representatives as delegates, elected to represent their constituent's preferences. Here, representation is a principal-agent relationship between voters, the principals, and their elected representative, the agent (Pitkin 1967). As Madison outlined in Federalist Papers 10 and 51, elected officials are held accountable through regular elections. This provides clear incentives to be responsive to public opinion.

Representation can take varying forms (Pitkin 1967). One of these is substantive representation, the degree to which elected officials represent and work to enact the policy preferences and views of their constituents (Pitkin 1967). To do this well, elected officials need to know what their constituents think. This poses a challenge. The typical public opinion poll tells elected officials the *collective* preferences of Americans. Their constituents in their district may or may not share these views. Conducting regular scientific polls of districts costs money and members of Congress instead devote much of their budget to constituent service.[2] Thus, communication from constituents becomes an important gauge for judging constituent opinion and determining how to vote (Kingdon 1989; Bergan 2009; Congressional Management Foundation 2011).

Contacting Elected Officials

Constituents contact their elected officials for many reasons including dissatisfaction in dealing with government agencies (Moon, Serra, and West 1993) and sharing their political views in the hopes of influencing how a legislator votes on an upcoming bill. These contacts can be particularized, to address the needs of an individual, or generalized to address broader needs in society (Verba and Nie 1972; Hirlinger 1992).

Efficacy and political ties have been found to increase the likelihood of contacting elected officials about general issues (Verba and Nie 1972; Zuckerman and West 1985; Hirlinger 1992). So, too, does the perceived receptiveness of the member of Congress as signaled by legislators that share constituents' partisanship (Broockman and Ryan 2016). Socioeconomic status also affects the likelihood of contacting elected officials (Verba and Nie 1972; Vedlitz and Veblen 1980; Sharp 1982). And, as Figure 7.1 suggested, age is a significant predictor of contacting elected officials. This holds true even when controlling for a variety of other factors, with increased age associated with greater likelihood of contacting elected officials (Verba and Nie 1972; Hero 1986).[3]

Whatever the cause, these contacts matter. Senator roll call voting shows responsiveness to the ideology of voters, but not those who fail to vote (Griffin and Newman 2005). It also shows strong responsiveness to the ideology of those who contact senators (Griffin and Newman 2005). Experiments also show that legislators respond to constituent contact. Bergan and Cole (2015) found that constituent contact in favor of an anti-bullying bill increased legislators' likelihood of voting in favor of it by 11–12%. Another field experiment showed that both members of Congress and state legislators are more responsive to letters making service requests of them than they are to policy letters (Butler, Karpowitz, and Pope 2012). Still, they do respond to policy letters. In Butler, Karpowitz, and Pope's (2012) experiment, members of Congress' staff responded to 52% of the constituency service letters and 38% of the policy letters. Although letters don't always yield a reply, voting patterns by legislators suggest policy responsiveness (Griffin and Newman 2005). Thus, if young adults vote at lower rates and contact elected officials less than their elders, then previous research suggests they will be far less likely to be listened to.

Online Posts as Messages to Elected Officials

Elected officials have worked to be accessible online. These efforts include developing web pages sharing their positions on issues and using interactive features on these web pages that allow constituents to click a button to send a message to legislators. Yet, as the data presented in Figure 7.1 suggest, young adults were not as quick to take to online methods for contacting elected officials as older generations. As it showed, whether online or offline, young adults were significantly less likely to directly contact elected officials than older generations. Instead, young adults have flocked to social media to share their political views.

Yet, unless young adults use social media to direct message (dm) elected officials, these messages are far less likely to make their way to elected officials' eyes. After all, elected officials do not follow all of their constituents' social media accounts, nor can they even if they wanted to do so. Most constituents' posts online likely will never be seen by their elected representatives. And, even those who do reach elected officials through their online posts are likely to be taken less seriously than messages sent by other communication forms. Part of this reflects generational gaps in communication preferences. After all, at the start of the 115th Congress, the average age of members of the House of Representatives was 57.8, and in the Senate, 61.8 (Manning 2018). This age group has a less positive view of the internet than do young adults (Vogels 2019). In addition, social media posts are sometimes seen as less costly, and therefore taken less seriously, than other forms of communication because typing and posting a few sentences online takes less time and effort than making a phone call or writing a letter.

There are ways of tracking social media posts in the aggregate as a rough gauge of public opinion. To date, these methods have been better at revealing the level of interest in an issue and what topics are popularly discussed, rather than specific messages about these topics. For example, Twitter hashtags have been used to track interest in presidential elections (Zhang, Seltzer, and Bichard 2013), the spread of the flu (Cheng et al. 2011), and the prevalence of the MeToo movement (Anderson and Toor 2018). While new methods of gaining insights into political opinions through analyzing social media posts continue to be developed, the most effective way to get a clear message to members of Congress remains sharing it with them directly. Thus, if young adults remain reluctant to contact elected officials, then their voices are less likely to be heard.

Why Posting Should Lead to Contacting

If the messages young adults post online are going to be effective at moving elected officials, their messages must first reach them. One way of examining whether this occurs is to see whether posting online about politics makes young adults more likely to contact elected officials. There is good reason to think it might. Those who consume political information online are more likely to share their political views online via social media (Moffett and Rice 2016, 2018). Expressing oneself online can boost efficacy (Yang and DeHart 2016), increasing the belief that one's actions can make a difference. This increases the likelihood of thinking that it is worth contacting elected officials. In addition, exposure to political information can help lead to political action. In fact, in 2013, 19% of 18–29-year-olds reported deciding to act on an issue because of what they read on social media (Smith 2013).[4] At the same time, posting one's views online typically involves some level of public expression. When young adults post their views on social media, they become much easier for individuals and groups with similar views to identify and mobilize to contact elected officials. For example, interest groups routinely share calls via their websites and their social media accounts to contact elected officials over specific legislation and some also engage in advertising targeted at likely supporters. Thus, those active politically online become more likely to get steered to contact their elected officials directly. This increased likelihood of exposure to pleas to contact elected officials, paired with increased efficacy, should combine to make those who post about issues more likely to contact elected officials about them.

Data

To test our primary hypothesis, we performed online surveys on November 7, 2018, and November 4, 2020, of Americans between 18 and 25 years old – an age range that includes both younger Millennials and older members of Generation Z.[5] We used Amazon's Mechanical Turk (mTurk) platform to carry out this survey, a website that allows members of the public to earn money for completing many kinds of tasks, including participating in survey research. Each participant was paid $1.50 for completing the survey. A total of 1,010 participants in 2018 completed the survey after we removed any incomplete responses, and a total of 969 participants completed the survey after eliminating any incomplete responses in 2020.[6]

Dependent Variables

The dependent variables measure the extent to which each respondent contacted government, either in general or about specific issues. The first dependent variable measures how often each respondent contacted or visited someone in government who represents their community. Each person was asked about the frequency with which they have engaged in this activity on a five-point scale but to facilitate a straightforward interpretation using matching, we collapsed this variable into a binary that is coded one when a respondent contacted government officials with any frequency, and zero if they never had. Only 38.92% of our respondents reported having contacted government officials with any frequency in 2018, while 71.29% of our respondents reported having performed this same behavior in 2020.[7]

To examine issue-specific variation, we asked respondents five separate questions about the frequency with which they contacted elected officials about Black Lives Matter (in 2020 only), gun control, immigration or family separation, Supreme Court nominations (Kavanaugh in 2018, Barrett in 2020), and the MeToo movement, respectively. We collapsed the measurement for these issue-specific variables into a series of binaries coded one if the respondent contacted elected officials about the relevant issue at least once, and zero if they never had. The means for most of these binaries suggest relatively low levels of contacting elected officials, as the averages range from 21.62% (contacting elected officials about the MeToo movement in 2018) to 62.53% (contacting elected officials about gun control in 2020). The online appendix contains additional details about question wording and variable measurement. To test our theoretical expectations, we use a series of matching routines.

Treatment Variables

To test our hypothesis, we asked each respondent about the extent to which they posted about politics on social media. However, it is likely that young adults post about varying political issues with differential frequencies. We followed up with separate questions that asked respondents about how often they posted messages on social media about gun control, immigration or family separation, Supreme Court nominations (Kavanaugh in 2018, Barrett in 2020), the MeToo movement, or Black Lives Matter (in 2020 only). We utilize each of these separate questions as a unique treatment variable in our follow-up analyses in this chapter. The response options for each of these questions about the respective issues were never, posted once, posted two or three times, and posted four or more times.

Matching Covariates

We used two variables to investigate the effects of political engagement apart from the internet. First, we asked each respondent about the extent to which they are interested in politics. Second, each respondent was asked three questions about the extent to which their friends engaged in a set of activities and used these responses to build an additive index of peer civic activities ($\alpha = .63$, 2018; $\alpha = .58$, 2020).[8,9]

In addition, we used several variables to query the effects of political engagement using the internet. First, we asked each respondent how often they read blogs online about politics as Moffett and Rice (2018) and Kerbel and Bloom (2005) uncover evidence that blogs can act as outlets that encourage enhanced civic activity, either online or offline. Second, each respondent was asked how frequently they read news on the internet about politics.

Third, we constructed an additive index of online civic activity consisting of four items, as several researchers have found a link between activities on social media and offline civic engagement (see e.g., Kahne and Bowyer 2018; Ley and Brewer 2018; Loader, Vromen, and Xenos 2014). Through separate questions, each respondent was asked about the extent to which they had relied on social media for news, read social media feeds about politics, liked or shared posts about politics on social media, or read or watched posts about politics on social media , and we summed the values for each of the items ($\alpha = .81$, 2018; $\alpha = .78$, 2020).

We employed four variables to account for the effects of issue importance, as issues can sometimes prime higher levels of political participation (Converse 1964; Carmines and Stimson 1989; Reny, Collingwood, and Valenzuela 2019). Using separate questions, we asked each respondent about the importance of congressional stances on immigration,[10] as well as, gun control,[11] in influencing their vote choice. Third, we asked each respondent about the extent to which they supported or opposed the family separation policy implementation under the Trump administration. Fourth, we asked each respondent whether they supported or opposed the DACA program.

Moreover, we employed several variables to account for the effects of personal characteristics on offline civic activity. First, we create a binary measuring strong partisanship, as this attachment is associated with an array of other political activities (see e.g., Flavin and Griffin 2009; Verba, Brady, and Schlozman 1995). Second, we examined the effects of ideology on civic engagement, as Achen and Bartels (2016) discover that self-identifying as either conservative or liberal shapes political participation. For those who did not initially indicate liberal or conservative, we asked a follow-up question requiring them to choose between liberal or conservative. Then, we create a binary for liberals.

Third, we asked each respondent for their sex, and we coded this variable one for females, two for males, and three for those who self-identified in another category. Fourth, we acquired data on each respondent's age by asking each to report their month and year of birth. Then, we computed each respondent's age based on the month and year of the 2018 midterm election in 2018 and on the month and year of the presidential election in 2020.[12] Fifth, we asked each respondent for their race and collapsed that information into a binary that is coded one for whites, and zero otherwise. Sixth, we asked each respondent for their level of education.

Finally, we used four variables to control for the effects of underlying political attitudes, as these can affect participation patterns. First, we asked each respondent whether they approved or disapproved of the job that Donald Trump is doing as president, as presidential approval is connected with changes in participatory patterns (Abramowitz and Stone 2006). Third, we include separate binaries for those who self-identified as MeToo supporters and as Black Lives Matter supporters.[13]

Matching Covariate Differences across Models

There are two primary differences in the covariates that we used across the different models beyond those that we specify above. First, we included separate measures in the models about the extent to which respondents posted messages about gun control, immigration, the MeToo movement, Supreme Court nominations, Black Lives Matter, and other political issues. The response options for these questions were "never," "once," "two or three times," and "four or more times." The models in Table 7.1 exclude all of these measures, as we do not want to include component parts of the treatment variable (posting about politics on social media) in this table as a matching covariate, as this violates the underlying assumptions of our matching technique.

The models in Tables 7.2 through 7.4 include these measures, but with some important variations. These models all include the variable for having posted messages about other political issues. However, the models exclude the variable about posting about the issue being examined in the table as a matching covariate, as that variable acts as a treatment variable in that table. However, the variables that query the extent to which one posts about the remaining issues beyond the "other" category are included. In Table 7.2, for example, we examine the effects of posting about the MeToo movement (treatment variable) on contacting elected officials about that movement. Consequently, we exclude posting about the MeToo movement as a matching covariate, since it is a treatment variable. However, we include posting about Supreme Court nominations (Kavanaugh in 2018, Barrett in 2020), gun control, immigration or family separation, Black Lives Matter (in 2020 only), and other political issues in this model. The reason that we do so is that we want to examine the effects of posting about the MeToo movement on contacting elected officials *over and beyond* respondents' baseline inclinations toward posting about other political issues. We perform analogous routines for the models in Tables 7.2 through 7.4.

Second, we included separate measures in the models about the extent to which respondents participated in protests about gun control, immigration, the MeToo movement, Supreme Court nominations (Kavanaugh in 2018, Barrett in 2020), Black Lives Matter (in 2020 only), and other political issues. The response options for these items were "never," "once," "two or three times," and "four or more times." The models in Table 7.1 include all of these items as matching covariates.

The models in Tables 7.2 through 7.4 include these measures, but with some substantial variations. These models all include the variable for having participated in protests about other political issues. However, the models exclude the variable about participating in protests related to the issue being examined in the table as a matching covariate, as that variable is connected with contacting elected officials related to that issue (the dependent variable),[14] and with posting about that issue (our treatment variable). However, the variables that query the extent to which one posts about the remaining issues beyond the "other" category are included. We do this because we want to be appropriately sensitive to the underlying assumptions of the matching approach (see e.g., Imbens and Rubin 2015).

In Table 7.2, for example, we examine the effects of posting about the MeToo movement (treatment variable) on contacting elected officials about that movement. Consequently, we exclude participating in protests related to the MeToo movement as a matching covariate, since it is connected with both the dependent and treatment variables. However, we include participating in protests about Kavanaugh's nomination, gun control, immigration or family separation, and other political issues in this model. We perform analogous routines for the models in Tables 7.2 through 7.4.

Methods

To investigate whether the treatment variables are associated with contacting elected officials, we use a matching analysis to compute the ATET. We choose a matching estimator for several reasons. First, nearly all regression-based techniques (including OLS) assume that there exists a linear relationship between the dependent and independent variables (see Greene 2011). Our theory posits a positive relationship between each of our treatment variables and contacting elected officials, but makes no prediction about the remaining response options contained in any of the treatment variables. Consequently, the phenomenon that we examine is nonlinear by construction, and is ill suited to investigate using a method that assumes linearity (like OLS). Fortunately, matching analyses do not assume linearity, allow for a more flexible functional form, and have other statistical properties that make them a more appropriate choice to test our theory (Imbens and Rubin 2015).

In addition, individuals have differing probabilities of contacting elected government officials in general, or about specific issues or movements. OLS estimators presume treatment homogeneity, which is unlikely to hold in the analyses that we present. It is likely that individuals have different treatment effects, particularly depending on the frequency with which they post online in general, or about specific issues or social movements (see Abadie and Imbens 2011). Thus, the effects of posting online about politics (more generally, or about specific issues or social movements) vary with the frequency with which one has performed this activity. For instance, we expect that those who posted more frequently about politics (or about specific political issues/social movements) are more likely to contact government officials (either in general or about the specific issue about which they posted) than those who have not posted at all.

By construction, OLS-based estimators assume that we observe a linear, homogeneous relationship between posting about politics (or specified issues/ social movements) and contacting elected government officials. Matching-based approaches deal effectively with this issue because they assume neither linearity nor homogeneity (Imbens and Rubin 2015). Rather, matching-based approaches produce several treatment estimates depending on the level of treatment that a respondent received (Imbens and Rubin 2015). Thus, we can generate several, more accurate estimates of the effect that posting had on contacting elected government officials.

Also, OLS does not allow us to estimate what happens to the probability of contacting elected government officials in the absence of posting about politics (or alternatively, about specific issues or social movements) (Nichols 2007). Matching analyses use the existing data to produce a dataset that includes observations that are as alike as possible, given the values of the remaining predictors (Stuart 2010). Thus, we can estimate what would have happened in the absence of any level of posting about politics, or about any specific issue or social movement (see Gelman and Hill 2007). Then, we can use this dataset to estimate the effects of a specified level of posting on contacting elected government officials. We iterate this procedure for each level of posting about politics, or for any specific issue or social movement. Finally, if we used OLS estimates to obtain the results, our results would likely be biased because any estimate of the treatment effect is conditioned on the values of the remaining independent variables. Consequently, OLS-based approaches do not compute ATETs.

Matching analyses deal nicely with each of these issues because they permit us to investigate whether posting about politics (or about a specific issue or social movement) is connected with contacting elected government officials. By matching based on each of the predictor variables to make inferences, we can separate the effect of posting about an issue beyond individuals' other predispositions to contact elected government officials. Thus, doing so enables us to compare people with similar inclinations to contact elected government officials who only vary in the level at which they post about politics or about any specified political issue or social movement. Moreover, matching allows us to calculate ATETs for each treatment level, and by doing so, to calculate more precise effect estimates with observational data.

Assumptions

Before performing our matching analyses, we must meet four assumptions. First, we presume that all sets of treatment variables are binary. To make each set of treatment variables binary, we generated a series of dichotomous variables for each response option, relative to never having posted about politics in general, or about each of the issues or social movements that we examine in this chapter. For instance, the binary for having posted rarely about politics is coded one for those who did so, zero for never having done so, and missing for those who declined to answer this question, and for those who reported having posted more than once. Similarly, the dichotomous variable for having posted about Kavanaugh's nomination (in 2018) once is coded one for those who did so, zero for never having done so, and missing for those who reported having posted more than once, or for those who did not answer this question. We performed analogous routines for posting about the remaining issue areas or social movements that we explore in this chapter. We expect positive signs for the ATET for all variables.

Second, we assume common support (or overlap), which means that it is possible that treated units may face an intervention that could have assigned them to the control group (see Imbens and Rubin 2015; King, Lucas, and Nielsen 2017). The data that we use meet this requirement because all respondents could have chosen not to post about politics, a political issue, or a social movement.

Third, we must fulfill the SUTVA assumption, which means that "the potential outcomes for any unit do not vary with the treatments assigned to other units, and for each unit, there are no different forms or versions of each treatment level, which lead to different potential outcomes" (Imbens and Rubin 2015, 10). We have met the first part of this assumption because the possible outcomes for civic activity do not vary with the extent to which one posted about politics more broadly, or about any issue or social movement.[15]

The second aspect of this assumption is more intricate because we have different variations on all of our treatment variables. For our first treatment variable, the variations are rarely, sometimes, frequently, and very often. Our remaining treatment variables vary with respect to posting once, posting two or three times, and posting four or more times about an issue or social movement. Yet, we can compare the effects of having posted with varying frequencies about politics, a political issue, or a social movement relative to those who never did so. For example, we can compare those who posted rarely about politics to those who never did so, provided that we exclude those who posted at all other frequencies from that analysis.[16] We have to perform an analogous procedure to compare those who had posted about politics rarely, frequently, or very often if we hope to perform a matching analysis without an alternative treatment.

In a similar vein, we can compare the effects of having posted with varying frequencies about a political issue or social movement relative to those who never did so. For example, we can compare those who posted once about Barrett's nomination (in 2020) to those who never did so, provided that we exclude those who posted at all other frequencies from that analysis. We must perform an analogous procedure to compare those who had posted two or three times, and those who posted four or more times about her nomination if we hope to perform a matching analysis absent an alternative treatment. We also must perform the procedure outlined in this paragraph on all other treatment variables related to political issues or social movements. When we compute our ATETs in the manner prescribed above for all sets of models, we ultimately satisfy the SUTVA assumption because we have neither interference nor any hidden variations of the treatments (Imbens and Rubin, 2015, 10–11).

Finally, the treatment assignment must be conditionally independent of the outcome variable given a set of matching covariates (D'Agostino 1998, 2266).

Thus, each respondent's assignment to treatment (i.e., posting about politics, a political issue, or a social movement) is unconnected with the extent to which they contact government officials, given the values of the remaining explanatory variables. We observed low levels of contacting government officials in 2018, but higher levels in 2020. In all cases, though, contacting government officials generally occurs with greater frequency than contacting government officials about any issue or social movement that we highlight in this chapter. In addition, contacting government officials does not cause an individual to post about politics, a political issue, or a social movement. In this way, contacting government officials does not cause an individual to be assigned to one or more treatment categories.

Matching Technique

Once we have met the statistical assumptions that underlie matching, we need to choose a method by which to execute the analysis. To perform our matching analyses, we use one-to-one genetic matching with replacement (Diamond and Sekhon 2013; Sekhon 2011). We incorporate a propensity score into the analysis, as knowing estimated values of this score meaningfully improves the accuracy of this method (Diamond and Sekhon 2013). Propensity score matching allows us to compare observations that are otherwise similar across other predictors, but have experienced different treatments. We perform our analysis with replacement, as matching discrepancies are reduced because we can use untreated units as a match multiple times (see Abadie and Imbens 2006).[17] To remove any bias that results due to the choice of the matching estimator without affecting the variance of that estimator, we employ a bias correction (Abadie and Imbens 2016).

Results

Before we discuss our results, we must examine how similar the treatment and control groups are to one another (King, Lucas, and Nielsen 2017). If these groups are substantially dissimilar, then we cannot use matching to estimate ATETs. The imbalance statistics for the models in Table 7.1 through 7.4 are contained in Tables A1 through A22 in the online appendix. In 2018, for 88.83% of the variables contained in the models in Tables 7.1 through 7.4, the KS tests are not significant at the .05 level after matching has occurred. For 2018, the remaining 41 of 367 cases (or 11.17%), the KS test is significant. Of these 41 cases, 21 of them (or 51.22%) involve issues that either have been examined in Chapters 2 through 6, or will be queried in Chapter 8. The remaining 20 variables are not distributed in a systematic pattern across any specific model or set of models.

In 2020, for 61.84% of the variables (or 316 out of 511) contained in the models in Tables 7.1 through 7.4, the KS tests are not significant at the .05 level after matching has occurred. For 2020, in the remaining 195 of 511 cases (or 38.16%), the KS test is significant. Of these 195 cases, 103 of them (or 52.81%)

involve issues that either have been examined in Chapters 2 through 5, or will be queried in Chapter 8. The remaining variables are not distributed in a systematic pattern across any specific model or set of models. Thus, we can be confident that we have reduced imbalance and have achieved balance across the model specifications in both 2018 and 2020. The matched groups have sufficiently similar observable characteristics such that we can attribute any remaining differences across levels of posting to posting about these issues, not to preexisting differences (Eggers and Hainmueller 2009).

Posting and Contacting Government Officials

In Table 7.1, we provide the results from the matching routines in which we examine the relationship between posting about politics and contacting government officials in 2018 and 2020. The results indicate that there is no statistically significant relationship between posting about politics and contacting elected government officials in 2018. In addition, the results indicate that higher levels of posting about politics are not associated with a higher propensity to contact government officials. This finding is interesting because it may appear that there is no relationship between online activity (like posting about politics) and an offline civic activity (contacting elected government officials) in 2018. However, it is possible that these effects differ by issue area or social movement, and if true, would be consistent with one of the themes of this book: different issues spurred civic activity among younger voters. Yet, those differing issues encouraged civic engagement in divergent ways. We will examine this more formally in subsequent models throughout this chapter.

Yet, in 2020, we find evidence that links posting about politics and contacting government officials. More specifically, posting very often about politics is connected with a 39.2% increase in the probability of contacting elected officials. Moreover, posting sometimes about politics is associated with a 33.5% increase in the likelihood of contacting elected officials. These results indicate that young adults are increasingly raising their voices in ways more likely to be heard by elected officials. Interestingly, posting frequently is not connected with an increase in the probability of posting about politics. However, the results for posting rarely about politics appear to be connected with a higher likelihood of contacting elected officials about politics. However, this particular result is not robust.

At best, we can conclude that there was a scant relationship between rarely posting about politics and contacting elected government officials in 2018. In all other cases in 2018, though, the robustness checks provide clear evidence that the results that we have obtained are robust, and that we can safely conclude that no statistically significant relationship exists between posting about politics and contacting elected government officials, at least at first glance. Yet, in 2020 posting sometimes and very often about politics result in significant gains in the likelihood

TABLE 7.1 Contacting Elected Officials and Posting about Politics

	2018				2020			
	Rarely	Sometimes	Frequently	Very Often	Rarely	Sometimes	Frequently	Very Often
Effect on Contacting Elected Officials	.127	-.029	-.244	.432	.296	.335	.259	.392
Abadie–Imbens Standard Error	.089	.092	.271	.520	.101	.088	.212	.098
95% Confidence Interval Lower Bound	-.045	-.211	-.782	-.605	.095	.160	-.161	.197
95% Confidence Interval Upper Bound	.299	.153	.294	1.469	.497	.510	.679	.587
T-Statistic	1.436	-.316	-.900	.831	2.922	3.800	1.221	4.005
P-Value (two-tailed)	.151	.752	.368	.406	.003	.0001	.222	$6.191*10^{-5}$
P-Value (one-tailed)	.076	.376	.184	.203	.002	.00005	.111	$3.100*10^{-6}$
N	135	153	98	72	75	79	120	75

Notes: In each column, the frequency with which one has posted about political issues is compared with one who has never done so. Second, the covariates on which the matching is based are described in the text. Third, the effects on contacting elected officials are the ATET. Finally, the matching results are from 1:1 genetic matching with post-matching bias adjustment. Thus, the N represents the matched number of observations.

Messages Received? 207

of contacting elected officials. We now turn to whether posting about the issues we focused on in Part I made young adults more likely to contact elected officials about these issues.

MeToo Movement

The MeToo movement has focused more on social reforms than political ones. Yet, 7% of #MeToo tweets mentioned politics or specific politicians (Anderson and Toor 2018). Young adults who posted about MeToo are likely to see other posts with the hashtag MeToo, and thus they may have an increased chance of seeing these tweets mentioning politics and elected officials. This might make them more likely to decide to contact an elected official about the MeToo movement.

The events of 2017 and 2018 suggest the MeToo movement drew attention from politicians. Although the political system has not been the primary focus of MeToo, it led to the downfall of some elected officials accused of inappropriate behavior. In addition, demands for change have been met with action by elected officials. For example, the MeToo movement helped increase the amount of legislation at the state level addressing sexual harassment and assault (Kelly and Hegarty 2018). This suggests MeToo messages have been received. Is there evidence that young adults who posted about MeToo were more likely to contact elected officials about MeToo?

In Table 7.2, we provide the results from the matching routines. The results indicate that in 2018, posting about the MeToo Movement is connected with contacting elected officials about the MeToo Movement. More specifically, those who posted once about this movement experienced a 12.5% increase in the probability that they contacted elected officials, relative to those who never posted about this movement. In addition, those who posted two or three times about this movement were 28.9% more likely to contact elected officials compared to those who never posted about this movement. Interestingly, though, those who posted four or more times about this movement were no more likely to contact elected government officials than those who had never posted about this movement. Yet in 2020, when the movement was much less salient and public interest was lower, posting about MeToo did not have a similar impact on young adults contacting elected officials about this movement. More specifically, there is no statistically significant connection between posting about MeToo and contacting elected officials about that movement in 2020.

Supreme Court Nominations

Owing to the emergence of allegations of sexual assault levied against Kavanaugh as his nomination was being considered by the Senate in 2018, his confirmation hearings generated even heavier media coverage than normal and caused many to tune in via television or watch online. The upcoming vote on Kavanaugh's

TABLE 7.2 Contacting Elected Officials about the MeToo Movement and Supreme Court Nominations and Posting about Those Issues

	MeToo Movement						Supreme Court Nominations					
	2018			2020			2018 (Kavanaugh)			2020 (Barrett)		
	Once	Two or Three Times	Four or More Times	Once	Two or Three Times	Four or More Times	Once	Two or Three Times	Four or More Times	Once	Two or Three Times	Four or More Times
Effect on Contacting Elected Officials	.125	.289	-.057	.017	.165	.168	.226	.271	.454	.257	.917	.495
Abadie–Imbens Standard Error	.060	.068	.318	.094	.114	.115	.076	.086	.098	.164	.340	.138
95% Confidence Interval Lower Bound	.006	.154	-.691	-.171	-.061	-.061	.075	.101	.259	-.070	.243	.220
95% Confidence Interval Upper Bound	.244	.424	.576	.205	.391	.397	.377	.441	.649	.584	1.591	.770
T-Statistic	2.089	4.259	-.181	.177	1.453	1.458	2.965	3.137	4.617	1.561	2.691	3.589
P-Value (two-tailed)	.037	2.053×10^{-5}	.857	.859	.146	.145	.003	.002	3.899×10^{-6}	.118	.007	.0003
P-Value (one-tailed)	.019	1.027×10^{-6}	.429	.430	.073	.073	.002	.001	1.950×10^{-7}	.059	.004	.0002
N	100	108	76	68	114	77	99	111	85	71	103	76

Notes: In each column, the number of times that one has posted about either the MeToo Movement or Supreme Court nominations is compared with one who has never done so. Second, the covariates on which the matching is based are described in the text. Third, the effects on contacting elected officials are the AITET. Finally, the matching results are from 1:1 genetic matching with post-matching bias adjustment. Thus, the N represents the matched number of observations.

nomination to the Supreme Court offered constituents a clear opportunity and limited window to try to influence their senators' votes. Further, interest groups spent hundreds of thousands of dollars targeting senators whose votes were likely to be pivotal in Kavanaugh's nomination (Stolberg, Fandos, and Edmonson 2018). Part of these efforts included mobilizing constituents to share their views directly with their senators. Thus, young adults who posted about Kavanaugh's nomination would be highly likely to know that contacting their senators might make a difference. Were those who posted online about the Kavanaugh nomination more likely to contact their elected officials about it?

Although Barrett's confirmation hearings lacked allegations of wrongdoing, they still provoked considerable controversy. Justice Ginsburg, a liberal justice and feminist icon, died just six weeks before the 2020 presidential election (Totenberg 2020a). Barrett, a conservative, would strengthen the conservative majority on the court and the Republican-controlled Senate rushed to confirm her before the election, despite arguing during a Democratic presidency four years earlier that a nomination should not proceed during a lame duck presidency when a presidential campaign was already underway (McConnell and Grassley 2016). Once again, her nomination offered constituents a clear opportunity and limited window to try to influence their senators' votes. In addition, after Barrett's nomination, interest groups also began mobilizing individuals to pressure senators regarding their upcoming confirmation vote (Walsh 2020). Those young adults who posted their views online would be more likely to know that contacting their senators might influence them. Were young adults who posted online about Barrett's nomination more likely to contact their elected officials about it?

In Table 7.2, we furnish the results of the matching routines. The results display substantial evidence that posting about Kavanaugh's nomination in 2018 was strongly connected with contacting elected government officials about this appointment. What is more, the likelihood of contacting elected officials increased with the number of times that respondents post about this issue. More specifically, those who posted once about the issue experienced increases in the probability that they contacted elected government officials by 22.6%. Those who posted two or three times about this issue were 27.1% more likely to contact elected government officials about this nomination, and those who posted four or more times were 45.4% more likely to contact elected government officials about this appointment.

The results also provide strong evidence that posting about Barrett's nomination in 2020 increased young adults' propensity to contact their elected officials about her nomination. Those who posted four or more times about her nomination experienced an increase in the probability that they contacted elected government officials about that nomination by 49.5%. However, those who posted just once about the nomination were no more likely to have contacted government officials about it than those who did not post at all. While the results seemingly indicate that those who posted two or three times about her nomination are connected with higher levels of contacting elected government officials, this result is not robust. Overall, the evidence supports our hypothesis: that posting about Supreme Court nominations is connected with a higher probability of contacting elected government officials about that issue. This connection, though, is stronger with Kavanaugh's nomination in 2018 than it was with Barrett's in 2020.

Gun Control

The founders of March for Our Lives began mobilizing against gun violence hours after a gunman killed 17 at their high school in Parkland, Florida. While protests may have received the most media attention, Jaclyn Corin began telling her Instagram followers that night that they should contact their elected officials in favor of stricter gun laws (Jones 2018). Corin soon organized lobbying trips and participated in a nationwide bus tour encouraging local leaders to adopt similar tactics to change gun laws (Jones 2018). Thus, contacting elected officials was a key, underreported part of the movement. Most of those who posted about gun control in 2018 would likely be aware of these efforts, as well as of opposition by the NRA, and would become more likely to be exposed to messages requesting they contact their elected officials to share their views about guns. Were those who posted online about gun control more likely to contact elected officials to share these views?

In Table 7.3, we display the results from the matching routines for gun control. The results provide evidence that posting about gun control is connected with contacting elected government officials about that issue. More specifically, in 2018 the probability of contacting government officials about gun control increases by 14% when one posted once about this issue, 22.6% for posting two or three times about this issue, and by 51.6% for posting four or more times about this issue. In 2020, when the issue had moved off center stage, posting only four or more times about gun control was associated with a heightened likelihood of contacting elected officials. Those young adults who posted at these high rates were 76.9% more likely to contact elected officials about gun control in 2020.

Immigration and Family Separation

The controversial policy of separating children from parents when crossing the border illegally produced numerous calls to contact elected officials in 2018, appearing in sources ranging from *The New York Times* to *Elle* magazine. A variety of groups including the Refugee and Immigrant Center for Education and Legal Services (RAICES), ACLU, and the Lutheran Immigration and Refugee Service urged people to contact their elected officials, even including sample wording they might use on the phone or in a letter or e-mail. Those who cared enough to post online about this issue are likely to be more receptive to these calls to contact elected officials.

Of all the issues we examined in Part I, immigration and family separation is the only one for which posting was not associated with greater civic engagement

TABLE 7.3 Contacting Elected Officials about Gun Control or Immigration and Family Separation and Posting about Those Issues

	Gun Control						Immigration and Family Separation					
	2018			2020			2018			2020		
	Once	Two or Three Times	Four or More Times	Once	Two or Three Times	Four or More Times	Once	Two or Three Times	Four or More Times	Once	Two or Three Times	Four or More Times
Effect on Contacting Elected Officials about Gun Control	.140	.226	.516	.342	-.027	.769	-.121	.324	.331	.182	-.211	.539
Abadie–Imbens Standard Error	.067	.072	.160	.306	.557	.163	.101	.142	.142	.143	.214	.167
95% Confidence Interval Lower Bound	.007	.084	.197	-.271	-1.132	.444	-.327	.043	.049	-.104	-.635	.207
95% Confidence Interval Upper Bound	.273	.368	.835	.955	1.078	1.094	.085	.605	.613	.468	.213	.871
T-Statistic	2.085	3.139	3.220	1.116	-.049	4.720	-1.168	2.275	2.325	1.273	-.989	3.234
P-Value (two-tailed)	.037	.002	.001	.265	.961	2.355×10^{-6}	.243	.023	.020	.203	.323	.001
P-Value (one-tailed)	.019	.001	.0005	.133	.481	1.178×10^{-7}	.122	.012	.010	.102	.162	.0005
N	100	142	75	59	107	77	99	110	94	63	114	82

Notes: In each column, the number of times that one has posted about gun control or immigration and family separation is compared with one who has never done so. Second, the covariates on which the matching is based are described in the text. Third, the effects on contacting elected officials are the ATET. Finally, the matching results are from 1:1 genetic matching with post-matching bias adjustment. Thus, the N represents the matched number of observations.

in 2018. Despite that, did posting about this issue result in a greater likelihood of contacting elected officials about it? Meanwhile, in 2020, posting four or more times about immigration and family separation was associated with higher rates of civic engagement. Did posting on this issue at these high rates in 2020 also lead to contacting elected officials about it?

In Table 7.3, we display the results from the matching routines to examine this point. The results provide evidence that posting about immigration or family separation is connected with contacting elected government officials about immigration or family separation when a respondent posts at least twice about this issue in 2018. More specifically, the probability of contacting government officials about immigration or family separation increases by 32.4% when one posted two or three times about this issue, and by 33.1% for posting four or more times about this issue in 2018. Meanwhile, the probability of contacting elected officials about immigration and family separation increased by 53.9% when one posted four or more times about this issue in 2020. At a minimum, we can conclude that posting multiple times with varying frequencies in both 2018 and 2020 about immigration or family separation is associated with an increase in the probability of contacting elected government officials about that issue.

Black Lives Matter

While Black Lives Matter protests dominated the news cycle beginning in May of 2020 after a series of tragic events in quick succession demonstrated the prevalence of societal racism and the continued tragic death of black people at the hands of police, posting one's views online were also commonplace, and even served as a key way young adults organized protests (Faguy 2020; Grimsley 2020). Compared to other age groups, young adults supported the Black Lives Matter movement at much higher rates (CBS News Poll 2020). Yet, if young adults remained less likely to contact elected officials than other age groups, politicians might be less likely to receive their messages. Was posting about Black Lives Matter by young people associated with higher likelihoods of contacting elected officials about Black Lives Matter?

Table 7.4 shows the results from the matching routines to query this point. The results indicate that posting once or four or more times about Black Lives Matter has no statistically significant connection with contacting elected government officials. Also, posting two or three times about Black Lives Matter appears to be connected with an increase in contacting elected government officials about that social movement. However, this result is not robust, and accordingly, we cannot conclude that there is a relationship between posting about Black Lives Matter and contacting elected government officials. This makes sense because the primary intended recipient of posting about Black Lives Mattter was the public, not elected officials.[18]

TABLE 7.4 Contacting Elected Officials about Black Lives Matter and Posting about that Social Movement in 2020

	Once	Two or Three Times	Four or More Times
Effect on Contacting Elected Officials about Black Lives Matter	-.566	.812	.140
Abadie-Imbens Standard Error	1.227	.226	.126
95% Confidence Interval Lower Bound	-3.011	.364	-.110
95% Confidence Interval Upper Bound	1.879	1.260	.390
T-Statistic	-.461	3.592	1.113
P-Value (two-tailed)	.645	.0003	.266
P-Value (one-tailed)	.323	.0002	.133
N	75	104	102

Notes: In each column, the number of times that one has posted about Black Lives Matter is compared with one who has never done so. Second, the covariates on which the matching is based are described in the text. Third, the effects on contacting elected officials are the ATET. Finally, the matching results are from 1:1 genetic matching with post-matching bias adjustment. Thus, the N represents the matched number of observations

Robustness Checks

To verify whether the results that we have obtained in the tables are model-dependent (Ho et al. 2007), we tested each model for robustness by removing one matching covariate at a time from the models. Then, we re-ran the matching routines with the remaining predictors.[19] These results are contained in the online appendix.[20] When we examine the models in Table 7.1 relative to that which we report here, 70.21% (or 132/188) of the models contained results that mirrored those reported here. Around 16 of the remaining 20 cases occurred where the treatment was rarely posting about politics in 2018. In each of these cases, the sign was positive, indicating a statistically significant connection between rarely posting about politics and contacting elected government officials. Thus, in 16 out of 22 possible model specifications where contacting government officials was the dependent variable and rarely posting about politics was the treatment variable, we observe a statistically significant connection between the treatment and dependent variables in 2018.

Of the remaining 36 models in 2020 where the results diverged from those that we report, 26 (or 72.22%) involve the models for rarely and sometimes posting about politics. Moreover, 14 of these robustness checks for rarely posting (out of the 25 possible, or 56%) contain a set of results that diverge from what we reported for 2020. Thus, we cannot conclude with scientific certainty that there is a connection between rarely posting about politics and contacting elected government officials in 2020. In addition, 12 of the robustness checks for sometimes posting (out of the 25 possible, or 48%) contain a set of results that differ from what is contained in Table 7.1 in 2020. While the majority of these robustness checks contain results that are consistent with what we report for sometimes posting in 2020, one should exercise appropriate caution in drawing strong conclusions from this result.

When we tested the models for posting about the MeToo movement in Table 7.2 for robustness, 69.33% (or 104/150) of the models contained results that mirrored those that we reported in this table. In 2018, there was no underlying systematic pattern that would change the ultimate conclusions that we derive from these models. In 2020, however, 36 (or 44.44%) furnish results that counter that which is contained in Table 7.2. Of these 36, 24 of them (or 75%) are for having posted once about MeToo and subsequently, contacting elected government officials about that movement. This indicates that the majority (24/27 specifications, or 88.89%) of specifications for having posted once provide a set of results that points toward the existence of a relationship between posting once about the MeToo and subsequently contacting elected officials about that movement. That said, because the model we report contains a set of results that indicates no relationship between having posted once about MeToo and contacting elected government officials about this movement, the most conservative approach is to conclude that there is no relationship between posting about MeToo and contacting elected government officials about that movement in 2020.

Moreover, when we investigate the models for posting about Supreme Court nominations and compare them to what we report here, we discovered that 76.67% (or 115/150) of the functional forms contained results that were consistent in terms of the signs and significance patterns to those that we report. When we examine the results for posting two or three times in 2020 and those that we report here, 55.56% (or 15/27) diverge from what we report in Table 7.2. Because of these robustness check results, we cannot conclude that a statistically significant relationship exists between posting about Barrett's nomination two or three times and contacting elected officials about her nomination. That said, the remaining robustness checks are scattered across the remaining models such that no systematic patterns emerge.

When we investigate whether the models that we report in Table 7.3 for posting about gun control are robust, we discovered that 58.97% (or 92/156) of the models contained results that are displayed. In 2018, 17 out of 24 (or 70.83%) of the robustness checks that correspond with having posted once indicate statistically insignificant results compared with what we report. Using the most conservative interpretation, we conclude that there is no statistically significant relationship between posting once about gun control and contacting elected government officials about that issue. In addition, 10 of the 24 (or 41.67%) of the robustness checks that correspond to posting four or more times about gun control provide results that diverge from what we report in 2018. Though this percentage is nontrivial, it does indicate that a majority of the models in the robustness checks for posting four plus times about gun control in 2018 yield results that are consistent with what are reported here.

Accordingly, we conclude that posting two or more times about gun control in 2018 was connected with an increased probability of contacting elected government officials about this issue.

In 2020, 92.11% (or 35/38) of the robustness checks that diverge from what we report here occur with the models for posting once or two or three times about gun control. What is more, these 35 models show statistically significant results in all cases, which ends up providing some indirect evidence that favors our argument. When viewed in this way, 96.43% (or 81/84) of the results in 2020 are either consistent with what we report here or have inconsistencies that end up aiding the argument. What is more, only 10.71% of the robustness checks (or 3/28) for the models for posting four or more times contain results that diverge from what we report here. Altogether, we can conclude that posting about gun control multiple times with varying frequencies in both 2018 and 2020 is connected with higher levels of contacting elected government officials about this issue.

When we examine the models reported in Table 7.3 for robustness and examine the relationship between posting about immigration and contacting elected government officials, 61.33% (or 92/150) of the functional forms contained results that mirrored those that we reported. Of the remaining 20 results for 2018 that diverge from what we report here, 16 of them (or 80%) occur where we examine whether posting four or more times about immigration or family separation is associated with contacting elected government officials about this issue. What is more, 16 out of the 23 (or 69.57%) functional forms in the robustness checks occur when we investigate the effects of posting four or more times about immigration or family separation. Consequently, we err conservatively and conclude that there is no statistically significant relationship between posting four or more times about immigration or family separation and contacting elected government officials about this issue in 2018.

Of the 38 models that diverge from what we report in 2020 for immigration, 27 of them (or 71.05%) are contained in posting three or fewer times about immigration or family separation. All 27 of these models show statistically significant relationships that provide indirect evidence that favors the hypothesis that we advance here. When viewed in this way, 70 out of 81 models in 2020 (or 86.42%) either provide results that are consistent with what we report in Table 7.3 or provide evidence that helps the argument.

When we examine the results compared to what are reported in Table 7.4 for posting about Black Lives Matter, 63.10% (or 53/84) provide results that mirror those that are reported in the table. Of the remaining 31 results that diverge from what is reported, 20 of remainder (or 64.52%) involve posting two or three times about Black Lives Matter. Because 71.43% (or 20/28) of the results for posting two or three times diverge from what we report in Table 7.4, we cannot conclude that a statistically significant connection exists between posting about Black Lives Matter and contacting elected government officials about this social movement.

Implications and Conclusions for Responsiveness

The results indicate that posting about political issues relates to an increased probability of contacting elected government officials about these issues. The strongest evidence occurs with respect to Kavanaugh's nomination in 2018, as posting about the nomination at any frequency was connected with higher probabilities of contacting elected government officials about that issue. In addition, there is also strong evidence that posting about the MeToo movement either once or two or three times is connected with a higher likelihood of contacting elected officials about that movement in 2018. These findings are not surprising, as Kavanaugh's nomination was an issue just prior to the 2018 election, and the MeToo Movement was one of the headlining social movements during 2018. Yet, as attention to the MeToo movement faded, we found no significant evidence in 2020 linking posting about this issue to heightened rates of contacting elected officials. However, posting four or more times about another Supreme Court nomination in 2020, this time Barrett's, was also associated with heightened likelihood of contacting elected officials about her nomination.

We had found in Part I that posting four or more times about another salient issue in 2018, gun violence, was associated with heightened levels of civic engagement. However, we found no relationship between other levels of posting and civic engagement, suggesting the movement had limited impact. Yet, we find that posting about this issue multiple times was connected with increased probabilities of contacting elected officials about gun violence. This shows the impact of this movement was narrow and focused in a way that increases the likelihood of young adults' voices being heard in the halls of power. Thus, while the movement appeared to have limited impact in our findings in Chapter 4, here we find that posting about gun control made a difference in a way that mattered. More specifically, posting at least twice about gun control in 2018 was associated with an enhanced probability that respondents contact elected government officials about that issue. Meanwhile, by 2020, this issue had been replaced by other more pressing and salient issues and only posting four or more times about gun control was associated with heightened levels of contacting elected officials about this issue. However, those who remained strongly concerned about this issue, as measured by high rates of posting, saw particularly high increases in their probability of making their views known to elected officials.

Also, while immigration and family separation did not exhibit the same link to heightened civic engagement in 2018 as other issues did in Part I, a different story emerges when investigating the links between these issues and contacting elected officials. Posting about immigration and family separation two or three times in 2018 and four or more times in 2020 is connected with a greater likelihood of contacting elected government officials about that issue as well. Thus, even those issues that show little to no evidence of expanding civic engagement more broadly show strong links to heightened levels of contacting elected officials about these issues. Finally, in 2020 we find no connection between posting about Black Lives Matter and contacting elected officials about this issue. Yet, if the primary intended audience of the movement was the public and not elected officials, this lack of connection should come as little surprise.

Altogether, we see a strong connection between posting about an array of political issues or social movements and contacting elected government officials about those movements. For every issue we examined in 2018, posting at some level about it was associated with increased probabilities of contacting elected officials about that issue. In 2020, for every issue except MeToo and Black Lives Matter, posting at some level about an issue had a robust association with increased probabilities of contacting elected officials about that issue. These results suggest that young adults are learning to express their political views in ways likely to reach elected officials. In turn, this may make elected officials more likely to be responsive to the concerns of young adults. In the next chapter, we examine whether another route by which young people commonly express themselves politically, protesting, leads to higher levels of contacting elected government officials. It is to that task that we now turn.

Notes

1 See Dovi (2018) for a good discussion of the distinctions between these varying views of political representation.
2 A search of the House of Representatives' Statement of Disbursements for the words "poll" and "survey" during the first and second quarters of 2019 found only four survey-related disbursement records.
3 However, one study did find that young adults were more likely to contact local government officials, especially about particularized issues (Hirlinger 1992).
4 This was a slightly higher percentage than other age groups.
5 These generations have concordant views on social issues (Parker, Graf, and Igielnik 2019).
6 We constrained the eligibility of participants in this survey to those with HIT approval rates of at least 95% and whose location is in the United States. While we were unable to constrain by age here, we did so through the first question asking respondents whether they were between the ages of 18 and 25. If they responded no, then the survey ended.
7 This suggests a significant increase in contacting elected officials between 2018 and 2020. This is consistent with an increasing number of young adults finding their political voice, as more members of Generation Z reach political age. Yet, it is possible these self-reports of activity are inflated. Still, self-reports of political activity in internet surveys have been found to suffer less from social desirability bias than other methods of surveying individuals (Holbrook and Krosnick 2010). Instead, internet surveys can disproportionately draw those who participate at higher rates (Holbrook and Krosnick 2010). We acknowledge this may be an issue, especially in 2020, as it is highly unlikely that this percentage of 18–25-year-olds in the population contacted their elected officials. Yet, as long as there is sufficient variation in activity levels, which there is, we can still use this data to test the hypothesis that posting about political issues enhances the probability of contacting elected officials about these issues.

8 These were the only questions in the survey about peer civic experiences. Some participants responded that they did not know for one or more of these questions. When building our index, we coded values for these variables as missing. Thus, no peer civic engagement score is present for those who answered "don't know" on a minimum of one of these questions.

9 This also acts as an indirect indicator with respect to mobilization, as people frequently act politically when others around them do so (see e.g., Gimpel, Lee, and Kamiski 2006). Yet, it is possible that mobilization efforts by those other than peers, like interest groups and political parties, also yield higher levels of participation (Rosenstone and Hansen 2002). There are no questions in this survey that allow us to directly account for the effects of mobilization on civic activity. That said, we do consider many other covariates that also affect mobilization as part of the matching routines in this analysis.

10 We excluded the variables about the importance of congressional stances on immigration and the extent to which one supports or opposes the family separation policy implementation under the Trump administration from the models reported in Table 7.3, as they are a common connector between both the treatment (posting about immigration and family separation) and dependent variables (contacting elected officials about immigration and family separation) in these models. The excluded variables are included in the remaining models in this chapter.

11 We excluded the variable about the importance of congressional stances on gun control from the models reported in Table 7.3, as this is a common connector between the treatment (posting about gun control) and dependent variables (contacting elected officials about gun control) in these models. We include this omitted variable in the remaining models in this chapter.

12 We asked an initial screening question that identified those who were between the ages of 18 and 25, and those who responded that they were not in this age range were excluded from further participation in the survey. When we performed the age computations based on the year and month that respondents selected, though, there were 49 respondents who stated that they were older than 25 in 2018. In the year-month calculation, there was usually about a six-month variance between the reported and actual age among those 49 respondents. Since we asked about both year and month of birth based on drop-down menus, it is possible that a substantial portion of these respondents misreported their year and/or month of birth in 2018 (see Gendall and Healey 2008). We have no reason to believe that this error is systematic, and did not encounter the same concern in 2020. Thus, nonsystematic measurement error in an independent variable does not bias any conclusions in research studies (see King, Keohane, and Verba 1994).

13 The binary for MeToo movement supporters is excluded for those models in which we examine the effects of posting about the MeToo movement. In addition, the binary for Black Lives Matter supporters is excluded from those models in which we query the effects of posting about Black Lives Matter. In all other models, though, these binaries are included as part of the matching specification.

14 Chapter 8 addresses the link between participating in protests and contacting elected officials.

15 If posting about politics or any specific issue were related to contacting elected government officials, then these quantities would be highly correlated. To test whether this happens, we correlated our dependent variable (contacting government officials, either on its own or about particular issues) and posting about politics (either on its own or

about varying issues). In 2018, the correlations are .372 (contacting elected government officials and posting about politics), .521 (contacting elected government officials about the MeToo movement and posting this movement), .540 (contacting elected government officials about Kavanaugh's nomination and posting about his nomination), .462 (contacting elected government officials about gun control and posting about this issue), and .476 (contacting elected government officials about immigration and family separation and posting about this issue). In 2020, the correlations are .531 (contacting elected government officials and posting about politics), .602 (contacting elected government officials about the MeToo movement and posting this movement), .640 (contacting elected government officials about Barrett's nomination and posting about her nomination), .648 (contacting elected government officials about gun control and posting about this issue), .569 (contacting elected government officials about immigration and family separation and posting about this issue, and .503 (contacting elected government officials about Black Lives Matter and posting about this movement). These correlations are sufficiently low such that we can conclude that the first part of the SUTVA assumption is satisfied.
16 If we do not conduct our analysis in this manner, then we cannot satisfy SUTVA, as there would be alternative treatment forms (see Imbens and Rubin 2015, 10–13).
17 However, we do not perform a regression following the matching analysis (as Ho et al. 2007 recommend), as Abadie and Spiess (2019) state that this is inappropriate when matching is done with replacement as researchers obtain inaccurate standard error estimates.
18 We thank Melissa Michelson for this insight.
19 One limitation of many matching analyses is that one can p-hack by varying the functional form of the matching algorithm to produce a set of results that coincidentally confirms a researcher's hypotheses (Head et al. 2015).
20 One limitation of many matching analyses is that one can p-hack by varying the functional form of the matching algorithm to produce a set of results that coincidentally confirms a researcher's hypotheses (Head et al. 2015).

References

Abadie, Alberto and Guido W. Imbens 2006. "Large Sample Properties of Matching Estimators for Average Treatment Effects." *Econometrica* 74(1): 235–267. https://doi.org/10.1111/j.1468-0262.2006.00655.x. Accessed online June 19, 2021.

Abadie, Alberto and Guido W. Imbens 2011. "Bias-Corrected Matching Estimators for Average Treatment Effects." *Journal of Business and Economic Statistics* 29(1): 1–11. https://doi.org/10.1198/jbes.2009.07333. Accessed online June 19, 2021.

Abadie, Alberto and Guido W. Imbens 2016. "Matching on the Estimated Propensity Score." *Econometrica* 84(2): 781–807. https://doi.org/10.3982/ECTA11293. Accessed online June 19, 2021.

Abadie, Alberto and Jann Spiess 2019. "Robust Post-Matching Inference." Forthcoming in the *Journal of the American Statistical Association*. https://doi.org/10.1080/01621459.2020.1840383. Accessed online June 19, 2021.

Abramowitz, Alan I. and Walter J. Stone 2006. "The Bush Effect: Polarization, Turnout, and Activism in the 2004 Presidential Election." *Presidential Studies Quarterly* 36(2): 141–154. https://doi.org/10.1111/j.1741-5705.2006.00295.x. Accessed online June 19, 2021.

Achen, Christopher H. and Larry M. Bartels 2016. *Democracy for Realists: Why Elections Do Not Produce Responsive Government*. Princeton, NJ: Princeton University Press.

Anderson, Monica and Brooke Auxier. 2020. "55% of U.S. Social Media Users Say They Are 'Worn Out' by Political Posts and Discussions." Pew Research Center. August 19. www.pewresearch.org/fact-tank/2020/08/19/55-of-u-s-social-media-users-say-they-are-worn-out-by-political-posts-and-discussions/. Accessed online January 25, 2021.

Anderson, Monica and Skye Toor 2018. "How Social Media Users Have Discussed Sexual Harassment since #MeToo Went Viral." Pew Research Center. October 11. www.pewresearch.org/fact-tank/2018/10/11/how-social-media-users-have-discussed-sexual-harassment-since-metoo-went-viral/. Accessed online June 6, 2019.

Bakshy, Eytan, Solomon Messing, and Lada A. Adamic 2015. "Exposure to Ideologically Diverse News and Opinion on Facebook." *Science* 348(6239): 1130–1132. 10.1126/science.aaa1160. Accessed online June 19, 2021.

Bergan, Daniel E. 2009. "Does Grassroots Lobbying Work? A Field Experiment Measuring the Effects of an E-Mail Lobbying Campaign on Legislative Behavior." *American Politics Research* 37(2): 327–352. https://doi.org/10.1177/1532673X08326967. Accessed online June 19, 2021.

Bergan, Daniel E. and Richard T. Cole. 2015. "Call Your Legislator: A Field Experimental Study of the Impact of Citizen Contacts on Legislative Voting." *Political Behavior* 37 (1): 27–42. https://doi.org/10.1007/s11109-014-9277-1. Accessed online June 19, 2021.

Boulianne, Shelly 2019. "Revolution in the Making? Social Media Effects across the Globe." *Information Communication and Society* 22(1): 39–54. https://doi.org/10.1080/1369118X.2017.1353641. Accessed online June 19, 2021.

Broockman, David E. and Timothy J. Ryan 2016. "Preaching to the Choir: Americans Prefer Communicating to Copartisan Elected Officials." *American Journal of Political Science* 60(4): 1093–1107. https://doi.org/10.1111/ajps.12228. Accessed online June 19, 2021.

Butler, Daniel M., Christopher F. Karpowitz, and Jeremy C. Pope 2012. "A Field Experiment on Legislators' Home Styles: Service versus Policy." *Journal of Politics* 74(2): 474–486. https://doi.org/10.1017/S0022381611001708. Accessed online June 19, 2021.

Carmines, Edward G. and James A. Stimson 1989. *Issue Evolution: Race and the Transformation of American Politics.* Princeton, NJ: Princeton University Press.

CBS News Poll. June 23–26, 2020. https://drive.google.com/file/d/1l0XruPxbVV8mBoT0mpmeLk4AmbnkIGeH/view. Accessed online January 12, 2021.

Cheng, Jiesi, Aaron Sun, Daning Hu, and Daneil Zeng 2011. "An Information Diffusion-Based Recommendation Framework for Micro-Blogging." *Journal of the Association of Information Systems* 12(7): 463–486. https://doi.org/10.17705/1jais.00271. Accessed online June 19, 2021.

Congressional Management Foundation 2011."Communicating with Congress: Perceptions of Citizen Advocacy on Capitol Hill." http://congressfoundation.org/storage/documents/CMFPubs/cwc-perceptions-of-citizen advocacy.pdf. Accessed online December 1, 2019.

Converse, Phillip 1964. "The Nature of Belief Systems in Mass Publics." In *Ideology and Its Discontents,* David E. Apter (Ed.). New York, NY: Free Press of Glencoe.

D'Agostino, Ralph B. 1998. "Propensity Score Methods for Bias Reduction in the Comparison of a Treatment to a Non-Randomized Control Group." *Statistics in Medicine* 17(9): 2265–2281. https://doi.org/10.1002/(SICI)1097-0258(19981015)17:19<2265::AID-SIM918>3.0.CO;2-B. Accessed online June 19, 2021.

Dann, Carrie 2016. "Unfriended: How the 2016 Election Made Us Battle, Avoid, and Block Each Other." NBC News. www.nbcnews.com/politics/first-read/unfriended-how-2016-election-made-us-battle-avoid-block-each-n698001. Accessed online November 18, 2019.

Del Vicario, Michela, Alessandro Bessi, Fabiana Zollo, Fabio Petroni, Antonio Scala, Guido Caldarelli, H. Eugene Stanley, and Walter Quattrociocchi 2016. "The Spreading of Misinformation Online." *Proceedings of the National Academy of Sciences* 113(3): 554–559. https://doi.org/10.1073/pnas.1517441113. Accessed online June 19, 2021.

Diamond, Alexis and Jasjeet J. Sekhon 2013. "Genetic Matching for Estimating Causal Effects: A General Multivariate Matching Method for Achieving Balance in Observational Studies." *Review of Economics and Statistics* 95(3): 932–945. https://doi.org/10.1162/REST_a_00318. Accessed online June 19, 2021.

Dovi, Suzanne 2018. "Political Representation." In *The Stanford Encyclopedia of Philosophy* (Fall 2018 Ed.), Edward N. Zalta (Ed.). https://plato.stanford.edu/archives/fall2018/entries/political-representation/. Accessed online December 1, 2019.

Dubois, Elizabeth and Grant Blank 2018. "The Echo Chamber Is Overstated: The Moderating Effect of Political Interest and Diverse Media." *Information, Communication, and Society* 21(5): 729–745. https://doi.org/10.1080/1369118X.2018.1428656. Accessed online June 19, 2021.

Duggan, Maeve and Aaron Smith 2016. "The Political Environment on Social Media." Pew Research Center for Internet and Technology. www.pewresearch.org/internet/2016/10/25/the-political-environment-on-social-media/. Accessed online August 27, 2020.

Eggers, Andrew C. and Jens Hainmueller 2009. "MPs for Sale? Returns to Office in Postwar British Politics." *American Political Science Review* 103(4): 513–533. https://doi.org/10.1017/S0003055409990190. Accessed online June 19, 2021.

Faguy, Ana 2020. "Youth-Led Group behind Columbia's Black Lives Matter Protests Discusses What It Takes to Organize in 2020." *Baltimore Sun.* www.baltimoresun.com/maryland/howard/cng-ho-youth-organizing-protests-20200605-gwfdwqdxmfaapkymmq2pvc27km-story.html. Accessed online June 9, 2020.

Flavin, Patrick and John D. Griffin 2009. "Policy, Preferences, and Participation: Government's Impact on Democratic Citizenship." *Journal of Politics* 71(2): 544–559. https://doi.org/10.1017/S0022381609090458. Accessed online June 19, 2021.

Flaxman, Seth, Sharad Goel, and Justin M. Rao 2016. "Filter Bubbles, Echo Chambers, and Online News Consumption." *Public Opinion Quarterly* 80(S1): 298–320. https://doi.org/10.1093/poq/nfw006. Accessed online June 19, 2021.

Gelman, Andrew and Jennifer Hill 2007. *Data Analysis Using Regression and Multilevel/Heiarchical Models*. New York, NY: Cambridge University Press.

Gendall, Philip and Benjamin Healey 2008. "Asking the Age Question in Mail and Online Surveys." *International Journal of Market Research* 50(3): 309–317. https://doi.org/10.1177/147078530805000303. Accessed online June 19, 2021.

Gimpel, James G., Frances E. Lee, and Joshua Kaminski 2006. "The Political Geography of Campaign Contributions in American Politics." *Journal of Politics* 68(3): 626–639. https://doi.org/10.1111/j.1468-2508.2006.00450.x. Accessed online June 19, 2021.

Greene, William H. 2011. *Econometric Analysis*. 7th Ed. New York, NY: Pearson Education.

Griffin, John D. and Brian Newman 2005. "Are Voters Better Represented?" *Journal of Politics* 67(4): 1206–1227. https://doi.org/10.1111/j.1468-2508.2005.00357.x. Accessed online June 19, 2021.

Grimsley, Brooke 2020. "Ft. Zumwalt West Grad Lead Peaceful Protest: 'It's Truly a Blessing to Bring People Together.'" KMOV News. www.kmov.com/news/ft-zumwalt-west-grad-leads-peaceful-protest-its-truly-a-blessing-to-bring-people-together/article_98d194b2-a913-11ea-8482-0387620ff5d0.html. Accessed online June 9, 2020.

Head, Megan L., Luke Holman, Rob Lanfear, Andrew T. Kahn, and Michael D. Jennions 2015. "The Extent and Consequences of P-Hacking in Science." *Plos Biology* 13(3): e1002106. https://doi.org/10.1371/journal.pbio.1002106. Accessed online June 19, 2021.

Hero, Rodney E. 1986. "Explaining Citizen-Initiated Contacting of Government Officials: Socioeconomic Status, Perceived Need, or Something Else?" *Social Science Quarterly* 67(3): 626–635. https://doi.org/10.1177/1532673X9302100205. Accessed online June 19, 2021.

Hirlinger, Michael W. 1992. "Citizen-Initiated Contacting of Local Government Officials: A Multivariate Explanation." *Journal of Politics* 54(2): 553–564. https://doi.org/10.2307/2132039. Accessed online June 19, 2021.

Ho, Daniel E., Kosuke Imai, Gary King, and Elizabeth A. Stuart 2007. "Matching as Nonparametric Preprocessing for Reducing Model Dependence in Parametric Causal Inference." *Political Analysis* 15(3): 199–236. https://doi.org/10.1093/pan/mpl013. Accessed online June 19, 2021.

Holbrook, Allyson L. and Jon A. Krosnick 2010. "Social Desirability Bias in Voter Turnout Reports: Tests Using the Item Count Technique." *Public Opinion Quarterly* 74(1): 37–67. https://doi.org/10.1093/poq/nfp065. Accessed online June 19, 2021.

Imbens, Guido W. and Donald B. Rubin 2015. *Causal Inference for Statistics, Social, and Biomedical Sciences: An Introduction.* New York, NY: Cambridge University Press.

Iyengar, Shanto and Kyu S. Hahn 2009. "Red Media, Blue Media: Evidence of Ideological Selectivity in Media Use." *Journal of Communication* 59(1): 19–39. https://doi.org/10.1111/j.1460-2466.2008.01402.x. Accessed online June 19, 2021.

Jacobson, Susan, Eunyoung Myung, and Steve L. Johnson 2016. "Open Media or Echo Chamber: The Use of Links in Audience Discussions on the Facebook Pages of Partisan News Organizations." *Information, Communication & Society* 19(7): 875–891. https://doi.org/10.1080/1369118X.2015.1064461. Accessed online June 19, 2021.

Jones, Maggie 2018. "The March for Our Lives Activists Showed Us How to Find Meaning in Tragedy." *Smithsonian Magazine.* December. www.smithsonianmag.com/innovation/march-for-our-lives-student-activists-showed-meaning-tragedy-180970717/. Accessed online November 20, 2019.

Kahne, Joseph and Benjamin Bowyer 2018. "The Political Significance of Social Media Activity and Social Networks." *Political Communication* 35(3): 470–493. https://doi.org/10.1080/10584609.2018.1426662. Accessed online June 19, 2021.

Kelly, Cara and Aaron Hegarty 2018. "#MeToo Was a Culture Chick: But Changing Laws Will Take More than a Year." *USA Today.* October 4. www.usatoday.com/story/news/investigations/2018/10/04/metoo-me-too-sexual-assault-survivors-rights-bill/1074976002/. Accessed online June 27, 2019.

Kerbel, Matthew R. and Joel David Bloom 2005. "Blog for America and Civic Involvement." *The International Journal of Press/Politics* 10(4): 3–27. https://doi.org/10.1177/1081180X05281395. Accessed online June 19, 2021.

King, Gary, Christopher Lucas, and Richard A. Nielsen 2017. "The Balance-Sample Size Frontier in Matching Methods for Causal Inference." *American Journal of Political Science* 61(2): 473–489. https://doi.org/10.1111/ajps.12272. Accessed online June 19, 2021.

King, Gary, Robert O. Keohane, and Sidney Verba 1994. *Designing Social Inquiry: Scientific Inference in Qualitative Research.* Princeton, NJ: Princeton University Press.

Kingdon, John 1989. *Congressman's Voting Decisions.* Ann Arbor, MI: University of Michigan Press.

Lawrence, Eric, John Sides, and Henry Farrell 2010. "Self-Segregation or Deliberation? Blog Readership, Participation, and Polarization in American Politics." *Perspectives on Politics* 8(1): 141–157. https://doi.org/10.1017/S1537592709992714. Accessed online June 19, 2021.

Lexico. 2020. "Slacktivism." www.lexico.com/en/definition/slacktivism. Accessed online November 20, 2019.

Ley, Barbara L. and Paul R. Brewer 2018. "Social Media, Networked Protest, and the March for Science." *Social Media and Society* 4(3): 1–12. https://doi.org/10.1177/2056305118793407. Accessed online June 19, 2021.

Loader, Brian D., Ariadne Vromen, and Michael A. Xenos 2014. "The Networked Young Citizen: Social Media, Political Participation and Civic Engagement." *Information, Communication and Society* 17(2): 143–150. https://doi.org/10.1080/1369118X.2013.871571. Accessed online June 19, 2021.

Manning, Jennifer E. 2018. "Membership of the 115th Congress: A Profile." *Congressional Research Service.* www.senate.gov/CRSpubs/b8f6293e-c235-40fd-b895-6474d0f8e809.pdf. Accessed online November 18, 2019.

McConnell, Mitch and Chuck Grassley 2016. "McConnell and Grassley: Democrats shouldn't rob voters of chance to replace Scalia." *The Washington Post.* February 18. www.washingtonpost.com/opinions/mcconnell-and-grassley-democrats-shouldnt-rob-voters-of-chance-to-replace-scalia/2016/02/18/e5ae9bdc-d68a-11e5-be55-2cc3c1e4b76b_story.html. Accessed online November 24, 2020.

Moffett, Kenneth W. and Laurie L. Rice 2016. *Web 2.0 and the Political Mobilization of College Students.* Lanham, MD: Lexington Books.

Moffett, Kenneth W. and Laurie L. Rice 2018. "College Students and Online Political Expression in the 2016 Election." *Social Science Computer Review* 36(4): 422–439. https://doi.org/10.1177/0894439317721186. Accessed online June 19, 2021.

Moon, David, George Serra, and Jonathan P. West 1993. "Citizens' Contacts with Bureaucratic and Legislative Officials." *Political Research Quarterly* 46(4): 931–941. https://doi.org/10.1177/106591299304600414. Accessed online June 19, 2021.

Nichols, Austin 2007. "Causal Inference with Observational Data." *The Stata Journal* 7(4): 507–541. https://doi.org/10.1177/1536867X0800700403. Accessed online June 19, 2021.

Parker, Kim, Nikki Graf, and Ruth Igielnik 2019. "Generation Z Looks a Lot Like Millennials on Key Social and Political Issues." Pew Research Center. www.pewsocialtrends.org/2019/01/17/generation-z-looks-a-lot-like-millennials-on-key-social-and-political-issues/. Accessed online February 12, 2019.

Pitkin, Hanna Fenichel 1967. *The Concept of Representation.* Berkeley, CA: University of California Press.

Rainie, Lee, Aaron Smith, Key Lehman Schlozman, Henry Brady, and Sidney Verba 2012. "Social Media and Political Engagement." Pew Research Center's Internet & American Life Project. http://pewinternet.org/Reports/2012/Political-Engagement.aspx. Accessed online August 24, 2019.

Reny, Tyler T., Loren Collingwood, and Ali A. Valenzuela 2019. "Vote Switching in the 2016 Election: How Racial and Immigration Attitudes, Not Economics, Explain Shifts in White Voting." *Public Opinion Quarterly* 83(1): 91–113. https://doi.org/10.1093/poq/nfz011. Accessed online June 19, 2021.

Rosenstone, Steven J. and John Mark Hansen 2002. *Mobilization, Participation, and Democracy in America*. New York, NY: Pearson-Longman.

Seelig, Michelle I. 2018. "Social Activism: Engaging Millennials in Social Causes." *First Monday* 23(2–5). https://journals.uic.edu/ojs/index.php/fm/article/view/8125/6642. Accessed online December 1, 2019.

Sekhon, Jasjeet S. 2011. "Multivariate and Propensity Score Matching Software with Automated Balance Optimization: The Matching Package for R." *Journal of Statistical Software* 42(7): 1–52.

Shah, Dhavan V., Jaeho Cho, William P. Eveland, Jr., and Nojin Kwak 2005. "Information and Expression in a Digital Age: Modeling Internet Effects on Civic Participation." *Communication Research* 32(5): 531–565. https://doi.org/10.1177/0093650205279209. Accessed online June 19, 2021.

Sharp, Elaine B. 1982. "Citizen-Initiated Contacting of Government Officials and Socioeconomic Status: Determining the Relationship and Accounting for It." *American Political Science Review* 76(1): 109–115. https://doi.org/10.1017/S0003055400186071. Accessed online June 19, 2021.

Smith, Aaron 2013. "Civic Engagement in the Digital Age." Pew Research Center. http://pewinternet.org/Reports/2013/Civic-Engagement.aspx. Accessed online November 18, 2019.

Stolberg, Sheryl Gay, Nicholas Fandos, and Catie Edmonson 2018. "Interest Groups Turn Up Pressure before Kavanaugh Vote." *The New York Times*. www.nytimes.com/2018/09/11/us/politics/brett-kavanaugh-confirmation-vote.html. Accessed online November 20, 2019.

Stuart, Elizabeth A. 2010. "Matching Methods for Causal Inference: A Review and a Look Forward." *Statistical Science* 25(1): 1–21. https://doi.org/10.1214/09-STS313. Accessed online June 19, 2021.

Totenberg, Nina 2016. "Justice Antonin Scalia, Known for Biting Dissents, Dies at 79." NPR. February 13. www.npr.org/2016/02/13/140647230/justice-antonin-scalia-known-for-biting-dissents-dies-at-79. Accessed online November 24, 2020.

Vedlitz, Arnold and Eric Veblen 1980. "Voting and Contacting: Two Forms of Political Participation in a Suburban Community." *Urban Affairs Quarterly* 16(1): 31–48.

Verba, Sidney and Norman Nie 1972. *Participation in America: Political Democracy and Social Equality*. New York, NY: Harper and Row.

Verba, Sidney, Henry E. Brady, and Kay L. Schlozman 1995. *Voice and Equality: Civic Voluntarism in American Democracy*. Cambridge, MA: Harvard University Press.

Vogels, Emily 2019. "Millennials Stand Out for Their Technology Use, but Older Generations also Embrace Digital Life." Pew Research Center. www.pewresearch.org/fact-tank/2019/09/09/us-generations-technology-use/. Accessed online November 20, 2019.

Walsh, Deidre 2020. "What Amy Coney Barrett's Supreme Court Nomination Means for the 2020 Election." NPR. September 27. www.npr.org/2020/09/27/917303199/what-amy-coney-barretts-supreme-court-nomination-means-for-the-2020-election. Accessed online November 24, 2020.

Yamamoto, Masahiro, Matthew J. Kushin, and Francis Dalisay 2013. "Social Media and Mobiles as Political Mobilization Forces for Young Adults: Examining the Moderating Role of Online Political Expression in Political Participation." *New Media and Society* 17(6): 880–898. https://doi.org/10.1177/1461444813518390. Accessed online June 19, 2021.

Yang, Hongwei "Chris" and Jean L. DeHart. 2016. "Social Media Use and Online Political Participation among College Students during the US Election 2012." *Social Media + Society* 2(1):.https://doi.org/10.1177/2056305115623802. Accessed online June 19, 2021.

Zhang, Weiwi, Trent Seltzer, and Shannon L. Bichard 2013. "Two Sides of the Coin: Assessing the Influence of Social Network Site Use during the 2012 U.S. Presidential Campaign." *Social Science Computer Review* 31(5): 542–551. https://doi.org/10.1177/0894439313489962. Accessed online June 19, 2021.

Zuckerman, Alan S. and Darrell M. West 1985. "The Political Bases of Citizen Contacting: A Cross-National Analysis." *American Political Science Review* 79(1): 117–131. https://doi.org/10.2307/1956122. Accessed online June 19, 2021.

Zukin, Cliff, Scott Keeter, Molly Andolina, Krista Jenkins, and Michael X. Delli Carpini 2006. *A New Engagement? Political Participation, Civic Life, & the Changing American Citizen*. New York, NY: Oxford University Press.

8
DISCONTENT HEARD?

Examining the Link between Young Adults Engaging in Protests and Sharing Views with Elected Officials

Introduction

While posting is among the most common ways young adults express their political views, protesting is the most visible. Organizers hope large crowds will draw media attention, shape public opinion, and pressure policymakers to act. The successful use of nonviolent protests in the civil rights movement inspired many other movements to adopt this tactic and participation in protests has increased. Between 1973 and 2008, the percentage of Americans reporting having ever attended a protest rose (Dalton 2008; Caren, Ghoshal, and Ribas 2011). This is part of a broader trend of increased participation in social movements across advanced industrial democracies (Dalton 2006). Some argue that this is due to the development of a social movement society in which protests have become a regular, mainstream form of political behavior (Tarrow 1994; Meyer and Tarrow 1998). Once seen as a risky endeavor, over time there has been a drop in the perceived risk of being arrested for protesting (Caren, et al. 2011). But questions remain about how effective protests are at producing policy change.

In 2011, "The Protester" was *Time* magazine's Person of the Year. This choice was inspired by both the Arab Spring protests and the Occupy Wall Street Movement that year. During the Arab Spring, popular uprisings demanding reform spread throughout the Middle East and North Africa. The protests, coordinated via social media and popular among young adults, successfully toppled regimes (Graham-Harrison 2018). However, eight years later, of all the countries where protesters pushed for democratic reforms, only Tunisia was classified by Freedom House as free (Freedom House 2019). Meanwhile, the Occupy Wall Street movement protested income inequality in the United States, with a growing crowd of protesters, a majority of whom were under the age of 35, camping out in New York's Zuccotti

Park and other locations around the nation (Da Silva 2018). Billed as a leaderless revolution, they rallied under the cry "we are the 99 percent" (Da Silva 2018). While some of the messages of this movement echoed in the rhetoric of Democratic presidential candidates like Bernie Sanders and Elizabeth Warren, eight years later income inequality in the United States reached its highest rate in more than 50 years (Picchi 2019). As these cases illustrate, protests do not always produce the immediate responsiveness from policymakers that protesters seek.

In 2018, *Time* could have easily chosen "The Protester" as Person of the Year again. The year began with the Women's March at which the Crowd Counting Consortium[1] estimates more than 1.8 million people in attendance at more than 400 events across the United States. Then, according to the Crowd Counting Consortium, the walkout to protest gun violence on March 14 drew over 1.1 million protesters and the March for Our Lives on March 20 attracted over 1.3 million protesters at 765 events across America. Additional student walkouts drew smaller crowds in April and May and on June 30 the Crowd Counting Consortium reports that Families Belong Together events protesting separating families at the border drew crowds of nearly half a million at more than 700 events across the United States. While the Fall of 2018 lacked such large protests, smaller ones focused on sexual assault and Kavanaugh's nomination to the Supreme Court. In total, the consortium logged more than 19,000 protests occurring in the United States in 2018. Young adults were part of many of these.

Although 2019 was comparatively quieter, it did not lack protests. One of the largest among these according to Crowd Counting Consortium estimates was the Women's March protest events in the United States in January 2019 that drew over 675,000. In 2020, concern over Covid-19 temporarily slowed participation in protests, especially as millions of Americans were under stay at home orders to help stop its spread. Yet, the murder of George Floyd provoked large crowds in cities across the United States to protest, often with young adults leading the way. The Crowd Counting Consortium identified more than 6,500 distinct antiracism protests in June 2020 alone.

Participating in protests may be more common among young adults. Millennials are more likely to have participated in a protest than Generation X (Caren, Ghoshal, and Ribas 2011) and compared to other generations, Millennials are particularly likely to believe that protest will bring about change (Rouse and Ross 2018). Yet, given young adults' lower probabilities of voting in elections, elected officials might easily write their protests off as unlikely to affect electoral success. Thus, if young adults rely on protests to advance change, these messages might easily be ignored. In this chapter, we consider whether young adults who protest, all else equal, are any more likely to contact elected officials. We begin by discussing how participation in protests varies by generation and age. We then turn to how three different theoretical perspectives on protest mobilization apply to protests in 2018 and 2020. We discuss the strengths and weaknesses in relying on protests to send a political message and influence policy and the importance of direct contacts from constituents. We develop a theory about why participating in protests should make contacting elected officials more likely and then we test whether protesting in general and on specific issues is associated with greater rates of contacting elected officials.

Protests, Generations, and Age

Some generations have protested at higher rates than others. Caren, Ghoshal, and Ribas (2011) find that those born between 1943 and 1954, most of whom would have been young adults during the Civil Rights Movement, are far more likely to report having ever participated in a protest. They find that compared to other generations, early Baby Boomers are far more likely to report having participated in protests, but that Generation Y, more commonly referred to as Millennials, show a higher rate of protest compared to others born outside the Baby Boom years (Caren, Ghoshal, and Ribas 2011). If the last few years are any indication, Generation Z seems to be joining the ranks of those generations more likely to protest.

Scholars point to several potential causes. Some identify temporal effects as a cause, arguing that some generations have had more opportunities to participate in protests than others (Dalton 2006). Similarly, Milkman (2017) argues that Millennials face an environment in which they contend with widening income inequality, persistent gender and racial disparities, and discrimination against the LGBTQ community. This environment differs from that which Generation X faced, and as such, creates an environment that fosters protests and countermobilization within a highly polarized political environment (Milkman 2017).

As evidence of this, more protests occurred when Baby Boomers and Millennials were young adults than when members of the Silent Generation or Generation X were young adults (Milkman 2017). Others point to distinct generational effects as a possible explanation, arguing that generations have different proclivities toward participation overall or to specific conceptions of participation (Putnam 2000; Dalton 2015). Millennials see protests as an obvious way to express their views and try to make a difference (Rouse and Ross 2018). This is an interesting preference for an age group who has often been characterized as politically uninterested and unengaged. Dalton (2015) argues that this is because the generation has been mischaracterized – they are engaged, just in different ways than their predecessors.

Generational differences aside, younger adults are more likely to participate in protests (McVeigh and Smith 1999; Dalton 2006; Schussman and Soule 2005). How much of this is due to youthful exuberance, a greater ability to absorb the costs of protests, educational experiences, or other factors is unclear. However, education has a strong, positive relationship with protesting (Dalton, Van Sickle, and Weldon 2010) and especially so for Baby Boomers, followed by Millennials (Caren, Ghoshal, and Ribas 2011). Standard courses in high school and college curricula cover how protests have made a difference in the past and most young adults have been exposed to this material more recently than older Americans. Caren, Ghoshal, and Ribas (2011, 147) conclude that "attending a protest represents a form of citizen engagement highly bounded by birth cohort, educational attainment, and political belief." This suggests that young college-educated Millennials and older members of Generation Z who care deeply about the issues that came to the forefront in 2018 and 2020 would be the ones most likely to participate.

Grievance, Mobilization, and Opportunity

Several theoretical perspectives helped explain the emergence of social movements, and the protests that frequently accompany them. Deprivation theories (see e.g., Gurr 1970; Piazza 2011) emphasize how discontent over the withholding of basic rights or resources in society sparks action. This may happen without a movement leader engaging in mobilization (Lohmann 1994). Conversely, resource mobilization theories (see e.g., McCarthy and Zald 1977) often examine how movement organizers recruit members and incentivize their participation as well as whether individuals have the resources necessary to participate. When conscience rather than life is threatened, the degree of injustice individuals feel is likely to affect how easy or hard it is to mobilize them (Kerbo 1982). In this respect, there is some linkage between resource mobilization and deprivation theories. Other scholars instead focused on developing process theory, a perspective that emphasizes both internal and external opportunities and constraints in shaping mobilization (Tilly 1978; Tarrow 2011). These opportunity-based explanations of activism investigate how the context shapes individuals' decisions to participate (Meyer 2004). The perceived likelihood of affecting the outcome seemingly influences individuals' calculation of whether to participate (Sears and Citrin 1982; Platt 2008). The cost-benefit calculation of whether protesting is worthwhile changes as government or society becomes more receptive to a cause (Platt 2008). However, activists are prone to be overly optimistic about opportunities (Gamson and Meyer 1996) and activism, even when the conditions seem favorable, does not always result in favorable policy changes (Platt 2008).

Empirical support for opportunity-based explanations has been mixed but so, too, has been how it is conceptualized and operationalized (Meyer 2004). For example, government openness (Eisinger 1973), changes in policy (Opp 2000), and the hostility of current government policy (Meyer 1993; Staggenborg 1991) have all been found to shape political activity. Meyer and Minkoff (2004) compare two opportunity models' ability to explain mobilization to participate in civil rights protests – changes in structural opportunities and changes in political signals. The presence of a Democratic president was the only structural opportunity that influenced protest levels while several issue-specific signals of openness were significantly related to protest activity (Meyer and Minkoff 2004).

Meanwhile, another opportunity-based study of black people's political participation found that participation increases with the presence of external threats, being a part of a social network, and having access to policymakers (Platt 2008). In short, protests occur under favorable conditions, but this can mean anything from the presence of political leaders prone to be receptive to the protesters' cause to the presence of a serious threat.

This leads some to suggest that a combination of these theoretical approaches is needed to fully explain protest movements (see e.g., Milkman 2017). For example, one study of women's protests around the world found that insights from deprivation theory, resource mobilization theory, and process theories all helped explain women's protest activity (Murdie and Peksen 2015). Consistent with deprivation theory, protests by women were more common in countries with higher women's rights violations. Also, consistent with resource mobilization theory, protests by women were more common in wealthier countries and in those with more women's organizations. And consistent with process theory, protests vary with regime type and are most common at mid-levels of openness (Murdie and Peksen 2015).

These differing theoretical perspectives could also be applied to explaining the emergence of protests in 2018 and 2020. Deprivation theories might point to women's experiences in organizational cultures that protect harassers to explain protests about sexual harassment and assault that sprung up during Kavanaugh's confirmation hearings, to students' feelings that society is failing to protect them in their schools to explain March for Our Lives, to the lack of basic human rights afforded to immigrant families crossing without papers at the southern border to explain participation in the Families Belong Together protests, or to a pattern of police use of force combined with systemic racism that repeatedly leads to unjustified deaths of black males to explain participation in Black Lives Matter protests in 2020.

Resource mobilization theories would instead point to how interest groups mobilized individuals to protest for and against Kavanaugh's nomination and to attend Families Belong Together protests, as well as the role young people played in planning March for Our Lives protests against gun violence and in planning Black Lives Matter protests. They might also acknowledge social media's role in helping to mobilize individuals to protest. Process or opportunity-based theories might point to the development of social media in changing the opportunity structure, how the Women's March helped pave the way for the MeToo movement by bringing women's issues to the forefront of conversation, the hostility of current policy or the amount of news coverage devoted to mass shootings, the MeToo movement, immigration and family separation, and the killing of George Floyd that primed society to be more responsive to these causes to explain these protests.

Process or opportunity-based theories might also identify how the prominence of cell phones with the capability of filming made it easier to document incidents of racism and of police brutality, how social media helps spread knowledge of these incidents to a wider audience, and how weeks or months of being stuck at home due to the Covid-19 pandemic meant people had less distractions competing for their time and attention and readied people to get out and be a part of something meaningful all helped make the resurgence of Black Lives Matter protests more likely. Process or opportunity-based explanations might also point to young adults' greater ability to shoulder the costs of protesting, their education levels, or higher optimism that protests might make a difference. Where these approaches seem to agree, though, is that protesting does not guarantee policy change.

Sending a Political Message

Unlike closed political systems where protest may be the only recourse (Dalton, Van Sickle, and Weldon 2010), open political systems like the United States provide citizens numerous routes to trying to influence policy. Introductory American government textbooks commonly follow Walker (1991) and distinguish between insider tactics, which work within government and involve direct contact with elected officials, and outsider tactics, which seek public attention and support that puts indirect pressure on policymakers. Protests are outsider tactics.

Instead of distinguishing activities by the intended audience, others use the terms conventional and unconventional to describe these two forms of engagement, with protests considered a more unconventional form of influencing policy (Craig 1980; Chong and Rogers 2005). Insider tactics might be replaced with more unconventional outsider tactics if elected officials do not listen or if they face new challenges from groups using outsider strategies to their advantage (Beyers, Eising, and Maloney 2008). Some outsider tactics are meant to threaten elected officials if they do not act and others are meant to persuade the public that an issue needs attention (Amenta et al. 2010).

Protests help raise awareness (Giugni 1998, 2004) and are particularly effective at doing so, even compared to attention to an issue from the president of the United States (Smidt 2012). For example, news coverage of the Million Mom March was associated with an increase in the percentage of people saying guns or gun control was the greatest problem facing the nation. This increase was larger than that produced by coverage of a school shooting in Michigan a few months earlier and of that produced by coverage of the first anniversary of the Columbine school shooting (Smidt 2012). Even though the media devoted more coverage to President Clinton's efforts to take on the NRA than it did any of these events, he was less effective at influencing public opinion (Smidt 2012). In another example of protests raising awareness and shaping opinions, exposure to protests of anti-undocumented immigrant legislation shaped Latinx opinions on immigration, increasing their support for amnesty for undocumented immigrants (Branton et al. 2015) and raising the perception that undocumented immigration is the most important problem facing the Latinx community (Carey, Branton, and Martinez-Ebers 2014). Protests have helped change public attitudes about civil rights (Mazumder 2018) and influence the voting decisions of the American public (Gillion 2020).

Mass political participation such as this also provides elected officials information about policy preferences (Verba and Nie 1972). Yet, protesting may not guarantee that policymakers receive protesters' intended message as protests often do not generate media coverage and the coverage they do receive is often negatively skewed (Smith et al. 2001; Di Cicco 2010). Further, protesters do not always advance specific policy demands, and even when they do, they might be subject to multiple interpretations, misinterpretation, or countermessaging. One potential example of a message open to multiple interpretations in the 2020 Black Lives Matter protests is the demand to "Defund the Police." Some elected officials and activists interpret these literally as a call to take away all funding from police departments, effectively eliminating them. Yet, most activists have something more nuanced in mind that involves reallocating part of police departments' budgets into increased funding for social services. Patrisse Cullors, who co-founded Black Lives Matter in 2013, described this demand:

> We're ready to chip away at the line items inside of a police budget that really are nonsensical. Police should not be in charge of mental health crises. They should not be in charge of dealing with homelessness. They should not be in charge of 'supporting' people with drug dependency and addiction. Those are three line-items which we can cut out of the police budget and then put that back into health care.
>
> *(Villa 2020)*

Others have called for eliminating problematic police departments that have lost their community's trust in places like Minneapolis but then replacing them with new community-oriented, nonviolent approaches to public safety (Fletcher 2020), along the lines of a model that Camden, New Jersey, implemented (Andrew 2020). Elected officials, especially those who only see the slogan, might reach many conclusions about what their constituents want. Other elected officials may take these slogans and use them as the basis of a countermobilization campaign. For instance, many Republican groups used this slogan to attack their Democratic opponents in competitive districts (Kertscher 2020). In fact, President Biden commented in a leaked recording shortly after the 2020 general election, "That's how they [Republicans] beat the living hell out of us across the country, saying that we're talking about defunding the police. We're not. We're talking about holding them accountable" (Memoli 2020).

Elected officials respond to what they think their constituents want (Broockman and Skovron 2018). However, they typically have limited information to work with (Fenno 1977) and elected officials sometimes get a skewed view of what their constituents want. Those with higher levels of trust in the political system are more likely to contact their elected officials (Cluverius and Banda 2018). Also, in 2008, 2012, and 2014 Republicans were far more likely than Democrats to contact elected officials, leading them to dramatically overestimate constituent support for conservative positions (Broockman and Skovron 2018). The issue on which state legislators overestimated conservative opinions most dramatically was background checks for guns but they also thought constituent opinion was more conservative than it was on other issues including banning assault rifles and amnesty for undocumented immigrants (Broockman and Skovron 2018). Broockman and Skovron (2018) speculate that protests may help shift these misperceptions of constituent opinions.[2] In fact, these were some of the same issues that generated protests in 2018. Protests can serve as meaningful signals of public opinion (Gillion 2013; Wouters and Walgrave 2017). Yet, unless protests occur within the contours of their congressional district, a factor which has been found to influence roll call votes (Gillion 2013), elected officials have no way of knowing if any of their constituents protested. Thus, letters from constituents may be perceived as a more reliable cue of constituent opinion than protests in Washington, DC, or other major cities.

Elected officials respond to the constituent cues they receive. Experiments show a very limited number of cues from constituents can produce changes in voting behavior (Bergan and Cole 2015). To be effective, legislators must believe they are receiving genuine grassroots messages rather than a manufactured astroturf campaign (Lyon and Maxwell 2004), even though genuine grassroots lobbying is also typically inspired by organized interest groups (Kollman 1998; Holyoke 2012). In fact, interest groups work to make these grassroots letters appear to come from individuals without prompting, sometimes even encouraging, individuals to include spelling and grammar errors (Schlozman and Tierney 1983).

Legislators' responsiveness to cues from protests and other sources vary over the course of the policymaking process. Scholars have found that protesting, particularly as part of social movements, can make an impact at the start of the policymaking process (Soule and King 2006; King, Bentele, and Soule 2007) and in congressional hearings (Olzak and Soule 2009). Later in the policy process, public opinion becomes more important (Soule and King 2006) and groups engaging in protests face increased competition from groups with greater institutional resources and entrenchment. This leads some to characterize protests as weapons of the weak who lack institutional recourse for their interests (Wouters and Walgrave 2017).

One analysis of 268 historical accounts of domestic policymaking between 1945 and 2004 credited congressional lobbying for helping produce 16% of policy enactments, constituent pressure for contributing to 9.4% of policy enactments, and protests for helping result in only 2.9% of policy enactments (Grossman 2012). Congressional lobbying is also particularly effective at stopping policy changes (Baumgartner et al. 2009). However, minority protests in congressional districts influence legislators' roll call votes on bills that address concerns of racial and ethnic minority groups (Gillion 2013).

Groups that start with unconventional outsider tactics might adapt, institutionalize, and turn toward increasingly insider tactics as they gain political power and resources (Beyers, Eising, and Maloney 2008). However, there has been little attention given to the movement from outsider to insider tactics at the individual level. To try to keep an issue moving forward in Congress, it makes sense to follow up expressing one's views in a protest with contacting an elected official to share these views more directly. After all, there is less danger that this message will be misinterpreted, as it does not rely on mediated communication. And, especially in the face of fierce opposition from entrenched interest groups and a general status quo bias in policy, direct communication to elected officials can help make sure the message of a protest does not get lost.

For young adults' voices, expressed so powerfully at protests, to carry weight in the halls of Congress and in state legislatures across the country, elected officials must both hear them and take them seriously. Contacting elected officials makes it more likely that this happens. It tells elected officials not just that some people in the country care deeply enough about this issue to protest, it also tells them that one of their constituents feels so strongly about this that they are taking the time to contact them and share their views. Yet, just because contacting elected officials makes strategic sense does not guarantee young adults will do so. As we saw previously, in 2012 older age groups contacted elected officials at much higher rates than did 18–29-year-olds. Thus, at least until recently elected officials have been hearing from an audience that is heavily skewed both in terms of partisanship (Broockman and Skovron 2018) and age.[3] Could these trends now be changing?

Next, we test whether participating in a protest made young adults more likely to contact elected officials. The results have important implications for the effectiveness of young adults' political voice. Yet, there is also good reason to expect that participating in a protest makes individuals more likely to contact elected officials. Connections with individuals and organizations influence whether an individual engages in protests, as groups employ a variety of mobilization strategies when planning protests (McAdam 1986; Murdie and Peksen 2015). These same connections might also help encourage individuals to contact elected officials. Participating in protests brings increased exposure to other more seasoned activists who care about the same issues. Owing to their political experience in trying to advance change, they are more likely to urge those they meet at the protest to follow up the mass message of the protest with individual messages to elected officials.

In addition, organizations have increased their involvement in protests since the 1960s (Soule and Earl 2005). These organizations are likely to actively recruit new members at these protests. Membership in political interest groups is associated with a higher likelihood of contacting elected officials and this membership can help counteract the biases that variations in socioeconomic status produce in contacting elected officials (Holyoke 2012). Also, young adults who meet representatives from interest groups at a protest may decide to follow the organization on social media, leading to exposure to additional pleas to contact elected officials. At least some young adults should respond favorably to these pleas, creating a link from protesting to contacting elected officials.

Data

To test our primary hypothesis in this chapter, we performed online surveys on November 7, 2018, and November 4, 2020, of Americans between 18 and 25 years old – an age range that includes both older members of Generation Z and younger Millennials.[4] We used Amazon's Mechanical Turk (mTurk) platform to execute this survey, a website that allows members of the public to earn money for completing many kinds of tasks, including participating in survey research. In both years, each participant was paid $1.50 for completing the survey. A total of 1,010 participants completed the survey in 2018 and 969 participants completed the survey in 2020 after we removed any incomplete responses.[5]

Dependent Variables

The dependent variables measure the extent to which each respondent contacted government officials, either in general or about specific issues. The first dependent variable measures how often each respondent contacted or visited someone in government who represents their community. Each person was asked about the frequency with which they have engaged in this activity on a five-point scale that ranged from "never" having done so to having done this "very often." To facilitate a straightforward interpretation using matching, we collapsed this variable into a dichotomous variable that is coded one when a respondent contacted government officials with any frequency, and zero if not. Only 38.92% of our respondents reported having contacted government officials with any frequency in 2018, while 71.29% of our respondents reported having performed this same behavior in 2020.[6]

To examine issue-specific variation, we asked respondents five separate questions about the frequency with which they contacted elected officials about Black Lives Matter (in 2020 only), gun control, immigration or family separation, Supreme Court nominations (Kavanaugh in 2018, Barrett in 2020), and the MeToo movement, respectively. To facilitate an easily interpretable set of results using matching, we collapsed the measurement for these issue-specific variables into a series of binaries. These binaries are coded one if the respondent contacted elected officials about the relevant issue at least once, and zero if they never had. The means for these binaries suggest relatively low levels of contacting elected officials, as the averages range from 21.62% (contacting elected officials about the MeToo movement in 2018) to 62.53% (contacting elected officials about gun control in 2020). Additional details about question wording and about variable measurement can be found in the online appendix. To test our theoretical expectations, we employ a series of matching routines.

Treatment Variables

To test our hypothesis, we asked each respondent about the frequency with which they protested using a five-point scale that ranged from "never" having done so to having done this activity "very often." However, it is probable that young adults protested about varying political issues with differential frequencies. We followed up with separate questions that asked respondents about how often they protested about gun control, immigration or family separation, Supreme Court nominations (Barrett in 2020, Kavanaugh in 2018), the MeToo movement, and the Black Lives Matter movement (2020 only). We employ each of these separate questions as a unique treatment variable in our follow-up analyses in this chapter. The response options for each of these questions about the respective issues were never, protested once, protested two or three times, and protested four or more times.

Matching Covariates

We used two variables to investigate the effects of political engagement away from the internet. First, we asked each respondent about the extent to which they are interested in politics on a four-point scale that ranged from four points for "Very interested" to zero points for "Not at all interested." Second, each respondent was asked three questions about the extent to which their friends engaged in a set of activities and from these responses we built an additive index of peer civic activities ($\alpha = .63, 2018; \alpha = .58, 2020$).[7,8]

In addition, we used several variables to query the effects of political engagement using the internet. First, we asked each respondent how often they read blogs online about politics as blogs can act as outlets that encourage enhanced civic activity, either online or offline (Moffett and Rice 2018; Kerbel and Bloom 2005). Second, each respondent was asked how frequently they read news on the internet about politics.

Third, we constructed an additive index of online civic activity that is composed of four items, as several researchers have found a connection between activities on social media and offline civic engagement (see e.g., Kahne and Bowyer 2018; Ley and Brewer 2018; Loader, Vromen, and Xenos 2014). Through separate questions, each respondent was asked about the extent to which they had relied on social media for news, read social media feeds about politics, liked or shared posts about politics on social media, or read or watched posts about politics on social media, and responses were added together ($\alpha = .81, 2018; \alpha = .78, 2020$).

We employed four variables to account for the effects of issue importance, as issues can sometimes prime higher levels of political participation (Converse 1964; Carmines and Stimson 1989; Reny, Collingwood, and Valenzuela 2019). Using separate questions, we asked each respondent about the importance of congressional stances on immigration,[9] as well as gun control,[10] in influencing their vote choice. Third, we asked each respondent whether they supported or opposed the DACA program. Fourth, we asked each respondent about the extent to which they supported or opposed the family separation policy implementation under the Trump administration.

In addition, we employed several variables to account for the effects of personal characteristics on offline civic activity. First, we examined the effects of ideology on civic engagement with a binary for liberals, as Achen and Bartels (2016) discover that ideological self-identification shapes political participation. Second, we create a binary for strong partisanship from answers to questions about party identification as strength of partisanship is associated with an array of other political activities (see e.g., Flavin and Griffin 2009; Verba, Brady, and Schlozman 1995).

Third, we asked each respondent for their sex, and we coded this variable one for females, two for males, and three for those who self-identified in another category. Fourth, we acquired data on each respondent's age by asking each to report their month and year of birth. Then, we computed each respondent's age based on the month and year of the 2018 midterm election in 2018 and the general election in 2020.[11] Fifth, we asked each respondent for their race and collapsed that information into a binary that is coded one for whites, and zero otherwise. Sixth, we asked each respondent for their level of education.

Finally, we used three variables to control for the effects of underlying political attitudes, as these can affect participation patterns. First, we asked each respondent whether they approved or disapproved of the job that Donald Trump is doing as president, as presidential approval is connected with changes in participatory patterns (Abramowitz and Stone 2006). Second, we include separate binaries for those who self-identified as MeToo supporters and as Black Lives Matter supporters.[12]

Matching Covariate Differences across Models

There are two primary differences in the covariates that we used across the different models beyond those that we specify above. First, we included separate measures in the models about the extent to which respondents posted messages about gun control, immigration, the MeToo movement, Supreme Court nominations, Black Lives Matter, and other political issues. The response options for these questions were "never," "once," "two or three times," and "four or more times." The models in Table 8.1 exclude these measures, as we do not want to include component parts of the treatment variable (protesting about politics) in this table as a matching covariate, as this violates the underlying matching assumptions.

The models in Tables 8.2 through 8.4 include these measures, but with important variations. These models all include the variable for having protested about other political issues. However, the models exclude the variable about protesting about the issue being examined in the table as a matching covariate, as that variable acts as a treatment variable in that table. However, the variables that query the extent to which one protests about the remaining issues beyond the "other" category are included. In Table 8.2, for example, we examine the effects of participating in protests related to the MeToo movement (treatment variable) on contacting elected officials about that movement. Consequently, we exclude participating in protests related to the MeToo movement as a matching covariate, since it is a treatment variable. However, we include protesting about Supreme Court nominations (Barrett in 2020, Kavanaugh in 2018), gun control, immigration or family separation, Black Lives Matter (in 2020 only), and other political issues in this model. The reason that we do so is that we want to examine the effects of participating in protests about the MeToo movement on contacting elected officials *over and beyond* respondents' baseline inclinations toward participating in protests about other political issues. We perform analogous routines for the models in Tables 8.2 through 8.4.

Second, we included separate measures in the models about the extent to which respondents posted about gun control, immigration, the MeToo movement, Supreme Court nominations (Barrett in 2020, Kavanaugh in 2018), Black Lives Matter (in 2020 only), and other political issues. The response options for these items were "never," "once," "two or three times," and "four or more times." The models in Table 8.1 include these items as matching covariates.

The models in Tables 8.2 through 8.4 include these measures, but with some meaningful variations. These models all include the variable for having posted about other political issues. However, the models exclude the variable about posting related to the issue being examined in the table as a matching covariate, as that variable is connected with contacting elected officials related to that issue (the dependent variable), and with posting about that issue (our treatment variable). However, the variables that query the extent to which one posts about the remaining issues beyond the "other" category are included. We do this because we want to be appropriately sensitive to the underlying assumptions of the matching approach (see e.g., Imbens and Rubin 2015).

In Table 8.2, for example, we examine the effects of posting about the MeToo movement (treatment variable) on contacting elected officials about that movement. Consequently, we exclude posting about the MeToo movement as a matching covariate, since it is connected with both the dependent and treatment variables. However, we include posting about Supreme Court nominations (Barrett in 2020; Kavanaugh in 2018), Black Lives Matter (in 2020 only), gun control, immigration or family separation, and other political issues in this model. We perform analogous routines for the models in Tables 8.2 through 8.4.

Methods

To investigate whether our treatment variables are associated with contacting elected officials, we use a matching analysis to compute the ATET. Several reasons drive the choice of a matching estimator. First, virtually all regression-based techniques (including OLS) assume that there exists a linear relationship between the dependent and independent variables (see Greene 2011). Our theory posits a positive relationship between each of our treatment variables and contacting elected officials, but makes no prediction about the remaining response options contained in any of the treatment variables. Consequently, the phenomenon that we examine is nonlinear by construction and is ill-suited to investigate using a method that assumes linearity. Fortunately, matching analyses do not assume linearity, allow for a more flexible functional form, and have other statistical properties that make them a more appropriate choice to test our theory (Imbens and Rubin 2015).

Moreover, individuals have differing probabilities of contacting elected government officials in general, or about specific issues or movements. OLS estimators presume treatment homogeneity, which is unlikely to hold in the analyses that are contained in this chapter. It is probable that individuals have different treatment effects, particularly depending on the frequency with which they participate in protests in general, or about specific social movements or issues (see Abadie and Imbens 2011). Thus, the effects of participating in protests (more generally, or about specific issues or social movements) vary with the frequency with which one has performed this activity. For instance, we expect that those who participated in protests more frequently (or about specific political issues or social movements) are more apt to contact government officials (either in general or about the specific issue about which they participated in protests) than those who did not participate in protests.

By construction, OLS-based estimators assume that we observe a linear, homogeneous relationship between protesting about politics (or specified issues or social movements) and contacting elected government officials. Matching-based approaches deal nicely with this issue because they assume neither linearity nor homogeneity (Imbens and Rubin 2015). Rather, matching-based approaches produce several treatment estimates depending on the level of treatment that a respondent received (Imbens and Rubin 2015). Thus, we can generate several, more accurate estimates of the effect that protesting had on contacting elected government officials.

Also, OLS does not permit us to estimate what happens to the probability of contacting elected government officials in the absence of participating in protests (or alternatively, about specific issues or social movements) (Nichols 2007). Matching analyses use the existing data to produce a dataset that includes observations that are as alike as possible, given the values of the remaining predictors (Stuart 2010). Thus, we can estimate what would have happened in the absence of any specific level of participating in protests generally, or about any specific issue or social movement (see Gelman and Hill 2007). Then, we can use this dataset to estimate the effects of a given level of participating in protests on contacting elected government officials. We iterate this procedure for each level of participating in protests, or for any specific issue or social movement. Finally, if we used OLS estimates to obtain the results, our results would likely be biased because any estimate of the treatment effect is conditioned on the values of the remaining independent variables. Consequently, OLS-based approaches do not compute ATETs.

Matching analyses handle each of these issues well because they permit us to investigate whether participating in protests (or about a specific issue or social movement) is associated with contacting elected government officials. By matching based on each of the predictor variables to generate inferences, we can separate the effect of participating in protests about an issue beyond individuals' other predispositions to contact elected government officials. Thus, doing so enables us to compare people with similar inclinations to contact elected government officials who only vary in the level at which they participate in protests in general, or about any specified political issue or social movement. Moreover, matching allows us to calculate ATETs for each treatment level, and by doing so, to calculate more precise effect estimates with observational data.

Assumptions

Before performing our matching analyses, we must meet four assumptions. The validity of the matching analyses in this chapter hinges upon fulfilling these assumptions. First, we presume that all sets of treatment variables are binary. To make each set of treatment variables binary, we generated several dichotomous variables for each response option, relative to never having participated in protests in general, or about each of the issues or social movements that we examine in this chapter. For instance, the binary for having participated in protests rarely is coded one for those who did so, zero for never having done so, and missing for those who declined to answer this question, and for those who reported having participated in protests more than once. Similarly, the dichotomous variable for having participated in protests about Black Lives Matter once is coded one for those who did so, zero for never having done so, and missing for those who reported having participated in protests more than once, or for those who did not answer this question. We performed analogous routines for protesting about the remaining issue areas or social movements that we explore in this chapter. We expect positive signs for the ATET for all variables.

Second, we assume common support (or overlap), which means that it is possible that treated units may face an intervention that could have assigned them to the control group (see Imbens and Rubin 2015; King, Lucas, and Nielsen 2017). The data that we use meet this requirement because all respondents could have chosen not to participate in protests in general, or about a political issue or social movement.

Third, we must fulfill the SUTVA assumption, which means that "the potential outcomes for any unit do not vary with the treatments assigned to other units, and for each unit, there are no different forms or versions of each treatment level, which lead to different potential outcomes" (Imbens and Rubin 2015, 10). We have met the first part of this assumption because the possible outcomes for civic activity do not vary with the extent to which one participated in protests generally, or about any issue or social movement.[13]

We must examine the second aspect of this assumption carefully because we have different variations on our treatment variables. For our first treatment variable, the variations are rarely, sometimes, frequently, and very often. Our remaining treatment variables vary with respect to participating in protests once, protesting two or three times, and protesting four or more times about an issue or social movement. Yet, we can compare the effects of having participated in protests with varying frequencies related to a political issue or a social movement relative to those who never did so. For example, we can compare those who participated in protests rarely to those who never did so, provided that we exclude those who participated in protests at all other frequencies from that analysis.[14] We have to perform an analogous procedure to compare those who had participated in protests rarely, frequently, or very often if we aspire to perform a matching analysis without an alternative treatment.

Similarly, we can compare the effects of having participated in protests with differing frequencies about a political issue or social movement relative to those who never did so. For example, we can compare those who participated in protests once about immigration or family separation to those who never did so, provided that we exclude those who participated in protests at all other frequencies from that analysis.[15] We need to perform an analogous procedure to compare those who participated in protests two or three times, and those who posted four or more times about this issue if we hope to perform a matching analysis absent an alternative treatment. We also must perform the procedure outlined in this paragraph on all other treatment variables related to political issues or social movements. When we compute our ATETs in the manner prescribed above for all sets of models, we ultimately satisfy the SUTVA assumption because we have neither interference nor any hidden variations of the treatments (Imbens and Rubin, 2015, 10–11).

Finally, the treatment assignment must be conditionally independent of the outcome variable given a set of matching covariates (D'Agostino 1998, 2266). Thus, each respondent's assignment to treatment (i.e., participating in protests in general, or about a specific political issue or social movement) is unconnected with the extent to which they contact government officials, given the values of the remaining explanatory variables. We observed low levels of contacting government officials in 2018, but higher levels in 2020. In all cases, though, contacting government officials generally occurs with greater frequency than contacting government officials about any issue or social movement that we highlight in this chapter. In addition, contacting government officials does not cause an individual to participate in protests in general, or about a political issue or a social movement. Thus, contacting government officials does not cause an individual to be assigned to one or more treatment categories.

Matching Technique

Once we have met the statistical assumptions that underlie matching, we must select a method by which to execute this type of analysis. To perform our matching analyses, we use one-to-one genetic matching with replacement (Diamond and Sekhon 2013; Sekhon 2011). We incorporate a propensity score into the analysis, as knowing estimated values of this score meaningfully improves the accuracy of this method (Diamond and Sekhon 2013). Propensity score matching allows us to compare observations that are otherwise similar across other predictors, but have experienced different treatments. We perform our analysis with replacement, as matching discrepancies are reduced because we can use untreated units as a match multiple times (see Abadie and Imbens 2006).[16] To remove any bias that results due to the choice of the matching estimator without affecting the variance of that estimator, we employ a bias correction (Abadie and Imbens 2016).

Results

Before we discuss our results, we must examine how similar the treatment and control groups are to one another (King, Lucas, and Nielsen 2017). If these groups are substantially dissimilar, then we cannot use matching to estimate ATETs. The imbalance statistics for the models in Table 8.1 through 8.4 are contained in Tables A1 through A22 in the online appendix. In 2018, for 83.92% of the variables contained in the models in Tables 8.1 through 8.4, the KS tests are not significant at the .05 level after matching has occurred. In the remaining 59 of 367 cases (or 16.07%), the KS test is significant. Of these 59 cases, 29 of them (or 49.15%) involve issues that have been examined in Chapters 2 through 7. In 2020, for 65.75% of the variables contained in the models in Tables 8.1 through 8.4, the KS tests are not significant at the .05 level after matching has taken place. In the remaining 175 of 511 cases, the KS test is significant. Of these 175 cases, 91 of them (or 52%) involve issues that have been investigated in Chapters 2 through 7.

The remaining 30 variables in 2018 and the remaining 84 variables in 2020 are not distributed in a systematic pattern across any specific model or set of models. Thus, we can be confident that we have reduced imbalance and have achieved balance across the model specifications. The matched groups have similar observable characteristics such that we can attribute any remaining differences across levels of protesting to protesting about these issues, not to preexisting differences (Eggers and Hainmueller 2009).

Participating in Protests and Contacting Government Officials

In Table 8.1, we provide the results from the matching routines in which we examine the relationship between participating in protests and contacting government officials. The results indicate that in 2018, those who rarely participated in protests were 17.1% more likely to contact elected officials. Moreover, those who participated in protests very often were 146.7% more likely to contact elected government officials. Meanwhile, in 2020 those who sometimes participated in protests were 53.7% more likely to contact elected officials while those who participated in protests very often were 49.9% more likely to participate in protests. In addition, it appears that there is a connection between participating in protests about politics and contacting elected government officials very often in 2018, and frequently in 2020. However, neither result is robust.

While we find some initial evidence that participating in protests is connected with contacting elected government officials, it is also possible that these effects differ by issue area or social movement, and if true, would be consistent with one of the themes that have emerged in this book: differing issues encourage young adult civic engagement in divergent ways. We will examine this more formally in subsequent models throughout this chapter.

MeToo Movement

The events of 2017 and 2018 suggest the MeToo movement and surrounding protests related to this issue attracted attention from officeholders. Although the political system was not necessarily the primary focus of MeToo, it has led to the downfall of several elected officials accused of inappropriate behavior. In addition, demands for change through protests and other mechanisms have been met with action by elected officials. For example, the MeToo Movement increased the amount of legislation at the state level addressing sexual harassment and assault (Kelly and Hegarty 2018). Is there evidence that young adults who participated in protests related to the MeToo Movement were more likely to contact elected officials about MeToo?

In Table 8.2, we provide the results from the matching routines. The results indicate that in 2018, participating in protests related to the MeToo Movement is connected with contacting elected officials about that movement. More specifically, those who participated in protests once in 2018 related to this movement experienced a 35.2% increase in the probability that they contacted elected officials about this movement, relative to those who never protested about this movement. In addition, those who participated in protests two or three times related to this movement in 2018 were 55.1% more likely to contact elected officials about this movement compared to those who never protested about this movement. What is more, those who participated in protests four or more times related to this movement in 2018 were 77.3% more likely to contact elected officials about this

TABLE 8.1 Contacting Elected Officials and Participating in Protests

	2018				2020			
	Rarely	Sometimes	Frequently	Very Often	Rarely	Sometimes	Frequently	Very Often
Effect on Contacting Elected Officials	.171	-.036	.030	1.467	.433	.537	.499	.499
Abadie-Imbens Standard Error	.070	.165	.158	.650	.333	.134	.126	.146
95% Confidence Interval Lower Bound	.033	-.362	-.283	.171	-.244	.270	.248	.206
95% Confidence Interval Upper Bound	.309	.290	.343	2.763	1.110	.804	.750	.792
T-Statistic	2.444	-.217	.189	2.257	1.301	4.003	3.957	3.428
P-Value (two-tailed)	.015	.828	.850	.024	.193	$6.250 \star 10^{-5}$	$7.589 \star 10^{-5}$	.0006
P-Value (one-tailed)	.008	.414	.425	.012	.097	$3.125 \star 10^{-6}$	$3.795 \star 10^{-6}$	.0003
N	135	147	102	72	35	85	76	51

Notes: In each two-column set, the frequency with which one has participated in protests is compared with one who has never done so. Second, the covariates on which the matching is based are described in the text. Third, the effects on contacting elected officials are the ATET. Finally, the matching results are from 1:1 genetic matching with post-matching bias adjustment. Thus, the N represents the matched number of observations.

movement, relative to those who never protested about this movement. In 2020, we found no statistically significant connection between participating in protests about the MeToo movement and contacting elected government officials about that movement.

Thus, the evidence supports our hypothesis: that protesting about the MeToo movement either one or four or more times in 2018 is associated with a higher propensity to contact elected government officials about that movement. Yet, in 2020, when the MeToo movement was crowded out by other issues and faded to the background in many voters' minds, there was no evidence of a link between protesting about MeToo and contacting elected officials about it.

Supreme Court Nominations

Owing to the emergence of allegations of sexual assault levied against Kavanaugh as the Senate considered his nomination in 2018, the confirmation hearings generated even more media coverage than usual and generated an audience. Meanwhile, the controversy over the timing of Barrett's nomination in 2020 and the fact that she would widen the conservative majority on the Court by replacing a liberal justice also drew significant attention. The pending votes on Kavanaugh's and Barrett's nominations to the Supreme Court offered constituents an opportunity and a limited window to influence their senators' votes. Further, interest groups spent millions targeting senators whose votes were likely to be crucial in both Kavanaugh's (Stolberg, Fandos, and Edmonson 2018) and Barrett's nominations (Miller 2020). Part of these efforts included mobilizing constituents to share their views directly with their senators. Were those who protested about Kavanaugh's or Barrett's nominations more likely to contact their elected officials about the nomination?

In Table 8.2, we furnish the results of the matching routines for Supreme Court nominations. The results seemingly provide evidence that those who protested four or more times about Kavanaugh's nomination in 2018 were 36.4% more likely than those who did not protest this nomination at all to contact government officials about that nomination. However, those who protested with lesser frequencies (once, or two or three times) were no more likely to have contacted government officials about his nomination than those who never posted at all. Meanwhile, in 2020 the results suggest that those who protested once about Barrett's nomination were 71.8% more likely to contact elected officials about it while those who protested her nomination four or more times were 39% more likely to contact elected officials about it compared to those who did not protest about her nomination.

Overall, the results indicate that participating in protests related to Supreme Court nominations is substantially related to a higher likelihood of contacting elected government officials about Barrett's nomination, but not about Kavanaugh's. This finding is interesting because protests related to Kavanaugh's

Discontent Heard? 247

TABLE 8.2 Contacting Elected Officials about the MeToo Movement or Supreme Court Nominations and Participating in Protests Related to Those Issues

	MeToo Movement							Supreme Court Nominations						
	2018			2020				2018			2020			
	Once	Two or Three Times	Four or More Times	Once	Two or Three Times	Four or More Times		Once	Two or Three Times	Four or More Times	Once	Two or Three Times	Four or More Times	
Effect on Contacting Elected Officials	.352	.551	.773	.162	.135	.151		.219	.091	.364	.718	.112	.390	
Abadie-Imbens Standard Error	.101	.268	.192	.144	1.065	.129		.169	.144	.133	.209	.179	.118	
95% Confidence Interval Lower Bound	.149	.012	.377	-.127	-1.980	-.107		-.120	-.203	.087	.298	-.244	.154	
95% Confidence Interval Upper Bound	.555	1.090	1.169	.451	2.250	.409		.558	.385	.641	1.138	.468	.626	
T-Statistic	3.498	2.056	4.033	1.125	1.127	1.166		1.299	.629	2.734	3.438	.626	3.319	
P-Value (two-tailed)	.0005	.040	$5.510*10^{-5}$	.261	.899	.244		.194	.529	.006	.001	.531	.001	
P-Value (one-tailed)	.0003	.020	$2.755*10^{-6}$	.131	.450	.122		.097	.265	.003	.0005	.266	.0005	
N	55	50	26	55	94	60		56	32	22	49	83	56	

Notes: In each two-column set, the number of times that one has participated in protests related to the MeToo Movement or Supreme Court nominations is compared with one who has never done so. Second, the covariates on which the matching is based are described in the text. Third, the effects on contacting elected officials are the AITET. Finally, the matching results are from 1:1 genetic matching with post-matching bias adjustment. Thus, the N represents the matched number of observations.

nomination were more widespread than protests related to Barrett's. Yet, young adults were more likely to contact elected officials when participating in protests related to Barrett's nomination. Perhaps they felt heightened responsibility to act, when part of protests made smaller in part due to the prevalence of the Covid-19 pandemic than when part of much larger protests related to Kavanaugh's nomination.

Gun Control

The founding members of March for Our Lives began mobilizing against gun violence hours after a gunman killed 17 at their high school in Parkland, Florida, and organized many protests around the United States thereafter. Jaclyn Corin soon organized lobbying trips and was part of a nationwide bus tour encouraging local leaders to adopt similar tactics to change gun laws (Jones 2018). Thus, contacting elected officials was a key, underreported part of the movement. Most of those who protested about gun control in 2018 would likely be aware of these efforts, as well as of NRA opposition, and would become more likely to be exposed to messages requesting they contact their elected officials to share their views about guns. Were those who protested about gun control more likely to contact elected officials to share these views? Meanwhile, in 2020, while public attention to March for Our Lives faded, some young activists remained highly engaged. Were those who engaged in related protests in 2020, despite the public's lessened attention to their cause, more likely to contact elected officials about gun control?

In Table 8.3, we display the results from the matching routines. The results provide evidence that participating in protests about gun control is connected with contacting elected government officials about that issue. More specifically, in 2018 the probability of contacting government officials about gun control increases by 26.7% when one protested once about this issue, 56% for protesting two or three times about this issue, and by 54.7% for protesting four or more times about this issue. Meanwhile in 2020, when fewer people were paying attention and messages to elected officials may have been increasingly critical for ensuring young activists' messages were heard, the probability of contacting elected officials about gun control increased by 64.2% among those who protested once about this issue, 95.4% among those who protested two or three times about this issue, and 82.1% among those who protested four or more times about this issue. Thus, we conclude that protesting once, or four or more times about gun control in 2018 is connected with an increased probability of contacting elected government officials about this issue. What is more, we can conclude that protesting at any frequency about gun control in 2020 is associated with an increased likelihood of contacting elected government officials about that issue.

TABLE 8.3 Contacting Elected Officials about Gun Control or Immigration and Family Separation and Participating in Protests about That Issue

	Gun Control						Immigration and Family Separation					
	2018			2020			2018			2020		
	Once	Two or Three Times	Four or More Times	Once	Two or Three Times	Four or More Times	Once	Two or Three Times	Four or More Times	Once	Two or Three Times	Four or More Times
Effect on Contacting Elected Officials	.267	.560	.547	.642	.954	.821	.094	1.289	.310	.263	.096	.360
Abadie-Imbens Standard Error	.128	.271	.244	.187	.198	.143	.135	.470	.159	.219	.148	.196
95% Confidence Interval Lower Bound	.012	.013	.044	.267	.561	.533	-.177	.341	-.019	-.175	-.198	-.034
95% Confidence Interval Upper Bound	.522	1.107	1.050	1.017	1.347	1.109	.365	2.237	.639	.701	.390	.754
T-Statistic	2.085	2.069	2.239	3.430	4.828	5.746	.697	2.744	1.954	1.199	.647	1.835
P-Value (two-tailed)	.037	.039	.025	.001	1.384×10^{-6}	9.156×10^{-9}	.486	.006	.051	.231	.518	.066
P-Value (one-tailed)	.019	.020	.013	.0005	6.920×10^{-7}	4.578×10^{-9}	.243	.003	.026	.116	.259	.033
N	72	44	26	57	94	44	52	43	24	58	86	50

Notes: In each two-column set, the number of times that one has participated in protests about gun control or immigration and family separation is compared with one who has never done so. Second, the covariates on which the matching is based are described in the text. Third, the effects on contacting elected officials are the AITE'T. Finally, the matching results are from 1:1 genetic matching with post-matching bias adjustment. Thus, the N represents the matched number of observations.

Immigration and Family Separation

The controversial policy of separating children from parents when crossing the border illegally produced numerous calls to contact elected officials that appeared in sources ranging from *The New York Times* to *Elle* magazine. A variety of groups including the RAICES, ACLU, and the Lutheran Immigration and Refugee Service urged people to contact their elected officials, even including sample wording they might use on the phone or in a letter or e-mail. Those who cared enough to attend a protest about this issue are likely to be more receptive to these calls to contact elected officials.

Compared to other issues we examined in Part I, there was less evidence that posting about immigration and family separation was associated with greater civic engagement. Despite that, did participating in protests about this issue yield a greater likelihood of contacting elected officials about it? In Table 8.3, we display the results from the matching routines to answer this query. The results for 2018 seemingly provide evidence that participating in protests more than once is connected with contacting government officials about that issue. The model coefficients indicate that protesting two or three times about immigration in 2018 is connected with a 128.9% increase in the probability that one contacts elected government officials about this issue, and a 31% increase in the likelihood that one contacts these government officials when they protest four or more times about this issue. Meanwhile, the results for 2020 indicate that protesting four or more times about immigration was associated with a 36% increase in contacting elected officials about that issue when we use a one-tailed test. Thus, participating in protests four or more times about immigration and family separation in 2020 was connected with a higher level of contacting elected government officials.

Black Lives Matter

As people took to the streets to protest the death of George Floyd, the conversation broadened to what could be done to prevent similar tragedies in the future and what actions individuals could take to counteract systemic racism. A variety of news sources and magazines from *USA Today* to *Cosmopolitan* published lists of concrete actions individuals could take to help make a difference. High on many of these lists was contacting elected officials. Social media played a key role in organizing protests on this issue, making those who protested also highly likely to see some of these lists of actions. Did those who protested become more likely to contact elected officials?

Table 8.4 displays the results of the matching routines used to test the impact of engaging in Black Lives Matter protests on contacting elected officials about issues related to Black Lives Matter. While we find no evidence that protesting multiple times is associated with greater rates of contacting elected officials, protesting once about this movement appears to be connected with higher levels of contacting

TABLE 8.4 Contacting Elected Officials about Black Lives Matter and Participating in Protests Related to That Movement in 2020

	Once	Two or Three Times	Four or More Times
Effect on Contacting Elected Officials about Black Lives Matter	.609	.054	-.055
Abadie-Imbens Standard Error	.205	.157	.194
95% Confidence Interval Lower Bound	.199	-.257	-.442
95% Confidence Interval Upper Bound	1.019	.366	.332
T-Statistic	2.967	.342	-.285
P-Value (two-tailed)	.003	.732	.776
P-Value (one-tailed)	.002	.366	.388
N	58	95	70

Notes: In each two-column set, the number of times that one has posted about Black Lives Matter is compared with one who has never done so. Second, the covariates on which the matching is based are described in the text. Third, the effects on contacting elected officials are the ATET. Finally, the matching results are from 1:1 genetic matching with post-matching bias adjustment. Thus, the N represents the matched number of observations.

elected officials about this movement. However, this result is not robust, and thus, we cannot conclude that a statistically significant connection exists between participating in protests related to Black Lives Matter and contacting elected government officials about this social movement. This result makes sense if the intended target of the protests was not elected officials, but rather, members of the public.[17]

Robustness Checks

It is possible that the results that we have obtained in this section are a function of the way in which we specified our models (Ho et al. 2007). To address this, we removed each matching covariate one at a time, and re-ran the matching routines with the remaining predictors for each model.[18] These results are contained in the online appendix.[19] When we examine the models in Table 8.1 relative to what we report here, 63.30% (or 119/188) contained results that mirrored those that we report. In addition, 18 of the remaining 25 cases (or 72%) in 2018 occurred where we had statistically significant results with rarely participating in protests or doing so very often. And, 8 of 22 results (or 36.36%) for rarely participating in protests deviated from what are reported in Table 8.1, while 10 of 22 results (or 45.45%) for participating in protests very often diverged in this manner in 2018. What is more, 17 of the remaining 44 cases (or 38.64%) of cases in 2020 when we examine frequently participating in protests deviate from what we reported here. Put differently, 17 of the 25 (or 68%) of cases for frequently participating in protests deviate from what we report in Table 8.1 in 2020. Because a majority of the robustness checks in 2020 for frequently participating in protests differ from what is contained in Table 8.1 in terms of the significance patterns, we cannot conclude that there is a relationship between frequently participating in protests and contacting elected government officials in 2020.

To err conservatively, we can conclude that there is a relationship between rarely participating in protests in and contacting government officials in 2018 as roughly 2/3 of the model specifications when we perform the robustness checks produce results consistent with what we report in Table 8.1 for both levels. We must be more cautious when drawing conclusions from our models for participating in protests very often in 2018, as slightly more than 50% of the robustness checks indicate results that are consistent with that which we report in Table 8.1. Similarly, we must be more cautious when drawing conclusions from our models for sometimes participating in protests in 2020, as slightly more than 50% of the robustness checks and model results indicate results that are consistent with that which we report in Table 8.1. To err on the safe side, we should not conclude much from the "very often" model Table 8.1 for 2018.

When we test the models for participating in protests related to the MeToo movement, 67.33% (or 101/150) of the models contained results that are consistent with those reported in Table 8.2. And, 14 of the remaining 17 results in 2018 (or 82.35%) occur where we examine whether participating in protests two or three times related to the MeToo Movement is associated with contacting elected government officials about this movement. When we remove 14 of the 23 matching covariates (or 60.87% of them) in the two or three times model, the results diverge from what is reported in Table 8.2. Thus, we should err conservatively with this model and conclude that participating in protests two or three times is unconnected with contacting elected government officials about this movement in 2018.

We examine whether the results for participating in protests related to Supreme Court justices are robust. When we investigate the models in Table 8.2, 72% (or 108/150) of the models contained results that were consistent in terms of signs and significance patterns to those that we report here. In 2018, 17 of the remaining 19 (or 89.47%) models where results diverged from what we report in Table 8.2 involve having protested four or more times about Kavanaugh's nomination. Put differently, 17 of 23 robustness checks (or 73.91%) for the model that corresponds to having protested four or more times about Kavanaugh's nomination in 2018 display results that diverge from what we report in Table 8.2. Altogether, these robustness checks clearly indicate that there is no relationship between protesting four or more times about Kavanaugh's nomination and the likelihood that one contacted elected officials about this appointment in 2018.

In 2020, 20 out of the 23 models (or 86.96%) where results differed from what we report in Table 8.2 occurred when we examined participating in protests two or three times about Barrett's nomination in 2020. Functionally, this means that the majority of specifications for two or three times in 2020 indicate support for our hypothesis. Nonetheless, because our table indicates that there is no relationship between participating in protests two or three times about Barrett's nomination and contacting elected government officials about that nomination, we cannot conclude that a relationship exists.

When we verify the robustness of our gun control models by comparing the results in Table 8.3 to what we report here, 91.67% (or 143/156) of the specifications furnish results that are consistent with those that we report in the table. In 2018, 10 of the remaining 11 models (or 90.91%) are centered around having protested about gun control two or three times. In addition, 10 of the 24 robustness checks (or 41.67%) in 2018 that involve the model for having protested two or three times have results that diverge from what we report here. Thus, the results from the models for having protested two or three times about gun control should be interpreted cautiously. Using the most conservative interpretation, we should conclude that there is no statistically significant relationship between protesting two or three times about gun control in 2018 and contacting elected government officials about that issue.

We verify the robustness of our immigration models by comparing the results in Table 8.3 with what we report here. When we do so, 69.33% (or 104/150) of the specifications provide results that are consistent with what we report in the table. When we examine the remaining 32 results where the results deviate from what we report in Table 8.3 in 2018, 27 of these results (or 84.38%) involve having participated in protests at least twice involving immigration or family separation. What is more, 27 out of 46 (or 58.7%) of the robustness checks for these models furnish results that diverge from that which we report in Table 8.3. Consequently, we conclude that there is no statistically significant relationship between participating in protests about immigration or family separation in 2018 and contacting elected government officials about this issue.

We check the robustness of our models for participating in protests related to Black Lives Matter in 2020 by comparing the results in Table 8.4 to what we report in this chapter. When we do so, 55 of them (or 65.48%) provide results that mirror those that are reported in the table. Of the remaining 29 results that diverge from what is reported in Table 8.4, 21 of them (or 72.41%) involve participating in protests once related to Black Lives Matter. Because 75% (or 21/28) of the results for participating in protests once diverge from what we report in Table 8.4, we cannot conclude that a statistically significant connection exists between participating in protests related to Black Lives Matter and contacting elected government officials about this social movement.

Conclusion

We found clear links between protesting and contacting elected officials on some of the issues and causes addressed in this chapter, while others showed little to no link. Specifically, in 2018 participating in protests related to the MeToo movement and the Never Again/March for Our Lives movement against gun violence at both low and high levels results in significantly higher probabilities of contacting elected officials about these issues. Meanwhile, we found little to no evidence that participating in protests related to the Kavanaugh nomination or to the policy of family separation was associated with significant increases in contacting elected officials about these issues. In 2020, participating in protests four or more times is connected with higher levels of contacting elected government officials. In addition, participating in protests related to Barrett's nomination, gun control, and immigration and family separation to varying degrees is also associated with statistically significant increases in contacting elected government officials about those issues.

This difference is striking for several reasons. Organized interests were heavily involved in working both for and against Kavanaugh's confirmation to the Supreme Court. Yet, there is little evidence that young adults who engaged in protests related to Kavanaugh became any more likely to contact elected officials, an action these organizations would have urged. Interest groups were also actively involved in protesting the Trump administration policy of separating children from parents when families crossed the southern border without documentation and worked to encourage people to contact elected officials to ask them to put a stop to this practice. Yet, we did not find robust evidence of a link between protesting and contacting elected officials about this issue in 2018, and only limited evidence of such activity in 2020.

Conversely, for several of those issues that sparked social movements in 2018 and 2020, protesting at both high and low levels resulted in robust and significant increases in the likelihood of contacting elected officials. Young adults who joined in these groundswells for change did not just take to the streets to express their views, they also turned their attention to the halls of power. We find that when it comes to young adults and social movements, those who engage in the outsider tactic of protest become more likely to engage in the insider tactic of contacting elected officials as well across an array of issues. This holds true for the MeToo movement in 2018 and the March for Our Lives movement against gun violence in both 2018 and 2020. Yet, in 2020 Black Lives Matter was an apparent outlier to this pattern. While there was scant evidence that protesting once related to Black Lives Matter was associated with higher rates of contacting elected officials about issues related to Black Lives Matter, this finding did not hold in a majority of our robustness checks. This may make it less likely that protestors' messages are clearly heard by elected officials when it comes to Black Lives Matter. Yet, the MeToo movement and March for Our Lives both show evidence of moving from protesting to a focus on elected officials.

This movement from the outside in helps amplify the signal of young adults' messages. After all, Tilly (2004) hypothesized that policymakers respond to protesters when they exhibit worthiness, unity, numbers, and commitment.

Wouters and Walgrave's (2017) experimental study of elected officials in Belgium found that among these, the unity in protestors' message and the number of protesters were most likely to influence elected officials. We note that of the issues we examined, some of those which drew the biggest crowds in protests – the Me Too movement in 2018, the Never Again/March for Our Lives movement against gun violence, and immigration and family separation in 2020 – were also the ones with the clearest and strongest links between protesting and contacting elected officials. Assuming American-elected officials respond similarly to protest cues as elected officials in Belgium (Wouters and Walgrave 2017), then those issues on which the crowd size of protests would already help prime elected officials to be more predisposed to be responsive were also the ones more likely to provoke young adult protesters to reiterate their protest message by directly contacting elected officials, increasing the probability of responsiveness to their concerns. Yet, while protests for Black Lives Matter drew large crowds in 2020, the evidence suggests most young protestors did not follow up by contacting elected officials. These differing patterns of participation have potential consequences for the responsiveness of elected officials to protestors' concerns, a subject we address further in Chapter 9.

Notes

1. The Crowd Counting Consortium offers both low and high estimates. We are reporting the low estimates here.
2. Although protests may also send skewed cues as strong partisanship is associated with higher rates of participating in protests (Finkel and Opp 1991).
3. Partisan identification itself is skewed by age. In 2018, there were twice as many Millennial Democrats as Millennial Republicans while among the Silent Generation (those born before 1946) Republicans have a five-point advantage over Democrats (Pew Research Center 2018a).
4. These generations have concordant views on social issues (Parker, Graf, and Igielnik 2019).
5. We constrained the eligibility of participants in this survey to those with HIT approval rates of at least 95% and whose location is in the United States. While we were unable to constrain by age here, we did so through the first question asking respondents whether they were between the ages of 18 and 25. If they responded no, then the survey ended.
6. The large increase in those reporting contacting elected officials between 2018 and 2020 may reflect an increasing number of young adults finding their political voice, as more members of Generation Z reached the age of 18. The reports for both years may be inflated due to social desirability bias, yet self-reports of political activity in internet surveys suffer less from this than other forms of surveys (Holbrook and Krosnick 2010). Our surveys, like other internet surveys, may disproportionately comprise those who participate at higher rates (Holbrook and Krosnick 2010). Yet, because there is sufficient variation in activity levels present in these surveys, they still allow us to test whether protesting about political issues increases the probability of contacting elected officials about these issues.

7 These were the sole questions in the survey about peer civic experiences. Some participants responded that they did not know for one or more of these questions. When constructing our index, we coded values for these variables as missing. Thus, no peer civic engagement score exists for those who answered "don't know" on a minimum of one of these questions.
8 This also acts as an indirect measure of mobilization, as people frequently act politically when others around them do so (see e.g., Gimpel, Lee, and Kamiski 2006). Yet, it is possible that mobilization efforts by those other than peers, like interest groups and political parties, also yield higher levels of participation (Rosenstone and Hansen 2002). There are no questions in this survey that allow us to directly account for the effects of mobilization on civic activity. That said, we do consider many other covariates that also affect mobilization as part of the matching routines in this analysis.
9 We excluded the variables about the importance of congressional stances on immigration and the extent to which one supports or opposes the family separation policy implementation under the Trump administration from the models reported in Table 8.3, as they are a common connector between both the treatment (protesting about immigration and family separation) and dependent variables (contacting elected officials about immigration and family separation) in these models. The excluded variables are included in the remaining models in this chapter.
10 We excluded the variable about the importance of congressional stances on gun control from the models reported in Table 8.3, as this is a common connector between the treatment (protesting about gun control) and dependent variables (contacting elected officials about gun control) in these models. We include this omitted variable in the remaining models in this chapter.
11 We asked an initial screening question that identified those who were between the ages of 18 and 25, and those who responded that they were not were excluded from the survey. When we performed the age computations based on the month and year that respondents identified, though, there were 49 respondents who reported that they were older than 25. Based on the month-year calculation, there was typically about a six-month variance between the reported and actual age among those 49 respondents. Since we asked about both month and year of birth based on drop-down menus, it is possible that a significant portion of these respondents misreported their month and/or year of birth (see Gendall and Healey 2008). There is no reason to believe that this error is systematic. Accordingly, nonsystematic measurement error in an independent variable does not bias any conclusions in research studies (see King, Keohane, and Verba 1994).
12 The binary for MeToo movement supporters is excluded for those models in which we examine the effects of posting about the MeToo movement. In addition, the binary for Black Lives Matter supporters is excluded from those models in which we query the effects of posting about Black Lives Matter. In all other models, though, these binaries are included as part of the matching specification.
13 If participating in protests in general or any specific issue were related to contacting elected government officials, then these quantities would be highly correlated. To test whether this happens, we correlated our dependent variable (contacting government officials, either on its own or about particular issues) and participating in protests (either generally or about varying issues). In 2018, the correlations are .372 (contacting elected government officials and protesting about politics), .742 (contacting elected government officials about the MeToo movement and participating in protest related to this

movement), .691 (contacting elected government officials about Kavanaugh's nomination and participating in protests related to his nomination), .686 (contacting elected government officials about gun control and participating in protests about this issue), and .697 (contacting elected government officials about immigration and family separation and participating in protests about this issue). In 2020, the correlations are .698 (contacting elected government officials and protesting about politics), .751 (contacting elected government officials about the MeToo movement and participating in protests related to this movement), .760 (contacting elected government officials about Barrett's nomination and participating in protests related to her nomination), .786 (contacting elected government officials about gun control and participating in protests about this issue), .770 (contacting elected government officials about immigration and family separation and participating in protests this issue), and .760 (contacting elected government officials about Black Lives Matter and participating in protest related to this movement). These correlations are low enough such that we can conclude that the first part of the SUTVA assumption is satisfied.
14 If we do not conduct our analysis in this manner, then we cannot satisfy SUTVA, as there would be alternative treatment forms (see Imbens and Rubin 2015, 10–13).
15 If we do not conduct our analysis in this manner, then we are unable to satisfy SUTVA, as there would be alternative forms of the treatment (see Imbens and Rubin 2015, 10–13).
16 However, we do not perform a regression following the matching analysis (as Ho et al. 2007 recommend), as Abadie and Spiess (2019) state that this is inappropriate when matching is done with replacement as researchers obtain inaccurate standard error estimates.
17 We thank Melissa Michelson for bringing this point to our attention.
18 A limitation of many matching analyses is that one can p-hack by varying the functional form of the matching algorithm to produce a set of results that coincidentally confirms a researcher's hypotheses (Head et al. 2015).
19 The online appendix for these and the other models in this chapter is available at www.kenmoffett.net/research.

References

Abadie, Alberto and Guido W. Imbens 2006. "Large Sample Properties of Matching Estimators for Average Treatment Effects." *Econometrica* 74(1): 235–267. https://doi.org/10.1111/j.1468-0262.2006.00655.x. Accessed online June 19, 2021.

Abadie, Alberto and Guido W. Imbens 2011. "Bias-Corrected Matching Estimators for Average Treatment Effects." *Journal of Business and Economic Statistics* 29(1): 1–11. https://doi.org/10.1198/jbes.2009.07333. Accessed online June 19, 2021.

Abadie, Alberto and Guido W. Imbens 2016. "Matching on the Estimated Propensity Score." *Econometrica* 84(2): 781–807. https://doi.org/10.3982/ECTA11293. Accessed online June 19, 2021.

Abadie, Alberto and Jann Spiess 2019. "Robust Post-Matching Inference." Forthcoming in the *Journal of the American Statistical Association.* https://doi.org/10.1080/01621459.2020.1840383. Accessed online June 19, 2021.

Abramowitz, Alan I. and Walter J. Stone 2006. "The Bush Effect: Polarization, Turnout, and Activism in the 2004 Presidential Election." *Presidential Studies Quarterly* 36(2): 141–154. https://doi.org/10.1111/j.1741-5705.2006.00295.x. Accessed online June 19, 2021.

Achen, Christopher H. and Larry M. Bartels 2016. *Democracy for Realists: Why Elections Do Not Produce Responsive Government*. Princeton, NJ: Princeton University Press.

Amenta, Edwin, Neal Caren, Elizabeth Chiarello, and Yang Su 2010. "The Political Consequences of Social Movements." *Annual Review of Sociology* 36(2010): 287–307. https://doi.org/10.1146/annurev-soc-070308-120029. Accessed online June 19, 2021.

Andrew, Scottie. 2020. "This City Disbanded Its Police Department 7 Years Ago. Here's What Happened Next." CNN. www.cnn.com/2020/06/09/us/disband-police-camden-new-jersey-trnd/index.html. Accessed online June 26, 2020.

Baumgartner, Frank R., Jeffrey M. Berry, Marie Hojnacki, David C. Kimball, and Beth L. Leech 2009. *Lobbying and Policy Change: Who Wins, Who Loses, and Why*. Chicago, IL: University of Chicago Press.

Bergan, Daniel E. and Richard T. Cole. 2015. "Call Your Legislator: A Field Experimental Study of the Impact of Citizen Contacts on Legislative Voting." *Political Behavior* 37(1): 27–42. https://doi.org/10.1007/s11109-014-9277-1. Accessed online June 19, 2021.

Beyers, Jan, Rainer Eising, and William Maloney 2008. "Researching Interest Group Politics in Europe and Elsewhere: Much We Study, Little We Know?" *West European Politics* 31(6): 1103–1128. https://doi.org/10.1080/01402380802370443. Accessed online June 19, 2021.

Branton, Regina, Valerie Martinez-Ebers, Tony E. Carey, Jr., and Tetsuya Matsubayashi 2015. "Social Protest and Policy Attitudes: The Case of the 2006 Immigrant Rallies." *American Journal of Political Science* 59(2): 390–402. https://doi.org/10.1111/ajps.12159. Accessed online June 19, 2021.

Broockman, David E. and Christopher Skovron 2018. "Bias in Perceptions of Public Opinion among Political Elites." *American Political Science Review* 112(2): 542–563. https://doi.org/10.1017/S0003055418000011. Accessed online June 19, 2021.

Caren, Neal, Raj Andrew Ghoshal, and Vanesa Ribas 2011. "A Social Movement Generation: Cohort and Period Trends in Protest Attendance and Petition Signing." *American Sociological Review* 76(1): 125–151. https://doi.org/10.1177/0003122410395369. Accessed online June 19, 2021.

Carey Jr., Tony E., Regina P. Branton, and Valerie Martinez-Ebers 2014. "The Influence of Social Protests on Issue Salience among Latinos." *Political Research Quarterly* 67(3): 615–627. https://doi.org/10.1177/1065912914534074. Accessed online June 19, 2021.

Carmines, Edward G. and James Stimson 1989. *Issue Evolution: Race and the Transformation of American Politics*. Princeton, NJ: Princeton University Press.

Chong, Dennis and Reuel Rogers 2005. "Racial Solidarity and Political Participation." *Political Behavior* 27(4): 347–374. https://doi.org/10.1007/s11109-005-5880-5. Accessed online June 19, 2021.

Cluverius, John and Kevin K. Banda 2018. "How Trust Attitudes Promote Grassroots Lobbying in the American States." *Social Science Quarterly* 99(3): 1006–1020. https://doi.org/10.1111/ssqu.12486. Accessed online June 19, 2021.

Converse, Phillip 1964. "The Nature of Belief Systems in Mass Publics." In *Ideology and Its Discontents*, David E. Apter (Ed.). New York, NY: Free Press of Glencoe.

Craig, Stephen C. 1980. "The Mobilization of Political Discontent." *Political Behavior* 2(2): 189–209. https://doi.org/10.1007/BF00989890. Accessed online June 19, 2021.

D'Agostino, Ralph B. 1998. "Propensity Score Methods for Bias Reduction in the Comparison of a Treatment to a Non-Randomized Control Group." *Statistics in Medicine* 17(9): 2265–2281. https://doi.org/10.1002/(SICI)1097-0258(19981015)17:19<2265::AID-SIM918>3.0.CO;2-B. Accessed online June 19, 2021.

Da Silva, Chantal 2018. "Has Occupy Wall Street Changed America?" *Newsweek* www.newsweek.com/has-occupy-wall-street-changed-america-seven-years-birth-political-movement-1126364. Accessed online December 17, 2019.

Dalton, Russell J. 2006. *Citizen Politics: Public Opinion and Political Parties in Advanced Industrial Democracies*. 4th Ed. Washington, DC: CQ Press.

Dalton, Russell J. 2008. "Citizenship Norms and the Expansion of Political Participation." *Political Studies* 56(1): 76–98. https://doi.org/10.1111/j.1467-9248.2007.00718.x. Accessed online June 19, 2021.

Dalton, Russell J. 2015. *The Good Citizen: How a Younger Generation Is Reshaping American Politics*. 2nd Ed. Thousand Oaks, CA: CA Press.

Dalton, Russell, Alix Van Sickle, and Steven Weldon 2010. "The Individual-Institutional Nexus of Protest Behaviour." *British Journal of Political Science* 40(1): 51–73. https://doi.org/10.1017/S000712340999038X. Accessed online June 19, 2021.

Di Cicco, Damon T. 2010. "The Public Nuisance Paradigm: Changes in Mass Media Coverage of Political Protest since the 1960s." *Journalism and Mass Communication Quarterly* 87(1): 135–153. https://doi.org/10.1177/107769901008700108. Accessed online June 19, 2021.

Diamond, Alexis and Jasjeet J. Sekhon 2013. "Genetic Matching for Estimating Causal Effects: A General Multivariate Matching Method for Achieving Balance in Observational Studies." *Review of Economics and Statistics* 95(3): 932–945. https://doi.org/10.1162/REST_a_00318. Accessed online June 19, 2021.

Eggers, Andrew C. and Jens Hainmueller 2009. "MPs for Sale? Returns to Office in Postwar British Politics." *American Political Science Review* 103(4): 513–533. https://doi.org/10.1017/S0003055409990190. Accessed online June 19, 2021.

Eisinger, Peter 1973. "The Conditions of Protest Behavior in American Cities." *American Political Science Review* 67(1): 11–28. https://doi.org/10.2307/1958525. Accessed online June 19, 2021.

Fenno, Richard. 1977. "U.S. House Members in Their Constituencies: An Exploration." *American Political Science Review* 71(3): 883–917. https://doi.org/10.1017/S0003055400265143. Accessed online June 19, 2021.

Finkel, Steven E. and Karl-Dieter Opp 1991. "Party Identification and Participation in Collective Political Action." *Journal of Politics* 53(2): 339–371. https://doi.org/10.2307/2131763. Accessed online June 19, 2021.

Flavin, Patrick and John D. Griffin 2009. "Policy, Preferences, and Participation: Government's Impact on Democratic Citizenship." *Journal of Politics* 71(2): 544–559. https://doi.org/10.1017/S0022381609090458. Accessed online June 19, 2021.

Fletcher, Steve. 2020. "I'm a Minneapolis City Council Member. We Must Disband the Police – Here's What could Come Next." *Time*. https://time.com/5848705/disband-and-replace-minneapolis-police/. Accessed online June 26, 2020.

Freedom House 2019. "Democracy in Retreat: Freedom in the World 2019." https://freedomhouse.org/sites/default/files/Feb2019_FH_FITW_2019_Report_ForWeb-compressed.pdf. Accessed online December 17, 2019.

Gamson, William A. and David S. Meyer 1996. "Framing Political Opportunity." Pp. 275–290 in *Comparative Perspectives on Social Movements*, edited by Doug McAdam, John D. McCarthy, and Mayer Zald. New York, NY: Cambridge University Press.

Gelman, Andrew and Jennifer Hill 2007. *Data Analysis Using Regression and Multilevel/Heiarchical Models*. New York: Cambridge University Press.

Gendall, Philip and Benjamin Healey 2008. "Asking the Age Question in Mail and Online Surveys." *International Journal of Market Research* 50(3): 309–317.

Gillion, Daniel Q. 2013. "Protest and Congressional Behavior: Assessing Racial and Ethnic Minority Protests in the District." *Journal of Politics* 74(4): 950–962. https://doi.org/10.1017/S0022381612000539. Accessed online June 19, 2021.

Gillion, Daniel Q. 2020. *The Loud Minority: Why Protests Matter in American Democracy*. Princeton, NJ: Princeton University Press.

Gimpel, James G., Frances E. Lee, and Joshua Kaminski 2006. "The Political Geography of Campaign Contributions in American Politics." *Journal of Politics* 68(3): 626–639. https://doi.org/10.1111/j.1468-2508.2006.00450.x. Accessed online June 19, 2021.

Giugni, Marco G. 1998. "Was It Worth the Effort? The Outcomes and Consequences of Social Movements." *Annual Review of Sociology* 24(1998): 371–379. https://doi.org/10.1146/annurev.soc.24.1.371. Accessed online June 19, 2021.

Giugni, Marco G. 2004. *Social Protest and Policy Change*. Oxford, UK: Rowman and Littlefield.

Graham-Harrison, Emma 2018. "Beyond Syria: The Arab Spring's Aftermath." *The Guardian*. www.theguardian.com/world/2018/dec/30/arab-spring-aftermath-syria-tunisia-egypt-yemen-libya. Accessed online December 17, 2019.

Greene, William H. 2011. *Econometric Analysis*. 7th Ed. New York City, NY: Pearson Education.

Grossmann, Matt 2012. "Interest Group Influence on US Policy Change: An Assessment Based on Policy History." *Interest Groups and Advocacy* 1(1): 171–192. https://doi.org/10.1057/iga.2012.9. Accessed online June 19, 2021.

Gurr, Ted-Robert 1970. *Why Men Rebel*. Princeton, NJ: Princeton University Press.

Head, Megan L., Luke Holman, Rob Lanfear, Andrew T. Kahn, and Michael D. Jennions 2015. "The Extent and Consequences of P-Hacking in Science." *Plos Biology* 13(3): e1002106. https://doi.org/10.1371/journal.pbio.1002106. Accessed online June 19, 2021.

Ho, Daniel E., Kosuke Imai, Gary King, and Elizabeth A. Stuart 2007. "Matching as Nonparametric Preprocessing for Reducing Model Dependence in Parametric Causal Inference." *Political Analysis* 15(3): 199–236. https://doi.org/10.1093/pan/mpl013. Accessed online June 19, 2021.

Holbrook, Allyson L. and Jon A. Krosnick 2010. "Social Desirability Bias in Voter Turnout Reports: Tests Using the Item Count Technique." *Public Opinion Quarterly* 74(1): 37–67. https://doi.org/10.1093/poq/nfp065. Accessed online June 19, 2021.

Holyoke, Thomas T. 2012. "The Interest Group Effect on Citizen Contact with Congress." *Party Politics* 19(6): 925–944. https://doi.org/10.1177/1354068811436036. Accessed online June 19, 2021.

Imbens, Guido W. and Donald B. Rubin 2015. *Causal Inference for Statistics, Social, and Biomedical Sciences: An Introduction*. New York, NY: Cambridge University Press.

Jones, Maggie 2018. "The March for Our Lives Activists Showed Us How to Find Meaning in Tragedy." *Smithsonian Magazine*. December. www.smithsonianmag.com/innovation/march-for-our-lives-student-activists-showed-meaning-tragedy-180970717/. Accessed online November 20, 2019.

Kahne, Joseph and Benjamin Bowyer 2018. "The Political Significance of Social Media Activity and Social Networks." *Political Communication* 35(3): 470–493. https://doi.org/10.1080/10584609.2018.1426662. Accessed online June 19, 2021.

Kelly, Cara and Aaron Hegarty 2018. "#MeToo Was a Culture Shock: But Changing Laws Will Take More than a Year." *USA Today*. October 4. www.usatoday.com/story/news/investigations/2018/10/04/metoo-me-too-sexual-assault-survivors-rights-bill/1074976002/. Accessed online June 27, 2019.

Kerbel, Matthew R. and Joel David Bloom 2005. "Blog for America and Civic Involvement." *The International Journal of Press/Politics* 10(4): 3–27. https://doi.org/10.1177/1081180X05281395. Accessed online June 19, 2021.

Kerbo, Harold R. 1982. "Movements of 'Crisis' and Movements of 'Affluence': A Critique of Deprivation and Resource Mobilization Theories." *Journal of Conflict Resolution* 26(4): 645–663. https://doi.org/10.1177/0022002782026004004. Accessed online June 19, 2021.

Kertscher, Tom 2020. "Republicans Using 'Defund the Police' Efforts to Attack Democrats in Key Congressional Races." *Politifact*. October 28. www.politifact.com/article/2020/oct/28/republicans-using-defund-police-efforts-attack-dem/. Accessed online February 4, 2021.

King, Brayden G., Keith G. Bentele, and Sarah A. Soule 2007. "Protest and Policymaking: Explaining Fluctuation in Congressional Attention to Rights Issues, 1960–1986." *Social Forces* 86(1): 137–163. https://doi.org/10.1353/sof.2007.0101. Accessed online June 19, 2021.

King, Gary, Christopher Lucas, and Richard A. Nielsen 2017. "The Balance-Sample Size Frontier in Matching Methods for Causal Inference." *American Journal of Political Science* 61(2): 473–489. https://doi.org/10.1111/ajps.12272. Accessed online June 19, 2021.

King, Gary, Robert O. Keohane, and Sidney Verba 1994. *Designing Social Inquiry: Scientific Inference in Qualitative Research*. Princeton, NJ: Princeton University Press.

Kollman, Ken 1998. *Outside Lobbying: Public Opinion and Interest Group Strategies*. Princeton, NJ: Princeton University Press.

Ley, Barbara L. and Paul R. Brewer 2018. "Social Media, Networked Protest, and the March for Science." *Social Media and Society* 4(3): 1–12. https://doi.org/10.1177/2056305118793407. Accessed online June 19, 2021.

Loader, Brian D., Ariadne Vromen, and Michael A. Xenos 2014. "The Networked Young Citizen: Social Media, Political Participation and Civic Engagement." *Information, Communication and Society* 17(2): 143–150. https://doi.org/10.1080/1369118X.2013.871571. Accessed online June 19, 2021.

Lohmann, Susanne 1994. "The Dynamics of Informational Cascades: The Monday Demonstrations in Leipzig, East Germany, 1989–1991." *World Politics* 47(1): 42–101.

Lyon, Thomas P. and John W. Maxwell 2004. "Astroturf: Interest Group Lobbying and Corporate Strategy." *Journal of Economics and Management Strategy* 13(4): 561–597. https://doi.org/10.1111/j.1430-9134.2004.00023.x. Accessed online June 19, 2021.

Mazumder, Soumyajit 2018. "The Persistent Effect of U.S. Civil Rights Protest on Political Attitudes." *American Journal of Political Science* 62(4): 922–935. https://doi.org/10.1111/ajps.12384. Accessed online June 19, 2021.

McAdam, Doug 1986. "Recruitment to High-Risk Activism: The Case of Freedom Summer." *American Journal of Sociology* 92(1): 64–90. https://doi.org/10.1086/228463. Accessed online June 19, 2021.

McCarthy, John D. and Mayer N. Zald 1977. "Resource Mobilization and Social Movements: A Partial Theory." *American Journal of Sociology* 82(6): 1212–1241. https://doi.org/10.1086/226464. Accessed online June 19, 2021.

McVeigh, Rory and Christian Smith 1999. "Who Protests in America: An Analysis of Three Political Alternatives – Inaction, Institutionalized Politics, or Protest." *Sociological Forum* 14(4): 685–702. https://doi.org/10.1023/A:1021656121301. Accessed online June 19, 2021.

Memoli, Mike 2020. "In Leaked Recording, Biden Says GOP Used 'Defund the Police' to 'Beat the Living Hell' Out of Democrats." NBC News. www.nbcnews.com/politics/2020-election/leaked-recording-biden-says-gop-used-defund-police-beat-living-n1250757. Accessed online February 4, 2021.

Meyer, David S. 1993. "Protest Cycles and Political Process: American Peace Movements in the Nuclear Age." *Political Research Quarterly* 46(3): 451–479. https://doi.org/10.1177/106591299304600302. Accessed online June 19, 2021.

Meyer, David S. 2004. "Protest and Political Opportunities." *Annual Review of Sociology* 30(2004): 125–145. https://doi.org/10.1146/annurev.soc.30.012703.110545. Accessed online June 19, 2021.

Meyer, David S. and Debra C. Minkoff 2004. "Conceptualizing Political Opportunity." *Social Forces* 82(4): 1457–1492. https://doi.org/10.1353/sof.2004.0082. Accessed online June 19, 2021.

Meyer, David S. and Sidney Tarrow (Eds.) 1998. *The Social Movement Society: Contentious Politics for a New Century*. Lanham, MD: Rowman & Littlefield.

Milkman, Ruth 2017. "A New Political Generation: Millennials and the Post-2018 Wave of Protest." *American Sociological Review* 82(1): 1–31. https://doi.org/10.1177/0003122416681031. Accessed online June 19, 2021.

Miller, Eliana 2020. "Political Ads Bombard Airwaves in Battle over Supreme Court." Center for Responsive Politics. www.opensecrets.org/news/2020/10/supreme-court-vacancy-acb/. Accessed online February 1, 2021.

Moffett, Kenneth W. and Laurie A. Rice 2018. "College Students and Online Political Expression in the 2016 Election." *Social Science Computer Review* 36(4): 422–439. https://doi.org/10.1177/0894439317721186. Accessed online June 19, 2021.

Murdie, Amanda and Dursun Peksen 2015. "Women and Contentious Politics: A Global Event-Data Approach to Understanding Women's Protest." *Political Research Quarterly* 68(1): 180–192. https://doi.org/10.1177/1065912914563547. Accessed online June 19, 2021.

Nichols, Austin 2007. "Causal Inference with Observational Data." *The Stata Journal* 7(4): 507–541. https://doi.org/10.1177/1536867X0800700403. Accessed online June 19, 2021.

Olzak, Susan and Sarah A. Soule 2009. "Cross-cutting Influences of Environmental Protest and Legislation." *Social Forces* 88(1): 201–225. https://doi.org/10.1353/sof.0.0236. Accessed online June 19, 2021.

Opp, Karl-Dieter 2000. "Adverse Living Conditions, Grievances, and Political Protest after Communism: The Example of East Germany." *Social Forces* 79(1): 29–65. https://doi.org/10.1093/sf/79.1.29. Accessed online June 19, 2021.

Parker, Kim, Nikki Graf, and Ruth Igielnik 2019. "Generation Z Looks a Lot Like Millennials on Key Social and Political Issues." Pew Research Center. www.pewsocialtrends.org/2019/01/17/generation-z-looks-a-lot-like-millennials-on-key-social-and-political-issues/. Accessed online February 12, 2019.

Pew Research Center 2018a. "Wide Gender Gap, Growing Educational Divide in Voters' Party Identification." www.people-press.org/2018/03/20/1-trends-in-party-affiliation-among-demographic-groups. Accessed online August 9, 2019.

Piazza, James A. 2011. "Poverty, Minority Economic Discrimination, and Domestic Terrorism." *Journal of Peace Research* 48(3): 339–353. https://doi.org/10.1177/0022343310397404. Accessed online June 19, 2021.

Picchi, Aimee 2019. "Income Inequality in America Is at Its Highest Level in More than 50 Years." CBS News www.cbsnews.com/news/income-inequality-in-america-is-at-its-highest-level-in-more-than-50-years-census-report-today-shows/. Accessed online December 17, 2019.

Platt, Matthew B. 2008. "Participation for What? A Policy-Motivated Approach to Political Activism." *Political Behavior* 30(3): 391–413. https://doi.org/10.1007/s11109-008-9054-0. Accessed online June 19, 2021.

Putnam, Robert D. 2000. *Bowling Alone: The Collapse and Revival of American Community*. New York, NY: Simon and Schuster.

Reny, Tyler T., Loren Collingwood and Ali A. Valenzuela 2019. "Vote Switching in the 2016 Election: How Racial and Immigration Attitudes, Not Economics, Explain Shifts in White Voting." *Public Opinion Quarterly* 83(1): 91–113. https://doi.org/10.1093/poq/nfz011. Accessed online June 19, 2021.

Rosenstone, Steven J. and John Mark Hansen 2002. *Mobilization, Participation, and Democracy in America*. New York, NY: Pearson-Longman.

Rouse, Stella M. and Ashley D. Ross 2018. *The Politics of Millennials: Political Beliefs and Policy Preferences of America's Most Diverse Generation*. Ann Arbor, MI: University of Michigan Press.

Schlozman, Kay Lehman and John T. Tierney 1983. "More of the Same: Washington Pressure Activity in a Decade of Change." *Journal of Politics* 45(2): 351–377.

Schussman, Alan and Sarah A. Soule 2005. "Process and Protest: Accounting for Individual Protest Participation." *Social Forces* 84(2): 1083–1108. https://doi.org/10.1353/sof.2006.0034. Accessed online June 19, 2021.

Sears, David O. and Jack Citrin 1982. *Tax Revolt: Something for Nothing in California*. Cambridge, MA: Harvard University Press.

Sekhon, Jasjeet S. 2011. "Multivariate and Propensity Score Matching Software with Automated Balance Optimization: The Matching Package for R." *Journal of Statistical Software* 42(7): 1–52.

Smidt, Corwin D. 2012. "Not All News Is the Same: Protests, Presidents, and the Mass Public Agenda." *Public Opinion Quarterly* 76(1): 72–84. https://doi.org/10.1093/poq/nfr019. Accessed online June 19, 2021.

Smith, Jackie, John D. McCarthy, Clark McPhail, and Boguslaw Augustyn 2001. "From Protest to Agenda Building: Description Bias in Media Coverage of Protest Events in Washington, D.C." *Social Forces* 79(4): 1397–1423. https://doi.org/10.1353/sof.2001.0053. Accessed online June 19, 2021.

Soule, Sarah A. and Brayden G. King 2006. "The Stages of the Policy Process and the Equal Rights Amendment, 1972–1982." *American Journal of Sociology* 111(6): 1871–909. https://doi.org/10.1086/499908. Accessed online June 19, 2021.

Soule, Sarah A. and Jennifer Earl 2005. "A Movement Society Evaluated: Collective Protest in the United States, 1960–1986." *Mobilization: An International Quarterly* 10(3): 345–364. https://doi.org/10.17813/maiq.10.3.7303503537531022. Accessed online June 19, 2021.

Staggenborg, Suzanne 1991. *The Pro-Choice Movement*. New York, NY: Oxford University Press.

Stolberg, Sheryl Gay, Nicholas Fandos, and Catie Edmonson 2018. "Interest Groups Turn Up Pressure before Kavanaugh Vote." *The New York Times*. www.nytimes.com/2018/09/11/us/politics/brett-kavanaugh-confirmation-vote.html. Accessed online November 20, 2019.

Stuart, Elizabeth A. 2010. "Matching Methods for Causal Inference: A Review and a Look Forward." *Statistical Science* 25(1): 1–21. https://doi.org/10.1214/09-STS313. Accessed online June 19, 2021.

Tarrow, Sidney G. 1994. *Power in Movement: Social Movements, Collective Action and Politics.* New York, NY: Cambridge University Press.

Tarrow, Sidney G. 2011. *Power in Movement: Social Movements and Contentious Politics.* 3rd Ed. New York, NY: Cambridge University Press.

Tilly, Charles 1978. *From Mobilization to Revolution.* New York, NY: McGraw-Hill.

Tilly, Charles 2004. *Social Movements, 1768–2004.* London, UK: Paradigm.

Verba, Sidney and Norman Nie 1972. *Participation in America: Political Democracy and Social Equality.* New York, NY: Harper and Row.

Verba, Sidney, Henry E. Brady, and Kay L. Schlozman 1995. *Voice and Equality: Civic Voluntarism in American Democracy.* Cambridge, MA: Harvard University Press.

Villa, Lissandra. 2020. "Why Protestors Want to Defund Police Departments." *Time.* https://time.com/5849495/black-lives-matter-defund-police-departments/. Accessed online June 26, 2020.

Walker, Jack L. 1991. *Mobilizing Interest Groups in America.* Ann Arbor, MI: University of Michigan Press.

Wouters, Ruud and Stefaan Walgrave. 2017. "Demonstrating Power: How Protest Persuades Political Representatives." *American Sociological Review* 82(2): 361–383. https://doi.org/10.1177/0003122417690325. Accessed online June 19, 2021.

9
CONCLUSION
Assessing Young Adult Political Power

Introduction

The period of young adult activism we describe coincides with Donald Trump's time as U.S. president. Thus, another potential explanation for young adults' increased activism deserves exploration before we conclude: views about then-President Trump's performance in office. While we considered the potential impact of views of then-President Trump in our models, we have yet to examine it as a potential treatment. However, it could be a common thread linking many of the issues we examined together. After all, at least 17 women have accused Trump of sexual harassment or assault (Keneally 2019). In addition, he nominated Brett Kavanaugh and Amy Coney Barrett to the Supreme Court, took a strong stance against illegal immigration, and implemented the family separation policy. He also called painting the phrase Black Lives Matter on New York City's Fifth Avenue "a symbol of hate" (Liptak and Holmes 2020) and referred to activists in the movement as "anarchists, not protesters" and "thugs" on Twitter (Villareal 2020). Thus, those who acted to support the MeToo and Black Lives Matter movements, who actively opposed Kavanaugh's and Barrett's confirmations, and who opposed the family separation policy might also share disapproval of then-President Trump. Meanwhile, young adult Trump supporters may have stood with him on at least some of these issues, acting in support of his position. Might views of then-President Trump, then, be responsible for young adults raising their political voice?

Compared to these issues, the potential link between views about then-President Trump and taking action related to the issue of gun violence is less clear as Trump and his administration made varying statements on this issue. Some of these statements strongly back the NRA and its opposition to gun control (Abramson 2018), while others expressed some support for the #NeverAgain movement and its goals (Jackson 2018). If gun violence had been the outlier issue in 2018 where posting was not related to higher civic engagement instead of family separation, this would have suggested that views of then-President Trump could be fueling increased engagement.

Still, there is reason to consider how views of then-President Trump may influence civic engagement, as he was a highly polarizing president. In his second year in office, his average partisan gap in presidential approval was 79, the highest on record (Jones 2018). Likewise, by 2020, Trump had set a new record for highest average gap in partisan approval, at 81 percentage points, 11 points higher than the previous high set by then-President Obama (Jones 2021). Abramowitz and Stone (2006) show that ideologically polarizing and divisive presidential candidates can help engage and mobilize the electorate by boosting voter turnout and activism (Abramowitz and Stone 2006). While Trump was not on the ballot in 2018, midterm elections are influenced by the prior presidential election (Campbell 1985, 1991). Although the effect of presidential approval tends not to be as strong in a president's first midterm as it is in subsequent midterm elections (Abramowitz, Cover, and Norputh 1986), midterm elections are often seen as referendums on the president and the economy (Kernell 1977; Tufte 1978). Thus, there is some reason to expect a divisive and polarizing president, like Trump, to not only stimulate participation in a presidential election year, but also help propel participation during midterm elections.

Yet, views of the president do not just differ by partisan affiliation, but also by age. As Figure 9.1 shows, while presidential approval among Democrats is

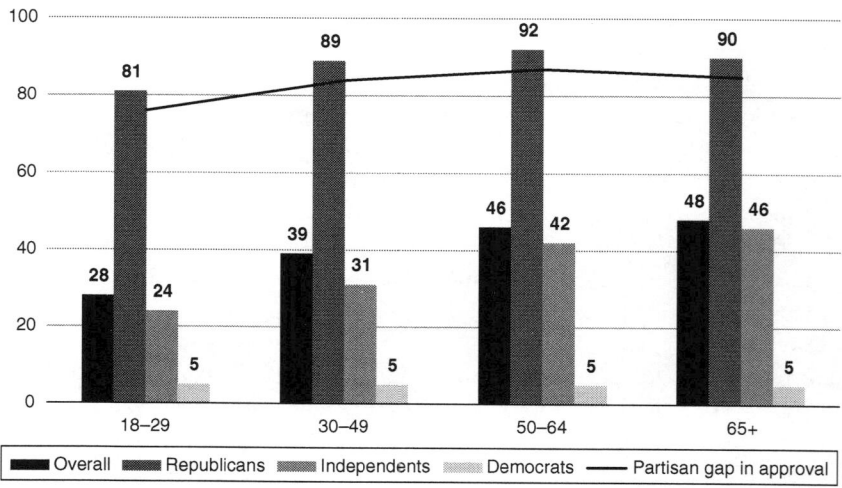

FIGURE 9.1 Job Approval of Then-President Trump by Age and Partisan Affiliation.
Source: Gallup March 2019 https://news.gallup.com/poll/248135/subgroup-differences-trump-approval-mostly-party-based.aspx.

steady across age groups[1] at 5%, both young independents and young Republicans approve of the president at substantially lower rates than their elders. This means that while young adults are still polarized in their evaluations of Trump, they are less so than older age groups. Figure 9.1 shows that the partisan gap in approval for younger adults is 76, compared to 84, 87, and 85 among the older age ranges. This suggests that if polarizing candidates help drive participation, this effect would be less pronounced among young adults than older age groups. Yet, if opposition to a president sparks participation, this effect would be most prevalent among young adults. Using the same data and basic model structures as in previous chapters, we test whether views about Trump are associated with heightened civic engagement. Specifically, we consider whether opposition to Trump among young adults might be responsible for heightened participation.

Data

To examine whether presidential approval drives civic activity and contacting elected government officials, we performed online surveys on November 7, 2018, and November 4, 2020 of Americans between 18 and 25 years old – an age range that includes both older members of Generation Z and younger Millennials.[2] We used Amazon's Mechanical Turk (mTurk) platform to execute this survey, a website that allows members of the public to earn money for completing a variety of tasks, including participating in survey research. In both years, each participant was paid $1.50 for completing the survey; 1,010 participants completed the survey in 2018 and 969 participants completed the survey in 2020 after removing any incomplete responses.[3]

Dependent and Treatment Variables

Our dependent variables measure the extent to which each respondent contacted government and each participant's level of civic activity. The first dependent variable is the extent to which each individual participated in civic and political activities away from the internet. Through separate questions, each respondent was asked about the frequency with which they have engaged in a variety of activities that included talking to people and explaining why they should vote for or against a specific candidate or party, attending political functions in support of a candidate or party and making purchasing decisions based on a company's conduct or values. To create a single measure of political and civic engagement, we added the values for each of the 12 activities to produce an index that was based on answers to this set of questions ($\alpha = .92$, 2018; $\alpha = .95$, 2020). The means of this index, 14.56 (2018) and 26.01 (2020), are relatively low compared to the maximum value of the index. The standard deviations, 10.75 (2018) and 14.61 (2020), indicate substantial variance around this mean. Thus, we have captured both low and high participators in our surveys.

The second dependent variable measures how often each respondent contacted or visited someone in government who represents their community. Each person was asked about the frequency with which they have engaged in this activity on a five-point scale but to facilitate a straightforward interpretation using matching, we collapsed this variable into a dichotomous variable that is coded one when a respondent contacted government officials with any frequency and zero if not. To test our theoretical expectations, we use a series of matching routines.[4] To investigate the link between presidential approval and our dependent variables, we asked each respondent whether they approved or disapproved of then-President Trump's job performance, coded one for those who approve and zero for those who indicated disapproval.

Matching Covariates

We used two variables to investigate the effects of political engagement away from the internet. First, we asked each respondent about the extent to which they are interested in politics on a four-point scale that ranged from "Very interested" (four points) to "Not at all interested" (zero points). Second, each respondent was asked three questions about the extent to which their friends engaged in a set of activities. We built an additive index based on the responses (α = .63, 2018; α = .58, 2020).[5,6]

In addition, we used many variables to investigate the effects of political engagement using the internet. First, we asked each respondent how often they read blogs online about politics. Kerbel and Bloom (2005) and Moffett and Rice (2018) found that blogs can foster enhanced civic activity. Second, each respondent was asked how frequently they read news on the internet about politics.

Third, we created an additive index of online civic activity consisting of five items, as several researchers have unearthed a link between activities on social media and offline civic engagement (see e.g., Kahne and Bowyer 2018; Ley and Brewer 2018; Loader, Vromen, and Xenos 2014). Through separate questions, we asked about the extent to which each respondent had relied on social media for news, posted about politics on social media, read social media feeds about politics, liked or shared posts about politics on social media, or read or watched posts about politics on social media and summed the responses (α = .84, 2018; α = .83, 2020).

Moreover, we employed several variables to consider the effects of personal characteristics on offline civic activity. First, we measured whether each respondent strongly identifies with either the Republican or Democratic parties, as this attachment is associated with an array of other political activities (see e.g., Flavin and Griffin 2009; Verba, Brady, and Schlozman 1995).

Second, we examined the effects of ideology on civic engagement, as Achen and Bartels (2016) find that self-identifying as either conservative or liberal shapes political participation. As the structure of the questions forced all respondents to choose between liberal or conservative, we created a binary variable for liberals.

Third, we asked each respondent for their sex, and we coded this variable one for females, two for males, and three for those who self-identified in another category. Fourth, we acquired data on each respondent's age by asking each to report their month and year of birth. Then, we computed each respondent's age based on the month and year of the 2018 midterm election for the 2018 data, and the month and year of the 2020 general election for the 2020 data.[7] Fifth, we asked each respondent for their race and collapsed that information into a binary that is coded one for whites, and zero otherwise. Sixth, we asked each respondent for their level of education.[8]

Methods

To investigate whether our treatment is associated with changes in civic activity and contacting elected government officials, we use a matching analysis to compute the ATET. We choose a matching estimator for several reasons. First, nearly all regression-based techniques (including OLS) assume that a linear relationship exists between the dependent and independent variables (see Greene 2011). Our theory makes no prediction about the relationship between the treatment variable and both dependent variables. Thus, the phenomenon that we examine is likely to be nonlinear and is poorly suited to investigate using a method that assumes linearity (like OLS). Fortunately, matching analyses do not assume linearity, allow for a more flexible functional form, and have other statistical properties that make them a better choice to test our hypothesis (Imbens and Rubin 2015).

In addition, individuals had differing probabilities of approving of then-President Trump's job performance. OLS estimators presume treatment homogeneity, which is unlikely to hold. Individuals likely have different treatment effects, particularly depending on their approval of then-President Trump's job performance (see Abadie and Imbens 2011). Thus, the effects of approving of then-President Trump's job performance may vary depending on the level of approval of his job performance that each respondent has. By construction, OLS-based estimators assume that we observe a linear, homogeneous relationship between our treatment variable and the dependent variables. Matching-based approaches deal effectively with this issue because they assume neither linearity nor homogeneity (Imbens and Rubin 2015). Rather, matching-based approaches produce several treatment estimates depending on the level of treatment that a respondent received (Imbens and Rubin 2015). Thus, we generate several, more accurate estimates of the effect that presidential approval has on our dependent variables (offline civic engagement and contacting elected government officials).

Moreover, OLS does not permit us to estimate what happens to either of our dependent variables in the absence of presidential approval (Nichols 2007). Matching analyses use the existing data to generate a dataset that includes observations that are as similar as possible, given the values of the remaining predictors (Stuart 2010). Thus, we can estimate what would have happened in the absence of presidential approval (see Gelman and Hill 2007). Then, we can use this dataset to estimate the effects of a specific level of presidential approval on the dependent variables. Finally, if we used OLS estimates to obtain the results, our results would likely be biased because any estimate of the treatment effect is conditioned on the values of the remaining independent variables. Consequently, OLS-based approaches do not compute ATETs.

Matching analyses manage each of these issues because they let us examine whether differing levels of presidential approval are associated with higher levels of civic engagement or contacting elected government officials. By matching based on each of the predictor variables, we can disentangle the effect of presidential approval beyond individuals' other predispositions to participate or contact elected government officials. Thus, doing so enables us to compare people with similar inclinations to civic activity or contacting elected government officials who only vary in their approval of then-President Trump's job performance. Moreover, matching allows us to calculate ATETs for each treatment level, and by doing so, to calculate more precise effect sizes with observational data.

Assumptions

Before performing our matching analyses, we must fulfill four assumptions.[9] First, we presume that each treatment variable is binary. The treatment variable in this chapter is already binary. Second, we assume common support (or overlap), which means that it is possible that treated units may face an intervention that could have assigned them to the control group (see Imbens and Rubin 2015; King, Lucas, and Nielsen 2017). The data that we use meets this requirement because all respondents could have chosen not to approve of then-President Trump's job performance.

Third, we must fulfill the SUTVA assumption, which means that "the potential outcomes for any unit do not vary with the treatments assigned to other units, and for each unit, there are no different forms or versions of each treatment level, which lead to different potential outcomes" (Imbens and Rubin 2015, 10). We meet this assumption because the possible outcomes for our dependent variables do not vary with the levels of presidential approval.[10]

Finally, the treatment assignment must be conditionally independent of the outcome variable given a set of matching covariates (D'Agostino 1998, 2266). Thus, each respondent's assignment to treatment (i.e., presidential approval) is unconnected with their level of civic engagement or contacting elected government officials, given the values of the remaining explanatory variables. We observe greatly varied participatory levels with respect to civic activity, and the mean level of civic activity is fairly low (M = 14.56, 2018; M = 26.01, 2020), given the minimum (0) and maximum values (48) possible with this index. We observed low levels of contacting government officials in 2018, but higher levels in 2020. In all cases, though, contacting government officials generally occurs with greater frequency than contacting government officials about any issue or social movement that we highlight in this volume. Moreover, the activities that comprise offline civic activity or contacting elected government officials do not cause an individual to be assigned to one or more treatment categories.

Matching Technique

To perform matching, we use one-to-one genetic matching with replacement (Diamond and Sekhon 2013; Sekhon 2011). We incorporate a propensity score into the analysis, as knowing estimated values of this score meaningfully improves the accuracy of this method (Diamond and Sekhon 2013). Propensity score matching allows us to compare observations that are otherwise similar across other predictors, but experienced different treatments. We perform our analysis with replacement, as matching discrepancies are reduced because we can use untreated units as a match multiple times (see Abadie and Imbens 2006).[11] To remove any bias that results due to the choice of the matching estimator without affecting the variance of that estimator, we employ a bias correction (Abadie and Imbens 2016).

Results

Before discussing our results, we must examine how similar the treatment and control groups are to one another (King, Lucas, and Nielsen 2017). If these groups are substantially dissimilar, then we cannot use matching to estimate ATETs. The imbalance statistics for the models in Table 9.1 are contained in Tables A1 through A4 in the online appendix. For 97.72% (or 43/44) of the variables contained in the models in Table 9.1, the KS tests are not significant at the .05 level after matching has occurred. When we examine a secondary test, the t-test, 86.36% (or 38/44) of the variables contained in the models in Table 9.1 contain results that are not statistically significant. Thus, we can be confident that we have reduced imbalance and have achieved balance across the model specifications. The matched groups have similar observable characteristics such that we can attribute any remaining differences across views of then-President Trump's job in office to views of his job performance, not to preexisting differences (Eggers and Hainmueller 2009).

Table 9.1 displays the results from the matching routines in both years for both dependent variables. The results indicate that presidential approval is not connected with higher levels of civic activity. Moreover, the models indicate that there was no association between presidential approval and contacting elected government officials in 2018, but there appears to be one in 2020. However, this result is not robust.

To examine whether the way in which we specified our models affects the results that we have obtained (Ho et al. 2007), we tested our models for robustness by removing one matching covariate at a time from each model. Then, we re-ran the matching routines with the remaining predictors. These results are

TABLE 9.1 Civic Engagement, Contacting Elected Government Officials, and Presidential Approval

	Civic Engagement		Contacting Elected Government Officials	
	2018	2020	2018	2020
Effect Size	1.852	1.484	.053	.102
Abadie-Imbens Standard Error	1.293	1.207	.079	.049
95% Confidence Interval Lower Bound	-.697	-1.338	-.103	.006
95% Confidence Interval Upper Bound	4.401	4.386	.209	.198
T-Statistic	1.433	1.230	.676	2.102
P-Value (two-tailed)	.152	.219	.499	.036
P-Value (one-tailed)	.076	.110	.250	.018
N	213	242	228	257

Notes: In each two-column set, approving of then-President Trump's job performance is compared to one who does not. Second, the covariates on which the matching is based are described in the text. Third, the effects on contacting elected officials are the ATET. Finally, the matching results are from 1:1 genetic matching with post-matching bias adjustment. Thus, the N represents the matched number of observations.

contained in the online appendix. The results indicate that 52.27% (or 23/44) of the results from the robustness checks mirror those that we report in Table 9.1. Of the remaining 21 models whose results deviate from what we report here, 15 of them are concentrated in 2020 (or 68.18% of the 22 2020 models), and 7 of 11 (or 63.64%) models are for contacting elected government officials in 2020. Thus, we cannot conclude that the 2020 results are robust, and by extension, cannot conclude that any statistically significant connection exists between presidential approval and either treatment variable in 2020. When paired with the 2018 results, we find no evidence that opposition to then-President Trump is what was driving the results evident in prior chapters.

What We Have Learned

Having an opinion about a salient issue alone, even one that inspires activism in society and disproportionately interests young adults, is rarely enough to expand civic engagement among young adults. Of the issues we examined, there was only one issue for which opinions alone was associated with heightened activity – the family separation policy. The lack of significant relationships between most issues and civic engagement is consistent with Olson's (1973) free rider problem – a shared interest alone is insufficient to get most people to act to advance those interests. However, when young adults act on their opinions on some of these issues by posting their views online or engaging in protests, their civic engagement levels show significant increases compared to otherwise similar young adults who decline to act. In Part I, we found that both posting and protesting can serve as pathways to other forms of engagement, but they do not always do so.

Specifically, in Chapter 2, we found that posting once about the MeToo movement in 2018 and posting four times about MeToo in 2020 (when offline civic engagement was costlier, due to the prevalence of Covid-19) is connected with higher levels of civic activity. We also found that protesting two or more times about MeToo in 2020 was associated with higher civic engagement rates. In Chapter 3, we found that posting at any level about Kavanaugh's nomination was associated with heightened levels of civic engagement. Posting four or more times about Barrett's nomination was also associated with higher levels of civic engagement. Also, protesting more than once about Kavanaugh's (but not Barrett's) nomination is associated with even larger significant increases in civic engagement.

In Chapter 4, we found that posting at high levels about gun violence in 2018 (but not in 2020) was associated with heightened civic engagement. Conversely, protesting about gun control did not increase civic engagement levels among young adults in 2018, when protesting about this issue was commonplace, but did so in 2020 among those who protested four plus times. Then, in Chapter 5, we found no evidence linking posting or protesting about immigration and family separation to higher rates of civic engagement in 2018. However, posting four or more times in 2020 about immigration and family separation is associated with heightened civic engagement. Yet, we found no evidence linking protesting about immigration and family separation and civic engagement in 2020. In Chapter 6, we found evidence that protesting four or more times in relation to Black Lives Matter was associated with higher civic engagement levels.

In sum, posting with varying frequencies about four of the five issues we examined was associated with increased civic engagement and protesting about four of these five issues was linked with greater civic engagement levels, too. This provides evidence that both posting about issues and protesting about them serve as pathways to heightened civic and political activity among young adults. We find evidence of these links both in movements led by young adults, like March for Our Lives, and in movements led by other generations, like MeToo. We find evidence of these effects on issues where interest groups actively recruited participants, like the Supreme Court nominations and the family separation policy, and in movements that developed more organically, spreading virally through social media, like MeToo and Black Lives Matter.

In 2018, posting once about MeToo appeared enough to foster increased civic engagement while high levels of posting about gun violence were necessary for significant gains in other forms of civic activity. Meanwhile, posting at any level about Kavanaugh's nomination was associated with higher levels of civic engagement among young adults. In 2020, when offline civic engagement was made costlier by the prevalence of the Covid-19 pandemic, it took posting four or more times to see a significant increase in civic engagement. We saw these effects hold for the MeToo movement, which had faded in popularity, Barrett's nomination, and the family separation policy, which returned to public focus just before the 2020 presidential election. Meanwhile, any link between posting about Black Lives Matter or gun violence in 2020 and civic engagement was not robust. While posting about an issue does not always expand civic engagement among young adults, enough evidence of a link exists across different issues and years to establish that posting should not be dismissed as slacktivism. The links we find between posting about a variety of issues and civic engagement support a growing literature linking online political expression and civic engagement (Shah et al. 2005; Yamamoto, Kushin, and Dalisay 2013; Boulianne 2015). Among young adults, posting their views online serves as an important pathway to other forms of activity.

In fact, posting appears to offer a more consistent pathway to heightened civic engagement than protesting. In 2018, only protesting multiple times about the Kavanaugh nomination was associated with higher levels of civic engagement. Yet, in 2020, when both protesting and other offline forms of civic and political activity were made costly and difficult by the threat of Covid-19, protesting at high rates related to the three social movements we examine – MeToo, gun control, and Black Lives Matter – all yielded significantly higher rates of civic engagement among young adults. These findings suggest that McAdam and Tarrow's (2010, 528) concern that organizing activism on online platforms might trigger increasingly combative electoral politics but come "… at the cost of sustained social movements" has not hindered these movements.

These increases in civic engagement are a positive externality, but not the main intent of most social movements. Instead, movement organizers hope to provoke specific political and social changes. Many of these changes require action by elected officials to make legal changes. This makes contacting elected officials a potentially important part of the recipe for success. In Part II, we focused on the link between posting and protesting about the issues examined in Part I and contacting elected officials about those issues. In Chapter 7, we investigated the link between posting and contacting and found that posting about both Barrett's and Kavanaugh's nominations was connected with higher probabilities of contacting elected government officials about those appointments. Moreover, posting about gun control and immigration and family separation multiple times was connected with higher levels of contacting elected government officials, albeit with varying frequencies in 2018 relative to 2020. Finally, posting about the MeToo movement was more strongly connected with contacting elected government officials in 2018, when the movement was at its height. This suggests that while not all these issues and the movements surrounding them helped broaden civic engagement, they helped channel young adult political participation to advance their causes. After all, posting about each of them was associated with increasing the probability of contacting elected officials about them.

Then, in Chapter 8, we investigated the links between protesting about these issues and contacting elected officials about them. In addition, we found several links between participating in protests related to political issues or social movements and contacting elected government officials. More specifically, participating in protests related to Barrett's nomination in 2020, MeToo in 2018, gun control (both 2018 and 2020), and immigration and family separation (both 2020 and to some extent in 2018) to varying degrees is connected with statistically significant increases in contacting elected government officials about those issues. This provides evidence that instead of limiting their activism to outsider tactics like protests, young adults are also turning their eyes inward to the halls of power.

The matching analyses we employed provide a causal inference method using observational data. They can only do so provided certain assumptions are met, which is why we devoted portions of each chapter to discussing how our data structure and treatments satisfy these assumptions. Then, to avoid the potential danger of p-hacking which involves varying the functional form of the matching algorithm to produce a set of results that coincidentally confirms a researcher's hypotheses (Head et al. 2015), we conducted robustness checks for every model, removing one variable at a time. The results we have highlighted in this section survive these robustness checks, retaining their significant effects across a substantial majority of alternate potential specifications.

Some may still question our findings because they rely on self-reports of political activity. Such self-reports can be notoriously biased, especially when it comes to voter turnout because most respondents know it is a socially desirable behavior (Traugott and Katosh 1979; Silver, Anderson, and Abramson 1986). This might pose a problem, when reporting the percentage of respondents who report engaging in a specific form of engagement and assuming it is also true of the population of interest. Yet, internet surveys seem less susceptible to social desirability bias (Holbrook and Krosnick 2010). However, there is a potential danger of internet surveys attracting those who vote at higher rates (Holbrook and Krosnick 2010) and exhibit higher levels of civic engagement (Kennedy et al. 2016). While our surveys might also fall prey to this issue, they contain substantial variation in participation rates. This variation allows us to successfully test our hypotheses (see e.g., Boulianne 2020).

Others may question our findings because they rely on survey data taken at single time points. While matching analyses are a method of causal inference, provided key assumptions are met, they do not eliminate the possibility of reverse causality. In Part I, we examined whether reverse causality occurs with respect to whether civic engagement leads to posting or protesting, and we found that in most cases, it did not. Might contacting elected government officials, though, lead to posting or protesting? We investigated this possibility with respect to each of the issues that we examined in Chapters 7 and 8. We found that for Black Lives Matter and immigration, it did not. For gun control, only contacting elected government officials in 2018 led to higher levels of protesting, but otherwise we saw no reverse causality.

When we examine the MeToo movement and Supreme Court justices, though, questions of reverse causality become more complex. For both issues, contacting elected government officials was not connected with higher levels of posting about these issues in 2020, but was in 2018. Moreover, contacting elected government officials was connected with higher levels of participating in protests about these issues in both 2018 and 2020. Thus, for at least some of the issues we examine, the causal arrow likely points both ways. This is unsurprising, as the path from insider to outsider tactics by organized interests when elected officials do not act is well established (Beyers, Eising, and Maloney 2008). The potential presence of reverse causality does not negate any of the theories or findings that we advance; it only suggests that there are multiple pathways to activism, and we leave some of the complexities of this to other scholars to more fully uncover.

Others might build on our research by testing our findings via experimental research. For example, Bennion (2013, 416) recommends that researchers use randomized field experiments to isolate the effects of a treatment on voting or civic engagement. To date, such experimental research has focused primarily on the impact of various interventions on voting. This research is particularly useful in identifying actions that might increase voter registration and voter turnout. For example, face-to-face voter registration efforts can help increase voter registration (Nickerson 2015). Experiments also show that personal canvassing increases voter turnout, especially for those unaffiliated with a political party (Gerber and Green 1999). Reminding people of their own history of voting (or not voting) also enhances voter turnout (Panagopoulos, Larimer, and Condon 2014). These studies suggest interventions that might help young adults vote at higher rates, another key piece in potentially influencing policy.

Policy Consequences

The successful bridges among young adults that we uncovered between posting and protesting about issues and contacting elected officials about them heighten the likelihood that young adults can successfully help advance change. Yet, as a brief review of the policy consequences that have emerged in the wake of this activity reveals, change is difficult but possible, not guaranteed, and when it occurs, it tends to happen incrementally, leaving more work to happen.

The MeToo Movement

Though much work remains to curtail the prevalence of sexual harassment and assault in society, the MeToo movement made significant gains. It sparked meaningful conversations about acceptable behavior in many sectors from entertainment to government. Also, in the year after Alyssa Milano's tweet first went viral in 2017, MeToo was responsible for over 200 prominent men losing their jobs after being publicly accused of sexual harassment or assault, with women making up almost half of their replacements (Carlsen et al. 2018). During the 115th Congress (2017–2018), eight members of Congress resigned or declined to seek reelection after sexual misconduct allegations became public and another decided not to seek reelection after reports emerged that she failed to act on serious allegations against her chief of staff (Cranley 2018). In addition, 33 state legislators resigned or were removed from office due to allegations of sexual misconduct and another 33 faced disciplinary actions short of removal for alleged misconduct (Associated Press 2019c).

In the midst of the MeToo Movement, the 2018 election (and appointments to fill open seats) propelled a record number of women into Congress with women making up 23.2% of the House of Representatives and 26% of the Senate (Center for American Women and Politics 2020). There was also a significant increase in the number of women serving in state legislatures, with women filling 25.8% of the seats in state Senates and 30% of the seats in state assemblies (Center for American Women and Politics 2019).

The number of laws passed by state legislatures addressing issues raised by the MeToo Movement increased (Kelly and Hegarty 2018). For example, Washington, DC, California, and Arizona enacted limits on the use of nondisclosure agreements in civil proceedings against alleged harassers or perpetrators of sexual assault while Vermont and Delaware passed laws with multiple provisions that would make it harder for employers to cover up incidents of harassment (Kelly and Hegarty 2018). By July 2019, the number of states with limitations or prohibitions on the use of nondisclosure agreements by employers grew to 13 (Johnson, Menefee, and Sekaran 2019). Meanwhile, five states expanded workplace harassment protections to previously unprotected groups (Johnson, Menefee, and Sekaran 2019).

Yet, other changes illustrate just how far society has to go in its efforts to prevent harassment and assault. In the year after Milano's tweet, five states made it illegal for members of law enforcement to have sex with those in their custody, bringing the number of states with this protection only up to 20 (Kelly and Hegarty 2018). In 2018, Tennessee voided nondisclosures concealing child sexual abuse, and 21 states passed laws mandating reporting for sexual harassment, assault, and child sexual assault (Kelly and Hegarty 2018).

Despite these advances, bills related to the MeToo movement struggled to pass in Congress. A search of legislation (excluding resolutions) for the words sexual harassment in either the bill title or bill summary on the Library of Congress' website, congress.gov, turned up 48 bills in the 115th Congress (2017–2018). About 65% of these bills were introduced by female legislators. Of the 48 bills introduced, less than ten made it out of committee and only three became law. First, H.R. 1, a budget reconciliation bill introduced by Representative Kevin Brady (R-TX) and signed into law on December 22, 2017, included a provision prohibiting taking a tax deduction for trade or business expenses for settlements and payments relating to sexual harassment or assault that are subject to nondisclosure agreements.

Second, the Sam Farr and Nick Castle Peace Corps Reform Act of 2018 required that Peace Corps applicants be informed about crimes against volunteers and the frequency of reports of sexual harassment from volunteers in the country in which they are to serve and be given an option to apply to serve in a different country, as well as requiring each Peace Corps post to have a designated staff to assist victims of sexual assault. Finally, the Congressional Accountability Act of 1995 Reform Act removed a provision requiring congressional employees participate in counseling and mediation before filing sexual harassment claims and required Members of Congress to reimburse the Treasury for any award or settlement due to their misconduct. The same search for the 116th Congress turned up 41 bills, 29 of which were introduced by women. Of these, only seven were considered in committee, while two became law. The Empowering Olympic, Paralympic, and Amateur Athletes Act of 2020 enacted safeguards to protect amateur athletes from sexual harassment or abuse by coaching staff and was signed into law on October 30, 2020. The National Oceanic and Atmospheric Administration Commissioned Officer Corps Amendments Act of 2020 included requirements for sexual harassment and sexual assault prevention among National Oceanic and Atmospheric Administration (NOAA) commissioned officers.

A similar search for bills that contain the words sexual assault in their title or summary turned up 85 bills (excluding resolutions) introduced during the 115th Congress. Some of the most far reaching of these were among the roughly 44% of those introduced by women. Yet, only two of those introduced by women made it out of committee and only one passed, an appropriations bill. Of the 85 bills introduced in the 115th Congress, 15 made it out of committee and 9 became law, including the Peace Corps act mentioned previously. The SAFER Act of 2017 required the Department of Justice (DOJ) to provide information about both adult and pediatric forensic nurses and extended a grant program for processing backlogged rape kits. The POWER Act required the chief judge in each judicial district to promote pro bono legal services for sexual assault survivors. The SOAR to Health and Wellness Act of 2018 expanded training for health care workers and social service providers regarding sexual assault and human trafficking. The Frederick Douglass Trafficking Victims Prevention and Protection Reauthorization Act of 2018 reauthorized various government programs to combat human trafficking and created a mechanism for U.S. military personnel to report child sexual abuse by members of Afghan security forces. The other four bills that passed were continuing appropriations that included continued support for the Sexual Assault Special Victims Counsel Program.

Seventy-three bills (excluding resolutions) introduced in the 116th Congress contain the words sexual assault in their title or summary. About 64% of these were introduced by women. Only 7 of these 73 bills received any consideration in committee, and of these only 2 became law. One of these was the Debbie Smith Reauthorization Act of 2019, which reauthorized a program that provides grants to help states and localities process DNA evidence from rape kits. The other was the National Oceanic and Atmospheric Administration Commissioned Officer Corps Amendments Act of 2020 that was mentioned previously.

Bills commonly languish in committee like this. It is also notoriously difficult to pass legislation during divided government when gridlock often prevails (Baumgartner et al. 2014). Passing more significant reforms will become more likely if members of Congress continue to hear from their constituents that these issues matter. This is one issue where the sustained involvement of young adults could help make a difference.

Kavanaugh and Barrett's Nominations

Despite protests and the allegations of sexual assault that emerged during Brett Kavanaugh's confirmation hearings, the Senate confirmed him on a 50–48 vote (Tatum 2018). While those seeking to stop his nomination faced defeat, this was the narrowest successful roll call confirmation vote margin since that for President James Garfield's nomination of Stanley Matthews on May 12, 1881 (United States Senate 2018). The party balance in the Senate in 2018 was 51 Republicans and 49 Democrats (or Independents who caucused with the Democrats). This fact suggested a close vote. Interest groups seeking to sway the outcome turned their attention to potentially vulnerable senators. Conservative groups lobbied and engaged in pressure campaigns aimed at Democrats in states Trump carried to break ranks with their party and vote for Kavanaugh. Conversely, liberal groups lobbied and pressured Republicans in states where Trump was less popular to cross their party and vote against his confirmation (McCammon 2018). Yet, as allegations from Dr. Christine Blasey Ford and others emerged, Republicans Susan Collins (ME) and Lisa Murkowski (AK) came under intense pressure to break with their party and vote to defeat Kavanaugh's nomination (Schor 2018). In the end, Senator Joe Manchin (D-WV) joined 49 Republicans, including Collins, in voting to confirm. The remaining 48 Democrats voted nay, Senator Murkowski (R-AK) voted present, and Senator Daines (R-MT) was absent from the vote to walk his daughter down the aisle (Senate Roll Call Vote 223; Molina and Hayes 2018). Kavanaugh's confirmation is likely to give him long-lasting influence on the Court, moving rulings in a more conservative direction.

Yet, while Kavanaugh was confirmed, the work of Caldeira and Wright (1998) suggests it is possible that changes in levels of mobilization could have swayed the outcome of the vote. Young adults were more likely to have a very unfavorable opinion of Kavanaugh, to see him as not qualified to serve on the Supreme Court, and to support an FBI investigation into the sexual assault allegations than older age groups (The Economist/YouGov 2018). While roughly 25% of the young adults we surveyed reported contacting elected officials about Kavanaugh's nomination, perhaps if even more young adults had gotten involved, the outcome may have differed. Specifically, had interest groups effectively encouraged young adults who protested Kavanaugh's nomination to contact their elected officials about the nomination, some senators may have been pressured to vote differently.

Likewise, Kavanaugh's confirmation vote may have carried consequences for some senators. Four Senate Democrats representing red states lost in 2018 after voting against Kavanaugh's nomination (Hayes and Cummings 2018). In Missouri, incumbent Democrat Claire McCaskill was upset by Republican Josh Hawley; 45.6% of voters chose McCaskill while 51.4% chose Hawley. Yet exit polls indicated that McCaskill led among voters under 45 years old (CNN 2018). Had they voted at rates more closely matching their percentage of the population, she might have retained her seat. In Indiana, exit polls showed the Democratic incumbent did not win more than 50% of the votes of any age group and in North Dakota the race was less close with the Democratic incumbent having a significant advantage only among the youngest age group. In these states, it is far less likely changes in turnout levels by age would have made a difference. Yet in Florida, where the difference between incumbent Democrat Bill Nelson and challenger Rick Scott was so narrow the election result triggered a recount, exit polls showed 62% of voters in the ages 18–24, 71% of voters in the ages 25–29, and 61% of voters in the ages 30–39 voted for Nelson. Had there been higher voter turnout among these ages, Nelson would likely have retained his seat.

Those who opposed Kavanaugh's confirmation may take comfort in at least one silver lining, though. Kavanaugh's confirmation despite allegations of sexual assault may have also helped propel more women into elected office, just as Clarence Thomas' confirmation despite allegations of sexual harassment did 26 years prior (Delli Carpini and Fuchs 1993). The 117th Congress, beginning in January of 2021, set a new record for the number of women serving in the House of Representatives (Blazina and Desilver 2021).

Barrett's confirmation, adding to the conservative Supreme Court majority, may also have helped inspire this surge in women in Congress, albeit for different reasons. For example, while opposition to her policy positions may have contributed to a surge in Democratic women in the House, her successful confirmation may have helped propel a record number of Republican women into the House (Blazina and Desilver 2021). Barrett was confirmed 52–48 with only Senator Susan Collins (R-ME), who faced a tough reelection battle, crossing party lines (Kapur, Tsirkin, and Shabad 2020). Some noted a surge in donations to Democratic candidates after Ginsburg's death and a bounce in the polls for Democratic challengers (Wu 2020). Yet, although opposing Barrett may have helped Collins save her Senate seat, it is unclear how heavily the Barrett confirmation vote figured into the small handful of Senate seats where party control flipped in 2020. Including the Georgia runoffs, Democrats gained four seats previously held by Republicans, and Republicans successfully flipped one seat previously held by Democrats, resulting in a Senate split 50–50. Unlike the 2018 Senate races, higher turnout by young adults would have been unlikely to change these outcomes. And, while changes in mobilization levels can potentially sway the outcome of confirmation votes (Caldeira and Wright 1998), Kavanaugh and Barrett's nominations also show how difficult it is to do so during unified government due to the positivity bias surrounding Supreme Court nominations (Gibson and Caldiera 2009; Krutz, Fleisher, and Bond 1998).

Gun Violence, #NeverAgain and the March for Our Lives Movement

The #NeverAgain movement against gun violence saw some significant gains in its first year. In the first year after it held the March for Our Lives on March 24, 2018, 26 state governors signed 67 gun safety bills into law (Peters 2019). The Giffords Law Center noted that eight states improved in their Annual Gun Law Scorecard and it was the first year since 2012 that no state was downgraded a full letter grade (Peters 2019). The most substantial changes were in Florida, where the movement originated. There, Republican Governor Rick Scott signed a bill that increased the legal age for firearms purchases to 21, banned bump stocks, enacted a three-day waiting period between the time that a firearm is purchased to when it is acquired, created a "red flag" initiative that allows for courts to seize firearms from those who are suspected of being a danger to themselves or others, and allowed school districts to arm nonteachers to protect children (National Public Radio 2018), resulting in the Giffords Law Center moving Florida's grade on its Annual Gun Law Scorecard from an F to a C- (Peters 2019). In addition to actions by state legislatures, major corporations such as Delta Air Lines, Hertz, and MetLife cut their ties with the NRA and Dick's Sporting Goods stopped selling assault weapons (Alter 2018). Nationally, at Trump's direction, the Department of Justice and the Bureau of Alcohol, Tobacco, Firearms and Explosives banned bump stocks (Crocker and Penzenstadler 2019).

Congress considered reforms as well. A search of legislation in Congress (excluding resolutions) performed on the Library of Congress website congress.gov for bills that contained the words gun violence in their titles or summaries turned up 33 bills introduced in the 115th Congress and 28 bills introduced in the 116th Congress. Of the 61 bills across two sessions of Congress, only one, a continuing appropriations act, passed but not before these words were removed from the legislation. The other bills, some of which contain significant reforms, have not moved out of committee.

The NRA spent over $5 million in lobbying in 2018 and $3.2 million in lobbying in 2019 and its associated political action committee (PAC) made $878,521 in campaign contributions and spent over $9 million in outside spending in the 2018 election cycle (Center for Responsive Politics 2021). Meanwhile, the March for Our Lives Action Fund spent $30,000 in lobbying in 2018 and $250,000 in 2019. While it is not the only group lobbying on behalf of gun control, the Center for Responsive Politics (2021) identifies a total of just over $2 million spent on lobbying on gun control in 2018 and $2.3 million in 2019. One side of this policy debate is clearly better funded and is investing more money in its efforts than the other.

Schattschneider (1960) warned that the side with more resources usually prevails unless the side with less funding can successfully expand the audience and draw them into the fight. This is precisely what the less well funded young adult-led movement against gun violence has sought to do. Similarly, Arnold (1990) identified that while policies with particularized benefits often prevail, there are circumstances under which the public can prevail despite opposition by interest groups because members of Congress estimate the potential electoral consequences before voting. This suggests that for Congress to pass meaningful reforms to address gun violence, they must see an enhanced electoral risk for not doing so. If young adults who support this movement continue to contact elected officials and begin voting at significantly higher rates, members of Congress' estimation of electoral risk if they continue not to act would increase substantially, heightening their likelihood of enacting reforms.

Immigration and Family Separations

As president, Trump advanced several policies that sought to stop unauthorized immigration. One of these was the construction of a wall along the country's southern border. Of the young adults we surveyed, the number of people who strongly opposed the border wall in 2018 was more than twice the amount that strongly supported it. The most common response among the American public was also strong opposition (Norman 2019), albeit not nearly at the levels seen among young adults. Congress appeared to have this strong opposition in mind when it came to the wall. When Congress would not provide the funds that then-President Trump wanted for the border wall he had campaigned on building, he declared an emergency and took funds Congress had appropriated to other agencies to use for wall construction (Cowan and Cornwall 2019). In late 2019, Congress allocated $1.37 billion for border security to get then-President Trump to sign appropriations bills to avoid a government shutdown (Cowan and Cornwall 2019). However, this number was less than what Trump had requested, so he diverted $3.8 billion in funds in 2020 from the funds Congress appropriated for the Department of Defense to help build the border wall (Booker 2020). Congress passed resolutions twice to end Trump's declaration of a national emergency at the southern border (and thus stop him from diverting funds to pay for the wall) but he vetoed both (Beech 2019). Yet, Congress lacked the two-thirds of each chamber needed to override these vetoes as overriding it would also be electorally risky, especially for Republicans.

Then-President Trump's controversial family separation policy was instead blocked by a court ruling in June of 2018. Yet, the district court ruling also set limited circumstances under which family separations could continue and at least 389 additional children were separated from families between the court ruling and May of 2019 (Jervis and Gomez 2019). A search of legislation (excluding resolutions) for the words "family separation" performed on the Library of Congress website congress.gov resulted in five bills introduced in the 115th

Congress and two in the 116th Congress. These sought to either block family separations entirely or to increase protections for migrant children. Yet, none of these bills made it past committee or subcommittee referral.

In this case, the family separation policy was limited by court ruling rather than elected officials. After the court ruling limited the use of family separations and the Trump administration began, again under court direction, to reunite children and parents, public pressure to act subsided. Yet, news of the continued failure to successfully reunite some children with their families two years after the policy ended returned this policy to public focus. This return to public focus might make congressional action more likely since significant majorities opposed this policy. However, additional congressional action may not be needed as President Biden officially rescinded the policy that led to family separations and established a task force to focus on reuniting separated families (Rose 2021; Rodriguez 2021).

Black Lives Matter

The Black Lives Matter movement sparked conversations about racism in American society and drew pledges of support from both corporate America and city officials (Adams 2020; Somvichian-Clausen 2020). Derek Chauvin was charged with second degree murder of George Floyd, the three other officers present were charged with aiding and abetting second degree murder, and a police officer involved in the shooting death of Breonna Taylor was fired (Ankel 2020). Several city councils including Mobile, Alabama, and Jacksonville, Florida, voted to remove a statue of a Confederate officer, while other Confederate statues were torn down by protestors (Ankel 2020; Somvichian-Clausen 2020). City officials in Minneapolis, Dallas, and Washington, DC, banned chokeholds while more than a dozen police departments in California as well as in Reno, Nevada, pledged to do the same (Ankel 2020; Somvichian-Clausen 2020). The New York legislature repealed a measure that had made it difficult to hold officers accountable for misconduct and the New York City mayor pledged to shift some police funding to funds for youth and social services (Ankel 2020).

Yet, reform efforts at the national level have been stymied by partisan gridlock. Democrats introduced the Justice in Policing Act of 2020. Without limitation, the bill includes several measures meant to increase police accountability and eliminate discriminatory practices including changes to the standards needed to convict police officers of misconduct and prohibiting racial profiling. It passed 236–81 in the House but stalled in the Senate. Meanwhile, Republicans introduced the JUSTICE Act in the Senate. Among other measures, this bill included data reporting requirements, grants for the purchase of body cameras, and incentives for limiting the use of chokeholds. The JUSTICE Act has been stalled in the Senate by an inability to secure the 60 votes needed to break any potential filibuster.

A search of legislation on congress.gov reveals that other narrower reform efforts such as closing the law enforcement consent loophole, antilynching legislation, banning chokeholds, and ending racial profiling have also stalled. For example, 14 bills were introduced in the 116th Congress that included a provision related to chokeholds. Two of these passed the House but have not received consideration in the Senate. Despite the demands for reform, few reforms related to Black Lives Matter were successful in the 116th Congress aside from a bill establishing the Commission on the Social Status of Black Men and Boys and directing it to conduct:

> ...a systematic study of the conditions affecting Black men and boys, including homicide rates, arrest and incarceration rates, poverty, violence, fatherhood, mentorship, drug abuse, death rates, disparate income and wealth levels, school performance in all grade levels including postsecondary education and college, and health issues.
>
> *(Public Law, 116–156)*

A common story emerges across the MeToo Movement, the #NeverAgain and March for Our Lives Movement against gun violence, the battle against Trump administration policies to curb illegal immigration, and the Black Lives Matter movement: activism has resulted in some policy changes, but more work remains to be done, especially in Congress. This fits with Mayhew's (1974) supposition that members of Congress would be more likely to engage in position taking than action because position taking allows them to show responsiveness while avoiding any negative electoral repercussions from acting. It also fits with a general struggle in Congress to pass laws. Only a small percentage of bills introduced in Congress make it through the legislative process successfully. With over 10,000 bills introduced each session, there were just 417 bills (not including resolutions) signed into law in the 115th Congress and 333 (not including resolutions) in the 116th Congress.

Policy Change Favorability Moving Beyond 2020

Yet, the 2020 election brought a unified government to power, with Democrat Joe Biden in the White House, a Democratic majority in the House, and a Senate split 50–50, with Democratic Vice President Kamala Harris providing the tiebreaking vote. While narrow majorities will still make passing legislation difficult, those in power after the 2020 election hold more favorable views toward the issue priorities shared by a majority of young Americans. In such an environment, contacting elected officials may be particularly important.

For the young adults we surveyed, in 2018 between 21.6% and 28.6% reported contacting elected officials about the issues we examined. While we acknowledge that this number may be inflated, as self-reports of activities tend to be, it is significantly higher than the percentages reported by 18–29-year-olds in 2012 and rivals that reported by those ages 50 and over (Smith 2013). We found that posting about a variety of political issues, particularly a common political activity among young adults, leads to enhanced probabilities of contacting elected officials about those issues. We also found evidence that young adults who attend protests about various issues and causes are more likely to contact elected officials about these issues and causes. More specifically, participating in protests related to Amy Coney Barrett's nomination in 2020, gun control (both 2018 and 2020), and immigration and family separation (both 2020 and 2018) to differing degrees is also connected with statistically significant increases in contacting elected government officials about those issues. These findings linking posting and protesting to contacting elected officials bode well for the effectiveness of young adults' political voice.

Climate Change and Generational Activity

A brief look at the movement to fight climate change also yields insights about what the future of this generation's political voice and power may entail. Climate change was important to young adults in 2018 and 2020 but, due to sharp differences in opinion by age and partisan affiliation on this issue, it only came in twelfth on the list of most important issues to voters in the midterm elections, with a slim majority saying this issue would be extremely or very important to their vote (Newport 2018). In 2020, climate change moved up one place to eleventh with 42% of voters identifying it as very important to their vote (Pew 2020a). The lower priority voters gave to this issue was one of the reasons we did not include it in our study. The second is that much of the climate-related activism has been concentrated among members of Generation Z that are still years away from reaching 18. Research of adolescents shows they have meaningful opinions about Trump (Metzger et al. 2020) and some have suggested lowering the voting age to 16 to increase young adult engagement (Maheo and Belanger 2020). However, with the voting age currently at 18, a study of voters on this issue would miss the action of teenagers and even preteens who led the movement.

In August 2018, Greta Thunberg, then aged 15, protested outside the Swedish parliament on Fridays, often with a sign that read "School Strike for Climate," vowing to continue until Sweden met the carbon emission goals agreed to in the Paris Climate Agreement (BBC News 2020). The hashtag #FridaysForFuture soon went viral and by December 2018 more than 20,000 students, from elementary schools to high schools, had joined her in their own school strikes (BBC News 2020). Among these was 13-year-old New Yorker Alexandria Villasenor, who began protesting on Fridays on a bench in front of the United Nations (Borunda 2019). Within months, she collaborated with Haven Coleman, aged 12, from Denver and Isri Hirsi, aged 16 and from Minneapolis, to organize American young people to engage in the U.S. Youth Climate Strike on March 15, 2019 (Borunda 2019). Events were held in Washington, DC, and nearly all of the 50 states with students from high schools down to elementary schools skipping school to attend protests or staging walkouts (Kaur and Park 2019). A few months later, on September 20, 2019, when another global youth climate strike was scheduled, there were more than 800 events scheduled in the United States and American young people joined millions around the world in protest (Neuman and Chappel 2019). Clearly, this issue matters intensely to Generation Z, who will feel the effects of climate change longer than older generations.

Age gaps in opinions about this issue have already become evident among the generations that precede Generation Z, but only when looking at age groups by partisan affiliation. Democrats, across generations, have very similar views on climate change but Republicans differ dramatically by age (Funk and Hefferon 2019). Figure 9.2 displays the percentages by partisan age group that think the federal government is doing too little to reduce the effects of climate change and think that the priority for the U.S. energy supply should be developing alternative energy. As it shows, nearly all Democrats and a slim majority of young Republicans think that the federal government is doing too little to reduce the effects of climate change, and on the issue of energy, young Republicans' opinions are more similar to Democrats than they are to either Generation X or the oldest generations. There are also generational differences in the willingness to act, with 37% of Millennials indicating a willingness to contact government officials about global warming, compared to 32% of Generation X, 30% of Baby Boomers, and 28% of the Silent Generation (Ballew et al. 2019). However, just 13% of Millennials reported having actually contacted government officials about climate change, a rate statistically indistinguishable from that of Generation X and Boomers (Ballew et al. 2019).

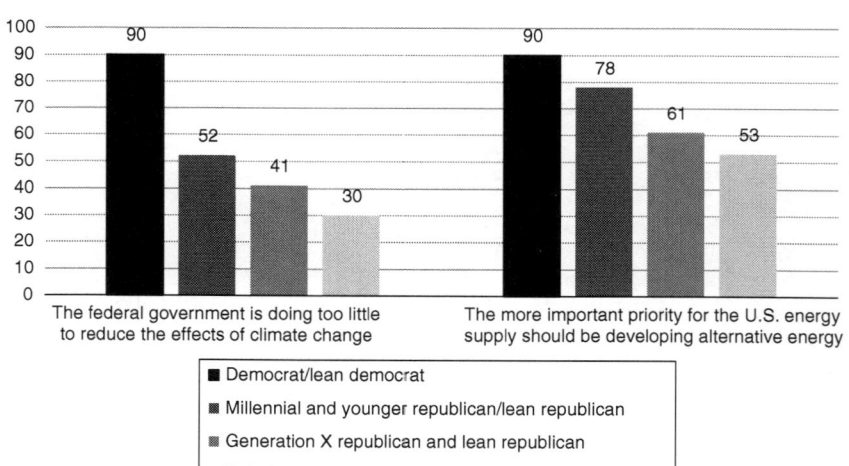

FIGURE 9.2 Views of Global Warming by Party and Generation.

Source: Pew Research Center. U.S. Public Views on Climate and Energy. October 1, 2019– October 13, 2019.

Yet, Generation Z has already displayed its willingness to protest to pressure government officials to take action to fight climate change. The evidence links protesting about issues and contacting elected officials about those issues and suggests that Generation Z will follow through at higher rates. This increases the likelihood that Congress will act on this issue in the future.

Generation Z: Looking Forward

The Covid-19 pandemic temporarily slowed activism, shifting most people's focus to their health and financial well-being. Thus, not surprisingly, concerns about health care, the economy, and Covid-19 took high priority over other issues in most voters' minds in the 2020 election (Hamel et al. 2020). With people confined to their residences for extended periods, protests temporarily stopped. Yet, it did not take long for protests to emerge about stay at home orders, drawing deep concern from public health officials that they might help spread Covid-19 (Smith 2020). Other events soon sparked protests, too. On May 5, 2020, protesters gathered (many of them taking social distancing precautions) to call for justice for Ahmaud Arbery after a video emerged appearing to show him being attacked and shot while jogging (Burke 2020). The protests helped lead to the Georgia Bureau of Investigation taking over the case and making arrests. Protests soon followed demanding justice for George Floyd and Breonna Taylor.

The pandemic produced declines in air pollution around the world (Regan 2020) and a drop in mass shootings in the United States (Dolmetsch 2020). Yet, it took just five days after Arizona lifted its stay-at-home order before a gunman armed with an AR-15 went to an Arizona shopping mall and attempted to carry out a mass shooting (Keeley 2020). The work of supporters of the #NeverAgain movement against gun violence is not done. Neither is the work of supporters of the #MeToo Movement. Immigration issues have yet to be settled. Approximately 700,000 DREAMers await actions that will determine whether they are able to stay in the country they have grown up in or face deportation (Ramos 2020). And despite the temporary reprieve to the environment caused by millions around the world staying home, the effects of climate change continue.

Other issues of importance to young adults will join these as objects of policy debate. While Covid-19 may have temporarily slowed their activism, Generation Z has already shown its willingness to act. They are quick to post about issues of concern to them, eager to protest when they think it can make a difference, and willing to contact elected officials to make sure their voices are heard. And, while we have focused on the political voices of Generation Z in the United States in this book, the climate strike movement provides but one example of the widespread activism seen among young people around the globe. These characteristics suggest that a more fitting name for Generation Z might be Generation Zeal. If they can successfully put this energy and enthusiasm for causes that matter to them into the voting booth, too, their voice has the potential to effectively shape public policy for years to come.

Notes

1. We rely here on the age ranges reported by Gallup.
2. These generations have concordant views on social issues (Parker, Graf, and Igielnik 2019).
3. We constrained the eligibility of participants in this survey to those with HIT approval rates of at least 95% and whose location is in the United States. While we were unable to constrain by age here, we did so through the first question asking respondents whether they were between the ages of 18 and 25. If they responded no, then the survey ended.
4. The online appendix contains the complete wording for each of the questions for the mTurk sample, along with a more extensive discussion of the variables that we used.
5. These were the only questions in the survey about peer civic experiences. Some participants responded that they did not know for one or more of these questions. When constructing our index, we coded values for these variables as missing. Consequently, no peer civic engagement score is present for those who answered "don't know" on a minimum of one of these questions.
6. This also acts as an indirect indicator with respect to mobilization, as people frequently act politically when others around them do so (see e.g., Gimpel, Lee, and Kamiski 2006). Yet, it is possible that mobilization efforts by those other than peers, like interest groups and political parties, also yield higher levels of participation (Rosenstone and Hansen 2002). There are no questions in this survey that allow us to directly account for the effects of mobilization on civic activity. That said, we do consider many other covariates that also affect mobilization as part of the matching routines in this analysis.
7. We asked an initial screening question that identified those who were between the ages of 18 and 25, and those who responded that they were not in this age range were excluded from further participation in the survey. When we performed the age computations based on the year and month that respondents selected, though, there were 49 respondents who stated that they were older than 25 in 2018. In the year-month calculation, there was usually about a six-month variance between the reported and actual age among those 49 respondents. Since we asked about both year and month of birth based on drop-down menus, it is possible that a substantial portion of these respondents misreported their year and/or month of birth in 2018 (see Gendall and Healey 2008). We have no reason to believe that this error is systematic, and did not encounter the same concern in 2020. Thus, nonsystematic measurement error in an independent variable does not bias any conclusions in research studies (see King, Keohane, and Verba 1994).
8. We did not include as matching covariates any of the issue-specific questions that we examined in the previous chapter. We did not do so because many of these issue-specific variables are inexorably connected to presidential approval, as then-President Trump made many policy decisions that generated strong reactions in several of those areas. In situations like this, it is inadvisable to include matching covariates that are connected to both the treatment and dependent variables, as this can make subsequent causal inference less clear than it should be. Similarly, several of the issue-specific variables examined in previous chapters directly asked about opinions of varying actions that then-President Trump performed.

9 Matching analyses are highly sensitive to even minor violations of these assumptions (Imbens and Rubin 2015).
10 If presidential approval were related to offline civic engagement or contacting elected government officials, then presidential approval would be highly correlated to both of our dependent variables. To examine whether this happens, we correlated our treatment variable (presidential approval) and our dependent variables (offline civic activity and contacting elected government officials). These correlations are low enough given our number of observations in both cases (offline civic engagement: .156 (2018), .428 (2020); contacting elected government officials: .102 (2018), .387 (2020)) such that we can conclude that we have satisfied the SUTVA assumption.
11 However, we do not generate a regression following the matching analysis (as Ho et al. 2007 advise), as Abadie and Spiess (2019) say that this is not appropriate when matching is performed with replacement as researchers obtain inaccurate estimates of their standard errors.

References

Abadie, Alberto and Guido W. Imbens 2006. "Large Sample Properties of Matching Estimators for Average Treatment Effects." *Econometrica* 74(1): 235–267. https://doi.org/10.1111/j.1468-0262.2006.00655.x. Accessed online June 19, 2021.

Abadie, Alberto and Guido W. Imbens 2011. "Bias-Corrected Matching Estimators for Average Treatment Effects." *Journal of Business and Economic Statistics* 29(1): 1–11. https://doi.org/10.1198/jbes.2009.07333. Accessed online June 19, 2021.

Abadie, Alberto and Guido W. Imbens 2016. "Matching on the Estimated Propensity Score." *Econometrica* 84(2): 781–807. https://doi.org/10.3982/ECTA11293. Accessed online June 19, 2021.

Abadie, Alberto and Jann Spiess 2019. "Robust Post-Matching Inference." Forthcoming in the *Journal of the American Statistical Association*. https://doi.org/10.1080/01621459.2020.1840383. Accessed online June 19, 2021.

Abramowitz, Alan I., Albert D. Cover, and Helmut Norpoth 1986. "The President's Party in Midterm Elections: Going from Bad to Worse." *American Journal of Political Science* 30(3): 562–576.

Abramowitz, Alan I. and Walter J. Stone 2006. "The Bush Effect: Polarization, Turnout, and Activism in the 2004 Presidential Election." *Presidential Studies Quarterly* 36(2): 141–154. https://doi.org/10.1111/j.1741-5705.2006.00295.x. Accessed online June 19, 2021.

Abramson, Alana 2018. "Trump Says Second Amendment Rights Are 'Under Siege.' But He Vowed to Defend Them in Defiant NRA Speech." *Time*. https://time.com/5265969/donald-trump-nra-convention-speech/. Accessed online May 15, 2020.

Achen, Christopher H. and Larry M. Bartels 2016. *Democracy for Realists: Why Elections Do Not Produce Responsive Government*. Princeton, NJ: Princeton University Press.

Adams, Char 2020. "A Movement, a Slogan, a Rallying Cry: How Black Lives Matter Changed America's Views on Race." NBC News. www.nbcnews.com/news/nbcblk/movement-slogan-rallying-cry-how-black-lives-matter-changed-america-n1252434. Accessed online February 2, 2021.

Alter, Charlotte 2018. "The School Shooting Generation Has Had Enough." *Time*. March 22, 2018. https://time.com/longform/never-again-movement/. Accessed online January 30, 2020.

Ankel, Sophia 2020. "30 Days that Shook America: Since the Death of George Floyd, the Black Lives Matter Movement Has Already Changed the Country." *Business Insider.* www.businessinsider.com/13-concrete-changes-sparked-by-george-floyd-protests-so-far-2020-6. Accessed online February 2, 2021.

Arnold, R. Douglas 1990. *The Logic of Congressional Action.* New Haven, CT: Yale University Press.

Associated Press 2019c. "90 State Lawmakers Accused of Sexual Misconduct since 2017." https://apnews.com/a3377d14856e4f4fb584509963a7a223. Accessed online May 21, 2020.

Ballew, Matthew, Jennifer Marlon, Seth Rosenthal, Abel Gustafson, John Kotcher, Edward Maibach, and Anthony Leiserowitz 2019. "Do Younger Generations Care More about Global Warming?" *Yale Program on Climate Change Communication.* https://climatecommunication.yale.edu/publications/do-younger-generations-care-more-about-global-warming/. Accessed online May 22, 2020.

Baumgartner, Frank R., Sylvain Brouard, Emiliano Gossman, Sebastien G. Lazardeux, and Jonathan Moody 2014. "Divided Government, Legislative Productivity, and Policy Change in the USA and France." *Governance* 27(3): 423–447. https://doi.org/10.1111/gove.12047. Accessed online June 19, 2021.

BBC 2020. "Greta Thunberg: Who Is She and What Does She Want?" BBC News. www.bbc.com/news/world-europe-49918719. Accessed online January 12, 2021.

Beech, Eric 2019. "Trump Vetoes Measure to End His Emergency Declaration on Border Wall." www.reuters.com/article/us-usa-trump-congress-emergency/trump-vetoes-measure-to-end-his-emergency-declaration-on-border-wall-idUSKBN1WV06P. Accessed online May 21, 2020.

Bennion, Elizabeth A. 2013. "Assessing Civic and Political Engagement Activities: A Toolkit." In *Teaching Civic Engagement: From Student to Active Citizen,* Alison Rios, Millett McCartney, Elizabeth A. Bennion, and Dick Simpson (Eds.). Washington, DC: American Political Science Association.

Beyers, Jan, Rainer Eising, and William Maloney 2008. "Researching Interest Group Politics in Europe and Elsewhere: Much We Study, Little We Know?" *West European Politics* 31(6): 1103–1128. https://doi.org/10.1080/01402380802370443. Accessed online June 19, 2021.

Blazina, Carrie Elizabeth and Drew Desilver 2021. "A Record Number of Women Are Serving in the 117th Congress." Pew Research Center. www.pewresearch.org/fact-tank/2021/01/15/a-record-number-of-women-are-serving-in-the-117th-congress. Accessed online February 2, 2021.

Booker, Brakkton 2020. "Trump Administration Diverts $3.8 Billion in Pentagon Funding to Border Wall." NPR. www.npr.org/2020/02/13/805796618/trump-administration-diverts-3-8-billion-in-pentagon-funding-to-border-wall. Accessed online May 21, 2020.

Borunda, Alejandra 2019. "These Young Activists Are Striking to Save Their Planet from Climate Change." *National Geographic.* www.nationalgeographic.com/environment/2019/03/youth-climate-strike-kids-save-the-world/. Accessed online May 22, 2020.

Boulianne, Shelley 2015. "Social Media Use and Participation: A Meta-Analysis of Current Research." *Information, Communication & Society* 18(5): 524–538. https://doi.org/10.1080/1369118X.2015.1008542. Accessed online June 19, 2021.

Boulianne, Shelley 2020. "Twenty Years of Digital Media Effects on Civic and Political Participation." *Communication Research* 47(7): 947–966. https://doi.org/10.1177/0093650218808186. Accessed online June 19, 2021.

Burke, Minyvonne. 2020. "Video Appears to Show Georgia Man Shot While Jogging; Lawyers Call for Arrests." NBC News. www.nbcnews.com/news/nbcblk/video-appears-show-georgia-man-shot-while-jogging-lawyers-call-n120130. Accessed online May 22, 2020.

Caldeira, Gregory A. and John R. Wright. 1998. "Lobbying for Justice: Organized Interests Supreme Court Nominations, and United States Senate." *American Journal of Political Science* 42(2): 499–523.

Campbell, James E. 1985. "Explaining Presidential Losses in Midterm Congressional Elections." *The Journal of Politics* 47(4): 1140–1157. https://doi.org/10.2307/2130810. Accessed online June 19, 2021.

Cambell, James E. 1991. "The Presidential Surge and Its Midterm Decline in Congressional Elections, 1868–1988." *The Journal of Politics* 53(2): 477–487. https://doi.org/10.1017/S0022381600048404. Accessed online June 19, 2021.

Carlsen, Audrey, Maya Salam, Clair Cain Miller, Denise Lu, Ash Bgu, Jugal K. Patel, and Zach Wichter 2018. "#MeToo Brought Down 201 Powerful Men. Nearly Half of Their Replacements are Women." *The New York Times*. October 29, 2018. www.nytimes.com/interactive/2018/10/23/us/metoo-replacements.html. Accessed online June 27, 2019.

Center for American Women in Politics 2019. "Women in State Legislatures 2019." https://cawp.rutgers.edu/women-state-legislature-2019. Accessed online May 21, 2020.

Center for American Women in Politics 2020. "History of Women in the U.S. Congress." www.cawp.rutgers.edu/history-women-us-congress. Accessed online May 21, 2020.

Center for Responsive Politics 2021. "Campaign Finance Data on the Internet." www.opensecrets.org. Accessed online February 8, 2021.

CNN 2018. "Missouri Election Results in 2018." www.cnn.com/election/2018/results/missouri. Accessed online February 1, 2021.

Cowan, Richard and Susan Cornwell. 2019. "U.S. Lawmakers Reach Tentative Deal to Avoid Government Shutdown." Reuters. www.reuters.com/article/instant-article/idUSKCN1Q01NV. Accessed online May 21, 2020.

Cranley, Ellen 2018. "9 Members of Congress Who Were Forced Out of Office by Sexual Misconduct Scandals." *Business Insider*. www.businessinsider.com/congress-sex-scandals-forced-out-of-office-2018-5. Accessed online May 21, 2020.

Crocker, Brittany and Nick Pensenstadler 2019. "Bump Stocks, Which Allow Rifles to Mimic Automatic Weapons, Are Now Illegal to Own, Buy, or Sell." *USA Today*. www.usatoday.com/story/news/politics/2019/03/26/bump-stock-ban-where-to-turn-in-knox-atf/3274917002/. Accessed online May 21, 2020.

D'Agostino, Ralph B. 1998. "Propensity Score Methods for Bias Reduction in the Comparison of a Treatment to a Non-Randomized Control Group." *Statistics in Medicine* 17(9): 2265–2281. https://doi.org/10.1002/(SICI)1097-0258(19981015)17:19<2265::AID-SIM918>3.0.CO;2-B. Accessed online June 19, 2021.

Delli Carpini, Michael X. and Ester R. Fuchs 1993. "The Year of the Woman? Candidates, Voters, and the 1992 Elections." *Political Science Quarterly* 108(1): 29–36.

Diamond, Alexis and Jasjeet J. Sekhon 2013. "Genetic Matching for Estimating Causal Effects: A General Multivariate Matching Method for Achieving Balance in Observational Studies." *Review of Economics and Statistics* 95(3): 932–945. https://doi.org/10.1162/REST_a_00318. Accessed online June 19, 2021.

Dolmetsch, Chris 2020. "One Good Thing from the Pandemic: Mass Shootings in the U.S. Plunge." *Bloomberg*. www.bloomberg.com/news/articles/2020-05-09/one-good-thing-from-the-pandemic-mass-shootings-in-u-s-plunge. Accessed online May 22, 2020.

Eggers, Andrew C. and Jens Hainmueller 2009. "MPs for Sale? Returns to Office in Postwar British Politics." *American Political Science Review* 103(4): 513–533. https://doi.org/10.1017/S0003055409990190. Accessed online June 19, 2021.

Flavin, Patrick and John D. Griffin 2009. "Policy, Preferences, and Participation: Government's Impact on Democratic Citizenship." *Journal of Politics* 71(2): 544–559. https://doi.org/10.1017/S0022381609090458. Accessed online June 19, 2021.

Funk, Cary and Meg Hefferon 2019. "U.S. Public Views on Climate and Energy." Pew Research Center. www.pewresearch.org/science/2019/11/25/u-s-public-views-on-climate-and-energy/. Accessed online May 22, 2020.

Gelman, Andrew and Jennifer Hill 2007. *Data Analysis Using Regression and Multilevel/Heiarchical Models*. New York: Cambridge University Press.

Gendall, Philip and Benjamin Healey 2008. "Asking the Age Question in Mail and Online Surveys." *International Journal of Market Research* 50(3): 309–317. https://doi.org/10.1177/147078530805000303. Accessed online June 19, 2021.

Gerber, Alan S. and Donald P. Green 1999. "Does Canvassing Increase Voter Turnout? A Field Experiment." *Proceedings of the National Academy of Sciences of the United States of America* 96(19): 10939–10942. https://doi.org/10.1073/pnas.96.19.10939. Accessed online June 19, 2021.

Gibson, James L. and Gregory A. Caldeira 2009. "Confirmation Politics and the Legitimacy of the U.S. Supreme Court: Institutional Loyalty, Positivity Bias, and the Alito Nomination." *American Journal of Political Science* 53(1): 139–155. https://doi.org/10.1111/j.1540-5907.2008.00362.x. Accessed online June 19, 2021.

Gimpel, James G., Frances E. Lee, and Joshua Kaminski 2006. "The Political Geography of Campaign Contributions in American Politics." *Journal of Politics* 68(3): 626–639. https://doi.org/10.1111/j.1468-2508.2006.00450.x. Accessed online June 19, 2021.

Greene, William H. 2011. *Econometric Analysis*. 7th Ed. New York City, NY: Pearson Education.

Hamel, Liz, Audrey Kearney, Ashley Kirzinger, Lunna Lopes, Cailey Munana, and Mollyann Brodie 2020. "KFF Health Tracking Poll – May 2020." Kaiser Family Foundation. www.kff.org/coronavirus-covid-19/report/kff-health-tracking-poll-may-2020/. Accessed online May 22, 2020.

Hayes, Christal and William Cummings 2018. "Democratic Senators Lost in Battleground States after Voting against Kavanaugh." *USA Today*. www.usatoday.com/story/news/politics/elections/2018/11/07/kavanaugh-effect-midterm-elections/1915457002/. Accessed online May 21, 2020.

Head, Megan L., Luke Holman, Rob Lanfear, Andrew T. Kahn, and Michael D. Jennions 2015. "The Extent and Consequences of P-Hacking in Science." *Plos Biology* 13(3): e1002106. https://doi.org/10.1371/journal.pbio.1002106. Accessed online June 19, 2021.

Ho, Daniel E., Kosuke Imai, Gary King, and Elizabeth A. Stuart 2007. "Matching as Nonparametric Preprocessing for Reducing Model Dependence in Parametric Causal Inference." *Political Analysis* 15(3): 199–236. https://doi.org/10.1093/pan/mpl013. Accessed online June 19, 2021.

Holbrook, Allyson L. and Jon A. Krosnick 2010. "Social Desirability Bias in Voter Turnout Reports: Tests Using the Item Count Technique." *Public Opinion Quarterly* 74(1): 37–67. https://doi.org/10.1093/poq/nfp065. Accessed online June 19, 2021.

Imbens, Guido W. and Donald B. Rubin 2015. *Causal Inference for Statistics, Social, and Biomedical Sciences: An Introduction*. New York, NY: Cambridge University Press.

Jackson, David 2018. "Trump at Mar-a-Lago as Thousands March in D.C. White House Applauds 'Courageous Young Americans.'" *USA Today*. www.usatoday.com/story/news/politics/2018/03/24/trump-mar-lago-thousands-march-our-lives-white-house-applauds-courages-young-americans/455506002/. Accessed online May 15, 2020.

Jervis, Rick and Alan Gomez 2019. "Trump Administration Has Separated Hundreds of Children from Their Migrant Families since 2018." *USA Today*. www.usatoday.com/story/news/nation/2019/05/02/border-family-separations-trump-administration-border-patrol/3563990002/. Accessed online October 23, 2019.

Johnson, Andrea, Kathryn Menefee, and Ramya Sekaran 2019. "Progress in Advancing Me Too Workplace Reforms in #20Statesby2020." National Women's Law Center. https://nwlc-ciw49tixgw5lbab.stackpathdns.com/wp-content/uploads/2019/07/20-States-By-2020-report.pdf. Accessed online May 20, 2020.

Jones, Jeffrey M. 2021. "Last Trump Job Approval 34%; Average Is Record-Low 41%." Gallup. https://news.gallup.com/poll/328637/last-trump-job-approval-average-record-low.aspx. Accessed online February 2, 2021.

Jones, Maggie 2018. "The March for Our Lives Activists Showed Us How to Find Meaning in Tragedy." *Smithsonian Magazine*. December. www.smithsonianmag.com/innovation/march-for-our-lives-student-activists-showed-meaning-tragedy-180970717/. Accessed online November 20, 2019.

Kahne, Joseph and Benjamin Bowyer 2018. "The Political Significance of Social Media Activity and Social Networks." *Political Communication* 35(3): 470–493. https://doi.org/10.1080/10584609.2018.1426662. Accessed online June 19, 2021.

Kapur, Sahil, Julie Tsirkin, and Rebecca Shabad 2020. "Senate confirms Amy Coney Barrett, Heralding New Conservative Era for Supreme Court." NBC News. www.nbcnews.com/politics/congress/amy-coney-barrett-set-be-confirmed-supreme-court-monday-n1244748. Accessed online February 2, 2021.

Kaur, Harmeet and Madison Park 2019. "Young Environmental Activists across the World Skip School in a Call to Action." CNN. www.cnn.com/2019/03/15/world/climate-strike-students/index.html. Accessed online May 22, 2020.

Keeley, Matt 2020. "At Least Three Shot in Arizona Shopping Mall: Suspect in Custody." *Newsweek*. www.newsweek.com/least-two-shot-arizona-shopping-mall-one-suspect-custody-1505587. Accessed online May 22, 2020.

Kelly, Cara and Aaron Hegarty 2018. "#MeToo Was a Culture Shock: But Changing Laws will Take More than a Year." *USA Today*. October 4, 2018. www.usatoday.com/story/news/investigations/2018/10/04/metoo-me-too-sexual-assault-survivors-rights-bill/1074976002/. Accessed online June 27, 2019.

Keneally, Meghan 2019. "List of Trump's Accusers and Their Allegations of Sexual Misconduct." ABC News. abcnews.go.com/Politics/list-trumps-accusers-allegations-sexual-misconduct/story?id=51956410. Accessed online May 15, 2020.

Kennedy, Courtney, Andrew Mercer, Scott Keeter, Nick Hatley, Kyle McGeeney, and Alejandra Gimenez 2016. "Evaluating Online Nonprobability Surveys." Pew Research Center. www.pewresearch.org/methods/2016/05/02/evaluating-online-nonprobability-surveys. Accessed online February 2, 2021.

Kerbel, Matthew R. and Joel David Bloom 2005. "Blog for America and Civic Involvement." *The International Journal of Press/Politics* 10(4): 3–27.

Kernell, Samuel 1977. "Presidential Popularity and Negative Voting: An Alternative Explanation of the Midterm Congressional Decline of the President's Party." *American Political Science Review* 71(1): 44–66. https://doi.org/10.1017/S0003055400259297. Accessed online June 19, 2021.

King, Gary, Christopher Lucas, and Richard A. Nielsen 2017. "The Balance-Sample Size Frontier in Matching Methods for Causal Inference." *American Journal of Political Science* 61(2): 473–489. https://doi.org/10.1111/ajps.12272 Accessed online June 19, 2021.

King, Gary, Robert O. Keohane, and Sidney Verba 1994. *Designing Social Inquiry: Scientific Inference in Qualitative Research*. Princeton, NJ: Princeton University Press.

Krutz, Glen S., Richard Fleisher, and Jon R. Bond 1998. "From Abe Fortas to Zöe Baird: Why Some Presidential Nominations Fail in the Senate." *American Political Science Review* 92(4): 871–881. https://doi.org/10.2307/2586309 Accessed online June 19, 2021.

Ley, Barbara L. and Paul R. Brewer 2018. "Social Media, Networked Protest, and the March for Science." *Social Media and Society* 4(3): 1–12. https://doi.org/10.1177/2056305118793407. Accessed online June 19, 2021.

Liptak, Kevin and Kristen Holmes 2020. "Trump Calls Black Lives Matter a 'Symbol of Hate' as He Digs in on Race." CNN. www.cnn.com/2020/07/01/politics/donald-trump-black-lives-matter-confederate-race/index.html. Accessed online February 2, 2021.

Loader, Brian D.; Ariadne Vromen and Michael A. Xenos 2014. "The Networked Young Citizen: Social Media, Political Participation and Civic Engagement." *Information, Communication and Society* 17(2): 143–150. https://doi.org/10.1080/1369118X.2013.871571. Accessed online June 19, 2021.

Mahéo, Valérie-Anne and Éric Bélanger 2020. "Lowering the Voting Age to 16? A Comparative Study on the Political Competence and Engagement of Underage and Adult Youth." *Canadian Journal of Political Science* 53(3): 596–616. 1–22. https://doi.org/10.1017/S0008423920000232. Accessed online June 19, 2021.

Mayhew, David R. 1974. *Congress: The Electoral Connection*. New Haven, CT: Yale University Press.

McAdam, Doug and Sidney Tarrow 2010. "Ballots and Barricades: On the Reciprocal Relationship between Elections and Social Movements." *Perspectives on Politics* 8(2): 529–542. https://doi.org/10.1017/S1537592710001234. Accessed online June 19, 2021.

McCammon, Sarah 2018. "Kavanaugh Fight Puts Vulnerable Senators in a Tight Spot." NPR. www.npr.org/2018/08/15/638644504/supreme-court-fight-focuses-on-states-that-could-decide-senate-control. Accessed online May 21, 2020.

Metzger, Aaron, Lauren Alvis, Katelyn F. Romm, Laura Wray-Lake, and Amy K. Syvertsen 2020. "Adolsescents' Evaluations of Political Leaders: The Case of President Donald Trump." *Journal of Research on Adolescence* 30(1): 314–330. https://doi.org/10.1111/jora.12544. Accessed online June 19, 2021.

Moffett, Kenneth W. and Laurie L. Rice 2018. "College Students and Online Political Expression in the 2016 Election." *Social Science Computer Review* 36(4): 422–439. https://doi.org/10.1177/0894439317721186. Accessed online June 19, 2021.

Molina, Brett and Christal Hayes 2018. "Republican Senator Offered Private Jet to Vote on Kavanaugh and Be at Daughter's Wedding." *USA Today*. www.usatoday.com/story/news/politics/onpolitics/2018/10/05/kavanaugh-vote-steve-daines-daughters-wedding/1532320002/. Accessed online May 21, 2020.

National Public Radio 2018. "Florida Governor Signs Package of New Gun Restrictions." www.npr.org/sections/thetwo-way/2018/03/09/592393010/florida-gov-rick-scott-signs-gun-package. Accessed online December 13, 2019.

Neuman, Scott and Bill Chappell 2019. "Young People Lead Millions to Protest Global Inaction on Climate Change." NPR. www.npr.org/2019/09/20/762629200/mass-protests-in-australia-kick-off-global-climate-strike-ahead-of-u-n-summit. Accessed online May 22, 2020.

Newport, Frank 2018. "Top Issues for Voters: Healthcare, Economy, Immigration." https://news.gallup.com/poll/244367/top-issues-voters-healthcare-economy-immigration.aspx. Accessed online May 12, 2020.

Nichols, Austin 2007. "Causal Inference with Observational Data." *The Stata Journal* 7(4): 507–541. https://doi.org/10.1177/1536867X0800700403. Accessed online June 19, 2021.

Nickerson, David W. 2015. "Do Voter Registration Drives Increase Participation? For Whom and When?" *The Journal of Politics* 77(1): 88–101. https://doi.org/10.1086/678391. Accessed online June 19, 2021.

Norman, Jim. 2019. "Solid Majority Still Opposes New Construction on Border Wall. Gallup. https://news.gallup.com/poll/246455/solid-majority-opposes-new-construction-border-wall.aspx. Accessed online May 20, 2010.

Olson, Mancur 1973. *The Logic of Collective Action: Public Goods and the Theory of Groups*. Cambridge, MA: Harvard University Press.

Panagopoulos, Costas, Christopher W. Larimer, and Meghan Condon 2014. "Social Pressure, Descriptive Norms, and Voter Mobilization." *Political Behavior* 36(2): 451–469. https://doi.org/10.1007/s11109-013-9234-4. Accessed online June 19, 2021.

Parker, Kim, Nikki Graf, and Ruth Igielnik 2019. "Generation Z Looks a Lot Like Millennials on Key Social and Political Issues" Pew Research Center www.pewsocialtrends.org/2019/01/17/generation-z-looks-a-lot-like-millennials-on-key-social-and-political-issues/. Accessed online February 12, 2019.

Peters, Katie 2019. "7 Ways American Has Changed since the March for Our Lives." Giffords Law Center. https://giffords.org/blog/2019/03/7-ways-america-changed-since-the-march-for-our-lives/. Accessed online May 20, 2020.

Pew Research Center. 2020a. "Election 2020: Voters Are Highly Engaged, but Nearly Half Expect to Have Difficulties Voting." www.pewresearch.org/politics/2020/08/13/important-issues-in-the-2020-election/. Accessed online December 21, 2020.

Ramos, Annie Rose 2020. "'I Try Not to Think about It': DREAMers Await Supreme Court Decision to Continue or End DACA." CBS Baltimore. https://baltimore.cbslocal.com/2020/05/18/coronavirus-nurse-dreamer-jose-aguiluz-daca-ruling/. Accessed online May 22, 2020.

Regan, Helen 2020. "Air Pollution Falls by Unprecedented Levels in Major Global Cities during Coronavirus Lockdowns." CNN. www.cnn.com/2020/04/22/world/air-pollution-reduction-cities-coronavirus-intl-hnk/index.html. Accessed online May 22, 2020.

Rodriguez, Sabrina 2021. "Biden to Sign Executive Orders on Family Separation and Asylum." *Politico*. www.politico.com/news/2021/02/02/biden-executive-orders-family-separation-464816. Accessed online February 2, 2021.

Rose, Joel 2021. "Families Separated at Border Hope Biden Reunites Them, Bringing Deported Parents Back." NPR. www.npr.org/2021/01/28/961301353/families-separated-at-border-hope-biden-reunites-them-bringing-deported-parents. Accessed online February 2, 2021.

Rosenstone, Steven J. and John Mark Hansen 2002. *Mobilization, Participation, and Democracy in America*. New York, NY: Pearson-Longman.

Schattschneider, Elmer Eric 1960. *The Semi-Sovereign People: A Realist's View of Democracy in America*. New York, NY: Holt, Rinehart, and Winston.

Schor, Elana 2018. "'They Expect More from Women': Collins and Murkowski Face Extra Pressure in Kavanaugh Fight." *Politico*. www.politico.com/story/2018/10/03/collins-murkowski-kavanaugh-ford-867740. Accessed online May 21, 2020.

Sekhon, Jasjeet S. 2011. "Multivariate and Propensity Score Matching Software with Automated Balance Optimization: The Matching Package for R." *Journal of Statistical Software* 42(7): 1–52.

Shah, Dhavan V., Jaeho Cho, William P. Eveland, Jr. and Nojin Kwak 2005. "Information and Expression in a Digital Age: Modeling Internet Effects on Civic Participation." *Communication Research* 32(5): 531–565. https://doi.org/10.1177/0093650205279209. Accessed online June 19, 2021.

Silver, Brian D., Barbara A. Anderson, and Paul R. Abramson 1986. "Who Overreports Voting?" *American Political Science Review* 80(2): 613–624.

Smith, Aaron 2013. "Civic Engagement in the Digital Age." Pew Research Center. http://pewinternet.org/Reports/2013/Civic-Engagement.aspx. Accessed online November 18, 2019.

Smith, Allen 2020. "Birx Says Protesters Not Practicing Social Distancing Are 'Devastatingly Worrying.'" NBC News. www.nbcnews.com/politics/politics-news/birx-says-protesters-not-practicing-social-distancing-are-devastatingly-worrisome-n1198991. Accessed online May 22, 2020.

Somvichian-Clausen, Austa 2020. "What the 2020 Black Lives Matter Protests Have Achieved so Far." *The Hill*. https://thehill.com/changing-america/respect/equality/502121-what-the-2020-black-lives-matter-protests-have-achieved-so. Accessed online February 2, 2021.

Stuart, Elizabeth A. 2010. "Matching Methods for Causal Inference: A Review and a Look Forward." *Statistical Science* 25(1): 1–21. https://doi.org/10.1214/09-STS313. Accessed online June 19, 2021.

Tatum, Sophia 2018. "Brett Kavanaugh's Nomination: A Timeline." www.cnn.com/interactive/2018/10/politics/timeline-kavanaugh/. Accessed online February 5, 2019.

Traugott, Michael W. and John P. Katosh 1979. "Response Validity in Surveys of Voting Behavior." *Public Opinion Quarterly* 43(3): 359–377. https://doi.org/10.1086/268527. Accessed online June 19, 2021.

Tufte, Edward R. 1978. *Political Control of the Economy*. Princeton, NJ: Princeton University Press.

United States Senate 2018. "Supreme Court Nominations (Present–1789)." www.senate.gov/legislative/nominations/SupremeCourtNominations1789present.htm. Accessed online May 21, 2020.

Verba, Sidney, Henry E. Brady, and Kay L. Schlozman 1995. *Voice and Equality: Civic Voluntarism in American Democracy*. Cambridge, MA: Harvard University Press.

Villareal, Daniel. 2020. "Trump Says the Black Lives Matter Movement Is 'Destroying Many Black Lives.'" *Newsweek*. www.newsweek.com/trump-says-black-lives-matter-movement-destroying-many-black-lives-1534411. Accessed online February 2, 2021.

Wu, Nicholas. 2020. "How Will Amy Coney Barrett's Confirmation Battle Affect Senate Races?" *USA Today*. www.usatoday.com/story/news/politics/2020/10/28/amy-coney-barrett-supreme-court-battle-flip-senate/6007519002. Accessed online February 2, 2021.

Yamamoto, Masahiro, Matthew J. Kushin, and Francis Dalisay 2013. "Social Media and Mobiles as Political Mobilization Forces for Young Adults: Examining the Moderating Role of Online Political Expression in Political Participation." *New Media and Society* 17(6): 880–898. https://doi.org/10.1177/1461444813518390. Accessed online June 19, 2021.

YouGov 2018. *The Economist*/YouGov Poll. September 23–25.

INDEX

Note: Page numbers in italics indicate figures and page numbers in bold indicate tables.

ACLU (American Civil Liberties Union) 136, 138, 211, 250
activism: core values and 21, 36, 50, 68, 86, 128, 134–38, 151, 161; generational shift and 6–14; increase in 265; "lateral connections" and 107; new wave of 2–3, 12–13; opportunity-based perspectives 230–32; slacktivism 50, 85, 117, 194, 274; success of 284
Adigwe, Dumebi 2
African American men, risk and 11, 166
African Americans, political participation 231
agenda setting 100–101
"all lives matter" 163, 164
Amato, Timothy 103, 105
American National Election Studies 20
Amnesty International USA 136
anti-Vietnam war movement 2, 37, 169
anxiety, threat-based narratives and 11, 21, 103, 105–7, 127–28, 133–34, 136
Aquarius, Adriana 168
Arab Spring 227–28
Arbery, Ahmaud 163–64, 287
Arnold, R. Douglas 68, 282
Asian/Pacific Islander men, risk and 11

Baby Boomers 2, 229–30, *286–287*
Barrett, Amy Coney *see* U.S. Supreme Court nominations

Bennion, Elizabeth A. 276
Bergan, Daniel E. 196
Biden, Joe 63, 64, 233, 284
Birkland, Thomas A. 104
Black Boston 2020 1, 5
Black Lives Matter (BLM) movement 160–89; "all lives matter" vs. 163, 164; *Black Lives Matter* as phrase 163; "Defund the Police" and 233; Google Trends and *161*, 162–63; news coverage *161*, 162–63, 167–68, 213, 250; overview 1–2, 5–6, 10, 21, 86, 160–67; protesting 165, 170–71, 231–32; public opinion and 167–69; social media 2, 5–6, 160, 168–70, 171; as social movement 11, 21; statistics and 11, 166; success of 283–84, 287–88; survey methods and results 170–83, **178**, 213–14, 216–20, 250–51, 253–55, 272–76; voter turnout and 169
blogs 12–13, 36
Bloom, Joel David 73, 110, 140, 172, 199
Bond, Jon R. 66–67
border wall *see* immigration policy movement
Brady, Kevin 277
Broockman, David E. 234
Brown, Michael 10, 162
Bryan, William 164
Burke, Tarana 31
Burney, Jamel 168–69

Bush tax cuts 137
Butler, Daniel M. 196

Caldeira, Gregory A. 66, 279
Caren, Neal 229, 230
Carlson, Tucker 167–68
Castile, Philando 163
Castle, Nick 278
CBS news poll 168, 213
Center for Popular Democracy Action 71
Center for Responsive Politics 281
Chase, Garrett 161
Chauvin, Derek 5–6, 163, 165, 283
Chavira, Daniele 132
civic engagement: activities of 20, 21; defined 19–20; *see also* survey methods
civil rights movement 2, 21, 33, 36, 37, 169, 170, 227
climate change *see* environmental movement
Clinton, Bill 232
Clinton, Hillary 7
Clothier, Tim 170–71
CNN: BLM movement coverage *161*, 162–63; DACA coverage *131*; school shootings coverage 98, *100*, 108
Cole, Richard T. 196
Coleman, Haven 285
collective action 21, 36, 38, 102, 103, 169, 181; *see also* mobilization
Collins, Susan 70, 279, 280
Columbine High School (Colo.) shooting 101–2, 232
confirmation bias 134
Cooper, Amy 164–65
Cooper, Christian 164–65
core values 21, 36, 50, 68, 86, 128, 134–38, 151, 161
Corin, Jaclyn 2, 96–97, 211, 248
countermobilization 33, 119n3, 134, 229, 233
Covid-19 pandemic: BLM movement and 5, 165, 181, 228, 232, 274; gun control protesting and 108–9, 117, 118, 274; immigration policy movement and 130; MeToo protesting and 37, 39, 49, 82, 248, 273–74; as protesting risk 39, 49, 71, 228, 287; Women's March and 39, 71
credible risk 104, 105
Crowd Counting Consortium 165, 228
Cruz, Nicholas 96
Cullors, Patrice 160, 233

DACA (Deferred Action for Childhood Arrivals Act): courts and 8, 10–11, 131–32; news coverage 98, *100*, *131*; overview 3, 128, 130–33; social media and 136; survey methods and results 146, **148**, 150–51; *see also* immigration policy movement
Daines, Steve 279
Dees, Donna 102–3
"Defund the Police" 233
Democratic Party 7–8, 17, **18**, 134, 167, 168, 234, 266–67, 286
deprivation theory 230–32
discrimination 10, 166, 229, 283
DREAMers 3, 287

Economist/YouGov Poll 64
Edwards, Frank 166
elected officials, contacting: as civic engagement 19–20; generational patterns 194–95; lobbying and 67, 211, 234–35, 248, 279, 281; as political expression 12, 18–19, 21–22; success of 13, 195–96, 276–85; survey methods and results 265–96, *266*, **272**, 284–85
elected officials, protesting and 227–64; effects on policy 232–36; letters vs. 234; lobbying vs. 234–35; overview 227–36; survey methods and results 236–57, **245**, **247**, **249**, **251**, 274–75, 284–85; theoretical perspectives 230–32
elected officials, social media and 193–226; accessibility and 197; generational patterns 194–95; overview 193–94; political efficacy and 197–98; responsiveness 195–96, 197; survey methods and results 198–220, **207**, **209**, **212**, **214**, 274, 284–85
empathy 11, 21, 128, 134–38
"engaged observers" 37, 169
environmental movement 6, 36, 39, 285–87, *286*
Eshoo, Anna 61
Esposito, Michael 166
ethnic stereotyping 133–34, 166

Facebook: BLM movement and 2, 6, 160, 168–69, 171; generational definitions and 14, *15*; gun control movement 2; MeToo movement 4, 35–36
Fair Housing Act 166
Families Belong Together protests 138, 228, 231

family separation *see* immigration policy movement
Farr, Sam 278
Feinstein, Dianne 61–62
Flake, Jeff 70
Flavin, Patrick 137
Fleisher, Richard 66–67
Floyd, George 5–6, 10, 163, 165, 228, 283, 287; *see also* Black Lives Matter (BLM) movement
focusing events 101, 104
Ford, Christine Blasey 4, 62, 279; *see also* U.S. Supreme Court nominations
Fox News: BLM movement coverage *161*, 162–63, 167–68; DACA coverage 98, *100*, *131*; school shootings coverage 98, *100*
Franken, Al 31
Frattaroli, Shannon 103, 104
Frazier, Darnella 165
Freedom House 227–28
Freedom Summer 170
free rider problem 36, 272

Gaines, Haylee 168
Gallup Polls 9, *129*, *266*
Garland, Merrick 63, 64
Garner, Eric 10, 162, 165
Garza, Alicia 160–61
generational shift 6–14
Generation X 2, 11, 32, 228, 229–30, *286–287*
Generation Y *See* Millennials
Generation Z: defined 14, *15*; future of 287–88; as movement leaders 11
Ghoshal, Raj Andrew 229, 230
Gibson, James L. 66
Giffords Law Center 281
Gillion, Daniel Q. 12
Gimpel, James G. 66
Ginsburg, Ruth Bader 62, 64, 210, 280
global warming *see* environmental movement
Gonzales, Emma 2, 97
Google Trends 33, 34, *35*, *161*, 162–63
Gorsuch, Neil 63
Grassley, Chuck 64
Gray, Freddie 163
Green Party 7–8
Griffin, John D. 137
group identification 128, 134–38
gun control movement 96–126; diversity of voices in 105; legislation 8, 97, 101–2, 105, 211, 234, 281–82, 284; lobbying and 211, 248, 281; mobilization factors regarding 101–9, *106*; news coverage 98–109, *100*, 232; overview 2, 4–5, 21, 96–98, 102–3, 104; protesting 107–9, 228, 231; public opinion and 101–3; social media 2, 107–9, 211, **212**; statistics on 11, 98, *99*, *100*, 105, 108; strategy of 104, 105; success of 281–82, 284, 287–88; survey methods and results 109–20, **115**, 211, **212**, 215–20, 248–49, 253–55, 272–76, 274, 285; voter turnout and 7–9, 12, 105; *see also* March for Our Lives; Million Mom March; Never Again Movement

Hannity, Sean 167
Harris, Kamala 284
Harris Interactive 16
Havercroft, Jonathan 165–66
Hawley, Josh 280
Hirsi, Isri 285
HoCo for Justice 6, 10, 171
Hogg, David 96–97, 104, 105
housing discrimination 166
Huckabee, Mike 163
Human Rights Watch 136
Hutchings, Vincent L. 66

immigration policy movement 127–59; issue framing and 133–34; news coverage 3, 21, 98, *100*, *131*, 135, 137, 150–51, 250; overview 21, 127–32; protesting 138, 211–13, **212**, 228, 231, 232–33, 234; social media posting and 136–37; success of 282–83, 284, 287–88; survey methods and results 128–30, 131, 132–33, 135–36, 138–53, **147–48**, 211–13, **212**, 216–20, **249–250**, 253, 254, 272–76, 285; voter turnout and 7–9, 12, 128–32; *see also* DACA (Deferred Action for Childhood Act)
"I'm With Her!" rally 71
independents *266–267*
Independent Women's Forum 71
insider tactics 21–22, 232, 235, 254, 276
Instagram 6, 171, 211
internet-based surveying 16, 20
Ipsos 16
Iraq War 133, 137
issue framing 101–3, 104, 105, 133–34
issue importance 100–109

Jackson, Rachel 39
Jewish Community Center (Los Angeles) shooting 102

Kahneman, Daniel 68
Karpowitz, Christopher F. 196
Kasky, Cameron 2, 96–97
Kavanaugh, Brett *see* U.S. Supreme Court nominations
Kerbel, Matthew R. 73, 110, 140, 172, 199
King, Martin Luther, Jr. 163
Krutz, Glen S. 66–67
Kueng, J. A. 165

Lane, Thomas 165
"lateral connections" 107
Latinos, risk and 11, 166
Latinx Americans 134–35, 232–33
Lee, Amy 103–4
Lee, Hedwig 166
lobbying 67, 211, 234–35, 248, 279, 281
Lutheran Immigration and Refugee Service 211, 250

Manchin, Joe 279
March for Our Lives: attendance 108, 228; coalition building and 5–6, 39, 171; lobbying and 281; overview 2, 4–5, 11, 97, 211, 231, 248; participation costs and risks 104, 105, 108; as social movement 11, 254–55; success of 8, 253–55, 273, 281–82, 284; theoretical perspectives 231
Marjorie Stoneman Douglas school shooting (Parkland, Fla.) 96–126; as focusing event 104; news coverage 98–108; overview 2, 4–5, 6, 96–100, 103–4, 248; *see also* gun control movement; March for Our Lives; Never Again movement
Marshall County, Ky. shooting 98
Martin, Trayvon 10, 12, 160
mass shootings *see* gun control movement
Mayhew, David R. 284
McAdam, Doug 52n2, 170, 274
McCaskill, Claire 280
McConnell, Mitch 63, 64, 82
McDonald, Jermaine M. 163
McMichael, Travis 164
media framing 101–3, 104, 105, 133–34
Meehan, Pat 31
methodology *see* survey methods

MeToo movement 31–60; future of 51, 287; Google Trends and 33, 34, *35*; overview 4, 10–11, 12, 20–21, 31–33; protesting and 38–40, 228; role of responses to 32–33; social media 4, 35–36, 37, 208, **209**; as a social movement 11, 34–35; success of 31–33, 276–81, 284, 287–88; survey methods and results 33, 40–54, **47**, 208, **209**, 215, 217–20, 244–46, **247**, 252, 253–55, 272–79; voter turnout and 7–9, 12, 61; *see also* U.S. Supreme Court nominations
Meyer, David S. 230
Michelson, Melissa 257
Milano, Alyssa 4, 12, 31, 34, 276
Milkman, Ruth 229
Millennials 6–13; defined 14, *15*; ideology and 36, 67–68, 255n3; impact on current movements 11; mischaracterization of 7–9; political participation and 2, 6, 7, 12, 32, 97, 160, 194, 228, 229–30, *286–287*; protesting and 85, 228, 229–30
Million Mom March 102–3, 107, 232
Minkoff, Debra C. 230
mobilization: credible risk and 104, 105; free rider problem 36, 272; "need for a roar" and 104, 108; news media and 100, 101–3, 135, 137; social movements and 33; *see also* threat-based narratives
Moffet, Kenneth W. 73, 110, 140, 172, 199
MoveOn.org 35, 138
MSNBC: BLM movement coverage *161*, 162–63; DACA coverage *131*; school shootings coverage 98, *100*
Murkowski, Lisa 279
Myszkowski, Sophia 38

Nadeau, Richard 103, 105
National Organization for Women (NOW) 136
National Women's Law Center 71
Native American men, risk and 11, 166
Nelson, Bill 280
Nettekoven, Linda 102–3, 107
Never Again movement: civic engagement and 107–8, 253–54, 255; future of 287; overview 4, 12, 96–97, 105, 118; as social movement 11, 107; success of 103–4, 107–8, 253–54, 265–66, 281–82, 284, 287–88; survey methods 118; *see also* gun control movement; March for Our Lives

news media 98–109; agenda setting 100–101; confirmation bias and 134; focusing events 101, 104; issue framing 101–3, 104, 105, 133–34; issue importance and 98–109, *100*, 232; source of 41; Twitter as 102, 162–63; young adults and 102; *see also specific journal or network*
Niemi, Richard G. 103, 105
9/11, generational definitions and 14, *15*
NRA (National Rifle Association) 97, 211, 232, 265–66, 281

Obama, Barack 63, 266
Occupy Wall Street 227–28
offline engagement: costs and risks of 32, 37–40, 70, 108–9, 118, 138, 171, 227; as form of political expression 7, 12; online engagement as source of 4, 12–13; *see also* elected officials; protesting
Olson, Mancur 36
online engagement: costs and risks of 32, 37–40, 107, 108–9, 171; effectiveness of 13, 21–22; as form of political expression 12–13, 19–20; as source of offline engagement 4, 12–13; *see also* social media
opinion polls *see* public opinion polls
O'Reilly, Bill 167
Ortiz, David G. 181
Ostertag, Stephen F. 181
outsider tactics: insider tactics and 21–22, 235, 254, 275, 276; insider tactics vs. 232; voter turnout and 12, 13
Owen, David 165–66

Pantaleo, Daniel 162
Parkland (Fla.) shooting *see* Marjorie Stoneman Douglas school shooting (Parkland, Fla.)
Peace Corps 278
peace movement 2, 37, 169
Pew Research Center 14, 17, **18**, 167
Pineda, Estefany 132
Planned Parenthood 71
polarization, political 7, 62, 101–2, 129, 229, 266–67
police brutality 11, 162, 166, 232, 233; *see also* Black Lives Matter (BLM) movement
political efficacy 51, 70, 108, 137, 138, 170, 171, 196, 198

political expression/participation: analyzing 13–14, 18–19, 21; civic engagement and 19–20, 68, 97–98; forms of 12–13, 18–19, 21–22; generational shift and 6–14; low levels of 2; *see also* elected officials; protesting; social media; voter turnout
Pope, Jeremy C. 196
posting *see* social media; *specific media*
process theory 230–32
prospect theory 68, 84–85
protesting 227–64; attendance 39, 102, 108, 165, 228; commitment requirements 38, 39; effectiveness of 13, 21–22, 228, 232–36; as form of political expression 12, 18–20, 38–40, 70–71, 227, 228–30; generational patterns 227–30, 235; increase in 227; motivation for 38, 103, 230; news coverage and 102; organizational involvement in 235–36; as social activity 38–39; social media vs. 11; theoretical perspectives 230–32; *see also* elected officials, protesting and
public opinion polls 64, 130, 166–67, 168, 196, 213, 280; *see also* survey methods

Quinonez, Amanda 168

racism 6, 10, 11, 133–34, 166, 232; *see also* Black Lives Matter (BLM) movement; immigration policy movement
Ramirez, Deborah 62
redlining 166
Refugee and Immigrant Center for Education and Legal Services (RAICES) 211, 250
religion, core values and 135, 138
Republican Party **18**, 134, 135, 167–68, 234, 266–67, 286
resource mobilization theory 230–32
Ribas, Vanesa 229, 230
Rice, Laurie L. 73, 110, 140, 172, 199
Robinson, Alesia 1
Rodriguez, Luis 132

Sanders, Bernie 7, 228
Sandy Hook Elementary School (Newtown, Conn.) shooting 100, 101–2
Santa Fe High School shooting 98
Scalia, Antonin 63
Schattschneider, Elmer Eric 282
school shootings 97, 98–100; *see also* gun control movement; *specific location*

Scott, Rick 97, 280, 281
Scott, Walter 163
self-interest, threat-based narratives and 21, 97–99, 103, 128, 133–35, 136, 150–51
Selph, Jessie 168–69
September 11 terrorist attacks, generational definitions and 14, *15*
Service Employees International Union 32BJ 71
Sessions, Jeff 131
sexual harassment and assault 4, 10–11, 22nn1–2, 31–33, 265, 276–79; *see also* MeToo Movement; U.S. Supreme Court nominations
Silent Generation 229, 255n3, 286
Singleton, Keon 6
Skovron, Christopher 234
slacktivism 50, 85, 117, 194, 274
slogans, effectiveness of 233
Snow, David A. 103
social hostility 133
social identification 135, 136
social media 193–226; as echo chambers 193–94; as form of political expression 12–13, 18–19, 37, 69–70; generational patterns 14, 194–95; and leadership development 5–6; as organizational tool 2–3, 10, 35; preference for 102; protesting vs. 11; slacktivism and 50, 85, 117, 194, 274; as source of offline engagement 12–13; stress and 193–94; *see also* elected officials, social media and; *specific media*
social movements: characteristics of 11–12, 33, 34–35, 274; coalition building and 71, 105, 107, 136–37, 151; history of young people in 2–3, 21, 254–55; theoretical perspectives 230–32
Sokoya, Ibukun 171
Soule, Sarah A. 103
Staples, Ryan 6, 170–71
stereotyping 133–34, 166
Sterling, Alton 163
strategic framing 101–3, 104, 105, 133–34
survey methods 14–22; ATET (average treatment effect on the treated) 42; Chronbach's alpha 20; data 14–18, *15*; future research 51, 276; internet-based 16, 20; Kolomogorov-Smirnov (KS) test 46; Mechanical Turk (mTurk) 16–18; OLS (ordinary least squares) 18; random digit dialing (RDD) 16; self-reporting

and 17–18, 218n7, 255n6, 275, 284–85; SUTVA (stable unit treatment value) 44–45
Swetnick, Julie 62

Tarrow, Sidney 52n2, 274
Taylor, Breonna 163, 164, 283, 287
Teen Vogue 3
Thao, Tou 165
Thomas, Clarence 280
Thomas, Madison 38
threat-based narratives: anxiety and 11, 21, 103, 105–7, 127–28, 133–34, 136; motivational strength and 68–69, 127–28, 136, 230, 231; self-interest and 21, 97–99, 103, 128, 133–35, 136, 150–51; theoretical perspectives 230–32
Thunberg, Greta 6, 285
Tilly, Charles 254
Time magazine 227–28
Tometi, Opal 160
Traister, Rebecca 34, 51
Trump, Donald: election of 2, 7–8, 127–28, 130, 134; job approval of 17–18, 265–67, *266*, **272**; supporters of 7; Twitter and 265
Tversky, Amos 68
Twitter: BLM movement and 6, 12, 160, 162–63, 164, 170–71; generational patterns 14, *15*, 32, 36; gun control movement 12, 97, 102; immigration policy movement 12; MeToo movement 4, 12, 31, 32, 35, 36; as news source 102, 162–63; as organizing platform 4–5, 12–13, 35, 97, 160, 171, *195*; as tracking tool 197; Trump and 265

United We Dream 3, 136
U.S. Census Bureau Current Population Survey 8
U.S. Supreme Court, DACA case 10–11, 131–32
U.S. Supreme Court nominations 61–95; effects on public policy 62–64, 67–69; lobbying and 67, 279; outcomes regarding 279–81, 284; overview 4, 10–11, 21, 61–65; protesting 70–71, 228, 231; social media 69–70, 208–11, **209**; survey methods and results 65, 71–88, **79–80**, 208–11, **209**, 215, 217–20, 246–48, **247**, 252–53, 253–55, 272–79, 285; voter turnout and 7–9, 12, 61

Viaud, Amel 1, 5
Villasenor, Alexandria 285
voter turnout: age and 6–9, 12, 13–14, *15*, 17–18, 61, 128–32, 169, 228, 280, 285; future research 276; importance of 7; increasing 276; outsider tactics and 12, 13; polarizing candidates and 266; protesting and 12, 13; self-reporting surveys and 275

Walgrave, Stefaan 255
Walker, Jack L. 232
Wallack, Lawrence 102–4, 107
Warren, Elizabeth 228
Washington, Toiell 1
Wilson, Darren 10, 162

Wind, Alex 96–97
Winett, Liana 102–4, 107
Wolpert, Robin W. 66
Women's March 38–39, 71, 138, 228
women's movement 33, 37, 169, 231
Wouters, Ruud 255
Wright, John R. 279
Wunete, Sara 2, 10, 171

young adults, defining 13–19, *15*, **18**, 118
young adults, risk and 11, 166
Youth Violence Prevention Initiative 103–4

Zimmerman, George 10, 12, 160
Zukin, Cliff 19–20, 194